THE
SCIENCE
OF
CULTURE

A STUDY OF MAN AND CIVILIZATION

By LESLIE A. WHITE

NEW YORK CITY

FARRAR, STRAUS AND GIROUX

TO MY WIFE, MARY

CONTENTS

ACKNOWLEDGMENTS

The author wishes to thank the following publishers for permission to quote from their publications:

Appleton-Century-Crofts, Inc., for excerpts from Ralph Linton, *The Study of Man*, New York, 1936.

Cambridge University Press (England), for excerpts from G. H. Hardy, *A Mathematician's Apology*, Cambridge, 1941.

Geo. E. G. Catlin, for excerpts from Emile Durkheim, *The Rules of Sociological Method*, University of Chicago Press, 1938.

The University of Chicago Press, for excerpts from *The Nature of the World and Man*, H. H. Newman, ed., Chicago, 1926; Marc Ruffer, *Studies in the Palaeopathology of Egypt*, R. L. Woodie, ed., Chicago, 1921; and from Geo. Steindorff and K. C. Seele, *When Egypt Ruled the East*, Chicago, 1942.

Thomas Y. Crowell Co., for excerpts from Clark Wissler, *Man and Culture*, New York, 1923.

Crown Publishers, for excerpts from A. Einstein, *The World As I See It*, copyright 1934 by Covici-Friede, New York.

Doubleday and Co., Inc., for excerpts from Helen Keller, *The Story of My Life*, New York, 1903.

Eyre and Spottiswoode, Ltd., for excerpts from Arthur Weigall, *The Life and Times of Akhnaton*, London, 1923.

Harper and Brothers, for an excerpt from Thomas Wolfe, *You Can't Go Home Again*, copyright The Sun Dial Press, 1942, New York.

Henry Holt and Co., Inc., for an excerpt from John Dewey, *Reconstruction in Philosophy*, New York, 1920; and from Clark Wissler, *An Introduction to Social Anthropology*, New York, 1929.

Alfred A. Knopf, Inc., for excerpts from A. A. Moret, *The Nile and Egyptian Civilization*, New York, 1927.

McGraw-Hill Book Co., Inc., for excerpts from Wm. I. Thomas, *Primitive Behavior*, New York, 1937; and from *Recent Social Trends*, New York, 1933.

The Macmillan Co., for excerpts from E. A. Hooton, *Up From the Ape*, New York, 1931; F. H. Giddings, *Principles of Sociology*, New York, 1896; A. M. Schlesinger, *New Viewpoints in American History*, New York, 1922.

W. W. Norton and Co., Inc., for an excerpt from Erwin Schrödinger, *Science and the Human Temperament*, New York, 1935.

The Science Press, for excerpts from H. Poincaré, *Foundations of Science*, New York and Garrison, 1913.

Charles Scribner's Sons, for excerpts from James H. Breasted, *A History of Egypt*, revised edition, New York, 1909.

Simon and Schuster, Inc., for an excerpt from *Living Philosophies*, New York, 1931.

Stechert-Hafner, Inc., for excerpts from E. T. Bell, *The Queen of the Sciences*, Baltimore, 1931.

The Viking Press, Inc., for excerpts from Wm. F. Ogburn, *Social Change*, New York, 1922.

AUTHOR'S NOTE

Some time ago Mr. Arthur Orrmont, formerly a student at the University of Michigan, now on the editorial staff of Farrar, Straus and Company, suggested that certain articles of mine that have appeared in various journals might well be reprinted in a single volume. This book has grown out of his suggestion. The previously published articles that reappear here in more or less modified form are as follows:

1. "Science is *Sciencing*," (Philosophy of Science, Vol. 5, pp. 369-389, 1938).

2. "Mind is *Minding*," (The Scientific Monthly, Vol. 48, pp. 169-171, 1939).

3. "The Symbol: The Origin and Basis of Human Behavior," (Philosophy of Science, Vol. 7, pp. 451-463, 1940).

4. "On the Use of Tools by Primates," (Journal of Comparative Psychology, Vol. 34, pp. 369-374, 1942).

5. "The Expansion of the Scope of Science," (Journal of the Washington Academy of Sciences, Vol. 37, pp. 181-210, 1947).

6. "The Locus of Mathematical Reality: An Anthropological Footnote," (Philosophy of Science, Vol. 14, pp. 289-303, 1947).

7. "Culturological *vs.* Psychological Interpretations of Human Behavior," (American Sociological Review, Vol. 12, pp. 686-698, 1947).

8. "Man's Control over Civilization: An Anthropocentric Illusion," (The Scientific Monthly, Vol. 66, pp. 235-247, 1948).

9. "Ikhnaton: The Great Man *vs.* the Culture Process," (Journal of the American Oriental Society, Vol. 68, pp. 91-114, 1948).

10. "The Definition and Prohibition of Incest," (American Anthropologist, Vol. 50, pp. 416-435, 1948).

"Education: America's Magic," which appeared in *School and Society* (Vol. 61, pp. 353-354, 1945) has been incorporated in the chapter "Man's Control over Civilization: An Anthropocentric Illusion." Material from "Atomic Energy: An Anthropological Appraisal" and "Energy and the Development of Civilization" has been incorporated in the chapter "Energy and the Evolution of Culture." "Atomic Energy: An Anthropological Appraisal" was read before the annual meeting of the American Anthropological Association in Philadelphia on December 28, 1945. It was never published in a journal * but was printed in its entirety or large part in some newspapers, including: The Baltimore Sun, December 29, 1945; The Milwaukee Journal, January 10, 1946; and The Norfolk Virginian-Pilot, January 13, 1946. "Energy and the Development of Civilization" was a radio address delivered over the Columbia Broadcasting System in New York City on February 16, 1947, on a program sponsored by the United States Rubber Company. It was subsequently published with a series of

---

* The curious reader will find interesting comment on this talk by Dr. E. U. Condon, Director, National Bureau of Standards, in an address to the winners of a science scholarship contest in Science News Letter, March 16, 1946; Science, April 5, 1946; and the Bulletin of the Atomic Scientists of Chicago, March 15, 1946. Dr. Condon, in effect, advises the young men and women to have nothing to do with prophets of "fatalism" (i.e., determinism in human affairs) such as I. He quotes the Holy Scriptures, and concludes with an inspiring passage from Elizabeth Barrett Browning.

See, also, a reply to Dr. Condon by M. F. Ashley Montagu in Science, May 3, 1946, in which he tells of a resolution, proposed by himself, seconded by Margaret Mead, and adopted by the American Anthropological Association, pledging anthropologists to work with other scientists to make "appropriate social inventions" to "guard against the dangers . . . inherent in atomic use." No report on progress toward such inventions has appeared as yet.

talks on science in *The Scientists Speak*, Warren Weaver, editor (New York, 1947). It was also reprinted by Technocracy Digest, May, 1947, and The Great Lakes Technocrat, May-June, 1947.

I am grateful to the editors of the journals in which my articles originally appeared for their kind permission to reprint them here.

Two of the articles republished here were reprinted some time ago in ETC., a Review of General Semantics: "The Symbol" (Vol. 1, pp. 229-237, 1944), and "Mind is *Minding*" (Vol. 1, pp. 86-88, 1943-44). "The Symbol" was rewritten at the request of Dr. Wm. S. Knickerbocker and published in *Twentieth Century English*, which he edited (New York, 1946).

A number of the articles republished in this volume evoked comment when they originally appeared. "Mind is *Minding*" brought forth a harsh criticism from Professor Jared Sparkes Moore (Scientific Monthly, Vol. 50, p. 365, 1940) to which I replied briefly (*ibid.*, pp. 365-66). "The Expansion of the Scope of Science" was reviewed at length in a sympathetic article by Professor A. L. Kroeber, "White's View of Culture" (American Anthropologist, Vol. 50, pp. 405-415, 1948). It was reviewed briefly in *Man*, by Professor J. L. Myres (Vol. 48, p. 11, January, 1948). And it received brief comment in Science (Vol. 106, p. 84, 1947) from Mr. Alden A. Potter.

"Man's Control over Civilization" drew a reply entitled "Clotho, Lachesis, and Atropos" from Harold H. Steinour in Scientific Monthly (Vol. 66, pp. 447-48, 1948). Mr. Steinour argues that it would be a good thing to believe that the human will is free even though it were not. He believes, however, that it is, at least to a degree. And "Ikhnaton" moved a distinguished Egyptologist, Professor Wm. F. Edgerton, to criticize me severely for venturing "to oppose the opinions of competent scholars" although I am unable to read inscriptions in the Egyptian language (Journal of the American Oriental Society, December, 1948).

To the above list of articles I have added the following chapters, written expressly for this volume: "Cultural Determinants of Mind;" "Genius: Its Causes and Incidence;" "Energy and the Evolution of Culture;" "The Science of Culture."

"Energy and the Evolution of Culture" was written in its entirety for this volume although based upon the thesis of an earlier article by the same title published in the American Anthropologist, Vol. 45, pp. 335-356, 1943. Material from "Cultural Determinants of Mind" was used for a paper, "The Individual and the Culture Process," presented in the symposium on "Human Individuality" at the Centennial meeting of the American Association for the Advancement of Science in Washington, D. C., on September 14, 1948. An abstract of this paper appeared in Science, Vol. 108, pp. 585-86, Nov. 26, 1948.

Since each of the articles reprinted here was originally written to stand on its own feet and by itself, there is some duplication and overlapping among them when all are placed together. Thus, a number of them contain a definition, or a characterization, of *culture* as an order of phenomena; or, a description of the science of culture and how it will operate. In preparing these articles for republication I have tried to reduce duplication and overlapping among them to a minimum, but perhaps too much still remains. We hope the reader will keep in mind the fact that, with a few exceptions, each chapter was originally an independent article and will be correspondingly indulgent. We might add, however, that some repetition is often very desirable, especially when a relatively novel theme—such as the science of culture—is being treated.

The articles as originally published have undergone revision in other respects also. We have added new material in some places and have cut out passages in others. In some instances we have transferred material from one article to another. The extent to which the original articles have undergone alteration varies; some have changed considerably, others very little. In every case, however, the premises and point of view, as well as much of the formulation and presentation, of the original articles have remained substantially the same.

I am greatly indebted to many persons for sympathetic interest, encouragement and assistance tendered me in the labors represented by the material in the present volume, written during a period of more than a decade. No expression of thanks of which I am capable could encompass the magnitude of my obligation nor adequately convey my sense of gratitude. Nor can I name here all of those who have, in one way or another, contributed to the pages that follow. I would like, however, to mention a few to whom I am especially indebted. I have received much inspiration and encouragement from a warm friendship of many years with Dr. Harry Elmer Barnes. My colleague, Professor Volney H. Jones, has kindly and patiently read almost all of my manuscripts for over a decade and I have profited greatly from his wise and sympathetic counsel. Professor R. L. Wilder, of the Department of Mathematics, University of Michigan, kindly read "The Locus of Mathematical Reality" in manuscript and offered many helpful suggestions.

I believe, however, that my greatest obligation is to the many students in my courses during the last fifteen years upon whom I have, so to speak, "tried out" the ideas set forth in this book. They are too numerous to mention here singly and by name. I hope, therefore, that they will accept this simple statement of my gratitude and affection, both for their interest and constructive criticism and for their patience and forbearance.

In planning the arrangement of this volume, Mr. John Farrar and his son, Curtis Farrar, have assisted with valuable suggestions.

My wife has helped enormously in the preparation of the manuscript, not to mention the years of encouragement and loyal support during which time the articles were conceived and written.

I cannot find words to express the full sense of my obligation to her.

LESLIE A. WHITE

University of Michigan
Ann Arbor, Michigan

PREFACE

*C*ulture became differentiated as soon as it appeared. Ever since the earliest days of human history local groups of people have been distinguished from one another by differences in speech, custom, belief, and costume, in so far as any was worn. We may believe, also, that man has always been aware of those differences that set his own group apart from others. Thus we might say that, in a sense, mankind has always been culture conscious. And, ever since the time of Herodotus at least there have been attempts to account for cultural variations among mankind. Some thinkers accounted for cultural differences in terms of environmental influence; one kind of habitat would produce one type of culture, another habitat a different type. Others were inclined to attribute cultural variation to innate mental or temperamental differences. In comparatively recent times the new sciences of sociology and social psychology worked out general principles of a science of social behavior, but these were assumed to be common to all mankind and so could not account for cultural differences among tribes and nations. Social interaction is a universal process; conflict, co-operation, accommodation, the four wishes, etc., are worldwide; they might account for cultural uniformities, but not differences. True, these sciences did not address themselves to the problem of cultural variation; they were limited almost entirely to the framework of one culture, Western civilization. But when one turned to the question of cultural differences among peoples, it was found that sociology and social psychology had virtually nothing to offer.

Apart from theories of environmental determinism which considered merely the relationship between habitat and culture, all types of interpretation prior to the emergence of anthropology as a science thought of man and culture together; no one considered culture apart from its human carriers. With the advance of science, however, came a recognition of culture as a distinct class of events, as a distinct order of phenomena. It was seen that culture is not merely a reflex response to habitat, nor a simple and direct manifestation of "human nature." It came to be realized that culture is a continuum, a stream of events, that flows freely down through time from one generation to another and laterally from one race or habitat to another. One came eventually to understand that the determinants of culture lie within the stream of culture itself; that a language, custom, belief, tool or ceremony, is the product of antecedent and concomitant cultural elements and processes. In short, it was discovered that culture may be considered, from the standpoint of scientific analysis and interpretation, as a thing *sui generis*, as a class of events and processes that behaves in terms of its own principles and laws and which consequently can be explained only in terms of its own elements and processes. Culture may thus be considered as a self-contained, self-determined process; one that can be explained only in terms of itself.

This profound discovery and advance in science was the lot of anthropology: it was the anthropologists, as Kroeber has said, who "discovered culture." In contrast with the sister sciences of social psychology and sociology, the new science of anthropology found itself in the very midst of cultural differences; concern with such things was in fact a large part of its objective. It was in a position to note that, in many instances at least, marked cultural variation is associated with a uniformity of human physical type. Thus, among North American Indian tribes who were of a highly

uniform physical type, there was nevertheless a great variety of
cultural types. A biological constant could not account for a
cultural variable. The anthropologist was able to see also that,
whereas a certain type of habitat would condition the form and
content of a culture, it did not determine them. An arctic climate,
for example, did not necessarily mean tailored fur clothing and
snug dwellings. As a matter of fact, a great variety of cultures are
compatible with any given type of environment, as a comparative
survey of regions or the archeological record of a single area over
a long period of time will show. Thus anthropologists were able
to free themselves from the old interpretative biases—that culture
was determined by habitat or by "human nature"—and to discover
the culturological determination of culture.

The great English anthropologist, E. B. Tylor, seems to have
been the first clearly to grasp this new conception. In the first
chapter of his great work, *Primitive Culture* (1871), he formulated
in succinct fashion the culturological point of view and outlined
the scope of the science of culture. Tylor was followed by Durkheim, Kroeber, Lowie, Wissler, and many others in the development of this new science. But progress has not been steady and
continuous. Of late there has been a falling away from the culturological point of view and objectives. Instead of interpretation of
culture as such, many American anthropologists in recent years
have turned to the overt reactions of human organisms and to the
deep subconscious forces that underlie these reactions. Thus, many
men and women anthropologists, who are by training and tradition
best qualified to study culture, have abandoned it for adventures
in psychology or psychiatry for which they have had little or no
technical training and with but little equipment save a ready
intuition. They have sold their culturological birthright for a mess
of psychiatric pottage.

And who is to study culture if not the anthropologists, particularly the culturologists? We have witnessed a definite regression in
anthropology in America in recent years. But it will not last.

xx   PREFACE

Sooner or later the advance in science begun with Tylor will be resumed. As Kroeber has indicated in a recent article, fashions and fads come and go in science, but underneath the currents and eddies on the surface is the deep strong flow of scientific progress. "Personality," says Kroeber, "is the slogan of the moment . . . Devices like 'ink-blot tests' have some of the outward qualities of a gadget . . . [and] as a nation we love gadgets . . . In a decade or two Rohrschachs may have been displaced as stimuli of fashion response by their successor of the day."

In the chapters that follow we treat the Science of Culture in its several aspects: the origin and nature of culture, the emergence of the scientific interpretation of culture and an historical sketch of this new venture, the fundamental distinction between psychology and culturology, and, finally, a few demonstrations of the point of view and techniques of culturological interpretation.

Preface to the Second Edition

*I*n 1901 Émile Durkheim wrote a rather lengthy preface to
the second edition of *Les Règles de la Méthode Sociologique*
(1895). He observed that he had been widely misunderstood,
that views were imputed to him which he had never held, etc. This
preface was a masterpiece of clarification; it is, in my opinion, the
best statement of Durkheim's philosophy of the scientific study
of man and culture that we have. Now, twenty years after the
publication of *The Science of Culture*, I am faced with a somewhat similar experience of retrospective stocktaking.

It is not enough to say that many readers have misunderstood
portions of *The Science of Culture*; they have *anti*-understood
it. That is, they have not only failed to comprehend what was said;
they have flatly asserted that I have said something quite different
and have roundly condemned me for it. I shall try to clarify my
position on a number of points.

The Science of Culture is imbued with a point of view that
many people today find exceedingly repugnant; generations before
them have regarded this philosophic attitude with apprehension
and hostility; and tender souls for years to come will continue an
age-old effort to scotch it. This is the sweet, soothing, reassuring,
belief in the Freedom of Man and his Omnipotence; the apothe-
osis of the talking primate. I can do no better than to quote the
closing lines of Durkheim's *Preface* of sixty-seven years ago:

xxii   PREFACE

Thus the history of sociology is but a long endeavor to give
this principle [the objective reality of social facts] precision, to
deepen it, and to develop all the consequences it implies. In
spite of the great advances which have been made in this direction, it will be clear, from what follows in this work, that numerous survivals of the anthropocentric bias still remain and that
here, as elsewhere, they bar the way to science. It displeases man
to renounce the unlimited power over the social order he has so
long attributed to himself; and on the other hand, it seems to
him that, if collective [i.e., sociocultural, L.A.W.] forces really
exist, he is necessarily obliged to submit to them without being
able to modify them. This makes him inclined to deny their
existence. In vain have repeated experiences taught him that this
omnipotence, the illusion of which he complacently entertains,
has always been a cause of weakness in him, that his power over
things really began only when he recognized that they have a
nature of their own, and resigned himself to learning this nature
from them. Rejected by all other sciences, this deplorable prejudice stubbornly maintains itself in sociology. Nothing is more
urgent than to liberate our science from it, and this is the principal purpose of our efforts (lvii-lviii).

Cultural determinism, a fundamental doctrine of the science of
culture, has been widely regarded as fatalistic and therefore "defeatist." It still is. Cultural determinism says, or implies, three
things: (1) that a people speaks English, eats with chopsticks,
believes in the Resurrection or Quetzalcoatl, etc., because it was
born and reared in a certain kind of cultural tradition ("the behavior of peoples is a function of their respective cultures"); (2)
variations of culture are to be explained culturologically rather than
psychologically, other factors being constant (the invention of the
steam engine, the Crow type of kinship terminology, monarchy or
representative government, etc., are not explained scientifically by
saying that people needed, desired, or achieved these things); and
(3) man does not, and cannot, control his culture or direct its

course (his behavior, i.e., the behavior of *peoples*, is a function of —is determined by—his culture, not the other way around).

Everyone, probably, would admit that a people speaks English or Chinese because it was born and reared in an English or Chinese language tradition. That a people eats with chopsticks rather than with knives and forks because of cultural—rather than genetic—determinism would also meet with wide, but probably not complete, acceptance. But that belief in the Resurrection of a Savior and the life everlasting should depend upon so slender a thread as cultural tradition is a proposition so repugnant to many that they reject it out of hand. The second proposition—that variations of culture are to be explained culturologically rather than psychologically (other factors remaining constant), that "culture is a thing sui generis which can be explained only in terms of itself" (Lowie, 1917, p. 66)—is regarded by many as obviously false: "culture does not enamel its fingernails, or vote, or believe in capitalism, but people do" (Lynd, 1939, p. 22). The third proposition is regarded by some not only as wrong (George Gaylord Simpson, 1951, p. 143, finds it "essentially fallacious") but as fatalistic, defeatist, and therefore inimical to human welfare. Abram Kardiner and Edward Preble (1961, p. 223) declare that such culturological propositions "land us . . . in a hopeless predicament. In addition," they continue, "any doctrine which denies man responsibility for his own fate tends . . . to greatly augment his social anxiety and to make such anxiety the pretext for hopelessness, hedonism, or social ruthlessness." The late C. Judson Herrick, a distinguished neurologist, declared (1956, p. 196): "Professor White's contention that the individual is irrelevant to an explanation of the cultural process leads to a nihilism that would paralyze all man's efforts to improve his condition, and that is not what science is for. This reification of culture as an autonomous and self-sufficient entity leads to a dismal fatalism and is a confession of defeat."

Let me try to clarify the issues involved here. First of all, I have not said that man, or the individual, is not necessary to the existence of culture; culture was brought into existence by man and cannot endure and function without him. What I have said is that we cannot *explain variations of culture*—in time, place, or race —in terms of man, the human animal. Differences between the cultures of China and Scandinavia, between the culture of England in A.D. 800 and in A.D. 1000, between the cultures of Mongoloids of aboriginal America and Negroids of the Congo basin are not explainable in terms of people (i.e., in terms of physical type or genetic constitution). I have not asserted that there are no genetic differences among peoples such as would give rise to cultural differences. I would say, however, that at the present time we do not have evidence of such differences which would allow us to use them to explain cultural differences.

The culturologist knows full well who—or which—it is that enamels its fingernails, swallows the aspirin tablet, or eats with chopsticks, people or culture. Of course it is human beings who do these things. But, as I pointed out in *The Science of Culture* (p. 143), this is not the point. Why does one people take aspirin rather than wear a good-luck charm? Why does a people eat with chopsticks rather than with knives and forks? What are the *determinants* of their behavior? The answer is, of course, plain: *the behavior of peoples is determined by their respective cultural traditions.* Dr. Herrick not only exposes his inability to comprehend this kind of problem but plays directly into the hands of those whom he criticizes (culturologists) when he says, plaintively: "It is the individuals who are educated, not the culture" (1956, pp. 195-96).

Quite true. And it is the process of education that imposes a cultural tradition upon human beings, equips them with beliefs, values, tools, techniques, etc.; in short, causes them to behave in this way or that. Education is the name of the process by which culture is transmitted from one generation, or people, to another.

When we concern ourselves with questions pertaining to the origin and function of culture, we must take the biological factor of man into consideration, of course. Culture was brought into being by man, and its function is to serve the needs of the human animal: to make life secure and enduring. Therefore, there is—and of course must be—an intimate relationship between man as an animal species and culture-in-general. In this broad, general way, culture is a function of the animal man; if he were different, his culture would differ correspondingly. If we did not have stereoscopic, chromatic vision, for example, our culture would be different. If we could subsist only upon meat, or cereals, our culture would be different. And so on. But we need not, and should not, take man into consideration in our explanations of differences (variations) in culture in time or place. We do not explain why some sociocultural systems are patrilineal, or monarchical, or have steam engines, practice mummification, use metallic currency, etc., whereas other societies differ, in terms of peoples or individuals. "Man is necessary for the existence of culture; he is not necessary (relevant) to scientific explanations of differences (variations) of culture."

The culturological proposition that culture consists of a body, or a flow, of culture traits (objects, acts, ideas) which interact with one another, forming new permutations, combinations, and syntheses, and that this culture process is to be explained scientifically in terms of its interacting component parts, independently of the underlying neuro-sensory processes involved, has been widely misunderstood—and therefore rejected. Of course it was James Watt, Isaac Newton, Ludwig van Beethoven that "did" the things for which they are respectively remembered. But, even if we could ascertain the facts of the neuro-sensory processes, i.e., observe and measure them rather than infer them from the culture process, they could not tell us what, specifically, was achieved or why it took place where it did (in England or in China) or when it did (in the Christian era or the late Neolithic). The science of culture (which includes consideration of historical, ecological, and topological factors) would tell us what, why, when, and where. More than that, it would explain the neuro-sensory behavior of Watt, Newton, and Beethoven as responses to their respective cultural habitats.

Kardiner and Preble (1961, p. 198) admit that (quoting White) "the study and interpretation of these events can be carried on not only without reference to individuals, gifted or otherwise, but without reference to the human species." But, they demand, "What are they [such studies] good for?" The limitations of their outlook are indeed unfortunate. They appear to be wholly restricted to psychology, to the behavior of human organisms. They seem to be quite incapable of conceiving of a scientific study and interpretation of *cultural* things and events ("symbolates": White, 1959a, p. 231) as a distinct class of phenomena ("culture . . . [is] a distinct domain . . . that demands for its investigation a distinct science": Lowie; see p. 409, *The Science of Culture*). They cannot realize that James Watt is not necessary to an explanation of the evolution of the steam engine, or that Isaac Newton is not essential to an explanation of the formulation of the laws of gravitation. These innovations were syntheses of concepts and things existing in the cultures within which these men respectively lived, and it is the business of the psychologist to study the responses of these men to their respective cultures. But it is the *culturologist*, not the psychologist, who must explain the *culture* process. One does not bring the biological factor of man into a scientific explanation of the culture process—the evolution of clan organization, for example, or the development of representative government, the evolution of money or of corporate organization—any more than one introduces the pancreas into a consideration of the question why a person is a capitalist or a communist, a Baptist or a Buddhist. The science of linguistics proceeds "as if the human race did not exist"; i.e., it does not take the human organism into account in its treatment of grammatical or phonetic structure, syntax, etc. (see White, 1959a, p. 234). Similarly, the science of culture is concerned with culturological phenomena rather than with psychological or physiological phenomena.

As for determinism, fatalism, defeatism, nihilism, and paralysis of initiative, etc., does it paralyze one's initiative to know and to understand the cultural forces that make him what he is and does? Will my efforts to develop a vaccine that will prevent poliomyelitis become paralyzed by the knowledge that without my culture I would not be a human being at all, that I would have no ideals or goals, no motives except those of a beast; that my culture has set me to work in a research laboratory rather than equipping me with fetiches, charms, and spells?

Herrick tells us that the nihilism of culturology and its paralyzing effect upon human initiative are "not what science is for." But what is science for if not to enlarge and deepen our understanding? And science differs from theological and metaphysical explanations in that it explains things in terms of themselves, in terms of their own natures, rather than in terms of the action of gods, demons, and spirits, or of essences and "principles." Formerly, rains were caused by rain gods. Later, forces and essences were used to explain things: "fossils were formed by the congelation of lapidific juices"; the "separatism of the natives" in Polynesia kept them from forming large political groups. Science explains phenomena in terms of those phenomena themselves: meteorological phenomena in terms of meteorological phenomena, biological phenomena in terms of biological things and events. Similarly, culturology explains culture processes and variations in terms of cultural phenomena; its mode of explanation resembles that of every other science.

Why is cultural determinism felt to be an enemy of mankind? We are surrounded with determinism. Human life itself on this planet has been determined by solar and terrestrial forces and conditions of temperature, atmosphere, humidity, solar radiation, photosynthesis, etc., along with cosmos-wide gravitation. Each one of us is subject to genetic determinism: once the egg has been fertilized, we are fixed ("determined") for life within a vast area of existence and experience. We cannot escape from cosmic, solar, terrestrial determinism. We cannot escape from biological, genetic determinism. Why then should we deplore cultural determinism —and go on to deny its very existence? Is it fatalistic that solar energy and terrestrial gravitation have irresistibly affected our form and functions as material systems? Is it fatalism that DNA molecules have determined what kind of individuals we shall be? Is it defeatism to know this? Does it paralyze our effort to make our lives more secure and enduring and satisfying? Why, then, should knowledge and understanding of how clan organization, or the Ten Commandments, came into being, how currency systems arose —how cultures in general evolved and why they differ from one another, how they affect our behavior, our thoughts, ideals, and spiritual values—why should a knowledge and understanding of this be felt as hostile to man's welfare?

Perhaps the reason is that cultural determinism strikes at man the human being rather than man the material system, or man the animal organism, that makes it the most objectionable expression of determinism. It strikes at the age-old philosophy of anthropocentrism and free will. Almost exactly one hundred years ago Thomas H. Huxley predicted that the conceptions of matter and law would invade and possess the fields of physiology and psychology as they had done the areas of physics and chemistry. "The consciousness of this great truth," he remarked (1870, p. 31)

weighs like a nightmare, I believe, upon many of the best minds of these days. They watch what they conceive to be the progress of materialism, in such fear and powerless anger as a savage feels, when, during an eclipse, the great shadow creeps over the face of the sun. The advancing tide of matter threatens to drown their souls; the tightening grasp of law impedes their freedom; they are alarmed lest man's moral nature be debased by the increase of his wisdom ("The Physical Basis of Life" a lecture delivered in Edinburgh in 1868 and published in 1870).

And so today the tide of determinism is rising. It has long since conquered our physical habitat. It has established itself firmly in our biological existence. And it has at least invaded the citadel of man, "the master of his fate, the captain of his soul," the embodiment of virtue and human dignity. And good people "are alarmed lest man's moral nature be debased by the increase of his wisdom." I sincerely believe that this is the source of almost all the feelings of hostility and rejection toward *The Science of Culture*.

A full century has passed since Adolphe Quételet, the great Belgian statistician and astronomer, observed:

> It is curious to see man, proudly entitling himself King of Nature and fancying himself controlling all things by his free-will, yet submitting, unknown to himself, more rigorously than any other being in creation, to the laws he is under subjection to. These laws are co-ordinated with such wisdom that they even escape his attention (quoted by Tylor, 1872, p. 359).

"These laws" are, of course, the laws of sociocultural systems. The illusion of free will can flourish only in the fertile soil of ignorance.

It was Durkheim who pointed out that, "for those who profess the complete autonomy of the individual, man's dignity is diminished whenever he is made to feel that he is not completely self-determinant" (1938, p. 4). More recently we have heard a plaintive protest from a former president of the American Anthropological Association that "we are men, not computers."

The culturologist as a culturologist, as a scientist, has no desire or need whatever to disparage the human species either individually or collectively, to lessen man's dignity, his spiritual worth, or anything else of this sort. As a human being as well as a scientist, the culturologist is well aware of the incalculable value that is motherhood, the warmth and strength of brotherhood, the virtue of filial piety. He is familiar with human dignity and virtue as well as with meanness, treachery, and vice. The last thing that a culturologist would want to do would be to deprive men and women of these precious imponderables without which our lives would hold neither meaning nor value for us. A culturologist who says that "men are computers" is either careless in his wording or using an illuminating metaphor. But men *are* "like computers" in a number of very significant respects, and knowing this—and something about computers—helps us to understand human behavior. Data are fed into electronic devices and into neuro-sensory systems where they are ordered, synthesized, and reduced to a simple formula. The conception of men as mechanisms has contributed to scientific understanding from Descartes's *l'homme machine* to Norbert Wiener's *Cybernetics* (see Chap. V, "Computing Machines and the Nervous System"). Even Dr. Herrick approved of likening the human nervous system to a telephone switchboard (1926, pp. 26-27).

I have been accused of hostility toward psychology, of rejecting or opposing it. "I am in fundamental disagreement with Dr. White," says Weston LaBarre (1954, p. 351), "in his vehement and repeated rejection of the importance of psychology and psychiatry to an understanding of man and culture." Kardiner and Preble (1961, p. 203) tell us that Kroeber once "warned of ignoring psychological explanations, as Leslie White wants to do." Edward Bruner (1964, p. 71) asserts that I "take the position that we should study only social and cultural systems . . . that anthropologists should not be concerned with psychology, personality, or individuals."

Anyone who has read *The Science of Culture* can hardly have failed to note such statements as: "It should not be necessary to point out that the thesis here set forth is not in any sense a criticism, much less a belittling, of psychology. The position of this science is as honorable as it is secure" (p. 144). "Both sciences [psychology and culturology] are essential to a comprehensive interpretation of human behavior" (p. 145). I have always held that there is and can be no justifiable conflict between psychology and culturology—any more than there can be a justifiable conflict between psychology and physiology, or between physics and chemistry. My position on this point may be set forth as follows.

Anthropology is a congeries of many studies of very diverse kinds—from clay figurines in Ecuador to serological analyses of fossil remains, from the phonetics of Mohawk to the social organization of a hospital ward, from kinship terminologies to mental patients in a state hospital, from human genetics to kinship terminologies, the social life of baboons, the origin of the state, Rorschach tests, interpretation of dreams, Freudian symbolism, and ethnological theory. Most anthropological studies are duplicated by other sciences—or the humanities. Anthropology has only one unique contribution to its credit: the science of culture. "It was anthropologists who discovered culture," said Kroeber (1936, pp. 331, 333, 334), and, I would add, it was anthropologists who have created and developed the science of culture.

During the nineteen-thirties and early forties there was a great vogue of "personality and culture" among American anthropologists. Anyone who had not published an article in the *Journal of Orthopsychiatry* (or one like it) was an exception. Kroeber remained aloof and in his later years he looked back upon this movement as a fad: not "merely a fashion . . . much of its urge and support in an emotional attraction . . . the basis of the movement was not wholly intellectual . . ." (Kroeber, 1956, p. 155). Self-made psychologists and psychiatrists bloomed and flourished among the anthropological fraternity. In 1946 I deplored the fact that anthropologists were "selling their culturological birthright for a mess of psychiatric pottage" (White, 1946, p. 86). Why, I asked, should an anthropologist, who has had little or no training in psychology, devote himself to personality and other psychological matters rather than engage in the scientific pursuit that belongs to anthropology in a particular and exclusive way: the science of culture? Why not let psychologists do the psychologizing? And who is to develop the science of culture if not nonbiological anthropologists? Culturology is the unique achievement of anthropology and has been

the traditional occupation of nonbiological anthropologists since
E. B. Tylor's pioneer essay, *The Science of Culture* (1871).

LaBarre (1954, p. 351) asserted that I "vehemently reject the
importance of psychology and psychiatry to an understanding of
man and culture." But he has confused two quite different categories, or classes of phenomena: man, a biological system, and culture,
a suprabiological system composed of things and events dependent
upon symboling (tools, customs, beliefs). Psychology and psychiatry are, of course, relevant to the study of *man;* they are not perti-
nent to the solution of culturological problems. I had already
"answered" LaBarre in *The Science of Culture:* ". . . culturology
cannot tell us all that we want to know about incest . . . psychology must be enlisted in the inquiry also. But one must insist upon
a sharp and clear distinction between the psychological problem
and the culturological problem. Psychology cannot account for the
origin or the *form* of the prohibitions; only culturology can do this.
But for an understanding of the way the human primate organism
behaves—thinks, feels, and acts—within, or with reference to, one
of these cultural forms, we must go to psychology" (p. 312n.; see,
also, pp. 144-45).

Émile Durkheim carefully distinguished between psychological
and sociological problems in *The Rules of Sociological Method.*
A. R. Radcliffe-Brown did likewise in a number of his theoretical
essays and addresses. Robert H. Lowie drew this distinction sharply
in "Culture and Psychology" (in *Culture and Ethnology*). These
clear-eyed scholars felt it was necessary to distinguish between psychology and sociology (or culturology) because: (1) they are quite
different sciences, and (2) many anthropologists confuse the two.
Durkheim, Radcliffe-Brown, and Lowie distinguished these two
sciences from each other because they wished to make it clear that
they were concerned with sociocultural, or culturological, problems
and not with psychological problems and interpretations. Is one
to be criticized for preferring to do culturology rather than psychology? Or psychology rather than physiology or biochemistry? I have

preferred to follow the course taken by the distinguished scholars just mentioned. In doing culturology I have left psychology to others—after carefully defining its scope, the nature of its problems, and its relation to the science of culture. In doing culturology I have left physiology to others, also; one's pancreas is "important," too.

I have been taken to task for failure to give the "individual" full credit for his intrinsic worth and his contribution to civilization —or for stating that the culture process can be studied scientifically (and profitably) "not only without reference to individuals, gifted or otherwise, but without reference to the human species." This proposition has, apparently, been regarded as the height of absurdity by many students of "man and culture." How can you have culture without man? Hallowell (1954, p. 200, n. 116) finds it an "extreme" view. So does M. Brewster Smith (1954, p. 34). Sieber accuses me of "denigration of the importance of the human personality in culture studies" (1961, p. 295). Margaret Mead (1964, p. 23) avers that "one must regard as untenable Leslie White's contention that the individual, as such, is of no importance" (with reference to contributions to culture).

Anyone who consults the index of The Science of Culture will see that I have certainly not ignored the individual. I have had a great deal to say about him and I would not at this time, twenty years later, wish to make any significant changes in what I have said, or to add to or subtract therefrom. It would be tedious to summarize here what has been set forth at length in The Science of Culture. What I have done repeatedly is to distinguish man, the self-contained, autonomous, thermodynamic, biological system, from man as vehicle of culture, as the locus of syntheses of cultural elements (Newton, James Watt, Darwin), and as a catalyst of the culture process. These two individuals are quite different from each other; they have different roles in their respective fields (contexts). Relative to cultural matrix, man is a puppet: he does, feels, believes that which his culture requires of him. In the biological context (and when we hold the cultural factor constant), man is a thermodynamic system, a prime mover (Sapir's individual, the one who "always thinks, acts, dreams, and revolts" [*The Science of Culture*, p. 104]). In the context of human experience and values, the individual is the embodiment of all the virtues or vices of mankind ("not a computer"). It has been the confusion of these conceptions of man, confusion of the contexts in which we find him among the sciences of "man and culture" and the humanities, that has caused so much misunderstanding (and wounded feelings of William James's "tender minded" people). To say that a person believes and does what this culture requires of him is not to say that a woman is not a loving mother or the father a noble man.

According to the researches of Kluckhohn and Murray (1953, p. xvi), I seem to have been the first American anthropologist to write an article entitled "Personality and Culture." * It appeared in *The Open Court* in March 1925. I never wrote anything else on personality-and-culture, but I certainly have not ignored the individual. On the contrary, I have given this subject repeated, sustained, concentrated, critical thought. What I have argued is not that the individual is "not important" (Important to whom? in what context? Is a bicycle important? or a canoe?) but that he is irrelevant to a scientific explanation of certain cultural processes, to the solution of certain culturological problems. This proposition seems to be incomprehensible to some students of "man-and-culture"; and being incomprehensible, it must therefore be wrong; consequently it is rejected.

I published two different versions of "The Individual and the Culture Process" (White, 1949, 1950), which was presented, by invitation, at the Centennial Celebration of the American Associa-

---

* Kluckhohn and Murray go on to say: "Dr. White was then a student of the linguist-anthropologist, Professor Edward Sapir . . ." (p. xvi). The implication was that I had written up some lecture notes and published them. The fact is that my article was published several months before I first met Sapir (when he came to the University of Chicago to teach in the fall of 1925). Sapir and Benedict did not begin to publish on personality-and-culture until some years after my paper was published.

tion for the Advancement of Science in 1948. "Ikhnaton: The Great Man vs. the Culture Process" (1948) demonstrated the irrelevance of this Pharaoh to an *explanation* of Egyptian culture history. I was invited by the American Studies Association of Texas to participate in a symposium on "Individualism in Twentieth-Century America" (see White, 1963, 1965). In my monographs, *The Pueblo of Santa Ana, New Mexico* and *The Pueblo of Sia, New Mexico,* I have paid much attention to individuals as such, especially to "the most influential men" and the basis of their influence. I have even produced "An Autobiography of an Acoma Indian" (White, 1943, pp. 326-37), a difficult thing to do in a society that subordinates the individual.

Since *The Science of Culture* was published in 1949, I have discovered that Wilhelm Ostwald used the term "culturology" as early as 1909 in *Energetische Grundlagen der Kulturwissenschaft,* but this significant achievement remained unknown to anthropologists until I "rediscovered" Ostwald—as Kroeber and Kluckhohn (1952, p. 71) have put it—as *The Science of Culture* was going through the press (see p. 113). I introduced "culturology" into anthropological literature in "A Problem in Kinship Terminology" in 1939 (see *American Anthropologist,* 41:566-73, 1939, pp. 411-12). The word was harshly criticized before *The Science of Culture* was published. In reviewing *The Science of Culture,* Hart (1950, p. 88) called "culturology" "a new label for an old activity . . . horrible to look at and horrible to hear . . . more likely to obscure issues than to clarify them." Geza Roheim (1950, p. 439) made this almost incredible remark: "The unjustified form of a 'culturological' explanation is simply to use one's ignorance of psychology and then to call it an explanation in terms of culture." In August 1959, James Newman, reviewing in *Scientific American* (Vol. 201, No. 2, p. 164) the paperback issue of *The Science of Culture,* observed that ". . . 'culturology' (coined by the chemist Wilhelm Ostwald) is one of the most unattractive and unnecessary words ever coined, even by a German savant."

In view of the abuse and criticism that "culturology" (and I) have received, it is indeed gratifying to note the wide acceptance of the term since *The Science of Culture* was published. In 1954 it was included in the Addenda of the second edition of *Webster's New International Dictionary of the English Language*. In 1956 it was included in the *Dictionary of Anthropology*, Charles Winnick, ed.; in 1958, in *A Comprehensive Dictionary of Psychological and Psychoanalytical Terms*, Horace B. and Ava Champney English; in 1959, in *Dictionary of Social Science*, John T. Zadrozny; in 1960, as the subject of an article, in *International Dictionary of Regional European Ethnology and Folklore*, (Vol. I, pp. 86-87) (Copenhagen). In 1961 it was included as a full-fledged word in the English language, in the Third Edition of *Webster's New International Dictionary*, where, incidentally, it is attributed to me by name. In 1964 it appeared as the subject of a two-page article (which I wrote) in *A Dictionary of the Social Sciences*, Julius Gould and William L. Kolb, eds. And most recently, in 1968, the *International Encyclopedia of the Social Sciences*, David L. Sills, editor, contains an article on "culturology" written by me at the invitation of the editor (Vol. III, pp. 547-51). "Culturology" is, apparently, here to stay. The word has found wide and rapid acceptance because it has made explicit a fundamental distinction between the science of mind, the science of society, and the science of culture. As Henry Poincaré observed many years ago, the "true discoverer will not be the workman who has patiently built up some of these combinations, but the man who has brought out their relation . . . The invention of a new word will often be sufficient to bring out the relation, and the word will be creative" (*The Science of Culture*, p. 415).

If we cannot control our culture or direct its course, what is culturology good for? is a question that I have been asked many times. My answers are: 1. What is science good for? Why does society feel that it is worthwhile to observe, and try to explain, cosmic events that took place a trillion light-years away—and consequently

millions of years ago? Answer 2: The science of culture enables us
to make some reasonable and well-founded statements about the
future course of cultural development. Predictions restricted to particular areas such as population growth, exhaustion of fossil fuel
reserves, pollution of the atmosphere, etc., are commonplace today.
But the science of culture can do much more than this. The culturologist has at his disposal a vast amount of data on the evolution
of culture as a whole. On the basis of his knowledge of more than
a million years of cultural development he has been able to formulate some basic principles of culture growth (White, 1959b, as a
whole; p. 56 in particular). Extrapolation to the extent of a hundred years or so would seem to be both a modest and a realistic
achievement; alternative courses can be distinguished and probabilities roughly calculated. Answer 3: A sociocultural system which
possesses a relatively mature science of culture as an integral part
of itself will behave differently than a sociocultural system whose
philosophy of man-and-culture is anthropocentric and free-willistic.
A sociocultural system that has a mature science of diseases of the
body and maladies of the mind will behave differently from one
which treats the former with fetiches, charms, and spells and regards the latter as evidence of diabolic possession. Similarly, a sociocultural system (nation) equipped and guided by a fairly mature
and generally disseminated science of culture instead of ideologies
such as divine right of kings, sovereignty of the people, or dictatorship of the proletariat; instead of time-worn clichés, images of
Great Men, party passions and prejudices; instead of campaign
oratory and demagoguery. A science of culture would, in short,
enable a nation to behave in a more rational manner, with knowledge and intelligence taking the place, more and more, of simple
reflex and tropism.

Finally, after commenting upon criticisms of *The Science of
Culture* and objections to its point of view, I would like to make
a suggestion with regard to the terminology of discussions in the

future. The term "symbolic behavior" appears rather frequently in *The Science of Culture*. I believe, however, that it would be much better to say "symboling" than "symbolic behavior." "Symbolic behavior" is not sufficiently explicit and unambiguous; we define "symboling" with precision. Symboling is a kind of behavior in which imperceptible meanings are bestowed, freely and arbitrarily, upon things and events in the external world, or in which such meanings are grasped and comprehended. Holy water is a good example of this; thumbing one's nose is another. Symboling is a kind of behavior of which man (and only man) is capable. We symbol things and events in the external world (i.e., react to them) just as we see, hear, or smell them. And the proper word for this activity is "symboling," not "symbolizing." As I emphasized in "Symboling: A Kind of Behavior" (1962b, p. 314), symbolizing has a meaning well established by long usage, and it is not the meaning I have given to "symboling." And the use of words as verbs as well as nouns—hammer, comb, water, rope, and hundreds of others—is, of course, a fundamental feature of the English language.

Literature Cited in the Preface

Bruner, Edward M.
  1964. "The Psychological Approach in Anthropology" (in Horizons of Anthropology, Sol Tax, ed. Chicago).
Durkheim, Émile
  1938. The Rules of Sociological Method, edited with an introduction by George E. G. Catlin. Chicago.
Hallowell, A. Irving
  1954. "Psychology and Anthropology" (in For a Science of Social Man, John Gillin, ed. New York).
Hart, C. W. M.
  1950. Review of The Science of Culture (American Journal of Sociology, 56:88).
Herrick, C. Judson
  1926. Brains of Rats and Men. Chicago.
  1956. The Evolution of Human Nature. Austin, Texas.
Huxley, T. H.
  1870. The Physical Basis of Life. New Haven, Connecticut.
Kardiner, Abram and Preble, Edward
  1961. They Studied Man. Cleveland and New York.
Kluckhohn, Clyde and Murray, Henry A.
  1953. Introduction to first edition of Personality in Nature, Society, and Culture. New York.
Kroeber, A. L.
  1936. "So-Called Social Science" (Journal of Social Philosophy, 1:317-40).
  1956. "The Place of Boas in Anthropology" (American Anthropologist, 58:151-59).
Kroeber, A. L. and Kluckhohn, Clyde
  1952. Culture, A Critical Review of Concepts and Definitions. Papers of the Peabody Museum of American Archaeology and Ethnology, Harvard University, Vol. XLVII, No. 1.
LaBarre, Weston
  1954. The Human Animal. Chicago.
Lowie, Robert H.
  1917. Culture and Ethnology. New York.
Lynd, Robert S.

1939. Knowledge for What? Princeton.
Mead, Margaret
1964. Continuities in Cultural Evolution. New Haven and London.
Quételet, Adolphe (see E. B. Tylor)
Roheim, Geza
1950. Psychoanalysis and Anthropology. New York.
Sieber, Sylvester A.
1961. Review in Anthropos, 56:294-96.
Simpson, George G.
1951. The Meaning of Evolution, a special revised and abridged edition. A Mentor Book. New York.
Smith, M. Brewster
1954. "Anthropology and Psychology" (in For a Science of Social Man, John Gillin, ed. New York).
Tylor, Edward B.
1872. "Quetelet's Contribution to the Science of Man" (Nature, 5:358-63).
White, Leslie A.
1942. The Pueblo of Santa Ana, New Mexico. Memoir 60, American Anthropological Association.
1943. New Material from Acoma. Anthropological Papers, No. 32, Bulletin 136, Bureau of American Ethnology, Washington, D.C.
1946. "Kroeber's 'Configurations of Culture Growth'" (American Anthropologist, 48:78-93).
1949. "The Individual and the Culture Process" (Journal, American College of Dentists, 16:3-10).
1950. "The Individual and the Culture Process" (another version) (in Centennial, Collected Papers Presented at the Centennial Celebration, American Association for The Advancement of Science. Washington, D.C.).
1959a. "The Concept of Culture" (American Anthropologist, 61:227-51).
1959b. The Evolution of Culture. New York: McGraw-Hill Book Company, Inc.
1962a. The Pueblo of Sia, New Mexico. Bulletin 184, Bureau of American Ethnology. Washington, D.C.
1962b. "Symboling: A Kind of Behavior" (The Journal of Psychology, 53:311-17).
1963. "Individuality and Individualism: A Culturological Interpretation" (Texas Quarterly, 6:111-27, 168-69).
1965. "Individuality and Individualism: A Culturological Interpretation" (in Innocence and Power: Individualism in Twentieth-Century America, Gordon Mills, ed. Austin, Texas).

PART I SCIENCE AND SYMBOLS

Introduction

We preface our treatise on the Science of Culture with an essay on science in general, "Science is *Sciencing*." Science is not a body of data; it is a technique of interpretation. And this technique is as applicable to cultural phenomena as to any other class. The science of culture, or the science of psychology, is not as mature as astronomy or physics; neither is it nearly as old. But it is fallacious or chauvinistic to assert that "physics is a science, but psychology or culturology is not." One can *science* in any sector of experience.

In "The Symbol" we lay bare the mechanism that has brought culture, as a new and distinct order of phenomena, into being. We *discover* culture as a new field of scientific exploration and interpretation. "On the Use of Tools by Primates" attempts to show why man has a continuous, cumulative, and progressive material culture whereas the anthropoid apes, who are able to make tools and who use them with great skill and versatility, do not. The answer is, again, the Symbol. "Mind is *Minding*" breaks with the old-fashioned view which regarded mind as a thing, as an entity, and sees it merely as a process of reacting to external stimuli. This helps to clarify the relationship between man as organism and the extrasomatic cultural tradition to which he reacts as he does to his natural habitat.

In "The Expansion of the Scope of Science," we trace the course of the conquest of science of ever more and more of the terrain of human experience, first of the heavenly bodies in astronomy, then terrestrial physical phenomena, then the various sectors of biological phenomena, and, finally, the realm of *culture*. In tracing the course of the advance and progress of science we come face to face with its predecessor and rival: the philosophy of anthropomorphism, anthropocentrism, and Free Will. As subsequent chapters will bring out clearly and emphatically, this is the philosophy that science has had to contend every inch of the way. And it is this age-old and primitive philosophy that we still have to oppose until it is at last eradicated, root and branch.

CHAPTER ONE

SCIENCE IS *SCIENCING*

"Science is a kind of human behavior."

S cience is not merely a collection of facts and formulas. It is pre-eminently a way of dealing with experience. The word may be appropriately used as a verb: one *sciences*, i.e., deals with experience according to certain assumptions and with certain techniques. Science is one of two basic ways of dealing with experience. The other is art. And this word, too, may appropriately be used as a verb; one may *art* as well as science. The purpose of science and art is one: to render experience intelligible, i.e., to assist man to adjust himself to his environment in order that he may live. But although working toward the same goal, science and art approach it from opposite directions. Science deals with particulars in terms of universals: Uncle Tom disappears in the mass of Negro slaves. Art deals with universals in terms of particulars: the whole gamut of Negro slavery confronts us in the person of Uncle Tom. Art and science thus grasp a common experience, or reality, by opposite but inseparable poles.

To use the word science as a noun is not, however, without justification. The words chemistry, physiology, history, sociology, etc., are both legitimate and useful. As categories they are derived from two sources. On the one hand, they reflect analytical distinctions which may be made within the field of reality: erosion, respiration, hysteria, voting, etc., are phases or segments of experience which find their reflections in the categories geology, physiology, psychology, and political science, respectively. On the other hand, division of labor in society, essential in modern times, also finds its reflection in the same, or similar, categories. This is a fact often ignored. Psychology is a category that is a reflection of the division of society into disparate occupational groups just as truly as it is an expression of analytical distinctions which may be made in experience ("subject matter") itself. "Psychology is what *psychologists* (i.e., a guild of workers bearing the label 'psychologist') do," is as valid a definition as "psychology is the study of mind, or behavior." The one is an expression of social reality; the other derives from the nature of the subject matter of the study.

This dual nature of the categories becomes manifest in the recurrent protest against the partition of science into "watertight" compartments, in the impossibility of telling whether a given study is historical, sociological, or psychological. Does the story of John Brown's "insurrection" belong to psychology, sociology, economics, political science, or history? Obviously and equally to each. Nor can the distinction between inanimate, biologic and cultural withstand the categorizing process which is implicit in the division of labor in society. When Harlow Shapley studies the responses of ants to varying quantities of heat reaching them from the sun,[1] is he an astronomer or an entomologist? Obviously, he is contributing to an understanding of insects as well as stars; this thermodynamic process has both entomologic and astronomic aspects. Dr. A. E. Douglass, an astronomer at the University of Arizona, has, by working out a correlation between rainfall and growth of trees in the Southwest, provided archeologists with the most precise technique for dating prehistoric remains unaccompanied by written records that has yet been devised.[2] In this case an "astronomer" has become an archeologist via climatology and

---

[1] References are grouped by chapters and appear on pp. 416-424.

botany. Conventionally, however, "an astronomer" is any member of a certain group, formal or informal, of scientific workers produced by the social division of labor, even though he may contribute to an understanding of insects, the growth of forests, and the sequence of Indian cultures, as well as to our knowledge of heavenly bodies. Logically, astronomy is the scientific interpretation of the behavior of celestial bodies regardless of the professional label borne by the one who makes it.

The custom of viewing "science" as a vast terrain divided into a number of "fields" each tilled by its own appropriately named guild has a certain justification in utility and convenience. But it tends to obscure the nature of science as a way of interpreting reality and to spread confusion in the ranks of scientists and laymen alike. The use of the word science as a noun not only leads to jurisdictional disputes—does the study of juvenile delinquency belong to sociology or to psychology, the study of fossils to geology or to biology?—but to such questions as, is history a science? is sociology a science? There is a tendency to identify "science" with some of its techniques. For example, one can perform experiments in chemistry and make accurate predictions in astronomy. Chemistry and astronomy are "sciences." Experimentation is exceedingly limited in sociology and predictions in history are seldom more than guesses. Therefore, the tendency is to say, "history and sociology are not sciences." Despite the fact that much of geology is more historical than certain studies of human culture, there is a willingness to call the one "a science" but to deny this status to the other.

Then a distinction is made between the physical sciences (frequently called by the flattering term "the exact sciences") and the "social sciences." Implicit in this distinction is the assumption that a fundamental difference obtains between the nature of physical reality and human social reality. This assumption leads to, if indeed it does not include by implication, the further as-

sumption that the data of human society, being essentially different from the data of physics ("the exact sciences"), are really not
susceptible to scientific treatment, hence the social sciences are
really not sciences at all; * they are not and cannot be "scientific."
The same observations are made, although with less emphasis,
with reference to biology: "Biology is less scientific than physics,
but more scientific than sociology." These assumptions are not
only confusing; they are unwarranted. The basic assumptions and
techniques which comprise the scientific way of interpreting
reality are applicable equally to all of its phases, to the human-
social, or cultural, as well as to the biological and the physical.
This means that we must cease viewing science as an entity which
is divisible into a number of qualitatively different parts: some
wholly scientific (the "exact sciences"), some quasi-scientific, and
some only pseudo-scientific. We must cease identifying science
with one or another of its techniques, such as experimentation.
We must, in short, view science as a way of behaving, as a way of
interpreting reality, rather than as an entity in itself, as a segment
of that reality.

Science distinguishes living, sentient beings on the one hand,
and an external world independent of sentient organisms on the
other.** Reality in this context consists of the organisms' interaction with the external world. As such it may be regarded as a
one or as a many. It may be thought of as the totality of the interaction, or experience, of the organism; or, it may be analyzed into
its component parts. On the perceptual level reality is analyzed
into sense impressions—odors, tastes, colors, sounds, etc. On the
conceptual level it is analyzed with symbolic instruments—words,
mathematical symbols, etc. Matter, energy, time, space, motion,
etc., are conceptual devices with which we analyze reality and in

* ". . . I think that social science is like a Welsh rabbit—not really a rabbit at all." E. A. Hooton, in *Apes, Men, and Morons*, p. 62.
** "The belief in an external world independent of the perceiving subject is
the basis of all natural science." Einstein, 1934, p. 60.

terms of which we make our adjustments to it. Matter, energy, time, motion, and so on, are not therefore discrete entities, but aspects or phases of a common reality. We may also analyze the totality of reality, insofar as we can experience it, into equivalent component parts, or "units," which we may call *events*. Experience is therefore conceived by us on the one hand as a one, as a totality, and on the other as an infinite number of parts, or events.

"Whole and parts" means relationships. "Relationship," too, is another conceptual device, a symbolic instrument, with the aid of which we render experience intelligible to a degree, and by means of which we effect our adjustments to our environment. Events are related to each other. But how?

"Every event that happens in the world is determined by the space-co-ordinates x, y, z and the time-co-ordinate *t*," [3] The fundamental relationship, or "interval," between events is one of space-time. Whereas formerly space and time were thought of as properties of the external world independent of each other, they are now seen to be merely *aspects* of the basic and primary property, space-time. To quote Minkowski: "The views of space and time which I wish to lay before you have sprung from the soil of experimental physics, and therein lies their strength. They are radical. Henceforth space by itself, and time by itself, are doomed to fade into mere shadows, and only a kind of union of the two will preserve an independent reality." [4] Thus reality confronts us, in modern thought, as a four-dimensional continuum; the process of reality in which events are manifested is a temporal-spatial (or temporal-formal) one.

Thus the primary and fundamental relationship between events is temporal-formal. But by purely logical analysis, we may distinguish the temporal aspect of the process from the spatial; although inseparable in actuality, we may occupy ourselves with either to the exclusion of the other. Thus we may distinguish three kinds of processes, one primary, the temporal-formal, and two secondary and derivative, the temporal on the one hand and the spatial, or formal, on the other. In the first category we would deal with events as being related to one another by space-time intervals. In the other two we would in the one consider the interval (or relationship) in its temporal aspect only; and in the other the interval would be dealt with in its spatial, or formal, aspect alone.

Sciencing must adapt itself to the structure of reality; its tools must be so shaped and its techniques so ordered as to grasp reality effectively and render it intelligible to us. This means, therefore, that we shall have three ways of sciencing: one which grasps the space-time property of reality in its entirety, and two subsidiary and derivative ways, each of which deals with one of the two aspects of this property, viz., space and time. All of "science" or sciencing will be found to be assignable to one or another of these three categories; there is no way of sciencing apart from these three.

"History" is that way of sciencing in which events are dealt with in terms of their temporal relationships alone. Each event is unique. The one thing that history never does is to repeat itself: Lincoln is assassinated only once. To be sure, the events themselves that constitute history are related to one another in ways other than temporal. This must of necessity be true since all kinds of relationships are equally attributes of a common reality. But in "history-ing" we arbitrarily select for our consideration the connective tissue of time, and just as arbitrarily ignore the relationship of space.*

This process of reducing concrete experience to artificial abstractions, or, to put it more precisely, the act of substituting concepts, "free inventions of the human intellect" (to borrow Einstein's

---

* To be sure, those who bear the label "historian" concern themselves with relationships other than temporal: they wish to know where Lincoln was assassinated as well as when. "The temporal process" would probably be a better term for our purpose here than "history."

phrase), for the concrete experiences of the senses,[5] is not only unavoidable, it is the very essence of sciencing.

"History," or the temporal aspect of experience, is co-extensive with reality; it is a property common to the inanimate, biological, and cultural orders of phenomena. Stars, the solar system, the earth, rivers, lead, granite, plants and animals, species and individuals, customs and institutions, each have their respective histories. Astronomy, physics, geology, biology, psychology, sociology, and anthropology are therefore, in part at least, historical "sciences." There is no antagonism nor even distinction between history and science: history is simply one way of sciencing whether it be in geology or sociology. If we refuse to accept this conclusion we are forced to its alternative: "An astronomer is a scientist when he deals with a non-temporal, repetitive process, but when he concerns himself with a chronological sequence of events (the history of the solar system, e.g.) he is no longer a scientist."

Events are related to each other spatially, and we may deal with reality in terms of spatial, or formal, relationships, ignoring the aspect *time*.

Spatial relationships between events may be regarded as either constant or variable. Events, or material objects, whose mutual spatial relationships are regarded as constant, constitute a *structure*. This property is characteristic of all phases of reality. In the inanimate, biologic and cultural levels it manifests itself in such forms as atoms, molecules, stars, constellations, planets, orbits, strata, the elements; in skeletons, bones, muscles, organs, bodies, limbs; in families, clans, societies, grammars, constitutions. When the spatial relationships uniting a number of events, or material objects, are regarded as variable, then we speak of *function*. This property likewise manifests itself on all levels of reality in atomic, molecular, meteorological, astronomic behavior; in physiological and psychological processes; and on the supra-biological level, in cultural processes. Thus the physicist, chemist, astronomer, geologist, zoologist, botanist, physiologist, psychologist, sociologist, linguist, cultural anthropologist, etc., are all concerned with the spatial or formal * (non-temporal) aspect of reality, in its structural or functional aspects, or both.

We come now to the third kind of relationship, or process: the temporal-spatial. This is like the two preceding processes, but different from each. As we have already noted, all three kinds of relationships are always intrinsic in any series of actual events, in any phase of reality. The temporal process (or "history") is a selective arrangement of events according to the principle *time*. Spatial relationships, though actually existent in these events, are disregarded: in the history of thought it is immaterial whether Newton cogitates under an apple tree or in his bath. Similarly, when dealing with spatial relationships, i.e., with structure and function, the time relationships which are inseparable from these events in objective reality are here divorced by logical analysis: the structure of the crystal, the rusting of iron, respiration, cowardice, secret societies, may be studied without reference to clocks or calendars.

But in the temporal-spatial process both temporal and spatial relationships are simultaneously significant. And it is not a case of time *and* space—"up from the South at break of day . . . and Sheridan twenty miles away." The conventional historian wishes to know not only that Napoleon fought battles, but where he fought them. The zoologist and the ethnologist are interested in the distribution of species and culture traits as well as their history. These are examples of a simultaneous interest in both temporal and spatial relationships. But they are not examples of temporal-spatial relationships. Hydrogen + oxygen = hydrogen + oxygen; $t + s = t + s$. But hydrogen x oxygen = water (H_2O); $t \times s = ts$. The temporal-spatial process is not, then, equivalent to a space

---

* Structure and function are not confined to the realm of metric space. Structure or form is a characteristic of such non-spatial systems as language, music, kinship systems, social organization, poetry, and so on.

and time organization of phenomena; it is not the *sum* of these factors but their product.

It is of interest to note in passing that in many instances in which both temporal and spatial relations are involved, one is significant only in terms of the other. Thus the thickness of a geologic stratum measured in feet indicates its age measured in years. Similarly, the distribution of a plant or animal species may indicate its age: the wider the distribution the greater the age. And, using the same principle, the anthropologist has been able, in many instances, to reconstruct the history of a tool, myth, custom, or institution by inference from its geographic distribution.[6] And, of course, our clocks measure time by a repetitive movement of a mechanism through space.

But the temporal-formal process is more than a concern with temporal and formal relationships taken either alone or each in terms of the other. It is one in which both time and space, or form, are significant, a process in which both are integrated into a single, undifferentiated event.

The temporal-formal process is an evolutionary, or developmental process. It is distinguished from the temporal process on the one hand and the formal process on the other. Like the others, this process is inherent in all experience and is manifest in all realms of reality, inanimate, biological, and cultural. Thus we have stellar and cosmic evolution, biological evolution and cultural evolution. This process differs from the temporal and formal processes in that in the evolutionary process, time and space are both integrally involved, they are fused, inseparable. Evolution is temporal-alteration-of-forms. A comparison of these three processes will make each one more distinct.

The temporal process is non-repetitive. In the sequence or process that is temporal (and temporal only), each event is unique; it occurs only once. The Rocky Mountains are formed only once, there is only one Würm glaciation, each raindrop is unique, each movement of every living creature is distinguished

from every other movement,* John Brown is executed only once,
each meeting of the women's sewing circle is a unique event. The
spatial, or functional, process, being non-temporal, is repetitive;
mountain systems may be formed repeatedly, ice-age may follow
ice-age, raindrops fall again and again, water freezes, ice thaws and
water freezes again, metal may be melted and remelted, monkeys
sneeze, men die, insurrectionists are executed, prices rise and fall
and rise again, societies and clubs are organized in every age. The
evolutionary process, being in part temporal in character, is also
non-repetitive;** a reptile becomes a mammal only once; radium
decomposes only once; stars "die" only once.*** Growth is also a

---

* It may be. Actually they usually are not, for the reason that such distinctions except in rare instances—such as the real or imagined kick of Mrs.
O'Leary's cow that started the great Chicago fire, or the honking of the geese
who "saved Rome"—have no significance for us as ordinary human beings.
But for a philosophy of science the sneeze of an anonymous monkey in the
depths of a jungle is as significant as illustrating the uniqueness of each event
in a temporal series as is the birth of Christ or the death of Caesar.

** Actually, this may depend upon one's point of view, or more accurately,
upon the temporal scope of one's vision. To us, the cosmic process seems to
be evolutionary in character: the universe is expanding (it may be assumed),
or matter is being transmuted into energy. The process seems to be temporal-
formal in character: non-repetitive and irreversible. But this appearance may
be an illusion due to the temporal limits of our observation. Were the period
longer, sufficiently longer, the cosmic process might reveal itself as a repetitive
one: an era of contraction might follow expansion, and so on, in an endless
series of pulsations; matter may be transmuted into energy and re-congealed
into matter, an endless vibration of a cosmic pendulum. So, to a creature that,
compared with us, had an infinitesimally brief span of observation, the repetitive and rhythmic character of respiration or the heart beat or the rusting of
iron would appear to be evolutionary in character, for seeing only a minute
part of the process, neither the beginning nor the end, he would observe only
a temporal alteration of form, and might declare it to be a non-repetitive
process. And he would be correct too, for the process which he observes is
non-repetitive just as the dying star and the decomposing radium represent
non-repetitive processes to us. Thus, whether a process be labelled repetitive
or evolutionary depends upon the unit of measurement. Any repetitive process
is made up of a sequence of events which in themselves are non-repetitive.
Conversely, any repetitive process is but a segment of a larger one which is
evolutionary in character.

*** One must not confuse *duplication* with *repetition*: there may be transi-
tions from reptile to mammal in many different phyla. These are duplications,
not repetitions.

temporal-spatial process; the term, however, is usually applied to individuals rather than to classes. Growth is a non-repetitive process: one is a child only once—second childhood is always a novelty.

Even at the cost of repetition, it might be well, for the sake of clarity, to re-emphasize the nature of the distinctions just made. Actually, each event has a four-dimensional character and has its place in a four-dimensional, space-time continuum. Thus the rain-drop is an event in the process of cosmic evolution, and we may view it as such. But we may also view it in other contexts: in a purely temporal context, or in a wholly non-temporal context (in which we consider only the alteration in spatial relationships between the raindrop, the earth, the clouds, etc.). These contexts are, of course, devices of our own making. They are arbitrarily selected points of view from which we regard and consider reality; they are the forms, the channels, so to speak, within which we science.

The formal process is reversible as well as repetitive. Water freezes, ice thaws; iron rusts, iron oxide decomposes; hay becomes beef; beef may become hay again; revolt and reaction are cyclical and opposite processes in society; prices rise and fall, etc. But the temporal order of events remains immutable; it cannot be reversed. Only in *Through the Looking Glass* do Queens scream before they prick their fingers, or Alices pass the cake before they cut it. The evolutionary process, being temporal as well as formal, is likewise irreversible. The stars do not reabsorb energy once emanated, mammals do not return to reptilianism, the days when knighthood was in flower can never return, "make me a child again just for tonight" is an impossible request.

The historic process and the evolutionary process are alike in being temporal in character, i.e., non-repetitive and irreversible. But, whereas the historic process is merely temporal, the evolutionary process is formal as well: it is a *temporal-sequence-of-forms*. Historically Eli Whitney and the invention of the cotton gin are

inseparable events in a chronological sequence. But had Whitney
died in his cradle the evolutionary process expressed in technology
would have produced a machine for ginning cotton. Similarly,
although Lincoln is bound historically to the emancipation of
slaves and Darwin to the formulation of certain biological principles, the processes of politico-economic evolution would have
achieved the one without Lincoln just as evolution of thought
would have produced the other without Darwin. The invention
of the calculus, which took place almost simultaneously, and independently, in the activities of Newton and Leibnitz, was the logical expression of a developmental process, i.e., it was the emergence of a new mathematical form from previous forms. Just as
the invention of the calculus was not dependent upon either Newton or Leibnitz alone, so it was not necessarily dependent upon
them both; it would have occurred eventually if both Newton
and Leibnitz had died in infancy. The development of mathematics, like the development of technology or medicine, is an
evolutionary process:* new forms grow out of preceding forms.
But in whose person and labors a new form is to appear, and when
and where it is to appear is a matter that belongs to the context
history alone. From the point of view of the evolutionary process
every historical event is an accident and in a sense unpredictable.
We may predict that a cure for cancer will be found, but to predict who will make the discovery and when is impossible. That
the nations of Europe will be embroiled again in a great war in
the not distant future is as safe a prediction as one could make;
the development of technological, economic, political, and military
forces makes another war inevitable. But who will strike the spark
that will set off the conflagration, and when and where—what
archduke or official will be shot, when, where, and by whom—it
is utterly impossible to say. The passing of a star, drawing out from
the sun a gigantic filament from which the planets of our solar

* Einstein and Infeld have called their recent book The *Evolution* of
Physics, not the *History* of Physics, it is significant to note.

system were formed, if a fact, is an historic fact; the process is an historic process in which specific and severally unique events take place in a purely temporal context. But this is quite a different process from that of cosmic or galactic evolution as exemplified, for instance, by the equi-partition of energy, or the transmutation of matter into energy, the dying of a star. Similarly, in the biologic realm, the narrative of the specific wanderings over the face of the earth, the struggles, intermixture, vicissitudes, etc., of the various species and races of man is quite a different story from the account of the evolutionary development.

So far, we have spoken of the inorganic, organic, and superorganic realms, or levels, of reality as if these distinctions could be taken for granted. For the sake of completeness and clarity, however, a few words on this subject are desirable.

The distinctions between these levels, or strata, of reality are valid, and are fundamental for science. The phenomena of these three levels do not differ from each other in that one is composed of one kind of basic substance, another of a different kind. They differ in the manner in which their component parts are organized into patterns or forms, respectively. Basically all reality may be assumed to be made up of a common stuff; differences in various manifestations of reality are due to differences in the forms in which reality confronts us. There are classes, or kinds, of forms amid the infinite range of specific variation. Physical, biological, and cultural are labels for three qualitatively different and scientifically significant classes of forms of reality.

The physical category is composed of non-living phenomena or systems; the biological, of living organisms. The cultural category, or order, of phenomena is made up of events that are dependent upon a faculty peculiar to the human species, namely, the ability to use symbols. These events are the ideas, beliefs, languages, tools, utensils, customs, sentiments, and institutions that make up the civilization—or *culture*, to use the anthropological term—of any people, regardless of time, place, or degree of development.

Culture is passed down from one generation to another, or, it may be borrowed freely by one tribe from another. Its elements interact with one another in accordance with principles of their own. Culture thus constitutes a supra-biological, or extra-somatic, class of events, a process *sui generis*. We shall analyze this order of phenomena at some length in the following chapter on *The Symbol*.

Even a casual inspection of our three categories reveals the fact that biological and cultural phenomena are but particular kinds of organization of events in the inanimate, and the biological and physical categories, respectively. Thus, a plant or an animal is but a peculiar form of organization of carbon, oxygen, calcium, etc. Likewise a cultural phenomenon is but a manifestation of biological (human beings) and inanimate phenomena organized in a special manner. Thus events on the biologic level (for levels, or strata, are what these categories are in reality) can be dealt with in terms of inanimate phenomena: a plant or animal is so much carbon, nitrogen, hydrogen; it has weight, will fall as a rock, may be frozen, transformed by fire, and so on. Similarly, a cultural event—a man taking a Christian oath of office—may be dealt with in terms of his gestures, vocal and manual, and these, in turn, together with the book upon which the oath is taken, can be treated in terms of acoustics, mechanics, physical and chemical properties of the Bible, and so on.

But the fact that the phenomena of one category (except of course the first, the inanimate) can be "reduced" to the one, or ones, below it does not destroy the categories themselves, nor even minimize their distinctness. Meteors, bullets, pterodactyls, birds, squirrels, fish, bats, bees, and airplanes "fly" through the air. A physicist could deal with each as a material body, in terms of mass, momentum, acceleration, atmospheric resistance, and so on. Considered merely as material bodies the fact that some are animate, others inanimate, is of course irrelevant. But merely because this distinction is not significant to the physicist does not mean that it is not meaningful in other sectors of science. On the contrary, organizations of events cannot be fully understood unless they are interpreted upon the level of their organization. It is a fact, of course, that bees, bullets, and bats are composed of atoms and molecules, and this fact is not without significance. But we cannot appreciate the difference between bees and bullets on the one hand or between bees and bats on the other on the basis of physical organization alone. Living organisms constitute a distinct order of material systems and they must be interpreted as such. Cultural systems are composed of psycho-physical events, but we cannot comprehend such a thing as taking an oath of office and distinguish it from use of a formula to make beer merely by knowing that each is made up of neuro-sensory-muscular reactions and that these in turn are composed of molecular and atomic particles and processes. However illuminating it may be to reduce systems of one level to the events of the level below it—and this is unquestionably valuable—each order of events, each kind of system, must be comprehended on its own level also.

Thus we see that we have three qualitatively distinct levels or strata of phenomena: the cultural, which is characterized by the symbol; the biological, characterized by the cell; and the physical, characterized by the atom, proton, electron, wave, or whatever other unit, or units, the physicist decides upon.

There are, however, instances in which our ends are not served by maintaining the distinctions between these three levels. We may wish to inquire into the relationship between one level and another. Inquiries of this sort are, needless to say, as legitimate and potentially profitable as any other. Thus bio-chemistry inquires into the relationship between the inanimate and the living. Similar inquiries are directed to the relationship between the biological and cultural levels. Take the Oedipus complex of psychoanalysis, for example. A boy's love for his mother, hatred or hostility toward his father, is of course a reaction of his organism. But these attitudes are functions of the culture in which he was born, also. His culture not only channels the expression of these emotions but plays a part in their evocation as well. The attitude of a boy toward his parents will not be the same in a patriarchal society as in one matrilineally organized, or in one that recognizes both lines of descent equally. Thus the Oedipus or Electra complex, as well as all other examples of *human* behavior—i.e., human behavior as distinguished from non-human, or sub-human, behavior; there is nothing peculiarly *human* about a sneeze, e.g.—are made up of elements drawn from two different categories: the biological and the cultural. The formula for human behavior is: Human organism x Cultural stimuli → Human behavior.

Studies of soil erosion may inquire into the relationship between such things as farming or grazing methods, the lumber industry, prices of building materials, and reforestation; the quantity and frequency of rainfall, natural and artificial drainage structures; winds, and legislation. The search for a material that will destroy plant or animal pests may involve relationships between all three levels: the price of commodities, the biological organisms and the chemicals capable of killing them.

Here again, whether we deal with reality in terms of distinct categories, or levels, of phenomena, or in terms of relationships between them, depends upon our purposes and ends. Both approaches are equally legitimate and potentially profitable.

In summary, we see that we have two classifications of reality which cut across each other at right angles: the one has to do with structure (the atom, the cell, the symbol), the other has to do with process (temporal, formal, and temporal-formal). This gives us nine categories in which all reality and all manners of sciencing may be logically and consistently divided as indicated in the diagram on the opposite page.

On the inanimate level we have cosmic and galactic histories (such as they are or may be), the history of our solar system, the history of the earth or of a continent, a mountain chain, a river, or even a snowflake, encompassed within the purely temporal context. In the formal-functional context we have the non-temporal and repetitive, structural and functional aspects of astronomy, geology, chemistry, and physics. And in the primary category, the temporal-formal one, of which the other two are but aspects, we have cosmic, galactic, stellar,[7] and solar evolution, and the decomposition of radio-active substances.

	Temporal	*Spatial-Temporal*	*Spatial*
Cultural	"History," Culture History, or History of Civilization	Cultural Evolution	Non-temporal, repetitive, culturally determined processes in human society
Biological	Racial history of Man. History of animal and plant species, genera	Biological evolution. Growth of individuals	Non-temporal, repetitive processes in organic behavior: intra-organismal (physiology), extra-organismal (psychology)
Physical	History of solar system, of the earth, a continent, mountain system, river, drop of water, a grain of sand	Cosmic, solar, stellar, galactic evolution. Disintegration of radio-active substances	Non-temporal, repetitive processes in physics, chemistry, astronomy

On the biologic level, in the purely temporal context, we have the histories of plants and animals, of genera, species, and individuals, both human and non-human. Our greatest concern in this category is, perhaps, with human beings: we are intensely interested in the problems of the origin, diffusion, extinction, intermixture of various species and races of mankind. But a like interest in plants and sub-human animals is not insignificant. In the formal-functional category we have studies of morphology and function; the non-temporal, repetitive aspects of anatomy, physiology, and psychology belong here. And, in the temporal-formal category, we have evolution of biologic forms in general, of genera, species, varieties in particular. The growth of an individual also comes within this category.

Biography, the history of a human individual, should, in most instances, be regarded as dealing with both the biologic and the cultural levels since our interest in a human individual is seldom, if ever, divorced from the culture in which he has his human being. Similarly with significant individuals in the sub-human animal or plant world: the cow that started the Chicago fire, the goose that saved Rome, the wolf who suckled Romulus and Remus, Man o' War, the hemlock that killed Socrates, each is significant only because it enters the context of human cultural history.

On the cultural level we have culture history; a consideration of nations, reigns, tribes, institutions, tools, ideas, beliefs, etc., in the temporal context. In the formal-functional context, we have the studies of "social morphology" in sociology, cultural anthropology, and the other "social sciences." The so-called Functionalist schools of cultural anthropology—Radcliffe-Brown, Malinowski and their respective students and co-workers—and the "Chicago school" of sociology, as exemplified by Robert E. Park and E. W. Burgess and their students, belong here. In the basic category, that of evolution of culture, we have at present virtually nothing. After a vigorous and bitter struggle the philosophy of evolution conquered on the biological field, but, after a few brief advances it has been routed from the cultural level. A few giants like Herbert Spencer, E. B. Tylor, and Lewis H. Morgan, in the "boom" days of evolutionism in the second half of the nineteenth century were able to occupy the cultural field for a time. But the anti-evolutionists regained the field and have held it successfully since the turn of the century. To be sure both Morgan and Spencer committed errors in the use of their philosophy, but a mistake made in the use of a tool does not render the tool worthless. But cultural anthropologists—and many sociologists—have repudiated the philosophy of evolutionism along with the errors of some evolutionists: they have poured the baby out with the bath. But the victory of the anti-evolutionists on the cultural level is only temporary. As social science matures, the basic concept of science and philosophy, that reality is temporal-formal in character, will win its way on the cultural level as it has upon the biologic and inanimate levels.

It will be noted, of course, that the conventional names for "the sciences" do not readily fit our system of categories. But this is quite understandable: the terms *physics, zoology, sociology*, etc., have come into use as science has grown, and this growth has been more or less accidental. The concepts *time* and *space* existed long before it was discovered that *time* and *space* are but aspects of a third thing for which there is no more adequate a name than *space-time*. But the fact that the names of "the sciences" do not correspond to our nine categories in no way invalidates the categories. The maturity of science in any field can be rather accurately gauged by its vocabulary: as "a science" matures it develops its own terminology. This has taken place extensively in the physical and the biological sciences. And such words as *instinct, intelligence, race, society*, are now being found so difficult to use that it is likely they will give way soon to a more effective terminology.

For the scientific worker such terms as *psychology, botany, chemistry*, etc., will no doubt continue to be useful and satisfactory except in so far as further division of labor and specialization should make new terms necessary. But for the thinker, for the philosopher of science, new technical terms are needed. I shall not presume to supply names for our nine categories. But, since they represent a realistic and logical analysis of the field, it seems likely that as these categories obtrude themselves more and more into systematic thinking, they will eventually receive names.

CHAPTER TWO

THE SYMBOL:
The Origin and Basis of Human Behavior

"In the Word was the Beginning . . . the beginning of Man and of Culture."

I

*I*n July, 1939, a celebration was held at Leland Stanford University to commemorate the hundredth anniversary of the discovery that the cell is the basic unit of all living tissue. Today we are beginning to realize and to appreciate the fact that the symbol is the basic unit of all human behavior and civilization.

All human behavior originates in the use of symbols. It was the symbol which transformed our anthropoid ancestors into men and made them human. All civilizations have been generated, and are perpetuated, only by the use of symbols. It is the symbol which transforms an infant of Homo sapiens into a human being; deaf mutes who grow up without the use of symbols are not human beings. All human behavior consists of, or is dependent upon, the use of symbols. Human behavior is symbolic behavior; symbolic behavior is human behavior. The symbol is the universe of humanity.

II

The great Darwin declared in *The Descent of Man* that "there is no fundamental difference between man and the higher mammals in their mental faculties," that the difference between them consists "solely in his [man's] almost infinitely larger power of associating together the most diversified sounds and ideas . . . the mental powers of higher animals do not differ in kind, though greatly in degree, from the corresponding powers of man" (Chs. 3, 18; emphasis ours).

This view of comparative mentality is held by many scholars today. Thus, F. H. Hankins, a prominent sociologist, states that "in spite of his large brain, it cannot be said that man has any mental traits that are peculiar to him . . . All of these human superiorities are merely relative or differences of degree." Professor Ralph Linton, an anthropologist, writes in The Study of Man: "The differences between men and animals in all these [behavior] respects are enormous, but they seem to be differences in quantity rather than in quality." "Human and animal behavior can be shown to have so much in common," Linton observes, "that the gap [between them] ceases to be of great importance." Dr. Alexander Goldenweiser, likewise an anthropologist, believes that "In point of sheer psychology, mind as such, man is after all no more than a talented animal" and that "the difference between the mentality here displayed [by a horse and a chimpanzee] and that of man is merely one of degree." [1]

That there are numerous and impressive similarities between the behavior of man and that of ape is fairly obvious; it is quite possible that chimpanzees and gorillas in zoos have noted and appreciated them. Fairly apparent, too, are man's behavioral similarities to many other kinds of animals. Almost as obvious, but not easy to define, is a difference in behavior which distinguishes man from all other living creatures. I say 'obvious' because it is quite apparent to the common man that the non-human animals with which he is familiar do not and cannot enter, and participate in, the world in which he, as a human being, lives. It is impossible for a dog, horse, bird, or even an ape, to have any understanding of the meaning of the sign of the cross to a Christian, or of the

fact that black (white among the Chinese) is the color of mourning. No chimpanzee or laboratory rat can appreciate the difference
between Holy water and distilled water, or grasp the meaning of
Tuesday, 3, or sin. No animal save man can distinguish a cousin
from an uncle, or a cross cousin from a parallel cousin. Only man
can commit the crime of incest or adultery; only he can remember
the Sabbath and keep it Holy. It is not, as we well know, that the
lower animals can do these things but to a lesser degree than ourselves; they cannot perform these acts of appreciation and distinction at all. It is, as Descartes said long ago, "not only that the
brutes have less Reason than man, but that they have none at
all." [2]

But when the scholar attempts to define the mental difference
between man and other animals he sometimes encounters difficulties which he cannot surmount and, therefore, ends up by
saying that the difference is merely one of degree: man has a bigger
mind, "larger power of association," wider range of activities, etc.
We have a good example of this in the distinguished physiologist,
Anton J. Carlson. After taking note of "man's present achievements in science, in the arts (including oratory), in political and
social institutions," and noting "at the same time the apparent
paucity of such behavior in other animals," he, as a common man
"is tempted to conclude that in these capacities, at least, man has
a qualitative superiority over other mammals." But, since, as a
scientist, Professor Carlson cannot define this qualitative difference between man and other animals, since as a physiologist he
cannot explain it, he refuses to admit it— ". . . the physiologist
does not accept the great development of articulate speech in man
as something qualitatively new; . . ." —and suggests helplessly that
some day we may find some new "building stone," an "additional
lipoid, phosphatid, or potassium ion," in the human brain which
will explain it, and concludes by saying that the difference between the mind of man and that of non-man is "probably only
one of degree." [3]

The thesis that we shall advance and defend here is that there is a *fundamental* difference between the mind of man and the mind of non-man. This difference is one of kind, not one of degree. And the gap between the two types is of the greatest importance—at least to the science of comparative behavior. Man uses symbols; no other creature does. An organism has the ability to symbol or it does not; there are no intermediate stages.

III

A symbol may be defined as a thing the value or meaning of which is bestowed upon it by those who use it. I say 'thing' because a symbol may have any kind of physical form; it may have the form of a material object, a color, a sound, an odor, a motion of an object, a taste.

The meaning, or value, of a symbol is in no instance derived from or determined by properties intrinsic in its physical form: the color appropriate to mourning may be yellow, green, or any other color; purple need not be the color of royalty; among the Manchu rulers of China it was yellow. The meaning of the word "see" is not intrinsic in its phonetic (or pictorial) properties. "Biting one's thumb at" * someone might mean anything. The meanings of symbols are derived from and determined by the organisms who use them; meaning is bestowed by human organisms upon physical things or events which thereupon become symbols. Symbols "have their signification," to use John Locke's phrase, "from the arbitrary imposition of men." [4]

All symbols must have a physical form otherwise they could not enter our experience. This statement is valid regardless of our theory of experiencing. Even the exponents of "Extra-Sensory Perception" who have challenged Locke's dictum that "the knowledge of the existence of any other thing [besides ourselves and God] we can have only by sensation," [5] have been obliged to work

---

* "Do you bite your thumb at us, sir?"—*Romeo and Juliet*, Act I, Sc. 1.

with physical rather than ethereal forms. But the meaning of a symbol cannot be discovered by mere sensory examination of its physical form. One cannot tell by looking at an x in an algebraic equation what it stands for; one cannot ascertain with the ears alone the symbolic value of the phonetic compound *si*; one cannot tell merely by weighing a pig how much gold he will exchange for; one cannot tell from the wave length of a color whether it stands for courage or cowardice, "stop" or "go"; nor can one discover the spirit in a fetish by any amount of physical or chemical examination. The meaning of a symbol can be grasped only by non-sensory, symbolic means.

The nature of symbolic experience may be easily illustrated. When the Spaniards first encountered the Aztecs, neither could speak the language of the other. How could the Indians discover the meaning of santo, or the significance of the crucifix? How could the Spaniards learn the meaning of *calli*, or appreciate Tlaloc? These meanings and values could not be communicated by sensory experience of physical properties alone. The finest ears will not tell you whether *santo* means "holy" or "hungry." The keenest senses cannot capture the value of holy water. Yet, as we all know, the Spaniards and the Aztecs did discover each other's meanings and appreciate each other's values. But not with sensory means. Each was able to enter the world of the other only by virtue of a faculty for which we have no better name than *symbol*.

But a thing which in one context is a symbol is, in another context, not a symbol but a sign. Thus, a word is a symbol only when one is concerned with the distinction between its meaning and its physical form. This distinction must be made when one bestows value upon a sound-combination or when a previously bestowed value is discovered for the first time; it may be made at other times for certain purposes. But after value has been bestowed upon, or discovered in, a word, its meaning becomes identified, in use, with its physical form. The word then functions as a sign, rather than as a symbol. Its meaning is then grasped with the senses.

We define a *sign* as a physical thing or event whose function is to indicate some other thing or event. The meaning of a sign may be inherent in its physical form and its context, as in the case of the height of a column of mercury in a thermometer as an indication of temperature, or the return of robins in the spring. Or, the meaning of a sign may be merely identified with its physical form as in the case of a hurricane signal or a quarantine flag. But in either case, the meaning of the sign may be ascertained by sensory means. The fact that a thing may be both a symbol (in one context) and a sign (in another context) has led to confusion and misunderstanding.

Thus Darwin says: "That which distinguishes man from the lower animals is not the understanding of articulate sounds, for as everyone knows, dogs understand many words and sentences," (Ch. III, *The Descent of Man*).

It is perfectly true, of course, that dogs, apes, horses, birds, and perhaps creatures even lower in the evolutionary scale, can be taught to respond in a specific way to a vocal command. Little Gua, the infant chimpanzee in the Kelloggs' experiment, was, for a time, "considerably superior to the child in responding to human words." [6] But it does not follow that no difference exists between the meaning of "words and sentences" to a man and to an ape or dog. Words are both signs and symbols to man; they are merely signs to a dog. Let us analyze the situation of vocal stimulus and response.

A dog may be taught to roll over at the command "Roll over!" A man may be taught to stop at the command "Halt!" The fact that a dog can be taught to roll over in Chinese, or that he can be taught to "go fetch" at the command "roll over" (and, of course, the same is true for a man) shows that there is no necessary and invariable relationship between a particular sound combination and a specific reaction to it. The dog or the man can be taught to respond in a certain manner to any arbitrarily selected combination of sounds, for example, a group of nonsense syllables, coined for the occasion. On the other hand, any one of a great number and variety of responses may become evocable by a given stimulus. Thus, so far as the *origin* of the relationship between vocal stimulus and response is concerned, the nature of the relationship, i.e., the meaning of the stimulus, is not determined by properties intrinsic in the stimulus.

But, once the relationship has been established between vocal stimulus and response, the meaning of the stimulus becomes *identified with the sounds*; it is then as *if* the meaning were intrinsic in the sounds themselves. Thus, 'halt' does not have the same meaning as 'hilt' or 'malt,' and these stimuli are distinguished from one another with the auditory mechanism. A dog may be conditioned to respond in a certain way to a sound of a given wave length. Sufficiently alter the pitch of the sound and the response will cease to be forthcoming. The meaning of the stimulus has become identified with its physical form; its value is appreciated with the senses.

Thus in *sign* behavior we see that in *establishing* a relationship between a stimulus and a response the properties intrinsic in the stimulus do not determine the nature of the response. But, *after the relationship has been established* the meaning of the stimulus is as *if* it were *inherent* in its physical form. It does not make any difference what phonetic combination we select to evoke the response of terminating self-locomotion. We may teach a dog, horse, or man to stop at any vocal command we care to choose or devise. But once the relationship has been established between sound and response, the meaning of the stimulus becomes identified with its physical form and is, therefore, perceivable with the senses.

So far we have discovered no difference between the dog and the man; they appear to be exactly alike. And so they are as far as we have gone. But we have not told the whole story yet. No difference between dog and man is discoverable so far as learning to respond appropriately to a vocal stimulus is concerned. But we must not let an impressive similarity conceal an important difference. A porpoise is not yet a fish.

The man differs from the dog—and all other creatures—in that *he can and does play an active role in determining what value the vocal stimulus is to have, and the dog cannot.* The dog does not and cannot play an active part in determining the value of the vocal stimulus. Whether he is to roll over or go fetch at a given stimulus, or whether the stimulus for roll over be one combination of sounds or another is a matter in which the dog has nothing whatever to "say." He plays a purely passive role and can do nothing else. He learns the meaning of a vocal command just as his salivary glands may learn to respond to the sound of a bell. But man plays an active role and thus becomes a creator: let x equal three pounds of coal and it does equal three pounds of coal; let removal of the hat in a house of worship indicate respect and it becomes so. This creative faculty, that of freely, actively, and arbitrarily bestowing value upon things, is one of the most commonplace as well as *the* most important characteristic of man. Children employ it freely in their play: "Let's pretend that this rock is a wolf."

The difference between the behavior of man and other animals then, is that the lower animals may receive new values, may acquire new meanings, but they cannot create and bestow them. Only man can do this. To use a crude analogy, lower animals are like a person who has only the receiving apparatus for wireless messages: he can receive messages but cannot send them. Man can do both. And this difference is one of kind, not of degree: a creature can either "arbitrarily impose signification," can either create and bestow values, or he cannot. There are no intermediate stages. This difference may appear slight, but, as a carpenter once told William James in discussing differences between men, "It's very important." All *human* existence depends upon it and it alone.

The confusion regarding the nature of words and their significance to men and the lower animals is not hard to understand.
It arises, first of all, from a failure to distinguish between the two
quite different contexts in which words function. The statements,
"The meaning of a word cannot be grasped with the senses," and
"The meaning of a word can be grasped with the senses," though
contradictory, are nevertheless equally true. In the *symbol* context
the meaning cannot be perceived with the senses; in the *sign* context it can. This is confusing enough. But the situation has been
made worse by using the words 'symbol' and 'sign' to label, not
the *different contexts*, but *one and the same thing*: the word. Thus
a word is a symbol *and* a sign, two different things. It is like saying
that a vase is a *doli* and a *kana*—two different things—because it
may function in two contexts, esthetic and commercial.

IV

That man is unique among animal species with respect to
mental abilities, that a fundamental difference of kind—not of
degree—separates man from all other animals is a fact that has
long been appreciated, despite Darwin's pronouncement to the
contrary. Long ago, in his *Discourse on Method*, Descartes pointed
out that "there are no men so dull and stupid . . . as to be incapable of joining together different words . . . on the other hand, there
is no other animal, however perfect . . . which can do the like."
John Locke, too, saw clearly that "the power of abstracting is not
at all in them [i.e., beasts], and that the having of general ideas
is that which puts a perfect distinction between man and brutes,
and is an excellency which the faculties of brutes do by no means
attain to . . . they have no use of words or any other general
signs." [7] The great British anthropologist, E. B. Tylor, remarked
upon "the mental gulf that divides the lowest savage from the
highest ape . . . A young child can understand what is not proved
to have entered the mind of the cleverest dog, elephant, or ape." [8]

And, of course, there are many today who recognize the "mental gulf" between man and other species.

Thus, for over a century we have had, side by side, two traditions in comparative psychology. One has declared that man does not differ from other animals in mental abilities except in degree. The other has seen clearly that man is unique in at least one respect, that he possesses an ability that no other animal has. The difficulty of *defining* this difference adequately has kept this question open until the present day. The distinction between *sign* behavior and *symbol* behavior as drawn here may, we hope, contribute to a solution of this problem once and for all.

V

Very little indeed is known of the organic basis of the symbolic faculty: we know next to nothing of the neurology of "symbolling." And very few scientists—anatomists, neurologists or physical anthropologists—appear to be interested in the subject. Some, in fact, seem to be unaware of the existence of such a problem. The duty and task of giving an account of the neural basis of symbolling does not, however, fall within the province of the sociologist or the cultural anthropologist. On the contrary, he should scrupulously exclude it as irrelevant to his problems and interests; to introduce it would bring only confusion. It is enough for the sociologist or cultural anthropologist to take the ability to use symbols, possessed by man alone, as given. The use to which he puts this fact is in no way affected by his, or even the anatomist's, inability to describe the symbolic process in neurological terms. However, it is well for the social scientist to be acquainted with the little that neurologists and anatomists do know about the structural basis of symbolling. We, therefore, review briefly the chief relevant facts here.

The anatomist has not been able to discover why men can use symbols and apes cannot. So far as is known the only difference between the brain of man and the brain of an ape is a quantitative

one: ". . . man has no new kinds of brain cells or brain cell connections," as A. J. Carlson has remarked. Nor does man, as distinguished from other animals, possess a specialized "symbol-
mechanism." The so-called speech areas of the brain should not
be identified with symbolling. The notion that symbolling is
identified with, or dependent upon, the ability to utter articulate
sounds is not uncommon. Thus, L. L. Bernard lists as "the fourth
great organic asset of man . . . his vocal apparatus, . . . characteristic of him alone." But this is an erroneous conception. The great
apes have the mechanism necessary for the production of articulate
sounds. "It seemingly is well established," write R. M. and A. W.
Yerkes in *The Great Apes*, "that the motor mechanism of voice
in this ape [chimpanzee] is adequate not only to the production
of a considerable variety of sounds, but also to definite articula-
tions similar to those of man." And the physical anthropologist,
E. A. Hooton, asserts that "all of the anthropoid apes are vocally
and muscularly equipped so that they could have an articulate
language if they possessed the requisite intelligence." Furthermore,
as Descartes and Locke pointed out long ago, there are birds who
do actually utter articulate sounds, who duplicate the sounds of
human speech, but who of course are quite incapable of symbolling. The "speech areas" of the brain are merely areas associated
with the muscles of the tongue, with the larynx, etc. But, as we
know, symbolling is not at all confined to the use of these organs.
One may symbol with any part of the body that he can move at
will.[9]

To be sure, the symbolic faculty was brought into existence by
the natural processes of organic evolution. And we may reasonably
believe that the focal point, if not the locus, of this faculty is in
the brain, especially the forebrain. Man's brain is much larger than
that of an ape, both absolutely and relatively. The brain of the
average adult human male is about 1500 c.c. in size; brains of
gorillas seldom exceed 500 c.c. Relatively, the human brain weighs
about 1/50th of the entire body weight, while that of a gorilla

varies from 1/150th to 1/200th part of that weight.[10] And the forebrain especially is large in man as compared with ape. Now in many situations we know that quantitative changes give rise to qualitative differences. Water is transformed into steam by additional quantities of heat. Additional power and speed lift the taxiing airplane from the ground and transform terrestrial locomotion into flight. The difference between wood alcohol and grain alcohol is a qualitative expression of a quantitative difference in the proportions of carbon and hydrogen. Thus a marked growth in size of the brain in man may have brought forth a *new kind* of function.

VI

All culture (civilization) depends upon the symbol. It was the exercise of the symbolic faculty that brought culture into existence and it is the use of symbols that makes the perpetuation of culture possible. Without the symbol there would be no culture, and man would be merely an animal, not a human being.

Articulate speech is the most important form of symbolic expression. Remove speech from culture and what would remain? Let us see.

Without articulate speech we would have no *human* social organization. Families we might have, but this form of organization is not peculiar to man; it is not *per se*, *human*. But we would have no prohibitions of incest, no rules prescribing exogamy and endogamy, polygamy or monogamy. How could marriage with a cross cousin be prescribed, marriage with a parallel cousin proscribed, without articulate speech? How could rules which prohibit plural mates possessed simultaneously but permit them if possessed one at a time, exist without speech?

Without speech we would have no political, economic, ecclesiastic, or military organization; no codes of etiquette or ethics; no laws; no science, theology, or literature; no games or music, except on an ape level. Rituals and ceremonial paraphernalia would be meaningless without articulate speech. Indeed, without articulate speech we would be all but toolless: we would have only the occasional and insignificant use of the tool such as we find today among the higher apes, for it was articulate speech that transformed the non-progressive tool-using of the ape into the progressive, cumulative tool-using of man, the human being.

In short, without symbolic communication in some form, we would have no culture. "In the Word was the beginning" of culture—and its perpetuation also.

To be sure, with all his culture man is still an animal and strives for the same ends that all other living creatures strive for: the preservation of the individual and the perpetuation of the race. In concrete terms these ends are food, shelter from the elements, defense from enemies, health, and offspring. The fact that man strives for these ends just as all other animals do has, no doubt, led many to declare that there is "no fundamental difference between the behavior of man and of other creatures." But man does differ, not in *ends* but in *means*. Man's means are cultural means: culture is simply the human animal's way of living. And, since these means, culture, are dependent upon a faculty possessed by man alone, the ability to use symbols, the difference between the behavior of man and of all other creatures is not merely great, but basic and fundamental.

VII

The behavior of man is of two distinct kinds: symbolic and non-symbolic. Man yawns, stretches, coughs, scratches himself, cries out in pain, shrinks with fear, "bristles" with anger, and so on. Non-symbolic behavior of this sort is not peculiar to man; he shares it not only with the other primates but with many other animal species as well. But man communicates with his fellows with articulate speech, uses amulets, confesses sins, makes laws, observes codes of etiquette, explains his dreams, classifies his relatives in designated categories, and so on. This kind of behavior is unique; only man is capable of it; it is peculiar to man because it consists of, or is dependent upon, the use of symbols. The non-symbolic behavior of Homo sapiens is the behavior of man the animal; the symbolic behavior is that of man the human being. It is the symbol which has transformed man from a mere animal to a human animal.

Because *human* behavior is symbol behavior and since the behavior of infra-human species is non-symbolic, it follows that we can learn nothing about human behavior from observations upon or experiments with the lower animals. Experiments with rats and apes have indeed been illuminating. They have thrown much light upon mechanisms and processes of behavior among mammals or the higher vertebrates. But they have contributed nothing to an understanding of *human* behavior because the symbol mechanism and all of its consequences are totally lacking among the lower species. And as for neuroses in rats, it is of course interesting to know that rats can be made neurotic. But science probably had a better understanding of psychopathic behavior among human beings before neuroses were produced experimentally in rats than they now have of the neuroses of the rats. Our understanding of human neuroses has helped us to understand those of rats; we have, as a matter of fact, interpreted the latter in terms of *human* pathology. But I cannot see where the neurotic laboratory rats have served to deepen or enlarge our understanding of *human* behavior.

As it was the symbol that made *mankind* human, so it is with each member of the species. A baby is not a *human* being until he begins to symbol. Until the infant begins to talk there is nothing to distinguish his behavior qualitatively from that of a very young ape, as *The Ape and the Child* showed. As a matter of fact, one of the impressive results of this fascinating experiment by Professor and Mrs. Kellogg was the demonstration of how ape-like an infant of Homo sapiens is before he begins to talk. The baby boy acquired exceptional proficiency in climbing in association with the little chimpanzee, and even acquired her "food bark"! The Kelloggs speak of how the little ape became "humanized" during her sojourn in their home. But what the experiment demonstrated so conclusively was the ape's utter inability to learn to talk or even to make any progress in this direction—in short, her inability to become "humanized" at all.

The infant of the species *Homo sapiens* becomes human only when and as he exercises his symbol faculty. Only through articulate speech—not necessarily vocal—can he enter the world of human beings and take part in their affairs. The questions asked earlier may be repeated now. How could a growing child know and appreciate such things as social organization, ethics, etiquette, ritual, science, religion, art and games without symbolic communication? The answer is of course that he could know nothing of these things and have no appreciation of them at all.

The question of "wolf children" is relevant here. A belief in instances in which human children have been reared by wolves or other animals has flourished ever since the myth of Romulus and Remus—and long before that time. Despite the fact that accounts of "wolf children" have been shown repeatedly to be erroneous or unsupported by adequate evidence ever since Blumenbach discovered that "Wild Peter" was merely a half-witted boy ejected from his home at the instance of a newly acquired stepmother, this deplorable folk-tale still flourishes in certain "scientific" circles today. But the use to which these lupine wards and "feral men" are put by some sociologists and psychologists is a good one, namely, to show that a member of the species *Homo sapiens* who lives is a world without symbols is not a human being but a brute. To paraphrase Voltaire, one might say that if wolf children did not exist "social science" would have to invent them.

Children who have been cut off from human intercourse for years by blindness and deafness but who have eventually effected communication with their fellows on a symbolic level are exceedingly illuminating. The case of Helen Keller is exceptionally instructive, although those of Laura Bridgman, Marie Heurtin, and others [11] are very valuable also.

Helen Keller was rendered blind and deaf at a very early age by illness. She grew up as a child without symbolic contact with anyone. Descriptions of her at the age of seven, the time at which her teacher, Miss Sullivan, came to her home, disclose no human attributes of Helen's behavior at all. She was a headstrong, undisciplined and unruly little animal.[12]

Within a day or so after her arrival at the Keller home, Miss Sullivan taught Helen her first word, spelling it into her hand. But this word was merely a sign, not a symbol. A week later Helen knew several words but, as Miss Sullivan reports, she had "no idea how to use them or that everything has a name." Within three weeks Helen knew eighteen nouns and three verbs. But she was still on the level of signs: she still had no notion "that everything has a name."

Helen confused the word signs for "mug" and "water" because, apparently, both were associated with drinking. Miss Sullivan made a few attempts to clear up this confusion but without success. One morning, however, about a month after Miss Sullivan's arrival, the two went out to the pump in the garden. What happened then is best told in their own words:

> I made Helen hold her mug under the spout while I pumped. As the cold water gushed forth, filling the mug, I spelled 'w-a-t-e-r' into Helen's free hand. The word coming so close upon the sensation of cold water rushing over her hand seemed to startle her. She dropped the mug and stood as one transfixed. A new light came into her face. She spelled 'water' several times. Then she dropped on the ground and asked for its name and pointed to the pump and the trellis, and suddenly turning round she asked for my name . . . *In a few hours she had added thirty new words to her vocabulary.*

But these words were now more than mere signs as they are to a dog and as they had been to Helen up to then. They were symbols. Helen had at last grasped and turned the key that admitted her for the first time to a new universe: the world of human beings. Helen describes this marvellous experience herself:

> We walked down the path to the well-house, attracted by the fragrance of the honeysuckle with which it was covered. Someone was drawing water and my teacher placed my hand under the spout. As the cool stream gushed over one hand she spelled into the other the word *water*, first slowly, then rapidly. I stood still, my whole attention fixed upon the motion of her fingers. Suddenly I felt a misty consciousness as of something forgotten—a thrill of returning thought; and somehow *the mystery of language was revealed to me*. I knew then that 'w-a-t-e-r' meant the wonderful cool something that was flowing over my hand. That living word awakened my soul, gave it light, hope, joy, set it free!

Helen was transformed on the instant by this experience. Miss Sullivan had managed to touch Helen's symbol mechanism and set it in motion. Helen, on her part, grasped the external world with this mechanism that had lain dormant and inert all these years, sealed in dark and silent isolation by eyes that could not see and ears that heard not. But now she had crossed the boundary and entered a new land. Henceforth her progress would be rapid.

"I left the well-house," Helen reports, "eager to learn. Everything had a name, and each name gave birth to a new thought. As we returned to the house every object which I touched seemed to quiver with life. That was because I saw everything with the strange new sight that had come to me."

Helen became humanized rapidly. "I see an improvement in Helen from day to day," Miss Sullivan wrote in her diary, "*almost from hour to hour*. Everything must have a name now . . . She drops the signs and pantomime she used before as soon as she has words to supply their place . . . We notice her face grows more expressive each day . . ."

A more eloquent and convincing account of the significance of symbols and of the great gulf between the human mind and that of minds without symbols could hardly be imagined.

VIII

Summary. The natural processes of biologic evolution brought into existence in man, and man alone, a new and distinctive ability: the ability to use symbols. The most important form of symbolic expression is articulate speech. Articulate speech means communication of ideas; communication means preservation—tradition—and preservation means accumulation and progress. The emergence of the faculty of symbolling has resulted in the genesis of a new order of phenomena: an extra-somatic, cultural, order. All civilizations are born of, and are perpetuated by, the use of symbols. A culture, or civilization, is but a particular kind of form which the biologic, life-perpetuating activities of a particular animal, man, assume.

Human behavior is symbolic behavior; if it is not symbolic, it is not human. The infant of the genus Homo becomes a human being only as he is introduced into and participates in that order of phenomena which is culture. And the key to this world and the means of participation in it is—the symbol.

CHAPTER THREE

ON THE USE OF TOOLS BY PRIMATES

"Tools x Symbols = Culture."

*M*an has often been characterized as "the tool-using animal," the implication being that no other animal uses tools. Benjamin Franklin went farther, it is said,* and defined man as the tool-making animal. A century later, when everyone was discussing Darwinism, many learned men were willing to admit that other animals might use tools, but insisted that man alone was able to make them. The Duke of Argyll, for example, argued in his *Primeval Man* that a great "gulf," a "whole immeasurable distance," [1] lay between man and the brutes with respect to tools. He admitted that some of the lower animals use tools, but he insisted that "in no case whatever do they ever use an implement made by themselves." Edward Clodd also insisted that if man "is not the only tool-user, he is the only tool-maker among the Primates." [2] Darwin, unwilling to go farther than the evidence of his day would permit, wisely left the question open. Today, thanks particularly to the observations and experiments made among chimpanzees by Wolfgang Köhler and reported in his fascinating book, *The Mentality of Apes*, we know that apes can and do make tools. The evidence on this point is accepted as conclusive by such

***

* Anthologies of quotations and authors without number credit Franklin with this definition. The writer has not had time to plough through his Collected Works, but considerable research has failed to discover this statement in Franklin's writings. Someone asked for the reference in *Notes and Queries* years ago (Vol. 8, 1913), but received no answer, apparently. Did Franklin really say this, or is it merely scholars' folklore?

40

students of primates as R. W. Yerkes, E. A. Hooton, T. C. Schnierla, and A. L. Kroeber. However, we still find some reluctance to admit anthropoids to the category of tool-makers. Thus, the British anthropologist, Grahame Clark, in his recent *From Savagery to Civilization*, asserts that "the understanding use of tools and their purposive devising is a characteristic of man alone" (p. 7). And Wilhelm Schmidt, the leader of the so-called *Kulturkreis* school of anthropology, is unwilling to admit that the lower primates are able even to use "real tools," let alone make them.[3]

Scientific studies of apes during recent decades have disclosed a skill and a versatility in the use of tools that is quite remarkable. They readily employ sticks as levers; they build structures of boxes; use sticks in digging; and otherwise employ a great variety of materials as tools. More noteworthy still, apes (chimpanzees) have shown themselves capable of inventing—by a process of understanding and insight—tools, and of accomplishing their manufacture in instances that required the artificial shaping of materials. Sultan, one of the chimpanzees observed by Köhler, combined two sticks by inserting the end of one into the hollow end of the other, thus making a tool long enough to obtain food hitherto out of reach. "That the combined sticks were perceived and used as a true tool and not used simply by accident," writes the comparative psychologist Schnierla, "was indicated by the fact that when the sticks became separated, the animal straightway reconnected them in a manner that suggested an understanding of their function together." [4] He even contrived to put three sticks together in this manner. Once when the one stick was too large to be inserted into the hollow end of the other, Sultan chewed it down until it would fit. Chimpanzees readily build structures of boxes and crates, sometimes four or five storeys high, in order to obtain food originally suspended out of reach. They demonstrate in this way their ability to modify and to rearrange their environment, to relate one thing to another and to an objective in terms of their physical properties, which is the essence of the tool-process.

The question naturally arises, therefore, why do not apes have a culture, at least a material culture? Why is it that tool-using among apes is not a cumulative and progressive phenomenon as it is among mankind?

The limitations upon the use of tools by apes are not imposed, it appears, by anatomical or sensory shortcomings. The senses of apes, with the exception of the sense of statics, are quite as keen and as suitable for wielding material objects as are those of men. Nor are apes limited to coarse and crude implements, or to those requiring brute strength rather than delicacy. They can handle string and straws with skill; they are able deftly to remove slivers from their hands and feet. One chimpanzee under observation readily learned to thread a needle. Little Gua, the baby chimpanzee in the Kelloggs' experiment, learned to eat with a spoon more readily than did the child who was trained with her. She was more skillful and effective, too, in her solution of the "suspended cookie test," and in obtaining food by means of a hoe. Thus it appears that the limitations upon the use of tools among apes are not physical in character. As Professor E. A. Hooton has expressed it:

> . . . observation of the anthropoid apes does not make it seem probable that their tool-using abilities are strictly limited by the conformation of their hands or arms, in spite of the relative coarseness of these members, resulting, no doubt, from the locomotor and suspensory uses to which they are put . . . I do not believe that the anthropoid apes are manually incapable of most of the ordinary movements in which man employs his hands.[5]

Professor R. H. Lowie has suggested that the reason for the lack of culture among apes lies in their inability to transmit their tool knowledge and experience from one to another by imitation. "If his neighbors imitated him," says Professor Lowie, speaking of the chimpanzee who invents and uses a tool, "if he taught them his trick and they all passed it on to their offspring, chimpanzees would be on the highroad to culture. But they do nothing of the sort." [6] Professor Lowie seems to be misinformed concerning apes. According to such authorities as R. M. and A. W. Yerkes, "the chimpanzee commonly and with great facility imitates acts." [7] Numerous examples of communication of experience by imitation are to be found also in W. Köhler's *The Mentality of Apes*. Apes, it would appear, really do ape. As E. B. Tylor long ago observed, "the faculty of learning by imitation comes out in the apes in an almost human way." [8] Thus the reason for their lack of a material culture cannot lie in this direction.

It can hardly be argued that apes have no material culture because they have no need for one, or because they could derive no advantage or benefit from it. In the first place we must note that levers, hammers, digging sticks, poking sticks, missiles, etc., are actually used to practical advantage by apes. Why would not spears and daggers be useful to them in self-protection? Would not bags be useful to carry or store food or other things? To turn from the practical and utilitarian to the esthetic and recreational, and, noting the fondness of chimpanzees for games, dancing, and personal adornment, would not drums, rattles, necklaces, gorgets, and a hundred other similar things bring endless joy and satisfaction to the simian heart? Indeed, the ape could use and enjoy a culture quite as well as his human cousin.

Why, then, do apes lack a material culture? It is due to his "lack of brains," or "lack of intelligence," according to Professor Hooton.[9] This, in our opinion, is quite correct. But it is not a sufficient answer. Merely to say "lack of brains" tells us very little about the difference between the use of tools by man and ape.

The essential difference between apes and men with regard to use of tools is not, as we have seen, that man is more skillful, versatile, or even inventive. As a matter of fact, the inventive ability of man is frequently over-rated. The archeological record of cultural development makes it clear that until relatively recent times inventions were decidedly infrequent; thousands of years might elapse between the appearance of an awl and the invention of the needle—although all one had to do to effect this advance was to drill a hole in the blunt end of the awl. The invention of the steamboat is often regarded as a great achievement and indeed it was. Yet is consisted merely of combining already existing tools— an engine and a boat—of putting one and one together. Chimpanzees are able to do this. Nor does the difference between man and ape lie in an ability to imitate, to communicate tool-experience from one to another, for, as we have noted, apes freely do this. The fundamental difference consists in the fact that the use of tools among men is a cumulative and progressive process whereas among apes it is neither. This is not to say that an individual ape does not make progress in his use of tools nor that he cannot increase his repertory of tool behavior. What we are saying is that apes as species make no progress in tool-using; one generation is no further advanced than its predecessor. With man, of course, it is the reverse: each generation may build upon and add to the tools and techniques of its predecessors. It is precisely this process of accumulation and progress in technology that has lifted man from the level of the brute and carried him through savagery and barbarism to civilization.

But our question is still unanswered: Why does this difference between man and ape exist?

Tool-using among men is a different kind of activity, fundamentally and qualitatively different in a psychological sense, from tool-using among apes. Among apes the use of tools is a conceptual process as well as a neuro-sensory-muscular one. By conceptual we mean the formation by the ape of a configuration of behavior in which he, a tool, and the thing upon which the tool is to be used are functionally related to one another. The ape is able to solve his problem by means of insight and understanding, and to effect the solution implicitly before he executes it overtly. This is what we mean by *conceptual*. In the human species, the tool process is also conceptual and neuro-sensory-muscular in character. But it is

more than this; it is *symbolic* as well. Human beings express their
concepts in symbolic form. Thus they not only have tools and
concepts of tools, but they have and use *words* of tools—axe, knife,
hammer, etc. *It was the introduction of symbols, word-formed
symbols, into the tool process that transformed anthropoid tool-
behavior into human tool-behavior.*

We must distinguish two aspects of the tool-using process, the
intra-organismal and the extra-organismal, the subjective and the
overt or explicit. On the one hand we have the animal's sensory
perception of tools and other material objects in the external
world and his bodily reactions to them. On the other hand, are
the inner, neural processes of imagination and insight in which
patterns of behavior to be executed overtly are formed. In short,
we have the inner, mental aspect of tool-using and the outer,
motor aspect.

A significant characteristic of ape tool-behavior is that it is a
discontinuous psychological process. In its overt, motor aspect
the discontinuity of tool-experience is, of course, a necessity; one
cannot be engaged in wielding tools all the time. But in the ape,
tool-experience is discontinuous on the subjective side as well as
upon the objective. "Out of sight out of mind" fairly well characterizes the ape's mentality. Köhler observes that the "disappearance of a sick (or dying) animal [chimpanzee] has little effect
on the rest, so long as he is taken out of sight." [10] There is some
foresight and some hindsight in the ape. But the characteristic
feature of their mental life is the "extremely narrow limits" of
the temporal world in which they live; this, according to Köhler,
is "the chief difference . . . between anthropoids and even the
most primitive human beings." [11] The ape lives in a small world.
Spatially it is confined to the range of his senses; temporally it is
limited to the moment, with perhaps an occasional dawn of anticipation and a twilight of reminiscence. Thus, tool-experience in
the ape is a series of disconnected episodes. He wields a tool then
lays it down. When he is confronted by a "tool situation" he sizes

up the situation, formulates a plan, puts it into execution, solves
his problem, and that is the end of it. On the inner, subjective
side, the ape's tool-experience is limited to the external and overt
experience. Tool-using among apes is thus a discontinuous psychological process subjectively as well as objectively.

With man, tool-experience is quite different. Overtly, tool-
using is a discontinuous process as, of course, it must be. But
subjectively, tool-experience in man is continuous and enduring.

Man differs from the apes, and indeed all other living creatures
so far as we know, in that he is capable of symbolic behavior.
With words man creates a new world, a world of ideas and philosophies. In this world man lives just as truly as in the physical
world of his senses. Indeed, man feels that the essential quality
of his existence consists in his occupancy of this world of symbols
and ideas—or, as he sometimes calls it, the world of the mind or
spirit. This world of ideas comes to have a continuity and a per-
manence that the external world of the senses can never have.
It is not made up of the present only, but of a past and a future as
well. Temporally it is not a succession of disconnected episodes,
but a continuum extending to infinity in both directions, from
eternity to eternity. As John Dewey has aptly expressed it:

> Man differs from the lower animals because he preserves his
> past experiences . . . With the animals, an experience perishes
> as it happens, and each new doing or suffering stands alone.
> But man lives in a world where each occurrence is charged with
> echoes and reminiscences of what has gone before, where each
> event is a reminder of other things. Hence he lives not, like
> the beasts of the field, in a world of merely physical things but
> in a world of signs and symbols.[12]

This inner world of ideas in which man dwells seems more real
to him than the outer world of the senses. We have a classic
example of this in the philosophy of idealism: ideas come first;
they are the real things; they endure forever; material objects and
sensory experiences are merely imperfect and ephemeral manifesta-

tions of the Ideas.* We have essentially the same idea, though perhaps in a more primitive, and also more graphic, form in the Christian conception of the Word: "In the beginning was the Word." The Word is also creative: from the spoken word the world came into being. The Word also became flesh (John, I, 14). Thus, in man's naive philosophies, ideas and words come first. They are "more real" than the things of the senses. They are enduring and eternal.

It is in such a world as this that man knows and wields tools. To him a tool is not merely a material object, or even a sensory image as it may be to an ape. It is also an idea. It is a part of that timeless inner world in which man lives. It is not something that exists for the moment only: it functions in the living past and is projected into the unborn future. The tool in man's mind, like Plato's ideas in the mind of God, is eternal. Hence tool-experience for man is more than a series of disconnected episodes, of grasping and using tools and laying them down again. These overt acts are merely occasional expressions of an ideational experience within him that is continuous and unbroken.

Thus the difference between ape and man: In the ape, tool-experience is a series of discrete episodes; the inner experience begins and ends with the overt act. In man, tool-experience is a continuum. Though the overt expression of this experience is disconnected and episodic, the inner experience is an uninterrupted flow. And it is the symbol, the word-formed idea, that makes this continuity of experience possible.

When Professor Lowie endeavors to account for the ape's lack of culture by the inability to imitate, and hence to transmit and perpetuate tool-experience, he is really on the right track even though his premise is wrong. For what he is getting at is con-

---

* Plato thought of these ideas as "laid up in the mind of God" rather than originating and functioning in the minds of men. But it is not uncommon for man to mistake himself for God; even great philosophers are guilty of this error occasionally.

tinuity of experience. Similarly, Professor A. L. Kroeber in discussing "the inventive but cultureless ape," suggests that "perhaps the thing which essentially makes culture is precisely those transmissive and preservative elements, those relational or binding factors, which social scientists have indeed occupied themselves with, but have been inclined to regard as after all of secondary importance in comparison with the dynamic phenomenon of invention." [13]

Culture without continuity of experience is, of course, impossible. But what sort of continuity of experience is prerequisite to culture? It is not the continuity which comes from the communication of experience by imitation, for we find this among apes. Clearly, it is continuity on the subjective side rather than on the objective, or overt, that is essential. As we have shown, it is the symbol, particularly in word form, which provides this element of continuity in the tool-experience of man. And, finally, it is this factor of continuity in man's tool-experience that has made accumulation and progress, in short, a material culture, possible.

CHAPTER FOUR

MIND IS *MINDING*

"We should have a great many fewer disputes in the world if words were taken for what they are, signs of our ideas only, and not for things in themselves."—Locke, *An Essay Concerning Human Understanding.*

"*T*he problem of the relation between body and mind has occupied philosophers and scientists since the dawn of thought, and to many it appears no nearer a solution now than then. It has been named the central problem of all philosophy, fundamental alike in the theory of knowledge, in ethics and in religion. Not less fundamental, however, is it for psychology and for physical science . . ."

These are the opening words of the article "Body and Mind" in the *Encyclopedia of Religion and Ethics* by James Lewis McIntyre, Anderson lecturer in comparative psychology to the University of Aberdeen. Hundreds of books and thousands of lectures and articles have been devoted to the "mind-body" problem. How is it possible for the body to have a mind? How can the mind have a body? Which is the reality, the body or the mind? How are body and mind articulated with each other? These are some of the questions which have plagued mankind for many a century. And "to many they appear no nearer to solution now than then."

Why has the "solution" not been reached? Where is the difficulty?

It is the thesis of this essay that the "solution" has not been reached because the problem is a false one, somewhat like the paradoxes of Zeno. The difficulty is one of verbal origin; it is of our own making. By rewording the problem, the "problem" disappears: use the word *mind* as a verb instead of a noun and no "problem, fundamental either to the theory of knowledge, ethics, psychology, science" or to anything else, remains. Mind is *minding*; it is the behaving, reacting, of a living organism as a whole, as a unit.

Once upon a time, in a far-off land, a people was concerned with the problem of Golshok. No one knew *exactly* what Golshok was, but everyone agreed that he (she or it) was very important and that their existence and welfare depended in large measure upon Golshok. Many of the best minds among this people devoted their lives to the study of Golshok. Their lucubrations were recorded and their pronouncements carried great weight. It was decreed that all social life was to be conducted in accordance with the principles of Golshok as set forth by the wise men. Of course it was necessary to put people to death occasionally because of their failure to comply with these principles. This was usually done by burning them alive. This went on for centuries. But not all people were content. Some were bent upon discovering just what Golshok really was—if anything. But they never got any farther than words, save for an occasional burning of a rebel.

Finally some one broke a way out of the impasse. He declared in plain language that the whole Golshok business, from start to finish, was nothing but "words, words, words," that the wise men had been chasing their tails for centuries, with "the solution no nearer now than then." He declared, moreover, that if people would conduct their lives upon human principles instead of Golshok principles they would be much better off.

Of course the wise men had him burned to death and his ashes scattered to the four winds. But they were too late. The secret was out. The common people went around saying, "There ain't no Golshok." And they lived happily ever after.

And so it has been with "Mind." "Mind" is a noun. A noun is a name of something. Therefore there must be something in the cosmos that *is* mind.* A person has a mind; it is possible for him to "lose" it. Thus "mind," an entity, a "thing-in-itself," was created and projected into the cosmos. Then people set about trying to find it as they have been searching for Truth, the Good, and Beauty, these many weary years. One might as well search the cosmos for $\sqrt{-1}$. Philosophic tail chasing, nothing more.

Living organisms may be distinguished from non-living systems. The former appropriate materials from their environments and incorporate them into their own structures. They capture free energy from the external world and utilize it to maintain, extend, and multiply themselves. They eat, grow, and reproduce; and they have cellular structure. We may distinguish two classes of motions, or reactions, of living organisms, intra-organismic and extra-organismic. In the former class we have the relationships of part to part and of part to whole. In the latter, we have the relationship of the organism as a whole to the external world. It is the reactions of the organism as a whole, as a coherent unit, to the external world that we may call *mind,* or *minding.*

This commits us to such statements as "an oyster has a mind." Similarly, a paramecium, a radish, a lichen, etc., "have minds." It

---

* We have a parallel situation in the history of physical theory. "The unknown man who invented the word *heat,*" says Henri Poincaré in *The Value of Science,* "devoted many generations to error. Heat has been treated as a substance simply because it was designated by a substantive [noun]." Substances have weight. But when it was finally discovered that a body weighed no more when hot, i.e., when it "contained much heat," than when cold, i.e., contained little heat, the logical conclusion that heat is *not* a substance was not drawn. On the contrary, so much at the mercy of words is man that he continued to think of heat as a substance, but he concluded that there must be *weightless* substances. It took a long time to realize that *heat* is not a *thing* but a *doing.*

may sound ridiculous to say that a radish "has a mind." But it does not sound ridiculous at all to say that a radish minds, i.e., reacts as a living organism to its external world. So much are we at the mercy of words that even so slight a change as one from noun-use to verb-use makes the whole world look different. Mind, or minding, is thus co-extensive with life. It is the extra-organismal aspect of that class of motions peculiar to material systems of cellular structure.*

To return to our starting point: what is mind? How can a mind have a body? The solution: mind is minding, the reacting of an organism as a whole, as a coherent unit (as distinguished from the reacting of parts of the organism with reference to other parts). Mind is a function of the body. The "organ" of the mind is the entire organism functioning as a unit. Mind is to body as cutting is to a knife.**

But Alexander merely cut the Gordian knot; he did not untie it. Neither have we "solved" the mind-body problem, for in the form in which it has plagued the reflecting portion of mankind, it is insoluble. But we have disposed of it. We have not proved, nor can it be proved, that there is no cosmic entity, mind, which has an existence independent of bodies. We have not proved that the "fundamental reality" is not mind, of which bodies are but

---

* The Dictionary of Psychology, H. C. Warren, ed., defines mind as "the sum total of those activities of an organism by means of which it responds as an integrated, dynamic system to external forces."

** Since the above was written, I have learned that a Chinese philosopher, Fan Chen, of the fifth century A.D., said the same thing and in almost the same words: "The body is the material basis of the spirit, and the spirit is only the functioning of the body. The spirit is to the body what sharpness is to a sharp knife. We have never known the existence of sharpness after destruction of the knife. How can we admit the survival of the spirit when the body is gone?" Quoted by Hu Shih in the symposium Living Philosophies, (New York, 1931), pp. 243-44.

Aristotle, too, "rejected any attempt to make the soul a thing or entity." Instead he treated it as a "function of the organism," as "a class of motions," (Brett, 1929) p. 707.

material expressions. So far as I know, there is no convincing proof for the non-existence of Santa Claus. Mankind progresses, often, not by disproving propositions but by outgrowing them.

The "Mind-Body" problem is of one piece with the Vitalism-Mechanism controversy. No one has ever "disproved" the theory of Vitalism, but scientists, and many philosophers, are agreed that the time has come when it should be ignored as obsolete, outgrown and, above all, sterile. It is not that the philosophy of Mechanism is True (with a capital T) and that of Vitalism False. It is that Mechanism has been fruitful, productive; Vitalism barren and sterile. Vitalism as "a view is exactly opposite to those which *have led to all the scientific progress that has been made*," declares Professor H. H. Newman.[1] Biologists have "clung to the materialistic or mechanistic explanation of life, simply because *it was the only way in which progress could be made*"[2] (emphases ours), declares the distinguished paleobiologist, Professor Ermine C. Case. As T. H. Huxley long ago made clear,

> *In itself* it is of little moment whether we express the phenomena of matter in terms of spirit, or the phenomena of spirit in terms of matter; matter may be regarded as a form of thought, thought may be regarded as a property of matter . . . But with a view to the progress of science, the materialistic terminology is in every way to be preferred. For it connects thought with the other phenomena of the universe . . . whereas the spiritualistic terminology is utterly barren, and leads to nothing but obscurity and confusion of ideas.[3]

Thus the importance of terminology. Words are the channels as well as the tools of thought. Some lead us into blind alleys; others, to fertile fields. And so, while we have not "proved" that mind is not some cosmic entity, or proved that it is not the "real reality," we have shown that this view is barren and sterile at its best and confusing and paralyzing at its worst. The opposite view, that mind is *minding*, or behavior, that mind is a function of the body, releases us from the verbal bondage of a sterile and a paralyzing metaphysics, and sets us free to sow and reap in a field that will bear fruit.

CHAPTER FIVE

THE EXPANSION OF THE SCOPE OF SCIENCE

"Anyone who is acquainted with the history of science will admit that its progress has, in all ages, meant, and now more than ever means, the extension of the province of what we call matter and causation, and the concomitant gradual banishment from all regions of human thought of what we call spirit and spontaneity . . ."—T. H. Huxley, *The Physical Basis of Life.*

*W*hen we survey the history of science we see at a glance that progress has not been equal and uniform on all fronts. Advance has been more rapid in some quarters than in others. Greater progress has been made in astronomy and physics than in biology; physiology is more advanced, as a science, than psychology; and psychology is older and more mature than sociology. The birth of each science cannot be neatly marked with a precise date, of course; there has been overlapping, and growth has been simultaneous among many, if not all, of them. Nevertheless, it is clear that some sciences are older and more mature than others. Since there is a close correspondence between the age of a science and its degree of development, we may treat these two factors as one. We may thus arrange the sciences in a scale in the order of their respective ages and degrees of maturity.

Generalizing broadly, we may say that the physical sciences appeared earlier and have developed farther than the biological sciences; the biological sciences took form earlier and have developed farther than the social sciences. The question naturally

"Social" Sciences	Cultural Anthropology Sociology Social Psychology
Biological Sciences	Psychology Physiology Anatomy
Physical Sciences	Chemistry Physics Astronomy

arises: why has this been so? Why do we find this order, both with regard to time and to degree of development, in the history of science?

One of the most noteworthy attempts to answer this question is that of Auguste Comte. In his *Positive Philosophy*, Comte sets forth and explains the "hierarchy of the sciences." His arrangement is essentially the same as ours. He distinguishes, in order, "Five fundamental Sciences . . . Astronomy, Physics, Chemistry, Physiology, and finally Social Physics [i.e., Sociology]" (p. 46). But, instead of grouping the sciences into three categories, as we have done, he divides them into two: "inorganic physics," which includes astronomy, physics and chemistry; and "organic physics," which embraces physiology and sociology (pp. 44-45). Although he does not distinguish "psychology" from "physiology," Comte deals with psychological phenomena in Book V: *Biology*.

Herbert Spencer, also, concerned himself with the development of science and with the classification, or order, of the sciences. In 1854, in an essay "On the Genesis of Science," he attacked Comte's theory of the sequence of the sciences. Spencer declares that "throughout the whole course of their evolution there has been a continuous *consensus* of the sciences," (p. 143). He says:

The conception of a *serial* arrangement of the sciences is a vicious one . . . the sciences cannot be rightly placed in any linear order whatever . . . There is no "true *filiation* of the sciences." The whole hypothesis is fundamentally false (p. 144; see, also, pp. 190-193).

I am not sure that I fully understand Spencer's argument. Throughout this essay he exhibits science as the accumulating product of a many-sided psychological process. But with the possible exception of an allusion to "social science" in ancient times, he does not show, nor does he attempt to show, that the physical sciences have not matured earlier than the biological sciences, and these in turn earlier than the social sciences.

A decade later in "The Classification of the Sciences" (1864), Spencer again returns to the subject, and again opposes Comte's hierarchy. But he ends up with an order essentially like Comte's. Lester F. Ward noted the similarity of Comte and Spencer at this point in his *Dynamic Sociology.* When, however, he repeated the observation in "The Place of Sociology among the Sciences," he received a sharp letter from Spencer who again insists upon his distinctness from Comte. Ward made effective reply to Spencer and published both letters in *Pure Sociology.* Ward again points out that despite his vigorous opposition to Comte, Spencer adopts the Comtean order of the sciences. In "The Filiation of the Sciences," a paper read before the Philosophical Society of Washington in 1896, Ward exhibited the two systems, Comte's and Spencer's, in parallel columns for comparison. They are fundamentally alike.

It would probably be unfair to say that Spencer's opposition to Comte's hierarchy was due wholly to a jealous claim to independence and originality on Spencer's part, although it is difficult to escape the conclusion that jealousy played a part in the controversy. It does appear that Spencer viewed the problem from a somewhat different angle than Comte, that he started from a slightly different premise. But he ends up with much the same conclusion nevertheless, and it is hard not to believe that it was willful stubbornness on Spencer's part that kept him from recognizing his similarity to Comte as well as pointing out such differences as did exist.

We find, then, that both Comte and Spencer present the sciences in essentially the same order, the physical sciences coming first, the biological sciences next, and finally the social sciences. Spencer points out that physical *phenomena* must precede biological phenomena—that there must be atoms and molecules before we can have living cells and organisms—and that social systems must rest upon a biological basis. But he does not explain why scientific *interpretation* of physical phenomena should precede interpretation of biological events, or why interpretation of biological forms should come before interpretation of social phenomena. Auguste Comte, however, does precisely this. He *explains* the order of development of the sciences. Let us turn now to his theory.

Comte's conception of the hierarchy of the sciences differs somewhat from ours. He does not begin with the events of history, with dates and sequences, and with varying degrees of development among the sciences, and then proceed to consider what interpretation might be given to these facts. Rather, he begins with the nature of the sciences, as he conceives it, and with what he assumes to be their necessary logical relationships one to another. The "hierarchy" of the sciences is arrived at by deduction. It is a "rational order" to Comte (p. 43). He observes, however, that his "classification agrees in the main with the history of science; the more general and simple sciences actually occurring first and advancing best in human history, and being followed by the more complex and restricted," (p. 43). Thus, the general picture of the development of the sciences as seen by Comte is essentially the same as ours; the physical sciences appeared earlier and have developed farther than the biological sciences, as the latter have developed earlier and progressed farther than the social sciences.

Comte explains this chronological order and these varying

degrees of development in this way: The physical sciences deal with more simple and universal phenomena than the biological sciences; the biological sciences deal with more universal and simple phenomena than the social sciences. Since biological phenomena are made up of chemical and physical events, a science of biology cannot come into being until the sciences of chemistry and physics have been developed. Similarly, since social phenomena consist of, or are the expressions of, psychological responses, and these in turn rest upon physiological processes, a science of sociology cannot be achieved until the underlying sciences of psychology and physiology have been developed. He says:

> . . . every science is [rooted] in the one which precedes it . . . (p. 398) . . . no science can be effectually pursued without the preparation of a competent knowledge of the anterior sciences on which it depends (p. 48). We must begin then with the study of the most general or simple phenomena, going on successively to the more particular or complex. This must be the most methodical way, for this order of generality or simplicity fixes the degree of facility in the study of phenomena, while it determines the necessary connection of the sciences by the successive dependence of their phenomena (p. 44).

We seem to have here three closely related propositions: first, that sciences higher in the hierarchy deal with more "complex" phenomena than sciences lower in the scale; secondly, that differences in degree of complexity have determined the order of emergence and degree of maturity of the sciences; and thirdly, that one cannot "effectually pursue" a science "without the preparation of a competent knowledge of the anterior sciences on which it depends." We believe that these propositions are either unsound or definitely misleading. Let us examine them in turn.

In one sense, psychological phenomena may be regarded as more complex than those of physiology, as physiological events, in turn, may be considered more complex than chemical and physical events. By "complex" in these contexts we would mean "possessing more classes, or kinds, of factors." Thus, a psychological event, such as perceiving, approaching and grasping food, can, by logical analysis, be reduced to physiological, chemical, and physical processes: smelling or seeing the food and the various physiological responses which find overt expression in approaching and seizing it; and the physiological processes may be broken down into chemical reactions and physical events. In this sense, the phenomena of one science may be said to be more "complex" than those of another. And in this sense, also, one may say that one science "rests upon" another.

While the foregoing is perfectly true logically and philosophically, it is beside the point scientifically. From the standpoint of the scientist, there is only one class of phenomena to be considered in any given situation. Even in biochemistry, which might appear to include two classes of phenomena, we really have only one class; the possibility of referring biochemical events to chemistry on the one hand and to biology on the other in no way negates the integrity of biochemical events *as biochemical phenomena*. Let us illustrate the distinctness of levels of phenomena and the integrity of the class of events corresponding to each level with an example:

I give my broker an order to buy one hundred shares of stock. He telegraphs the order to the exchange in New York, a seller is found and the transaction completed. We may distinguish many classes of phenomena involved in this transaction taken as a whole and in its entire extent and depth. First there are the psychological motives for buying and selling: desire, anticipation of gain, fear of loss, excitement of risk-taking, etc. Underneath are physiological processes: the condition of my thyroid, my digestion, etc. And we can analyze the physiological processes into chemical reactions. Atomic motion, electrical tensions and discharges in my nervous system, and so on, give us a class of physical factors. But, for an understanding of the transfer of the stock *as an event of buying-and-selling,* as a *social* event, the scientist need not and does not concern himself with all of these kinds, or levels, of processes at all. The scientist *never* grapples with *all* of the interrelated phenomena that confront him in a given situation. To do so would be to embrace the cosmos every time a sparrow falls. This is undesirable as well as impossible. The scientist must always abstract a certain segment of reality, a certain class of phenomena, from all others, and deal with it as *if* it existed by itself, independent of the rest.*

Similarly the physiologist abstracts certain processes from the totality of reality and regards them as a closed system. Thus, the argument that the sciences higher in the hierarchy are more complex—i.e., consist of more classes of phenomena—than those on lower levels is irrelevant from the standpoint of science, since the scientist deals with only one class at a time anyway. Socio-psychological phenomena, such as the purchase-and-sale of stock, may be treated as a single, homogeneous, class of events despite the fact that physiological, chemical, electrical, and physical processes underlie it. In this respect psychology does not differ from physics.

Sociologists and cultural anthropologists are accustomed to account for the meagerness of their accomplishments, as compared with physicists or physiologists, by declaring that the phenomena with which they deal are so much more complex than the phenomena confronting the physicist or biologist.** They seldom explain what they mean by "complexity," and more rarely do they attempt to prove that complexity of phenomena must mean meagerness of scientific achievement. They merely assume, in the first place, that everyone knows what is meant by complexity, and,

---

* "In all scientific procedure we begin by marking out a certain region or subject as the field of our investigations. To this we must confine our attention, leaving the rest of the universe out of account till we have completed the investigation in which we are engaged," Clerk Maxwell, (1892), p. 11.

** "The facts of society are far more complex than those of physics, hence no laws have hitherto been discovered," Lowie, (1940), p. 384.

in the second place, they assume without argument that complexity means difficulty. We regard their reasoning as unsound. Social phenomena are no more complex in the sense of "difficult to treat scientifically" than physical or physiological phenomena. The social scientist's plea of "complexity" is usually an attempt, unconscious no doubt, to conceal his helplessness. The difference lies not in complexity of phenomena but in knowing what your problem is and how to attack it. The physicist knows what his problem is and how to go about solving it; the social scientist does not. And the reason for this is that the point of view and the techniques of science have been growing and maturing in the physical domain for centuries, whereas they were introduced into the social realm only yesterday. A science cannot be built in a year like a skyscraper. Indeed, it cannot be *built* at all; it must *grow*, and this requires time.

We have already seen that the purchase-and-sale of stock is a very simple affair; it is no more complex than an apple falling to the ground. And, what is more, we probably know more about stock markets than we do about gravitation. A war between two nations is really a very simple thing at bottom: two nations, A and B, want the same thing—a fertile river valley, an oil field, a foreign market, a seaport—and both are determined to have it. This is no more complex than the rusting of iron or the freezing of water. As a matter of fact, it may be simpler than the formation of ice or a snowflake. And it appears to be much simpler—simple in the sense of ease of scientific explanation—than matricide, masochism, or dementia praecox, events upon a *lower* level (psychological) than a war between nations (sociological level). We understand symbol behavior (e.g., articulate speech) much better on the psychological level than upon the lower level of neurology. We know more about the psychology of jealousy than its physiology. We understand the physiology of intoxication better than its chemistry, and the chemistry of the glands better than their physics.

As a matter of fact, one could make a good case for the exact opposite of the proposition that social scientists sometimes use to rationalize their shortcomings, and say that the complexity of phenomena and the difficulty of scientific interpretation increase rather than decrease as we descend the scale of the sciences. What is simpler than the purchase-and-sale of a share of stock? And what is more complex than a ray of light? Two hundred and sixteen years have passed since the great Newton died and we do not know how to describe light yet. One might well argue that as we approach "ultimate reality" in physics the complexity of phenomena increases and the difficulties of scientific explanation become greater.

Complexity is a *quality* of a phenomenon, not a measure of its size. An atom is as complex as a pebble, a cell as complex as a cow. Nor is complexity a function of the level on which the phenomena are found except in the sense of resolving a class of events into sub-classes as we have already noted. Complexity and simplicity obtain on all levels alike. So much for the concept of "complexity."

The third proposition, namely, Comte's contention that one cannot "effectually pursue a science" until he has a "competent knowledge of the anterior sciences," has been taken care of fairly well in our treatment of the first two propositions. Who would wish to argue that one cannot explain a transaction on the stock exchange until he had mastered physics and chemistry—or even the rudiments of those sciences? As we have previously pointed out, we often understand a phenomenon better on a higher level than upon a lower. Doris is jealous of Jane; Tom hates his father. We understand these events quite well psychologically; we know almost nothing about them on the physiological level. And, so far as we can see, anything that the physiologist might tell us would add little if anything to our understanding. And is the "chemistry," or "physics," of jealousy more than a metaphor?

We would reject, therefore, Comte's contention that preparation in sciences lower in the hierarchy must precede effective work in sciences higher in the scale. Since we have rejected Comte's premise that varying degrees of complexity have determined the order of filiation of the sciences, and since we admit differences in complexity only in so far as this term refers to the number of kinds of phenomena into which a situation can be analyzed, we have, in effect, rejected Comte's rationalization of his hierarchy almost *in toto*. In place of Comte's explanation of the order in which the various sciences have emerged and matured, we venture to propose the following theory.

Every living organism strives to evaluate the various items in its environment, to discover which are beneficial, which injurious, so that advantage may be derived from the one and injury from the latter avoided. In addition to the sensory means employed in this evaluating process by other animals, man employs verbal symbols. He not only translates the evaluations of his senses into words—"fire is hot," "thorns are sharp"—but he posits relational values between one thing and another. Thus he declares that the hoot of the owl presages death, a falling star means good luck, etc. In this manner, man creates a philosophy, a body of ideas and beliefs expressed in verbal form, which he employs as a means of adjustment to the world he lives in.

From our standpoint of analysis and classification, there have been, and logically can be, only two major types of philosophy: one in which the external world is interpreted in terms of the human ego; the other in which it is explained in terms of *itself*. In the first type, man unconsciously projects himself into the external world, describing and interpreting it in terms of his own psychic processes. The whole world is thus made alive and peopled with spirits who feel and behave as men do. They have desires like men, show preferences for certain foods and drink; they are susceptible to jealousy and flattery; they fight and make love. One spirit makes the earth, another brings rain, a third sends game or brings forth crops. The gods favor or oppose certain types of economic and political systems, and aid the armies of their chosen nations. Thus man creates the world in his own image. This is the philosophy of supernaturalism: of animism and anthropomorphism.

In the second type of philosophy, the phenomena of nature are explained in terms of themselves, in terms of the events of nature. Thus, rain falls because other meteorologic phenomena precede and accompany rainfall; a fossil is merely a link in a chain of paleontologic events. Explanation in this type of philosophy consists of a recitation of relevant events; scientific explanation is thus condensed description. This is the philosophy of naturalism.

Between these two major types, in the process of development of philosophy, lies an intermediate, or transitional type, which Comte has called "metaphysical." This may be illustrated by such statements as "fossils were produced by stone-making forces;" "opium puts one to sleep because of its dormative powers," "cattle graze together because of a gregarious instinct." * This kind of interpretation partakes of both of the major types of philosophy. It eschews animism, and points to the external world for its explanations. Thus it says that fossils are produced by stone-making forces—i.e., by natural phenomena that exist and function in the realm of nature—not by gods with minds like ours. But, the explanatory device, "stone-making forces," is merely a part of our selves, a verbal formula created *ad hoc*, and projected into the external world. *Functionally*, it is like the concept "spirit," and

---

* We occasionally find this kind of explanatory device used in cultural anthropology even today. Thus, Lowie says that "owing to the separatism of the natives, no large population was ever anciently brought under a common head" in Polynesia, (1940, p. 293). Radcliffe-Brown says that certain institutions "are the results of the action of sociological principles," (1930-31, p. 429). Franz Boas finds certain cultural phenomena "due to a classificatory tendency," (1940, p. 323). Herskovits tells us that "the essential democracy of the Plains Indian life . . . inhibited the development of economically privileged classes . . ." (1940, p. 393).

hence has affinity with the anthropomorphic philosophy of animism.

In the beginning of human history, man's philosophies were wholly animistic; he diffused his psyche throughout the cosmos; he confused the self with the not-self at almost every point.* As culture advanced philosophy grew and matured. Little by little the animistic philosophy was outgrown and the naturalistic philosophy developed. But progress in philosophic interpretation was not uniform in all fields of experience, it was greater in some sectors than others. The distinction between the self and the not-self—i.e., explanation of natural phenomena in terms of natural events rather than in terms of the human ego disguised as gods and spirits—was made first in the realm of celestial phenomena. This was followed by the distinction in the field of terrestrial physical phenomena. Then it was made in the biological field— in anatomical, physiological, and psychological phenomena, and in that order. The distinction between the self and the not-self was achieved in astronomy and physics before it was made in physiology and psychology because it was easier of accomplishment in the former than in the latter. And it was easier because *the phenomena of astronomy and physics are more remote and less significant as determinants of human behavior than are the processes of physiology and psychology.*

Man gradually learned, through ages of observation and experience, that all things do not affect his life equally. Some things are immediate and exert a powerful influence upon him; others are remote and affect his life but little. It is significant to

---

* "To the Omaha nothing is without life: the rock lives, so do the cloud, the tree, the animal. He projects his own consciousness upon all things, and ascribes to them experiences and characteristics with which he is familiar; there is to him something in common between all creatures and all natural forms, . . . this something he conceives of as akin to his own conscious being," Alice C. Fletcher, "Wakonda," in *Handbook of American Indians,* Part 2, (Bulletin 30, Bureau of American Ethnology, Washington, 1910).

note that systematic observation of the stars was begun under the belief that they exert a powerful influence upon man's daily life. Vestiges of this belief are still preserved in the names of the days of the week: Sun's day, Saturn's day, etc. And enough of this ancient belief still flourishes to make astrology a profitable business enterprise even today.*

But as mankind accumulated experience and compared one thing with another, he discovered that stars exert less influence upon his life than such terrestrial phenomena as those of climate, topography, flora and fauna. At the same time, systematic observation of planets and stars revealed regularities and an order that fostered description in terms of natural law rather than divine caprice. Thus astronomy was lost to animism, won for naturalism.**

As observation was continued and experience accumulated, it was discovered that, intimate as man is with his habitat, and influential as it is upon his life, there is yet another class of determinants of behavior even more immediate and significant: the human body. The man, the ox, the snake, and the bird all dwell in the same environmental setting, but they behave very differently. The deer is swift, the squirrel climbs trees, the bird flies, because they have different kinds of bodily structure. An appreciation of this fact was the dawn of the science of anatomy.

Anatomy developed before physiology, not because the structure of the body is "simpler" than its functioning, but because it is easier to distinguish between one's self (one's ego) and one's arms and legs than between one's self and one's glandular processes. The body, unsophisticated man feels, is but a shell, the house in which the true self dwells. The ego and the body, he

---

* According to *Time* Magazine for March 25, 1946, p. 23, there were 25,000 practicing astrologers in the United States at that time; the five leading astrological periodicals had a combined circulation of nearly one million; and one of the leading astrological manuals sold at least 1,000,000 copies of its 1945 issue for $1 per copy.
** See Henri Poincaré's fine essay on astronomy, the mother of science, in *The Value of Science*, Ch. VI.

feels, are two different things.* The self that he regards in "self-respect" is in no way affected by the amputation of a limb. One may lose both legs, his teeth, and even his eyes, but his "self" remains untouched and unscathed.** But when glands flow hot in anger or in love, naive man does not distinguish them from his ego; he identifies the process with himself.

Similarly, the science of physiology matures before psychology: it is easier to distinguish between the self and the not-self when dealing with physiological processes than with mental phenomena. We observe that a hungry man behaves one way, a well-filled man another. The effects of work and rest are obvious. Disposition is influenced by digestion. Profound changes in behavior can be effected by drugs and liquor. But, unsophisticated man feels, there is a point beyond which outside forces cannot go, boundaries which they cannot cross. Deep within him, naive man believes, is a citadel that is impregnable, a sanctuary inviolable. Here he lives—his real self, his essential character, his very soul. The "human spirit" or Will is free, he thinks, subject to no laws natural or physical. He sees himself as *subject* only; he is unable to regard the self as an *object*, as an event in the world of nature. The distinction between self and not-self at this point lies beyond his grasp and comprehension.

It was a great day for science when man became able to look upon mental processes as so many events in a world of nature, when, to use William James' apt phrase, minds could be studied "as *objects*, in a world of other objects." The distinction between subject and object was made. But the fight for naturalism has not

---

* It is not merely "unsophisticated man" who is sure that "mind" and "body" are two different things. Descartes, certainly one of the greatest minds of modern times, maintains that "it is certain that I, [that is, "my mind, by which I am what I am"], is entirely and truly distinct from my body, and may exist without it," *Meditations*, No. VI.

** ". . . and although the whole mind seems to be united to the whole body, yet, when a foot, an arm, or any other part is cut off, I am conscious that nothing has been taken from my mind," *idem.*

been wholly won yet. Mental life is still called "the human spirit" in many circles, and the soul and mind still walk hand in hand in psychologies, sociologies, and anthropologies even today.

Thus we find the reason for the order in which the sciences have made their appearance and the extent to which they have matured to consist, not in varying degrees of universality or complexity, but in the varying ability of mankind to distinguish between the self and the not-self in various sectors of experience. This distinction is made most easily when one deals with phenomena which play an insignificant role as determinants of human behavior. Conversely, it is difficult to distinguish between the self and the not-self where phenomena are intimate and powerful determinants. The human race has discovered which are the powerful determinants and which the insignificant through experience; there was no a priori way of knowing.

The heavenly bodies, being more remote and less significant as determinants of human behavior than the winds, rain, frost, and terrain, the science of astronomy appears earlier and matures faster than terrestrial physics, geology and geography. Anatomical determinants being more remote and less influential than physiological processes, the science of anatomy precedes physiology. Physiology comes before psychology for the same reason. We may conclude our argument by formulating the following law of development: *Science emerges first and matures fastest in fields where the determinants of human behavior are weakest and most remote; conversely, science appears latest and matures slowest in those portions of our experience where the most intimate and powerful determinants of our behavior are found.*

Auguste Comte recognizes this law when he observes:
It is worthy of remark in this place that the most general and simple phenomena are the furthest removed from Man's ordinary sphere, and must [it would be better to say "can," L.A.W.] thereby be studied in a calmer and more rational frame of mind than those in which he is more nearly implicated; and

this constitutes a new ground for the corresponding sciences being developed more rapidly (p. 44).

In explaining the "hierarchy of the sciences," however, Comte speaks of this "new ground" merely incidentally and in passing, while the argument based upon "the universal and the simple as opposed to the special and complex" is emphasized again and again. But in other portions of *Positive Philosophy*, Comte takes pains to point out repeatedly that the obstacles which oppose the growth of social science are the theological and metaphysical philosophies which must be driven from the field of social phenomena before a genuine social science can be achieved. Although we reject Comte's own explanation of the order of filiation of the sciences, we could, and indeed have, applied his theory of the three stages in the development of philosophy to the solution of this problem. What we have done, in effect, is to show that the "theological" (supernaturalistic) philosophy has been dislodged and driven first, and to the greatest extent, from interpretations of physical phenomena, next from biological studies, and last and to the least extent from explanations of human behavior. And, with the rejection of the theological philosophy and the decline of the metaphysical, there has been a growth and spread, *pari passu*, of the naturalistic, scientific philosophy. Thus, what we observe is a trend in philosophy from the theological through the metaphysical to the positivistic—from the supernaturalistic to the naturalistic, or scientific—sweeping across the field of experience from the physical through the biological to the social. Comte had all of the materials for this explanation of his hierarchy, and indeed, it is implicit in the *Positive Philosophy*. But so concerned is he with another rationalization that the true solution is all but obscured entirely.

We may illustrate the development and the sequence of the sciences in the accompanying diagram. In the center of the circle is man, surrounded by events which influence his behavior in varying degrees, some intimate, some remote. From this point of view, the advance of science has been more in the nature of expansion of scope than of growth or development. The cosmos lies everywhere about man. Science, a particular way of dealing

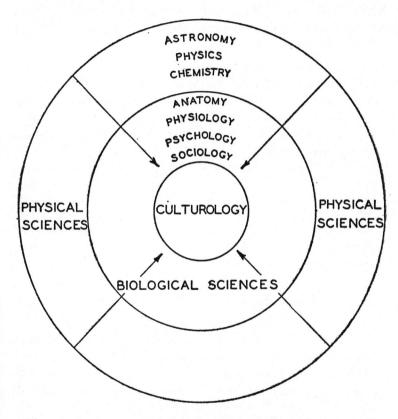

with experience, appeared first in interpretations of a particular portion of our field of experience, namely, in astronomy, where phenomena are most remote and insignificant as determinants of human behavior. From there its techniques have spread and extended to other segments of experience. As science advances and expands, the anthropomorphic philosophy of animism recedes and

contracts; as the concepts of natural law and determinism gain
ground, the philosophy of free will retreats. The logical conclusion is, of course, to have the whole field of human experience
embraced by the philosophy of science rather than that of
animism. It is interesting, in this connection, to recall the words
of the eminent Polish sociologist, Ludwig Gumplowicz, written
many years ago:

> Modern natural science has successfully demonstrated that even
> the 'human mind' is subject to physical laws . . . But in the
> domain of social phenomena unchangeable natural laws have
> not been completely demonstrated. Between 'mental' phe-
> nomena subject to the laws of matter and the social world
> strode the conception of human freedom to distract and
> confuse. It seemed to order and control social relations accord-
> ing to its own choice. In the domain of mental phenomena . . .
> monistic natural science has in part demonstrated the un-
> conditioned sway of natural laws . . . Dualism [i.e., law vs. free
> will], *driven from this domain, has retired to the domain of
> social phenomena, whence it must be dislodged,*[1] (emphasis
> ours).

We find the same view expressed by the great French social
scientist, Emile Durkheim, in *The Rules of Sociological Method:*

> Since the law of causality has been verified in the other realms
> of nature, and since it has progressively extended its authority
> from the physicochemical world to the biological, and from the
> latter to the psychological, we are justified in claiming that it is
> equally true of the social world; and it is possible to add today
> that the researches undertaken on the basis of this postulate
> tend to confirm it (p. 141). There was a time when sentiments
> relating to the things of the physical world opposed with equal
> energy the establishment of the physical sciences, because they,
> too, had a religious or moral character. We believe, therefore,
> that this prejudice, pursued from one science to the next, will
> finally disappear also from its last retreat, sociology, leaving a
> free field for the true scientific endeavor (p. 34).

According to Comte, Spencer, and others since their day, sociology is the last link in the logical chain of science, the final stage of its development. In terms of our theory, this would mean that when astronomical, geological, physical, chemical, anatomical, physiological, and psychological determinants of human behavior had been dealt with there would remain but one more class of determinants: the sociological. But are we willing to accept this conclusion? Is this classification adequate and final? We do not believe it is. On the contrary, we find it inadequate and immature. There is still another class of determinants of human behavior that lie outside and beyond the scope of psychology and, for the most part, sociology. These are the traditional customs, institutions, tools, philosophies, languages, etc., which we call, collectively, *culture*. Cultural phenomena are super-, or supra-, psychological determinants of human behavior. They are super-psychological in the sense that it is beyond the scope of psychology to account for them. Psychology cannot explain, e.g., why one people has clans (behaves "clanwise") while another does not; why one people eats with knives and forks, another with chopsticks; why a people prohibits marriage between parallel cousins but requires marriage between cross cousins; why a tribe practices polyandry, observes the mother-in-law taboo, forms plurals by affixation, uses money, etc. Culture *as culture* can be explained only in terms of culture. But let us return to the history of science and observe its expansion beyond the horizons of individual psychology.

For a long time, and until recent decades, psychology was *individual* psychology. The anatomical and physiological psychologists had, of necessity, to take the individual as their province. The same was true of the introspectionists and associationists. In the early years, the subject matter of psychology was "mind," and the mind was something that "went on" in the individual organism. It was to be studied in terms of anatomical structure and physiological processes, and by direct observation through introspection. In any event, psychology was the study of mind, and the mind was an individualistic phenomenon.

But as the scientific study of man's behavior advanced, it came to be recognized that there are important determinants of behavior lying outside and beyond the individual which, however, profoundly influence his conduct. With the appreciation of this fact, science undertook to grapple with these super-individual determinants and to bring them within the scope of scientific interpretation.

Professional psychologists were, however, slow to appreciate the significance of super-individual determinants of human behavior. Consequently science organized its forces under another banner, so to speak, to undertake this necessary task. This new movement was Sociology.* Sociology came into being as an organized attempt of science to deal with super-individual determinants of behavior. These determinants were social in nature. Consequently, sociology became the science of society. Early sociologists distinguished their science from psychology on the ground that the latter was limited to the individual whereas theirs was devoted to the group. As F. H. Giddings put it:

> . . . psychology [is] the study of the . . . individual mind . . . ; sociology . . . the investigation of the more special and complex phenomena of minds in association with one another . . . Psychology is the science of the association of ideas. Sociology is the science of the association of minds.[2]

Psychology bestirred itself meanwhile and gradually extended its scope to include super-individual determinants. William James displayed a fine appreciation of social factors in behavior in the

---

* "Precisely because the currents of thought ran too exclusively to analysis and explanations in terms of the *single* human being, Sociology arose as a discipline for the study of the *collective* life of man. In the early years it was considered as properly beginning at the point where Psychology left off," E. E. Eubank, *The Concepts of Sociology*, (1932), p. 90.

chapter "The Consciousness of Self" in his *Principles of Psychology* (1890). In 1904, at the Congress of Arts and Sciences at St. Louis, James McKeen Cattell stated that he was "not convinced that psychology should be limited to the study of consciousness as such." And at the same Congress, J. M. Baldwin predicted that "the psychology of the future will be social to the core." In 1908, William McDougall published his *Social Psychology*. This was the first work bearing this title written by a psychologist. It so happened that E. A. Ross's *Social Psychology*, the first work bearing this title by a sociologist, was published in the same year.[3]

Although psychology was able to expand its horizons sufficiently to take cognizance of group factors in behavior, it still remained anchored to the individual as the object of its studies. Thus G. F. Stout and C. A. Mace, in their article "Psychology" in the Encyclopaedia Britannica (14th ed.), declare that psychology is the "science of individual experience." And other psychologists even maintain that *social* psychology is after all a study of the individual. Thus F. H. Allport defines social psychology as "the science which studies the behavior of the individual" in so far as his behavior is related to that of other individuals. "Psychology in all its branches," he argues, "is a science of the individual." Similarly, Professor Margaret Floy Washburn declares that "all psychology deals with individuals." Social psychology, she says, is "that branch of psychology which deals with the mind as it is affected by and manifested in relations with other minds." To R. H. Gault, social psychology is but "an aspect of the psychology of the individual." Thus psychology was able to reach out and at least take cognizance of social factors in behavior. But it was so firmly anchored to the individual as its object of study that it was unable to free itself and envisage a psychological *system* composed of many individuals instead of only one, a *social* organism as well as a biological one. This field was left therefore pretty much to the sociologists.[4]

Sociology embarked upon its career with high hopes and

enthusiasm. Psychology had long devoted itself to the individual aspect of human behavior. Now sociology was to deal with the group aspect. Give sociology time to mature, many thought, and the science of human behavior would be complete, for with the individual and collective aspects of behavior taken care of, what else was there? To many sociologists of the late 1890's and early 1900's it appeared, as it had to Comte many decades earlier, that at last the "hierarchy" of the sciences was complete, that sociology was to be the crown or capstone of the great edifice that was science. But these hopes and aspirations have not been realized. Sociology has not become the head of an impressive hierarchy of sciences. On the contrary, many scholars, both within sociology and outside, raise the question, Is sociology a science at all? Whatever accomplishments sociology does have to its credit, it certainly has failed to fulfill the hopes and expectations of Comte and subsequent generations of sociologists. The reasons, we believe, are as follows:

Beyond the horizon of individual psychology lie not only super-individual psychological determinants of behavior, but super-psychological determinants as well. Sociology devoted itself to the interpretation of super-individual (i.e., social) psychological determinants of behavior, and in so doing became social psychology. But, with few and relatively insignificant exceptions, it failed to distinguish and to recognize super-psychological (i.e., cultural) determinants, and thus failed to complete the science of human behavior by becoming a science of culture (i.e., culturology). In short, sociology merely rounded out the science of psychology by making it the study of the collective aspect of behavior as well as of the individual aspect. But it failed to create or become a science of culture and thus left the science of human behavior incomplete. Another science beyond the horizon of sociology still remained to be realized, namely the science of culture (culturology). Before proceeding further let us see precisely what this class of super-psychological (cultural) determinants of behavior consists of, and what the nature and scope of a science of culture would be.

We may illustrate with the following example: a number of Navaho Indians were spending the night in a large house near their reservation when a party of other Navahos approached. Word of their approach was passed through the house whereupon a number of men quickly left by the back door and windows: their mothers-in-law were in the approaching group and they must not meet them face to face. How is their behavior to be explained?

Clearly there is a psychological reason for their behavior, and there are both individual and social aspects to their response. Each individual was influenced by his own organism and the experiences which it had undergone. And each individual was influenced by his fellow Navahos. The psychologist can properly deal with both aspects, the individual and the social, of this phenomenon. He can inquire into their feelings, ideas, and so on, and throw much light upon the matter. But there is a point beyond which the psychologist cannot go: He cannot explain why the Navahos observe the mother-in-law taboo whereas their close neighbors, the Hopi, do not. No amount of psychologizing will explain why one tribe has this custom while another does not. The psychologist does not always realize this. Sometimes he declares that the institution exists because the people think and feel and act in a certain way; that the institution is merely the crystallization of certain psychological processes. He fails to realize that it is the other way around: the people feel, think and act the way they do because they possess—or, more accurately, are possessed by—a certain custom. Manifestly, the psychologist cannot explain why the Indian organism in the Navaho tribe behaves in such a way as to produce the mother-in-law taboo while the Indian organism in the Hopi tribe does not behave in that manner.

If, therefore, psychology cannot explain why one tribe has a certain custom while another people does not, what science can? The answer is, the Science of Culture. A custom or institution is the product of the action and interaction of other customs and institutions. The mother-in-law taboo would have to be explained in terms of *other customs*—those of marriage, residence, sexual division of labor, mode of subsistence, and so on. Customs and institutions—culture traits in general—constitute a distinct class of phenomena. As such, it may be treated as a closed system. Culture is a thing *sui generis*; culture *as culture* can be explained only in terms of culture.* Let us illustrate with a few other examples.

Psychology cannot explain why the language of one people is agglutinative while that of another is inflective. This linguistic difference must be explained in terms of language, not in terms of mental processes or emotional states. Likewise, the psychologist cannot explain why a people practices polygyny rather than polyandry or monogamy; why it resorts to legal trial rather than to ordeals or covert black magic in the case of personal injury; or why it fights over money and debts instead of practicing communism.

Thus we see that over and above the individual and social psychological factor in human behavior, there is another factor which is not psychological at all. It is super-psychological or cultural. In addition to the individual organic component in human behavior and over and above the social factor which comes from the interaction of individuals, there is the influence of the traditional customs, institutions, tools, philosophies, etc. These things,** these culture traits, have an existence prior to the birth of any person living. They exist outside the human organism; they

---

* "Culture is a thing *sui generis* which can be explained only in terms of itself," (Lowie, 1917), p. 66.
** Durkheim calls "social facts" (i.e., culture traits) *things* (*choses*). "The proposition which states that social facts are to be treated as things," he says, lies "at the very basis of our method," (1938 p. xliii).

act upon him from the outside as meteorologic forces do.* Culture can be transferred freely, without migration, from one people to another. The culture of any people at any given time is the product of antecedent cultural forces, and consequently is to be explained only in cultural terms. The English language of New England in 1949 is to be explained in terms of antecedent linguistic processes and events, just as the automobile, paper currency, courts of law, Mormonism, relativity, and jazz music are to be explained in terms of their respective cultural antecedents.

We see, then, that in addition to the psychological factor, individual and social, in human behavior there is an important suprapsychological factor. The importance of this factor has only recently come to be recognized and appreciated. Everything that we do as human beings, individually and collectively, is profoundly influenced by our culture. Our food habits, marital customs, ideas of right and wrong, canons of beauty, mortuary practices, our philosophies and religions, in short, the whole gamut of our lives, is culturally determined. And, far from explaining our culture in terms of the way we think, feel and act, we can explain much of our thought, feelings and behavior in terms of our culture.

This is not to say that there is no further function for psychology in the modern science of human behavior. It will be noted above that we have said that "much," not "all," of our behavior can be explained culturally. There is still a place for psychology, of course. But its scope is not as extensive as was formerly supposed. The day of facile psychological explanations of customs and institutions is done. In the future, culture will have to be explained culturologically. But within any given cultural situation the operation of the psychological factors will still have to be observed and interpreted. For example, given Navaho culture, how

---

* "Collective tendencies [i.e., culture traits] have an existence of their own; they are forces as real as cosmic forces . . . they also act upon the individual from the outside . . .," translated from Durkheim, *Le Suicide*, p. 348.

will Indian organisms behave? In short, we can hold the cultural factor constant while we study the variable psychological factor.

Returning again to the history of science, we note that sociology was the new form taken by science in the extension of its scope to embrace super-individual determinants of behavior. Sociology became, for the most part, social psychology, and *social* psychology is of course psychology, just as ripe plums are plums, or honest men, men. But in going beyond the scope of individual determinants, sociology encountered super-psychological (cultural) determinants as well as super-individual psychological factors. But instead of dealing with cultural determinants upon their own level, i.e., culturologically, sociology brought them down to the socio-psychological level and attempted to interpret them in terms of "social process," or "interaction." Sociologists failed for the most part to realize that there is no such thing as social interaction among human beings as human beings (i.e., as organisms behaving in terms of symbols) that is not culturally determined. To say that social interaction produces matrilineal clans here, patrilineal clans there does not make sense. To say that one kind of process of interaction produces matrilineal, another kind of process patrilineal, clans is to put the cart before the horse. It is the type of clan, the culture trait, that determines the form of social interaction; matrilineal clans will produce one type of interaction, patrilineal clans another. And clans, as culture traits, cannot be accounted for in terms of individual psychological processes—hopes, desires, fears, etc.—or in terms of an abstract process of social interaction but in terms of other culture traits, such as customary division of labor between the sexes, which in turn is closely related to the mode of subsistence and the circumstances and means of defense against enemies; such as rules of marriage, place of residence of the married couple, and so on. And so it is with social interaction everywhere in human society. Whether it be in the family, clan or lineage, household or neighborhood, guild, lodge, church, market place or what not, the concrete processes of interaction that actually obtain in any given case have been determined, i.e., given form and content, by the culture that possesses the people, the culture that existed before they were born and into which they were introduced at birth, and which has given form and content to their behavior since that time. The attempt of sociologists to explain culture in terms of "social process" or "interaction" failed as of course it must. A sociological interpretation of culture does not and cannot give a scientific account of the origin and function of customs and institutions; it merely conceals their supra-psychological, supra-sociological nature. Thus we see that when science created sociology in its march of expansion, it rounded out the science of psychology, but failed to achieve a science of culture. Let us examine more fully the preceding propositions in turn.

The behavior of every living organism presents two aspects: inner and outer.* There are processes and relationships which take place within the organism; these we may call intra-organismal. Then there are reactions and relationships between the organism and the external world; these may be designated extra-organismal. We may define physiology as the scientific observation and interpretation of intra-organismal processes and relationships; psychology, as the study of the extra-organismal aspect of behavior.** Now extra-organismal behavior presents two aspects, individual and collective, and consequently can be studied from these two standpoints. In other words, we can have individual psychology and social psychology. But both are, of course, psychology—the scientific observation and interpretation of extra-organismal reactions. There is no such thing as an individual apart from the group, and

---

* "All relations or actions between one part of . . . [a material system] and another are called Internal relations or actions. Those between the whole or any part of the system, and bodies not included in the system, are called External relations or actions," Clerk Maxwell, (1892), p. 11-12.

** Herbert Spencer, too, distinguished physiology from psychology in terms of "internal relations" and "external relations," "The Classification of the Sciences," Table III.

no collectivity independent of individuals. *Individual* and *society* are but two poles of the same phenomenon: extra-organismal reactions of biological organisms.

When sociology took form as a distinct discipline it was dedicated, as we have seen, to the study of the collective aspect of behavior. It thus became social psychology. Because the psychology of that day was individualistic in character and outlook, the infant sociology took pains to distinguish itself from that science.

Professor F. W. Blackmar, as chairman of the session on Sociology at the St. Louis Congress of Arts and Sciences, protested against having sociology classified with the "mental sciences" on the program for the meeting. Notwithstanding all this, numerous sociologists have testified that the subject matter of sociology is "mental phenomena" and that sociology is, for the most part, social psychology. Thus Lester Ward speaks of "that collective psychology which constitutes so nearly the whole of sociology." Giddings declares that "society [is to be regarded] as a mode of mental activity . . . social life . . . is a phenomenon of the mind . . . common mental activity . . ." Accordingly, he regards sociology as "a psychological science." Hobhouse says that "fundamentally society is a psychological structure." American sociologists came to recognize that "social life is essentially psychical," according to Gottfried Salomon. At the St. Louis Congress of Arts and Sciences, C. A. Ellwood, speaking as chairman of the section on social psychology, refers to this science as "this most important part of sociology." Albion W. Small once defined sociology as "the science of the social process," but he also states that the interpretation of the social process is "social psychology." Thus, sociology and social psychology appear to be one and the same. To Giddings "societal psychology is substantially the same thing as sociology." And quite recently L. L. Bernard has declared that "modern sociology becomes largely social psychology." [5]

Thus sociology turns out to be social psychology, and social psychology is psychology, according to the testimony of sociologists as well as by our own definitions. E. A. Ross, the first sociologist to write a book entitled *Social Psychology*, defined social psychology as a subdivision of "general psychology." And more recently R. M. MacIver observes that "social psychology is a branch of psychology." We note therefore that in so far as sociology is the study of social interaction, social process, etc., it is merely a psychological science. But what of the study of super-psychological determinants of behavior? Where does sociology stand with reference to interpretation of cultural phenomena? [6]

Sociology was a quarter of a century old, if not more, before the concept of *culture* entered into its thinking to any appreciable extent. By degrees, however, the concept of culture—or, at least, the term—has become more common, and even popular. But, with few and relatively insignificant exceptions, sociologists have not been able to rise to a culturological point of view; they have not been able to envisage a science of culture as distinct from a science of society.

To most sociologists culture is merely behavior, a particular kind of behavior, perhaps, but the reactions and interactions of human organisms, nevertheless. Thus Kimball Young says that "culture consists of . . . learned behavior patterns." To Read Bain, "culture is all behavior mediated by social symbols . . . all culture patterns are resident in the organisms of persons." Ogburn and Nimkoff say that culture is "behavior transmitted by learning." Ellwood defines culture as "behavior patterns socially acquired and socially transmitted by means of symbols." [7]

There is also a tendency among sociologists to regard culture as merely a by-product of social interaction. Thus, E. R. Groves states that "culture is a product of human association." Kimball Young thinks of culture as "a precipitate of man's social life." [8]

To many sociologists, "cultural" has become merely another word for "social." Robert S. Lynd, for example, speaks of "the individual in our culture," "leaders of the culture," etc. As Jessie Bernard shrewdly observed many years ago, " 'culture' bids well to supersede 'society' and 'cultural,' 'social,' in the sociologist's vocabulary." [9]

The inability of sociologists to conceive of culture as a supra-psychological order, distinct from the process of "social inter-action," is well exemplified by the eminent German sociologist, Georg Simmel. When one considers, he says, "the development and character of language, morals, church, law, political and social organization," the conception that they constitute "a structure of independent reality, which leads its life after peculiar laws and by virtue of peculiar forces, independent of all its individual com-ponents" seems "inevitable." Simmel is here face to face with culture. Its independence of individuals is so plain that it compels recognition by itself. That culture has an existence of its own which is determined by its own laws, is also so plain as to make the conception "inevitable." Yet, so mired in individualistic psychology is Simmel, and so blinded by an obsolete metaphysics, that he cannot accept the conclusion to which his observations and reasoning "inevitably" lead him. "It is certain," he stubbornly maintains, "that in the last analysis only individuals exist." Even society exists only "in mental attitudes or psychological occur-rences within the minds of individuals." And culture, apart from material things, consists of "spiritual structures . . . [which] have their existence only in personal minds. Every attempt to think of them outside of persons is a mysticism . . ." [10]

The conception of a science of culture held by many American sociologists is expressed by Dorothy P. Gary in her essay "The Developing Study of Culture:" "A science of culture will be built up only when the analysis of culture is approached from the standpoint that culture itself is a social process growing out of and consisting of collective human behavior." [11] In other words, a science of culture will be realized only when it becomes a science of social process, of collective behavior, rather than a science of culture. Th. Abel considers the question of a science of culture in his essay, "Is a Cultural Sociology Possible?" and comes to the conclusion that it is not. To Abel, sociology is the study of "inter-human behavior" of which culture is but an aspect.

There have been, to be sure, sociologists who have a fine appreciation of the role of culture in human behavior. Professor C. A. Ellwood, for example, declares that "it is impossible to understand human society without understanding human culture; for the social behavior of man . . . is dominated by the culture of his group." But he, too, thinks of culture as human (organic) behavior rather than as a class of supra-psychologic, superorganic, phenomena. To Ellwood, "all culture is a product of the human mind [which means that] back of all historical interpretation, therefore, must be the method of psychological analysis . . . the development of culture is essentially a learning process." William F. Ogburn took a culturological point of view, to a certain extent at least, in his *Social Change*. But, as we have just seen, he and his collaborator, Nimkoff, think of culture as human behavior. Malcolm M. Willey is another sociologist who has done much to bring his science to an appreciation of culture. He has gone so far as to declare that "the study of culture—the processes of its origin and its growth, its spread and its perpetuation—constitutes the study of sociology." But in an earlier article written by Willey and Melville J. Herskovits (an anthropologist), we are told that "it must not be assumed, of course, that culture is a metaphysical entity which operates of itself. It is, rather, a generic term that covers an amazing number of types of behavior." [12]

Thus we see that sociologists think of culture as behavior, as social process or interaction, as a factor in human behavior, or as a by-product of human behavior. But they seldom, if ever, rise to the level of viewing culture as a distinct and separate class of supra-psychological, supra-social phenomena; as a process *sui generis* with its own laws. In short, they cannot rise above a science of society and envisage a science of culture. This is not, however, surprising. Being sociologists, they are by definition and tradition devoted to the study of society, of social interaction. It is not

surprising, therefore, to find that when they are confronted with
culture they translate it into the only language they know: the
idiom of social interaction. There is not a single sociologist that
we know of (Durkheim excepted) who has a clear conception of
what a science of culture would be and who has devoted himself
to the advancement of such a science.

A few sociologists have, however, been sufficiently exposed to
the culturological point of view to be disturbed by it. Professor
R. M. MacIver is concerned with the "disturbing effect" which
"the impact of anthropology" has had upon sociology; the "cultural approach," he says, "leaves sociology without a focus." Professor Robert S. Lynd issues a clear warning against the error of
"viewing culture as a self-contained force, operating by inner
laws of its own." He lists "four distinct advantages" which may be
gained from treating culture as human behavior instead of as
culture ("basically impersonal things"). Culture, he argues, does
not "enamel its fingernails, or vote, or believe in capitalism, but
people do." L. L. Bernard, too, argues against a science of culture,
denying that culture is a thing *sui generis*. He likewise thinks of
culture as "the impact of an intelligent organism . . . upon its
environment," in other words, as the reactions of the human
organism.[18]

Thus, among sociologists we find a recognition of cultural phenomena and an appreciation of the role of culture in human
behavior. But we find virtually no conception of a science of
culture among them, no appreciation of the fact that cultural
phenomena constitute a separate and distinct order; that cultural
elements act and react upon each other according to laws of their
own; that culture *as such* can be explained only in terms of culture; that culture not only *can* be studied apart from the psychological reactions of human organisms, apart from "social interaction," but that it *must* be so studied; in fine, that a special
science is required to study and interpret this special class of
phenomena, and that this science is not a science of psychology,

individual or social, or a science of society or "social interaction," but a supra-psychological science of culture: culturology.

With the creation of Sociology the boundaries of science were extended to embrace super-individual determinants of behavior. But, being but a science of group behavior, of collective psychological determinants, Sociology was unable to grasp and interpret super-psychological determinants. Science was, therefore, obliged once again to advance its frontiers by creating a new science. This time it was culturology.

It was the anthropologists who, as Professor A. L. Kroeber has observed, "discovered culture," [14] and it has been within the province of anthropology that the science of culture has had most of its growth. The eminent British anthropologist, Edward Burnett Tylor, was the first person, so far as we know, to formulate in an explicit and self-conscious manner, the point of view, the purpose, principles and scope, of a science of culture. He was the first, too, so far as we know, to use the phrase "science of culture:" it was the title of Chapter I of *Primitive Culture* (1871). We do not mean to assert that Tylor was the first to take a culturological point of view or to produce a culturological work; there were, of course, others before Tylor who did this to a greater or lesser extent. But so far as we are aware, Tylor was the first to define and describe the new science.

To begin with, Tylor gave us what has probably been the most satisfactory definition of culture that we have ever had until recently. "Culture," he says in the opening words of *Primitive Culture*, "is that complex whole which includes knowledge, belief, art, morals, law, custom, and any other capabilities and habits acquired by man as a member of society." Secondly, Tylor makes it clear that this new science will take as its object of study, not human behavior, nor social process or interaction, but culture traits themselves as a separate and distinct class of phenomena. The study "not of tribes and nations, but the condition of knowl-

edge, religion, art, custom, and the like among them" is the task
he sets for his science. He proposes first to classify culture traits
into categories such as weapons, myths, rites, social customs, etc.,
and then to "make out their distribution in geography and history
and the relations which exist among them." It is the *relations
between culture traits*, relations historic, geographic, and functional, that Tylor is concerned with, not relations between human
beings (i.e., "social interaction").[15]

The next noteworthy attempt to establish a science of culture
was that of Emile Durkheim.* In a great deal of his work, but
especially in *The Rules of Sociological Method*—above all in the
Preface to the second edition of this work—Durkheim endeavored
to formulate the premises and principles of culturology. His
phraseology was unfortunate, however, since it rather effectively
concealed his true thought.** In the first place he calls his science
"sociology" rather than a "science of culture" as Tylor did, and he
lacks the terminology to distinguish between the social and the
cultural. He designates the class of traditional super-psychologic
symbolic phenomena which we call "culture" by such terms as
"collective consciousness," which has not only obscured his
thought but has brought upon him the charge of mysticism. But
to one who can reach his thought and meaning through the
façade of inappropriate terminology, it will be quite apparent that
Durkheim is talking about *culture* rather than "society" or "social
interaction," and that he is trying to establish a science of culture.

---

* Having previously stated that the founding of the science of culture was
primarily the work of anthropology the question arises, Was not Durkheim a
sociologist? It is of course a fact that Durkheim called his science "sociology."
But it is also true that its nature and content was very different from the
works of most sociologists. As Bernard has put it, "the Durkheim school generally has been closer to anthropology than to sociology," (article "Social
Psychology," Encyclopedia of the Social Sciences, p. 154).

** See the opening words of Durkheim's Preface to the second edition of
The Rules for his own statement about how he was misunderstood by his
colleagues.

Durkheim is speaking of culture when he says:

> ... collective ways of acting or thinking have a reality outside the individuals who, at every moment of time, conform to it. These ways of thinking and acting exist in their own right. Collective representations are the result of an immense co-operation, which stretches out not only into space but into time as well; to make them, a multitude of minds have associated, united and combined their ideas and sentiments; for them, long generations have accumulated their experience and knowledge.[16]

Durkheim leaves no doubt that he is concerned with what anthropologists such as Tylor, Kroeber and Lowie have called *culture* even though he uses the term "society." "It is not true," he says, "that society is composed of individuals only; it also includes *material objects* which play an essential role in the common life," (emphasis ours). Among these material objects he lists "houses, buildings of all kinds which, once constructed, become autonomous realities, independent of individuals . . . lines of communication and transportation, . . . instruments and machines used in industry . . ." [17]

That Durkheim is interested in the behavior of culture traits rather than the behavior of human organisms ("social interaction") is made clear by the following:

> We need to investigate, by comparison of mythical themes, popular legends, traditions, and languages, the manner in which social representations [i.e., culture traits] adhere to and repel one another, how they fuse or separate from one another.[18]

Since culture is to be studied with reference to the ways in which traits act and react upon one another—"adhere to and repel one another"—it follows that culture is to be explained in terms of culture:

> Society [i.e., culture] is a reality *sui generis*; it has its own peculiar characteristics . . . The determining cause of a social fact [culture trait] should be sought among the social facts [culture

traits] preceding it . . . We must seek the explanation of social
life [culture] in the nature of society [culture] itself.[19]

A few sociologists have been able to see that Durkheim is talking about culture traits and their behavior rather than human
organisms and their interactions, but most of his successors have
either tried to reduce his culturology to the social psychology of
interaction or have dismissed it as "mysticism." Despite misunderstanding, however, Durkheim's influence has been considerable,
and he will eventually come to be recognized as one of the
founders of the science of culture.

In the works of Tylor and Durkheim the science of culture got
off to a good start in the nineteenth century. But progress in this
field has been rather meager in recent decades. A considerable
amount of work of a culturological nature has been produced by
American and European anthropologists. But little advance in the
development of the theory of such a science has been made.
There has, in fact, been considerable opposition to the culturological point of view, and numerous signs point to regression
from the level attained by Tylor and Durkheim.

Professor A. L. Kroeber has undertaken to formulate the philosophy of a science of culture on several occasions, notably in the
following essays: "The Superorganic," "The Possibility of a Social
Psychology," "On the Principle of Order in Civilization as Exemplified by Changes in Fashion," "Sub-Human Cultural Beginnings," "So-Called Social Science," and, finally in his recent huge
work, *Configurations of Culture Growth*. Like Comte, Kroeber
is concerned with the "hierarchy of the sciences." He distinguishes
cultural phenomena from psychological phenomena. "Civilization," he says, "is not mental action but a body or stream of
mental exercise." He distinguishes the psychological from the cultural in the instance of Darwin's formulation of the theory of
natural selection: the "reactions in Darwin's nervous system at the
moment when the thought of natural selection flashed upon him,"

are contrasted with "the relation of doctrines such as that of natural selection to other concepts and social [cultural] phenomena." In short, Kroeber envisages a science which would concern itself, not with psychological events, but with the actions and reactions of superorganic (cultural) phenomena.[20] In speaking of the reaction of one concept on another, Kroeber is thinking as Durkheim was when he spoke of the way in which "social representations [culture traits] adhere to and repel one another, how they fuse or separate from one another."

Culture, as a class of supra-psychic—or superorganic, to use Kroeber's term—phenomena constitutes a distinct order of reality, in Kroeber's conception. "The superorganic or super-psychic . . . that we call civilization [culture] appears to have an existence, an order, and a causality as objective and as determinable as those of the sub-psychic or inorganic," he says. He also thinks of culture as a "closed system of phenomena," which means that "the first explanation of cultural phenomena must be in cultural terms." [21]

Professor Kroeber is not able to hold consistently to the culturological point of view, however. He appears to think that culturological explanations can be only historical; "Anthropology belongs in the group of the historical sciences," he says. Generalizations dealing with non-temporal aspects of cultural phenomena would, he reasons, belong to psychology, as is indicated by the title of one of his essays, "The Possibility of a Social Psychology." He is not quite able to conceive of scientific laws of culture itself. Instead, he speaks of laws which *underlie* culture, and these are "the laws of psychology." [22]

Kroeber has pointed out in "The Possibility of a Social Psychology" "the fatal defect" of the term "sociology": its failure to distinguish the cultural from the social. But he does little to remedy this shortcoming, since in the same essay where the defect of "sociology" is exposed, he suggests that the science of culture be called "cultural mechanics," "social psychology," and even "sociology." If only he could have crystallized his thought in a new term: "culturology"! In a later essay, he does use the phrase "science of culture," however. And he displays a keen understanding of the direction that science is taking when he observes: "It does look as if the future science would be more concerned with culture than with society." [23]

Professor Robert H. Lowie gives us a clear expression of the culturological point of view in his various writings. To him, culture constitutes a distinct class of supra-psychological phenomena which requires a special science for its interpretation. "During the last hundred years," he writes, "it has become increasingly clear that culture . . . represents . . . a distinct domain. We have [in culture] a thing *sui generis* that demands for its investigation a distinct science." This distinct science is to be a "science of culture," as he calls it in a recent essay. The science of culture is to be distinguished sharply from a science of mental phenomena: "We cannot reduce cultural to psychological phenomena . . . Culture . . . can be explained only in terms of itself." Like Durkheim and Kroeber, Lowie sees that culture traits *as such* act and react upon each other: "culture thus appears as a closed system." It is therefore the business of the ethnologist [culturologist] to show how one cultural element is determined by, or influences, other culture traits. He shows, for example, how a type of kinship terminology is determined by rules of marriage and descent.[24]

Clark Wissler, likewise an anthropologist, takes the culturological point of view in much of his work. He regards the "culture concept [as] one of the most recent and important achievements in anthropological research." He distinguishes psychology, the scientific explanation of the way people behave, from anthropology, the study of the way culture traits, or cultures, behave. In fact, he advocates the study of "culture as independent of human beings." Like Tylor, Wissler states that the task of the anthropologist is to "describe and classify these inventions [culture traits], to study their distribution over the earth, and above all the gross outlines of their history." Wissler is interested in the evolution of culture, the history of specific traits and complexes, and in relationships obtaining between traits. "All cultures," he maintains, "follow out their careers according to discoverable laws," and it is the anthropologist's business to discover and to formulate these laws.[25]

Wissler does not, however, fully appreciate the extent to which the culturological point of view can be applied. Instead of trying to explain such traits as the couvade and incest prohibitions in terms of the interaction of other culture traits, he turns them over to the psychologist.[26] He would thus restrict the science of culture to an unwarranted and unfortunate degree, and deprive it of much opportunity for achievement. But this blind spot does not lessen the merit of his culturological work in other areas of interpretation.

Wissler's insight and understanding concerning the expansion of the scope of science and of the direction which this expansion is taking are shown in the following passage:

> Thus, it was an easy step from the realization of the individual to the conception of society . . . Such a consciousness of ourselves functioning as a group is coincident with the rise of sociology . . . and whereas a century or more ago men were thinking in terms of the individual, they came during the last half century to see themselves in society. It is then a curious fact that for a long time man was so intent upon his individualism, he failed to sense the existence of society, and that to such a thing as culture was totally blind. But we have seen how our people are just becoming conscious of the existence of culture . . . So while we have attained social consciousness . . . into culture consciousness we are just now groping our way.[27]

Professor G. P. Murdock has a fine exposition of the culturological point of view in his essay, "The Science of Culture." Dr. Bernhard J. Stern also touches upon it in an illuminating manner in his article, "Concerning the Distinction between the Social and the Cultural." It would be interesting to note expressions of the culturological point of view in the works of other men if sufficient space were at our disposal. But we have cited enough to show that some progress in the direction of a science of culture has been made since the days of Tylor and Durkheim.

But the new science has encountered considerable opposition as well as support. The extension of the point of view of science to the realm of human institutions has aroused the opposition and resentment of champions of the older philosophy of free will. As Durkheim has expressed it:

> The same antagonism breaks out each time a new science is founded . . . on more than one point, the natural sciences themselves found an obstacle in faith. But it is especially when man became an object of science that the resistance became fierce. The believer, indeed, cannot but find repugnant the idea that man is to be studied as a natural being, analogous to others, and moral facts as facts of nature. It is well known how these collective sentiments, under the different forms they have taken, have hindered the development of psychology and sociology [culturology].[28]

Opposition to a science of culture is not confined to non-scientists, however. We have already noted the opposition of certain sociologists, and there is considerable opposition to culturology among anthropologists themselves.

Kroeber's early attempt, in "The Superorganic" (1917), to formulate the culturological point of view and to advocate a science of culture was met with speedy and spirited opposition. Edward Sapir, in a skillfully argued essay entitled "Do We Need a Super-Organic?" tried to show that no such concept, and consequently no special science, was needed. Alexander Goldenweiser, also in a reply to Kroeber's essay "The Superorganic," likewise opposed a super-psychological science of culture. "The life of culture," he argues elsewhere, "belongs to the psychological level. It is in the minds of men in society . . . The historian, the anthropologist, are students of life. Life is psychology." [29]

It seems likely that Franz Boas had Kroeber in mind when he wrote, "It seems hardly necessary to consider culture a mystic entity that exists outside the society of its individual carriers and that moves by its own force." Like Lynd, Boas would insist that "cultures do not enamel their fingernails but that people do." Ruth Benedict, too, can see nothing but mysticism in Kroeber's attempt to formulate a science of culture as a class of phenomena *sui generis*. She speaks of those who "have often expressed themselves in mystical phraseology . . . like Kroeber they have called in a force he calls the superorganic to account for the cultural process." Being unable to understand or to appreciate a science of supra-psychological phenomena, Boas and Benedict simply brand the idea "mystical" and reject it. The inability of Boas to rise above the level of psychological interpretation and to grasp a culturological point of view is clearly set forth in a significant passage by Benedict. "It has never been sufficiently realized," she writes, "how consistently throughout his life Boas defined the task of ethnology as the study of 'man's mental life,' 'fundamental psychic attitudes of cultural groups,' 'man's subjective worlds.' " [30]

Father Wilhelm Schmidt defines ethnology as "a science of the mind." [31]

The reaction against the culturological point of view in American anthropology in recent years has gone so far as to receive the following summary expression in the words of David Bidney: "The tendency to hypostatize culture and to conceive it as a transcendental, super-organic, or super-psychic force . . . the assumption that culture is a force that may make and develop itself" is one of the major "cultural fallacies" of our day. It is the "culturalistic fallacy," to be specific, he tells us.[32] Dr. Bidney fails to appreciate the direction that science has been taking for more than a century, that it has been moving upward from the individual psychologic level to the social psychologic, and from there to the super-psychologic, or culturologic, level. He feels only the impact of the current reaction against this trend and consequently does no more than serve as the passive medium of its expression.

Many anthropologists are still unable to rise above the level of a sociological, or socio-psychological, conception of human behavior. Thus Radcliffe-Brown ridicules the notion that two cultures can react upon each other, or that a culture can exert an influence, or produce an effect, upon an individual human being. Culture, to Radcliffe-Brown, is merely "an abstraction," and he finds it "fantastic to imagine . . . two abstractions coming into contact and by an act of generation producing a third abstraction." The idea that a culture can "act upon an individual" is, to Radcliffe-Brown, "as absurd as to hold a quadratic equation capable of committing a murder." In theoretical outlook Radcliffe-Brown is merely a sociologist; he is incapable of envisaging a science of culture.* He asks: "Is a science of culture possible? Boas says it is not. I agree. You cannot have a science of culture." But, he says, a science of societies is possible and this is the proper goal of the social anthropologist.[33]

Radcliffe-Brown confuses the issue very effectively by calling culture an abstraction. Words are culture traits. Why call them abstractions any more than the bark of a dog or the quack of a duck? The fact that words have a symbolic significance as well as auditory and physical properties does not make them "abstractions," any more than the sexual significance of the mating call of frogs makes this an abstraction. Polygynous households are culture traits. But why call one husband and three wives an abstraction any more than one atomic nucleus and three electrons? Why should social or ceremonial forms be called abstractions any more than cellular or molecular forms? A wild horse is not an abstraction. Why call

---

* It is an interesting and noteworthy fact, however, that although Radcliffe-Brown has not been able to appreciate the concept of a science of culture and hence has repudiated and rejected such a concept, he has employed it effectively in some of his work. His "Social Organization of Australian Tribes" is a good example of a culturological interpretation of super-psychological phenomena.

a domesticated horse (a culture trait) one? Culture traits are very real things:* objects, acts, forms, sentiments and ideas which can be and are experienced as real things. There is no more reason for calling them abstractions than anything else in our experience.

As for culture's ability to "act upon an individual," it is remarkable to find a man who is so often identified with Durkheim arguing this question in the negative. It was one of Durkheim's chief theses that culture traits have an existence prior to and independent of the individual human organism, and that these traits impinge upon man from the outside and profoundly affect his behavior. And it is, of course, obvious that this is the case. From birth—and even before—culture traits in the form of ideas, sentiments, acts, and material objects act upon the human organism and cause it to behave in this way and that. And it is not as "absurd" as Radcliffe-Brown would have us think to "hold a quadratic equation [i.e., an idea or set of ideas] capable of committing a murder." A culture trait in the form of an idea may so stimulate the human organism as to cause it to kill another human being. This is in fact a very common thing in cases of witchcraft, the killing of one or both of twins at birth, and many other cultural situations. A culture trait in the form of a sentiment-charged idea will cause a Japanese general to disembowel himself in atonement for disgrace or failure, or an occidental officer to blow out his brains with a pistol. It would, of course, be silly to argue that it was the person, the human organism, that actually does the killing in the examples just cited. Of course it was the human being. But —and this is the point at issue in a scientific analysis of behavior— it was the culture trait, not the human being, that was the *determinant of the behavior*, and hence was the cause, scientifically speaking, of the homicides. The human organism does not kill witches or commit hara-kiri because of any inherent property or tendency.

---

* Recall Durkheim's emphasis upon the proposition that social facts are *things* (choses). This proposition was "at the very basis of . . . [his] method," (*The Rules*, p. xliii).

As a matter of fact, self-destruction runs counter to powerful and deep-seated organic tendencies. But, under the powerful stimulation of cultural traits, acting upon the organism from the outside, the human being can be brought to homicide or hara-kiri. These acts are the organic responses to cultural stimuli, and in scientific phraseology, it is quite proper to say that the culture traits are the *causes*, the killings the *results*. If different cultural stimuli are applied, different results will be forthcoming. Thus, we see that far from being absurd to think of a "quadratic equation, i.e., a culture trait in the form of an idea-sentiment, committing a murder," or a suicide, it is realistic and scientifically valid to think in precisely this way.*

Professor A. Irving Hallowell, too, emphasizes a point of view which would rule out a supra-psychologic science of culture. After quoting with approval Bidney's characterization of the culturological point of view as a fallacy, he says:

> Although anthropologists often speak of the "movements" of culture or the "meeting" of cultural traits or complexes, this manner of speaking must be understood as an economical mode of abstract speech. In a literal sense cultures never have met nor will ever meet. What is meant is that *peoples* meet and that, as a result of the processes of *social interaction*, acculturation—modifications in the mode of life of one or both peoples —may take place. *Individuals* are the dynamic centers of this process of interaction . . . it is hard to see how culture—an abstract summation of the mode of life of a people—can exert an influence except as it is a definable constituent of the

---

* We do not assert that the culturological point of view is nowhere implicit in Radcliffe-Brown's work. It is. As we have already noted, it permeates his fine study, "The Social Organization of Australian Tribes." When he distinguishes "social anthropology" from psychology in "The Methods of Ethnology and Social Anthropology," p. 133, he gives expression to the culturological point of view. What we have claimed here is that Radcliffe-Brown has explicitly and specifically opposed the theory of a science of culture. This is demonstrated by his own utterances. The fact that he not infrequently *does* culturology in no way invalidates this charge. Even scientists sometimes fail to square their behavior with their articulate theory.

activities of *human individuals* in interaction with each other. In the last analysis it is *individuals* who respond to and influence one another,[34] (emphasis ours).

We see here only the social psychologist, with, however, a marked individualistic bias. Hallowell thinks of culture only as the reactions of biological organisms. The interaction of culture traits as such seems utterly unrealistic to him. Hence he resolutely turns his back upon a science of culture.

Of course culture traits could do nothing were it not for human beings; they could not even exist. And who, we might ask, has ever thought otherwise? Certainly not Tylor, Durkheim, Kroeber, Lowie, Wissler, or any other culturologist that we know of. But it is a false realism to argue that culture traits do not react upon each other immediately and directly. A hoe is a culture trait. It acts directly upon and influences other culture traits such as division of labor between the sexes, customs of residence, food habits, religious beliefs and ceremonies, and so on. The introduction of the automobile in modern American culture directly affected many other culture traits: harness and carriage manufacture, the steel and rubber industries, road building, urban development, road houses and tourist camps, consolidated schools, etc. To be sure, these cultural events could not have taken place had it not been for human organisms. But is our account of the influence of the automobile upon other culture traits made any more realistic by introducing these organisms into it? Not one whit. The development of the symphony or non-Euclidean geometry could not have taken place without the respiratory and digestive processes of composers and mathematicians. But to inject these physiologic processes into a scientific explanation of these cultural processes would not add a single thing to our understanding of them. On the contrary, it would only confuse because of their irrelevance. Thus we see that, although culture traits have no existence, and hence can do nothing without the agency of human beings, we can treat them scientifically as if they had an independent existence. In fact, as we have shown, the problem of the direct and immediate influence of one trait upon another can be solved most effectively by eliminating the human organism from our consideration entirely. Far from being unrealistic—or fantastic or absurd, in the words of Radcliffe-Brown—it is a common procedure in science. The physicist may treat falling bodies as *if* they fell in a perfect vacuum; or imagine an airplane passing without friction through the atmosphere. But no physicist is so naive as to protest that such things simply don't occur; it goes without saying that they do not. Every physicist knows that the most effective—if not the only—way to arrive at the formulas and propositions necessary to explain physical phenomena is to substitute *ideal* situations for *real* ones.* The only way, for example, to arrive at a law of falling bodies is to imagine them falling through a perfect vacuum—a situation that does not and cannot exist on this earth.

Similarly the culturologist knows full well that culture traits do not go walking about like disembodied souls interacting with each other. But he realizes that he can explain cultural phenomena *as cultural phenomena* only when he treats them as *if* they had a life of their own, quite apart from the glands, nerves, muscles, etc., of human organisms. The remarkable thing about this argument is not that it is revolutionary, but that it should be necessary to defend it. It is neither revolutionary nor novel. As a matter of fact, scholars in many fields have been making culturological studies for decades. We have had studies of Indo-European and other languages on a purely linguistic, i.e., non-biological, level. We have had studies of the evolution of currency, the effect of telescopes upon theological beliefs; the influence of the industrial revolution

* Physics, says the distinguished physicist, Max Planck, "substitutes a new world in place of that given to us by the senses. . . . The other world is the so-called physical world image; it is merely an intellectual structure. To a certain extent it is arbitrary. It is a kind of model or idealization created in order to avoid the inaccuracy inherent in every measurement and to facilitate exact definition," *The Philosophy of Physics*, (New York, 1936), p. 53.

upon political institutions; the development of Greek tragedy, non-Euclidean geometry, Gothic architecture, and parliamentary government; the relationship between taxi dance halls and prostitution, delicatessens and the divorce rate; money spent on medical schools and death rates for contagious diseases, etc., etc. All of these are culturological problems and their solutions are culturological. Need one insist that none of these situations could exist were it not for human organisms? It is obvious of course that they could not. But it is equally obvious that the introduction of human organisms into a consideration of these problems is not only not necessary, it is irrelevant and confusing. It is only the traditional habit of thinking anthropomorphically which still clings to "social science" that keeps one from seeing that in the man-culture *system*, it is the cultural, rather than the organic, factor that is the *determinant* of the events within this system.

We see then that the culturological point of view, procedure and objective are not new. Actually, scholars in philology, musicology, philosophy, mathematics, political science, economics, literature, art, have been making culturological studies for years. Our argument in support of a science of culture is necessary now only because the theoretical position taken today by many psychologists, sociologists and anthropologists opposes this new science so vigorously.

The reaction against the culturological point of view has gone even farther than has been indicated above. Proceeding from the view that culture is "an abstraction," some anthropologists have argued that it is intangible and imperceptible and end up by questioning the very existence and reality of culture itself. Thus Ralph Linton observes:

Any investigator of culture is at once confronted with the problem of its reality. Do cultures actually exist, . . . ? Culture . . . is intangible and cannot be directly apprehended even by individuals who participate in it . . . If it [culture] can be said to exist at all . . .[35]

Herskovits regards culture as "intangible," but grants to culture patterns "the reality of any abstraction," [36] whatever this may mean. Thus culture is made virtually to disappear. And obviously if culture does not exist there can be no science of culture.

Vigorous opposition to a science of culture comes from Earnest Albert Hooton. Whereas anthropologists like Boas, Goldenweiser, Sapir and others have essentially a psychological point of view, Professor Hooton's outlook is on a still lower level: the biological. To him the study of culture is but a branch of biology. "Since man's behavior," he argues, "is a function of his organism . . . it is within the province of the physical anthropologist to survey also the cultural and psychological symptoms of the well-being or ill-being of the human animal." Just as Lynd deplores the "artificial" separation of culture from people, so does Hooton bewail the attempt to disjoint culture from the blood, bone, and muscle of the human organism. "My only quarrel with the ethnologist and with the social anthropologist," he says, "is that they willfully abstract social phenomena and divorce man's activities as a social animal from man himself. [He deplores] the old way of considering social institutions completely apart from the human animals which produce them, as if the former lived, died, propagated and evolved independently, like parasites upon their human hosts." Professor Hooton can see what culturologists are trying to do, but being unable to appreciate anything beyond the horizon of biology, he regards their objective as a great mistake. "We have been misled," he bemoans, "into the imbecilic assumption that culture, an inanimate thing consisting of humanly manipulated matter and disembodied ideas, evolves by itself ever onward and upward, and that all man has to do is to grease the wheels and ride." Hooton has even gone so far, in his anti-culturological attitude, as to suggest that "it is possibly more profitable for the sociologist and the social anthropologist to study monkeys [who are, of course, culture-less, L.A.W.] than savages." Needless to say, Professor Hooton's unfortunate attitude toward a science of culture in no way detracts from the excellence of his contributions in other fields.[37]

Professor C. W. M. Hart, too, deplores the separation of the cultural (or the social, for that matter) from the biological.[38]

Thus we see that although some progress has been made in the direction of realizing a science of culture in recent decades, there is also considerable opposition to it. Some, like Boas, are simply not able to grasp the concept of a special science devoted to a distinct and independent class of super-psychological determinants of behavior. Others, like Lynd and Hooton, see what culturologists are trying to do, but are convinced that they are on the wrong— a dangerously wrong—track.

As a matter of fact, anthropology has actually regressed in recent years from the levels attained by Tylor and Durkheim in the nineteenth century. We have, of course, an objective criterion and measure of advance and regression in the expansion of the scope of science. We may view the stages of this expansion as a series of strata, one laid upon another, the older strata on the bottom, the newer on top. Thus at one time we see the science of the behavior of man on the anatomical and physiological level. Subsequently science has advanced to the individual psychological level, then to the socio-psychological, and finally to the culturological, level. Thus by referring the point of view and objectives of anthropology at any given time to this developmental series, we can gauge its condition of advancement or regression.

Measured by this yardstick, anthropology has regressed considerably, especially since 1930.[39] Science attained the culturological level in anthropology. This is anthropology's distinctive achievement and mission: to formulate and develop a science of culture. Tylor and Durkheim formulated such a science. Kroeber, Lowie, Wissler, and others have carried it forward. But many students bearing the professional label of "anthropologist" have been unable to ascend to the culturological level and to grasp the concept of a supra-psychological science of cultural phenomena. Being unable to do this, they have opposed the culturological point of view. We have already seen how Boas, Sapir, Goldenweiser and Benedict opposed it. Culture, Goldenweiser argues, "belongs to the psychological level. It is in the minds of men." Sapir, apart from linguistics, was primarily a psychologist. We get some notion of how far the anthropology of today is from the culturological position of former years from the following statement by one of our younger anthropologists, Dr. John Gillin:

> One of the greatest recent advances [in anthropological theory] is the realization by anthropologists that culture is a psychological phenomenon.[40]

It is rather ironical that the article in which this observation appears should have been entitled "Some Unfinished Business of Cultural Anthropology." The "unfinished business" is, of course, the development of a science of culture. The realization that culture is a "psychological phenomenon" is not an advance but a regression to a lower level in the development of science.

More recently Professor M. J. Herskovits tells us that "the ultimate reality of culture is psychological." *

Not only has anthropology regressed to the psychological level; it has tended to go even below the *collective* psychological level and come to rest upon the level of *individual* psychology. "An analysis of culture," Goldenweiser argues, "if fully carried out, leads back to the individual mind." To Boas the "working of culture" meant "the life of the individual as controlled by culture and the effect of the individual upon culture. The causal conditions of cultural happenings lie always in the interaction between individual and society." "It is always the individual that really thinks and acts and dreams and revolts," Sapir maintained. Sapir's "ap-

---

* "The Processes of Cultural Change," p. 163. Why one should locate the "ultimate reality" of culture in psychological processes is not clear. If one reduces culture to the psychological level why not reduce psychological events to the physiological level, and these to the anatomical and these in turn to the chemical and physical levels—if one is concerned with ultimates.

proach to the problem was always through the individual," according to Ruth Benedict. Hallowell asserts that "in the last analysis it is individuals who respond to and influence one another." Linton takes the position that "culture . . . exists only in the minds of the individuals who compose a society. It derives all its qualities from their personalities and the interaction of these personalities." [41]

In line with this emphasis upon the individual, we note that the most popular trend in American anthropology today is the study of personality. "Depth psychology," ink-blot tests, psychiatry, etc., are almost de rigueur these days for the up-to-date anthropologist. Thus we see that much of anthropology today has regressed to a level even below that of most sociologists and some social psychologists. And in some of Hooton's work, anthropological theory has regressed even lower and has reached the biological level. His interpretation of social disorders in terms of inferior germ plasm and his advocacy of social reform through biological purges are expressions of this point of view.[42]

In a recent work, Kroeber has once again given expression to the culturological point of view: "I am convinced that, the phenomenon being cultural, the explanation must first of all be made in cultural terms . . . psychological explanations have not got anyone very far in reducing the phenomena of history to order, and I shall not fall back on them." [43] But in these days of personality studies and ink-blot tests, Kroeber stands almost alone. How is anthropology's regression from culturology to psychology and psychiatry to be explained?

Long ago Tylor remarked upon the repugnance with which otherwise enlightened persons will regard a science of culture. "To many educated minds," he wrote, "there seems something presumptuous and repulsive in the view that the history of mankind is part and parcel of the history of nature, that our thoughts, wills, and actions accord with laws as definite as those which govern the motion of waves, the combination of acids and bases, and the growth of plants and animals." [44]

Durkheim, too, noted that the old anthropocentric philosophy of free will, which still dominates our thinking about man and his behavior, generates vigorous opposition to a science of culture. He wrote:

> Numerous survivals of the anthropocentric bias still remain and . . . here as elsewhere, they bar the way to science. It displeases man to renounce the unlimited power over the social order he has so long attributed to himself; and on the other hand, it seems to him that, if collective forces really exist, he is necessarily obliged to submit to them without being able to modify them. This makes him inclined to deny their existence. In vain have repeated experiences taught him that this omnipotence, the illusion of which he complacently entertains, has always been a cause of weakness in him; that his power over things really began only when he recognized that they have a nature of their own, and resigned himself to learning this nature from them. Rejected by all other sciences, this deplorable prejudice stubbornly maintains itself in sociology [culturology]. Nothing is more urgent than to liberate our science from it, and this is the principal purpose of our efforts.[45]

And more recently A. L. Kroeber has observed that a science of culture will have to win its way against the older philosophy of human free will:

> Our minds instinctively resist the first shock of the recognition of a thing [cultural determinism] so intimately woven into us and yet so far above and so utterly uncontrollable by our wills. We feel driven to deny its reality, to deny even the validity of dealing with it as an entity; just as men at large have long and bitterly resented admitting the existence of purely automatic forces and system in the realm that underlies and carries and makes possible the existence of our personalities: the realm of nature.[46]

These quotations do not merely distinguish between "social" science and "natural" science. They also distinguish between the philosophy of determinism and the philosophy of free will that still permeates much of the thinking of today.* Social science had won its way to the philosophy of determinism in the anthropology of the 1880's and '90's: "If law is anywhere it is everywhere," said Tylor.

We find that anthropology has regressed at this point, too. We have exponents of free will in anthropology today, and this philosophy seems to be growing in strength and adherents. Dr. Margaret Mead believes that "man should democratically take control of his own destiny and build himself a world that is fit to live in." [47] Much of her book, *And Keep Your Powder Dry*, is permeated with the philosophy of Free Will. Dr. John R. Swanton closes his essay "Are Wars Inevitable?" with the assurance that "all that is needed [to terminate warfare] is the will to do so." Ralph Linton espouses the philosophy of free will and the theory of social change through education in his lecture to teachers entitled "Potential Contributions of Cultural Anthropology to Teacher Education." "I believe," he says, "that there are none of our current problems which cannot be solved if people will put their minds to them and it is the educator's task to make them willing and able to do this (p. 9) . . . If the educator can establish a particular value system in his pupils he can control the future of his society, not in detail but in gross. By the feeling

---

* On this point Alfred North Whitehead makes the following penetrating observation: "A scientific realism, based on mechanism, is conjoined with an unwavering belief in the world of men and of the higher animals as being composed of *self-determining organisms*. This *radical inconsistency* at the basis of modern thought accounts for much that is half-hearted and wavering in our civilization. It would be going too far to say that it distracts thought. It *enfeebles* it, by reason of the *inconsistency lurking in the background*," (*Science and the Modern World*, p. 94, emphasis ours).

Much of anthropological thought is enfeebled—not to say crippled—today by a belief in man as a "self-determining organism" as the following quotations will show.

which he establishes toward war, or toward unlimited accumulation of wealth, or toward social justice he can deflect culture
change in desirable or undesirable directions (p. 16) . . . A
society that genuinely believes in social justice can get social
justice and the educator can do more than anyone else to establish this belief (p. 17) . . ."

Professor Linton makes the control of culture change seem
very simple. Teachers, guided of course by a little coaching from
the cultural anthropologist, will direct the course of social change
as they please, "in desirable or undesirable directions," simply by
establishing the proper "value systems" in their pupils and insur-
ing the proper "feeling" toward social problems so that when
they grow up they will be "willing and able to put their minds to
these problems" and by so doing solve them. This view is faintly
reminiscent of what the clergy have been telling us for centuries:
"If we will but purpose in our hearts . . ." Or, as politicians,
columnists, and rhetoricians put it: "If the democracies (peace-
loving nations, the churches, the women, etc., etc.) of the world
would only take a firm stand against war . . ." To which one
might add: "If New England had a sub-tropical climate they
could grow grapefruit," or "if frogs grew fur the world might be
made safe for chinchillas."

But the crassest expression of the doctrine of Free Will that
we have seen recently is to be found in a recent article in the
American Anthropologist: "The Concept of Cultural Crisis."
Here we are told by Dr. David Bidney that "man, under God,*
controls his own cultural destiny and is free to choose and realize
the ends he would achieve," (p. 541). With the re-introduction

---

* We believe that it is not at all facetious—above all for an anthropologist
—to inquire of Dr. Bidney, "Whose God?" The God of the Christians or
the God of the Jews? Of the Catholics or of the Protestants? The God of
Mary Baker Eddy, Madame Blavatsky, or of Pius IX? Of Gandhi or of
Winston Churchill? Of William Jennings Bryan or of Robert Andrews Millikan—not to mention the Gods of millions upon millions of Mohammedans,
Hindus, Buddhists and others.

of God into ethnological theory, Bidney sets a new low in the present trend toward regression.*

We have, however, merely exhibited the opposition to a science of culture and demonstrated the occurrence of regression; we have not *explained* it. To undertake such an explanation would require another essay, but we might suggest here that the regression we are witnessing in social science in general and in cultural anthropology in particular is but one aspect of a reactionary tendency that pervades Western civilization today. The nineteenth century was one of expansion and growth of our social system as well as our technology; it was an era of progress. With the end of the period of colonization of backward lands and peoples in Asia and Africa, and the disappearance of the frontier in America, our social system reached the limits of its capacity for growth. Mass unemployment, over-production and glutted markets, relieved only by periodic World Wars, are the indexes of this condition. An obsolete social system is striving to maintain itself against technological imperatives for change. Although there have been some gains—the destruction of the feudal houses of Romanoff, Hapsburg and Hohenzollern—the *status quo* has had, on the whole, the better of it in the struggle. The powers victorious in the war just ended are dedicated to the *status quo ante bellum*, to the preservation of the old system of capitalism, empire and imperialism. Our whole life is pervaded, therefore, by reactionary

---

* Kroeber charitably grants Bidney his God, remarking that he does not see why he should be concerned with the use of God, by Bidney or Toynbee, in their interpretations of culture "until it is evident that their attitude affects the results of their studies" (1948, p. 413). But how could it be otherwise than to affect their interpretations? And do we not already know what this effect will be? The use of "God" as an explanatory device is hardly original with Bidney and Toynbee. Have we not had centuries and centuries of this kind of interpretation? And has not the development of science been, to a very great extent, an attempt to outgrow and get away from such sterile and mystical concepts as "God" as explanatory devices?

It is worth pointing out as a relevant fact in this connection that Bidney was not trained in anthropology but in philosophy, where, presumably, there is still a place and a use for "God" as an explanatory concept.

purposes and ideals and to a great extent dominated by them. The victors of World War II will probably effect a continuation of this political and philosophic atmosphere for some time to come.

It is therefore not surprising to discover reactionary and regressive tendencies in present-day anthropology.* It is both anti-evolutionist and anti-culturological. The outlook for the immediate future is not bright. But all science is still young and culturology is the youngest member of the family. Nor has social evolution reached the end of its rope. Culture is but a million years old and we have some twenty million years ahead of us—unless, of course, the techniques of destruction develop to the point of extermination. The way of life that "we fought to maintain" will eventually be discarded and forgotten. And with the advance of cultural and social evolution will go advance in philosophy and science. A science of culture will come eventually. Meanwhile, those who know what course the evolution of culture has taken in the past will know how best to serve the cause of science in the future.

Summary: Man is an animal, and like all other living beings he strives to live: to adapt himself to his habitat, to exercise some control over his environment so that life can be made secure and his kind perpetuated. Man has the same means of adjustment and control that other animals have: neuro-sensory-muscular-glandular, etc. But in addition to these purely animal means, he has a technique that is peculiarly human: articulate speech. With language man constructs philosophies in which the whole cosmos is evaluated and interpreted. In terms of these philosophies, man

---

* Note carefully that it is certain tendencies in ethnological theory that we characterize as reactionary and regressive. This characterization does not in any sense assert or imply that the men and women who bear the professional label "anthropologist" and who are primarily concerned with psychological or psychiatric studies are themselves reactionary. It is the trend in theory, not the human personnel, that we are concerned with here.

effects his adjustment to and control over his environment. The function of philosophy is at bottom a biological one.

The first philosophies of mankind were animistic, supernaturalistic and anthropomorphic. The external world was explained, not in terms of its own properties but in terms of human psychological forces, in terms of spiritual beings with minds like our own. This primitive type of philosophy, although emotionally satisfying, was, of course, ineffective practically, as a means of understanding and controlling the external world.

Gradually, after hundreds of thousands of years, a new type of philosophy was developed. It interpreted the external world in terms of its own properties instead of terms of wish and will projected from the human mind. Free will and caprice gave way to determinism and natural law. But this transition in point of view was not effected throughout the whole range of philosophy at once. On the contrary it began in certain areas of experience and spread from there to others. It got a foothold first in the study of the heavens and spread from there to other physical phenomena. Then it invaded the realm of biological phenomena, conquering first the anatomical, next the physiological, and finally the psychological levels. From the psychology of the individual, the new interpretation was extended to the psychology of society. And always, as the new naturalistic philosophy of science advanced, it pushed out and displaced the old philosophy of free will.

The order in which the various realms of nature were invaded and subdued by the new philosophy was determined by the following law: *Scientific interpretation will appear first and grow fastest in those areas where the determinants of human behavior are the weakest and least significant.* Since the primitive philosophy rested upon a projection of the human psyche into the external world, upon a confusion of the self with the not-self, the new philosophy would begin first and flourish best where the identification of the self with the external world was weakest, namely, in relation to the heavenly bodies and other inanimate objects. Biological phenomena were next brought within the scope of the new interpretation, and eventually social behavior.

But sociology, the science of society, was not the end of the road of science as Comte and many others supposed. There was one more class of determinants of human behavior to be dealt with, the most intimate and powerful of all: culture. Just as psychologists found it difficult to envisage a collective psychology beyond an individualistic one, so have sociologists found it hard to envisage a science of culture beyond the horizon of "social interaction." But science cannot and will not stop in its onward march, in its movement of expansion, until it has fulfilled its potentialities to the utmost, and this means until it has embraced and subdued the whole realm of human experience.

The science of culture is the next item of business on the agenda of science. Many of our "best minds" still talk as if the fate of civilization lay in the hands of man, to be wrecked or saved as he chooses of his own free will. Many are still prattling about how "we" are going to construct the post-war world, nursing, in Durkheim's phrase, the illusion of omnipotence. There is, as Tylor, Durkheim, Kroeber and a few others have pointed out, a powerful and sometimes bitter antagonism to the view that it is not "we" who control our culture but that our culture controls us. And our culture grows and changes according to its own laws. As we outgrow our primitive and infantile notion of mastery and set about to learn the nature of the culture in which we live, we will have a less flattering conception of ourselves, perhaps, but a greater capacity for rational and effective living.

And so today, we witness one of the most critical and dramatic episodes in the long and exciting history of science. Advancing over the charred bones of hapless astronomers, put to death in a frantic attempt to stem the tide of the new philosophy, science has gone on to new conquests. After a bitter battle over Darwinism, science has securely held the field of biology. Psychology has at last made it possible to regard "minds" as objects, and sociology has illuminated the laws of social interaction. It now remains to discover the principles of a million years of culture growth and to formulate the laws of this development. When this has been done, science will have captured the last remaining stronghold of the old philosophy; it will have reached its final boundary.

P.S. As these pages were going to press I made a discovery too important to pass by without mention here, namely, two significant essays by a distinguished German chemist and Nobel laureate, Wilhelm Ostwald (1853-1932), entitled "The System of the Sciences," and "Principles of the Theory of Education," addresses prepared for the inauguration of Rice Institute of Houston, Texas, and published in English translation in the Rice Institute Pamphlet, Vol. II, No. 3, November, 1915.

In "The System of the Sciences," Ostwald classifies the several sciences on a logical basis, arranging them in an order determined by the degree of generality or particularity of their basic concepts. All sciences are classified into three groups: (1) the sciences of order—logic and various forms of mathematics; (2) the energetical sciences—mechanics, physics, and chemistry; and (3) the biological sciences which he subdivides into physiology, psychology, and culturology. The sciences of order are the simplest as well as the most general in the application of their concepts; the biological sciences are the most complex as well as the most particular.

The logical arrangement of the sciences represents also their order of development, according to Ostwald. We "cannot fail," he says, "to recognize that an absolutely definite sequence can be shown in which the various scientific disciplines have appeared and have developed into their first florescence . . . the simplest arose and were developed first," and "in proportion as the reliability of the human mind in mental operations was developed, the more complicated and diversified fields of experience were gradually submitted to science" (pp. 118, 120).

Ostwald's "hierarchy" of the sciences is thus like those of Comte and Spencer in all fundamental respects, and his theory of the sequence of development is much the same as theirs: the physical sciences were developed before the biological sciences because they were simpler; the sociological, or culturological, sciences were developed last because they are the most complex. Like Comte, Ostwald says that "a sure mastery of at least the fundamental principles of all the sciences . . . is therefore a necessary presupposition for the scientific mastery of culturological problems" (p. 169).

We still prefer our own interpretation of the sequence in which the various sciences have developed. The simplicity-complexity factor is not irrelevant, but it is secondary in importance, we believe, to the varying roles that physical, physiological, psychological, and cultural phenomena play in the determination of human behavior. A fellow human being who is attracted by a smile, repelled by a scowl, is logically complex, i.e., analyzable into physiological, anatomical, chemical, and physical events. But experientially we feel the events of human cultural behavior to be as simple as physical phenomena, to consist of stimulus and response, attraction and repulsion.

One wonders what Ostwald's phrase "in proportion as the reliability of the human mind in mental operations was developed" might mean? Does he mean that the native mental ability of man increased? This can hardly have been appreciable within a period of time as brief as the history of science. If he means that man's techniques of interpretation of experience were improved, might this not well be that he learned to distinguish the self from the not-self in a series of sectors of experience?

It is significant to note in Ostwald's essay on pedagogy that the human mind is not "naturally attracted" first to physical phenomena, then to biological. On the contrary, he finds that "it is much easier . . . to awaken an interest in animals and plants than in minerals and physical experiments . . . zoology and botany can be taught with success at an age when systematic physics or chemistry could not be taught . . ." (pp. 204-05). Ostwald speaks of this as "a certain antithesis," a "seeming contradiction," and accounts for it by noting that plants and animals resemble man more closely than do inanimate phenomena. Thus the anthropomorphic, anthropocentric factor insinuates itself into Ostwald's discussion after all. Man is interested in himself and things like himself; but, *for this very reason*, is less able to understand them than things and events more remote because of the greater difficulty of disengaging himself, his ego, from the external world in the case of things close to, and like, himself.

At the top of "the pyramid of the sciences," Ostwald places—*culturology*, the science of civilization or culture, the science that has as its subject matter "those facts and relationships which have developed in *man*, in contradistinction to all other animals, and which form that which we specifically call human civilization" (p. 167). This science, he says, "is usually designated by the improper name of *sociology*" (p. 167). And here Ostwald, a chemist, demonstrates that he has seen clearly what virtually no sociologist has been able to grasp, namely, that it is *culture* as an extra-somatic tradition that is significant here—not social process or interaction; and what many a cultural anthropologist has failed to realize, namely, that it is a specific kind of behavior—symbolic —that is significant rather than how many individuals exhibit this kind of behavior. Let us deal with each of these points in turn.

To the sociologist the social process, social interaction, is the be all and end all of human behavior; he cannot escape from the confines of this concept. He cannot grasp the idea of an external, extra-somatic class of things called *culture* that determine the social process itself as well as the behavior of individual human beings. He can only translate culture into the coinage and

currency of social process; culture thus becomes a mere aspect or
a by-product of social interaction.

But Ostwald is far shrewder and wiser than this. He sees clearly
that it is not social process but civilization or culture that is the
distinctive characteristic of the human species. The term *sociology* has been used, he says, to designate the science peculiar to
man because of

> the fact that man, . . . even in the very early stages of his
> development, has unquestionably been a social being, so that,
> for much the greater part, specifically human culture has shown
> itself to be the culture of groups of people living together
> socially and busying themselves in common. This special nature
> of human culture, however, is relatively a secondary phe-
> nomenon; and it is, moreover, not entirely general, for certain
> cultural performances have been, and can in the future be, ac-
> complished by a single individual. Thus, socializing mankind is
> an important phenomenon in this field; indeed, it is one of the
> most important, but *not the most characteristic and universal
> one*. I proposed, therefore, a long while ago to call the field in
> question the science of civilization, or culturology (*Kulturol-
> ogie*) (p. 167).

It is *culture*, not society, that is the distinctive feature of man.
Therefore, the scientific study of this feature should be called
culturology rather than *sociology*.

Many cultural anthropologists take the position that an act
limited to a single individual cannot properly be called *culture*,
but when more than one person is involved it may be so called.
Thus, the number of expressions or manifestations of an event is
regarded as a distinctive feature of *culture*. Ostwald exposes this
fallacy also. It is not the *number of manifestations* of an event
that determines its cultural character; it is the *quality* of the event.
Ostwald says that the event must be peculiar to man "in contradistinction to all other animals." This quality is, to use our own
terminology, *the symbol*. Thus, an event is cultural because it

occurs in a context dependent upon symbolling, not upon how many human organisms produce it. As Ostwald observes, "Certain cultural performances have been, and can in the future be, accomplished by a single individual" (p. 167). If there were only a single atom of copper in the cosmos it would still be copper. Likewise, if there were only one expression of symbolling, it would still be *cultural*.

It is a bit discouraging to discover that a chemist has been able to see certain things in the sciences of man more clearly a third of a century ago than many sociologists and anthropologists can today. But it is gratifying indeed to discover, outside the anthropological tradition of Tylor, Durkheim and others, such a distinguished and substantial champion of the science of culture, and one who calls it by its proper name: *culturology*.

PART II MAN AND CULTURE

Introduction

*H*uman behavior is a compound made up of two quite different elements: a biological—neuro-sensory-muscular-glandular-etcetera—factor, and a supra-biological, extra-somatic cultural factor. But, in interpretations of human behavior these two factors have been fused and confused for decades or even ages. And they still are. It is still common to regard culture as a simple and direct expression of "human nature" or to explain it in terms of psychological mechanisms such as frustration, rejection of the father, or the traumatic experiences of bottle feeding in infancy. On the other hand, there is a very general failure to recognize the operation of cultural determinants of *mind*. We try to make clear the fundamental distinction between *mind* and *culture*, between psychology and culturology.

In this connection we examine the role of the Great Man in human affairs both generally and analytically in "Genius: Its Causes and Incidence," and specifically and illustratively in "Ikhnaton."

"The Locus of Mathematical Reality" and "The Definition and Prohibition of Incest" provide demonstrations of the technique of culturological interpretation of two major sectors of human experience, the intellectual and the social.

Finally, "Man's Control over Civilization" critically examines a conspicuous expression of the primitive, but still popular and respectable, philosophy of anthropocentrism. The illusion of Free Will and Omnipotence still hangs like a pall over much of our attempt to define the relationship between Man and the Culture Process and to evaluate his role in it.

CHAPTER SIX

CULTUROLOGICAL VS. PSYCHOLOGICAL INTERPRETATIONS OF HUMAN BEHAVIOR

"Social facts are not simply the development of psychic facts; the latter are in large part merely the continuation of the former inside people's minds. This proposition is extremely important, for the opposite point of view inclines the sociologist at every instant to take the cause for the effect and vice versa. For example, if, as often happens, one sees in the organization of the family the logically necessary expression of human sentiments inherent in every mind, the true order of facts is reversed. On the contrary, it is the social organization of the relationships of kinship which has determined the respective sentiments of parents and children . . . Every time that a social phenomenon is directly explained by a psychological phenomenon, we may be sure that the explanation is false."—Emile Durkheim.[1]

*H*uman behavior is not as simple as it seems. It is not a single homogeneous substance like copper or gold, but a compound like water or table salt. Human behavior is made up of two separate and distinct elements, the one biological, the other cultural. This is not obvious, however, any more than the fact that water is composed of two distinct elements, oxygen and hydrogen, is apparent to the observer. On the contrary, human behavior appears to be a simple, homogeneous stuff, just as water does. It is only through analysis of one kind or another that we can discover the true structure and composition of human behavior or of chemical compounds. And it is only through such knowledge that we can come to an understanding of either.

Human behavior constitutes a class of events and as such is distinguished from other classes, or kinds, of behavior such as simian, reptilian, plant, cellular, atomic, molecular, stellar, galactic, etc. Human behavior is confined to the genus *Homo* but it is not co-extensive with man's actions and reactions: *human* behavior and *man-animal* behavior are not synonymous. As we have already seen, only that portion of man's behavior which consists of or depends upon symbolling may properly be called human; the rest is merely animal behavior.

We have already seen also that the human species has, by the exercise of the symbol faculty, brought a class of phenomena into existence that is, in a real sense, supra-biological or extra-somatic. These are the languages, beliefs, customs, tools, dwellings, works of art, etc., that collectively we call *culture*. They are supra-biological in the sense that they are transmitted by the mechanisms of *social* heredity; they are extra-somatic in the sense that they have an existence independent of any individual organism and act upon it from the outside just as meteorologic forces do. Every individual of the human species is born into a cultural environment as well as a natural one. And the culture into which he is born embraces him and conditions his behavior.

We see then that any given specimen of human behavior is made up of two distinct factors proceeding from separate and independent sources. On the one hand is the organism, composed of bones, muscles, nerves, glands, and sense organs. This organism is a single coherent unit, a system, with definite properties of its own. On the other hand is the cultural tradition into which the organism is born. There is, of course, no necessary relation between the infant organism and the particular type of culture into which it is born. It could have been born into one cultural tradition as well as another, into Tibetan as well as American or Eskimoan culture. But, from the standpoint of subsequent behavior, everything depends upon the type of culture into which the baby is introduced by birth. If he is born into one culture he will think, feel and act in one way; if into another, his behavior will be correspondingly different. Human behavior is, therefore, always and everywhere, made up of these two ingredients: the dynamic organization of nerves, glands, muscles and sense organs that is man, and the extra-somatic cultural tradition.

Culture has been produced by man and consequently bears a close relationship to him as a genus or species. As a system culture is adapted to man rather than to apes, ants, or elephants. Conversely, if man's organism were not what it is, his culture would be different. As Clarence Day has shown in his deceptively profound little book, *This Simian World*, a civilization built by super-ants or super-cows would be very different from the culture of super-simians. There is then a close relationship between man and culture. But the relationship is general rather than specific. This or that culture cannot be explained by appealing to man's structure or nature, however varied we may conceive it. Culture may be regarded as a thing *sui generis*, with a life of its own and its own laws. But we shall return to this later.

Given a certain type of organism, a certain type of behavior will follow. But in the human species this type is very broad and contains infinite variation within itself. The relationship between man and culture seems close only when we contrast man with other animals. The picture is quite otherwise when we confine our observations to the human species. Within this category, what relationship can we discover between organism and type of culture? The answer is "None",—none, that is, of a functional nature; there are only chance, historical associations. There is, for example, no functional relationship between racial or physical type and language or dialect. Negroes may speak Bantu, French, or Chinese. The same will hold true of any other aspect of culture, whether it be form of family, ethics, music, or economics.

The human species is of course varied, not uniform. There are tall peoples and short peoples; round heads and long heads; black, yellow, and white skins; straight, wavy, and kinky hair; thick lips, long noses, blue eyes, "slant" eyes, relatively large livers, and so on. It may be assumed that functional variation accompanies structural variation. Thus it is reasonable to suppose that there are some innate psychological differences among the various races of mankind. But one must not be misled by appearances. The differences among races which are most easily observed are confined to superficial physical features such as color of skin, color and shape of hair, size of lip, shape of nose, and so on. In basic features, such as the nervous, glandular, and muscular systems, blood, bones, and sense organs, they are impressively uniform. From a biological standpoint, the differences among men appear to be insignificant indeed when compared with their similarities. From the standpoint of human behavior, too, all evidence points to an utter insignificance of biological factors as compared with culture in any consideration of behavior variations.* As a matter of fact, it cannot be shown that any variation of human behavior is due to variation of a biological nature. In other words, in the whole range and scope of human behavior, differences of custom or tradition can nowhere be correlated in a functional sense with differences of physical structure.

In a consideration of the differences of behavior between peoples, therefore, we may regard man as a constant, culture as a variable. This is to say that the differences in behavior that we observe between Chinese and Russians, between Eskimos and Hottentots, Mongoloid and Caucasoid, savage and civilized man, are due to their respective cultures rather than to biological—anatomical, physiological, or psychological—differences between them. The whole matter of interpretation of human behavior is thus put in quite a different light from the one in which it is frequently viewed. Instead of explaining cultural differences among peoples by saying that one is energetic, vivacious, Dionysian, and

---

* We are speaking here, as elsewhere in this chapter, of human behavior in the mass, in terms of societies, tribes or nations, not of individual organisms.

creative, whereas another is phlegmatic, taciturn, unimaginative and prosaic, we now see that the differences of behavior of various peoples are due to the differences among the cultural traditions that stimulate them respectively. Thus we explain the behavior of peoples in terms of their cultures; but we do not and cannot explain their cultures in terms of the respective "psychologies" of the peoples. The specific "psychologies" are psychosomatic expressions of the cultures, not their causes. The cultures must be explained in terms of culture; culturologically rather than psychologically.

Psychological explanations are however still prevalent and popular, among social scientists as well as among laymen. Thus, in a discussion of exogamy, the English anthropologist, B. Seligman, says: "It is obvious that if there is any general law underlying all marriage prohibitions it must be founded on human emotions and reactions." [2] Hitler's "rapid rise to power, the spread of his ideas to other countries, and the fanatical devotion to him of thousands upon thousands of men, women, and children in one of the most progressive and intelligent nations of the world —all this shows," says Raymond Dexter Havens, Caroline Donovan Professor of English Literature at Johns Hopkins University, "how deep is the craving for authority, for certitude, for intellectual and moral security. And not in Germany alone but in all of us. Which means that when the war is won in Germany and Japan it must still be carried on in America, and in our own hearts . . ." [3] David Lilienthal, chairman of the U. S. Atomic Energy Commission, is quoted by *Time* Magazine as saying that "What goes on in people's minds—and in their hearts—is more important in determining the fateful future than what goes on in laboratories and production centers" (February 16, 1948, p. 24). And the English ethnologist, the late W. H. R. Rivers, said: "To me, as to most students of the subject, the final aim of the study of society is the explanation of social behavior in terms of psychology." [4]

In addition to these *general* explanations of cultural phenomena in psychological terms, we have numerous psychological interpretations of specific institutions and of particular sociocultural phenomena. Thus, the institution of private property is often "explained"—and justified—by arguing that it is simply human nature. There is a natural desire, it is said, to own your own home, your own fields and herds, and to possess the products of your own labor. If it were not for private property, the argument continues, there would be no incentive to effort and consequently no progress.

Plausible as this theory may sound, it is not in accord with ethnographic fact. There are many societies in which there is no private property in the resources of nature at all; on the contrary, they are free and accessible to all members of the society. Customs of hospitality, exchange of gifts, ease of borrowing, and so on, make private property in food, clothing, tools, and ornaments little more than a fiction. Communism has been the dominant note in man's economic life for by far the greater part of human history so far. But this, too, is no more an expression of human nature than is feudalism or capitalism. Peoples do not have communal or private systems of property because they want them or because it is human nature to prefer one to the other. In a very realistic sense they do not "have them" at all; rather, *it is the cultures which possess the people who have been born into them.* Attitudes, sentiments, and behavior toward property are determined by the type of economic system into which one is born.

Similar observations may be made concerning competition, rivalry, and leadership. The basic principle of the socio-economic life of many peoples is mutual aid. It is doubtful if primitive groups could have held their own in difficult situations and with crude tools, weapons, and techniques if their social life had not been based upon this principle. The individual hunter was obliged by custom to share his kill with others. Indeed, in some instances he received the smallest portion of all. Prestige, social approval, moral codes provided the incentive. And he in turn was entitled to a portion of the kill of other hunters. The produce of the field or herds must likewise be shared.

The leader is often a necessary and an honored person, but not always. Among our Pueblo Indians, a "leader" is likely to be regarded as an obnoxious person, and may, in extreme cases, be done away with on a charge of sorcery. The ideal Pueblo Indian is not the go-getter, the leader, but a quiet unobtrusive person who does not provoke community discord. And psychologists who have sought to subject Pueblo Indian children to competitive tests have found that their project failed when the children learned the purpose of the tests. Far from trying to outdo the others so that they might come home triumphant to admiring parents, the children carefully refrained from doing their best lest they humiliate or embarrass their fellows, and in so doing bring odium upon themselves.

The institution of slavery has often been interpreted as the outcome of man's inherent tendencies to commit aggressions upon others—of "man's inhumanity to man." An eminent psychologist, Wm. McDougall, once went so far as to postulate a high degree of an instinct of submission among African peoples to account for the prevalence of Negro chattel slavery. We know, however, that the institution of slavery has not been universal by any means. As a matter of fact, it did not make its appearance until relatively recent times—since the beginning of the Neolithic at least; the hundreds of thousands of years of human history that went before had no slavery. And many peoples of the modern world have had no slaves. Are we to assume that the instinct of aggression—or of submission—was not sufficiently developed during the early eras of human history, or among some of the peoples of recent times, to find overt expression in a traffic in human chattels?

If the origin of the institution of slavery has been interpreted psychologically, so has its extinction. A growing consciousness of human rights, an appreciation of the essential dignity of man (whatever that is), or the rising spirit of Christianity have all been invoked to explain the decline of this institution. One scholar, writing in the Encyclopedia of the Social Sciences, has asserted that "the movement against slavery . . . was largely the result of the rising spirit of democracy, etc." [5] By the same token, the institution came into being as a consequence of the rising spirit of slavery. Obviously, psychological and spiritual interpretations do not tell us very much actually. Why have aggressive—or submissive—tendencies resulted in a certain type of social institution among some peoples but not among others? Why has the spirit of democracy asserted itself at one time, the spirit of slavery at another?

A culturological explanation of slavery makes the institution readily intelligible. Slavery as an institution will exist and endure only when the master can derive profit and advantage by exploiting the slave. This is possible only when a family group is able to produce considerably more than it requires for its continued existence. The efficiency of production is of course determined by the degree of technological development. Slavery did not exist during the hundreds of thousands of years before Neolithic times because culture had not developed sufficiently to make it possible for a producer to be more than self-supporting. There certainly would be no point—even if it were possible—in one tribe of savages enslaving another if the latter required all that they were able to produce in order to subsist. Consequently, we find no slavery in early periods of human history, nor, in the modern world, among peoples on low levels of technological development. But when in the course of cultural evolution the productivity of human labor was sufficiently increased by technological progress so as to make exploitation profitable and advantageous, the institution of slavery came into being. Correspondingly, when culture—particularly the technological culture—had reached a certain point where it could no longer be operated efficiently by a human chattel, then the institution of slavery became extinct. Slavery died out, not because someone discovered the essential dignity of man, or because of a rising spirit of Christianity or Democracy, but because, as Lewis H. Morgan put it long ago, a freeman is a better "property-making machine" than a slave.[6] Modern industrial technologies could not be operated by ignorant, illiterate human chattels. Also, the slave owner suffered a handicap which does not affect the employer of free labor: the slave owner had to feed and care for his slaves whether he made money out of them or not; he had a substantial investment in them and he must safeguard this investment. The employer of free labor, however, is under no such obligation to his employees. If his profits diminish he can lay off some workers; if they cease, he can close up his establishment entirely without assuming responsibility for his employees; they can shift for themselves—go hungry, go on public relief, or resort to begging or to theft. Thus, at a certain stage of cultural development, slavery comes into being as a consequence of the resources and imperatives of the cultural system. At a subsequent and higher stage of cultural development, the institution becomes extinct because it is no longer compatible with the resources and exigencies of the socio-cultural system.

War is a tremendously impressive expression of human behavior that is often "explained" psychologically. In addition to the Great Men who make wars at their own sweet will, we find more generalized psychological explanations. According to *Time* Magazine (Aug. 23, 1948), a UN-sponsored International Congress on Mental Health, attended by "2,000 of the world's foremost psychiatrists and psychologists," gave forth such interpretations of the cause of war as the following: Wars are caused by a sense of guilt which causes you to do something violent, which in turn creates a sense of guilt. Thus the repetition of wars is explained as well as their origin. Another psychologist attributed wars to restraint upon sexual impulses which causes frustration which causes people to become aggressive. Still another thought that people have been made aggressive and violent by corporeal punishment during childhood.

Professor Gordon W. Allport, a psychologist at Harvard, quotes with approval a passage from the preamble of the charter of UNESCO: "Since wars begin in the minds of men it is in the minds of men that the defences of peace must be constructed." [7] Monsignor Fulton J. Sheen expresses the same view in only slightly different words: "World wars are nothing but projections of the conflicts waged inside our own souls, for nothing happens in the world that does not first happen inside a soul." [8] "A burst of military enthusiasm and a line of able rulers enabled Egypt to assume for several centuries an imperial position," [9] according to an eminent orientalist, the late James H. Breasted. The common people were, however, "a naturally peaceful people," and consequently Egypt was not able to retain her position of pre-eminence. War has no "rational cause," said Franz Boas; it is due to a "mental attitude," the "emotional value of an idea." [10] Another anthropologist, Ralph Linton, finds that the Plains Indians did not fight for hunting grounds or other tangible advantages, but rather because they were "warlike." * To Ruth Benedict ". . . it is a commonplace that men like war . . . Over and over men have proved that they prefer war with all its suffering." [11] William James tells us, in "The Moral Equivalent of War," that "modern man inherits all the innate pugnacity and all the love of glory of his ancestors . . . Our ancestors have bred pugnacity

---

* "Superficially it might appear that the roving life of a Plains Indian tribe and the frequent contacts with other groups which this entailed would be likely to focus interest on war, but it need not have done so if the Plains Indians in general had not been warlike. After all, there was enough food and other natural resources in the Plains to take care of a much larger population than the area supported, and these tribes were not driven into war by economic needs," *The Study of Man*, p. 461.

Professor Lowie, too, thinks that the Plains Indians fought "just for fun": the "Plains Indians fought not for territorial aggrandizement nor for the victor's spoils, but above all because fighting was a game worth while because of the social recognition it brought when played according to the rules," *Primitive Society*, p. 356.

into our bone and marrow, and thousands of years of peace won't breed it out of us . . . The military instincts and ideals are as strong as ever." And the layman sums up his estimate of the future: "You can't do away with war; it's just human nature."

But *is* man by nature so pugnacious and militant? Compared with other animal orders, the Carnivores for example, the Primates are a rather timid lot. The "innate pugnacity" of which James speaks is often conspicuously lacking in the human species. Warfare is virtually non-existent among many primitive tribes. And in many instances where fighting does take place, the contestants do not meet each other face to face and slug it out man to man so that their "military instincts and ideals" can be exercised to the full. Instead, they resort to ambush, killing their victims before they have a chance to defend themselves. To slaughter helpless sleeping victims is quite sufficient to feed the "love of glory" of most peoples. And when free and open conflict does take place among primitive peoples, their pugnacity is often more vocal than military—as is usually the case among the lower primates. Often the fight ends when the first blood is drawn. And in modern nations pugnacity has been "bred so weakly in our bones and marrow" that every nation has to resort to conscription. And despite such stinging epithets as "draft dodger," the number of men who prefer the degradation of prison to the glory of war is considerable. Thus it would appear that the lust for fighting and killing is not over-riding in primates in general or in man in particular.

But even if it were, it would tell us very little about war, why it is fought and when, with whom and over what. To attempt to explain war by appeal to an innate pugnacity would be like explaining Egyptian, Gothic, and Mayan architecture by citing the physical properties of stone; or like explaining the industrial revolution by invoking an inventive tendency in the human mind. A culturological interpretation of war will, however, tell us something of significance. Wars are fought between societies, between sociocultural systems, between tribes and nations. It is the culture of any given situation that determines whether warfare shall be engaged in or not, and if so how, with whom and for what. In some cultural settings, warfare is non-existent; the mode of life as culturally defined has no place for it. In other situations there is only occasional skirmishing between tribes. Where rich hunting or fishing grounds are at stake, we can expect military contests. The same holds true for grazing lands and for fertile valleys when culture has reached the level of animal husbandry and agriculture. It may sound absurd and superfluous to say that peoples will not fight over grazing lands, fertile valleys, coal and iron deposits, foreign markets, oil reserves and uranium mines until culture has advanced to such levels of development as domestication of animals, cultivation of plants, steam and internal combustion engines, world trade, and uranium piles. But if one listens to those who talk about man's "innate pugnacity" he might easily get the impression that this was sufficient to account for everything.

Warfare is a struggle between social organisms, not individuals. Its explanation is therefore social or cultural, not psychological. We could never understand why the United States entered World War II—or any other war—by an inquiry into the psychological motives of men and women. One man wanted to quit his distasteful job as bank clerk, another wanted adventure, a third sought release from an unbearable domestic situation, another wanted to see what the women of France, Samoa, or China are like, another wanted to wear a uniform, another fought for God, for Country, and the New Deal, and so on. Of course, most men went to war because they were obliged to—or accept the degradation of imprisonment or worse. To picture the multitudes of docile serfs and peasants of ancient Egypt, pre-Columbian Peru, China, or Czarist Russia going to war because of an "innate pugnacity and a love of glory" (James), or as Benedict says because "men *like* war" is grotesque. They were forced to go, driven to the slaughter like sheep. And if any were animated by "the love of glory" it came to them from propagandists, not from their innermost selves.

Again, supposing we grant merely for the sake of argument an innate pugnacity to men: Whom will they fight? If a poll had been taken among Americans in 1939 to discover the objects of their hostility, it is likely that England would have received more votes than any other nation with the possible exception of Russia. Yet we entered the war on the side of these two nations. When Russia was fighting "gallant little Finland" in 1939-40 our pugnacious instincts were leveled squarely at the Kremlin. The non-aggression pact between Russia and Germany in 1939 aroused our indignation and anger. But after the Germans invaded Russia in 1941, the orientation of our instincts changed. We then found in Soviet Russia a stout champion of democracy.

Psychological explanations are not only irrelevant here, they are pathetic. The psychological orientations were the result of the intercourse of nations, not the cause. The lust for blood and glory was at low ebb in the military camps in the United States in November, 1941. An international event at Pearl Harbor transformed a listless, disgruntled mass of conscripts into a spirited fighting force. It would make more sense to say that it is war that breeds the martial spirit than to argue that pugnacious instincts cause wars.

To be sure, there would be no wars if there were no people— human organisms with their hungers and fears, hopes and inertia —to fight them. But to explain warfare in terms of psychology is illusion. War is a cultural phenomenon, and we can not only explain it in cultural terms, but we can account for the presence or absence of the pugnacious "instinct," the love of glory, or the loathing of slaughter, in cultural terms also. World peace will come, if it ever does, not because we shall have bred out the

pugnacious instinct, or sublimated it in mass athletic contests,*
but because cultural development, social evolution, will have
reached the ultimate conclusion of the age-old process of merging
smaller social groups into larger ones, eventually forming a single
political organization that will embrace the entire planet and the
whole human race.

The phenomenon of race prejudice and inter-racial antagonisms
is frequently regarded and explained as primarily a psychological
phenomenon. Since the phenomenon is manifested in acts and
attitudes of individual human organisms it is frequently taken for
granted that the problem of race prejudice and inter-racial antagonisms is psychological from the standpoint of scientific explanation, and psychiatric from the point of view of therapy.
Psychoanalysis has come forward with interpretations such as
these: The Jew is identified with the law-giving, super-ego forming father, and also with the unrepentant parricide. The hated
Jew is not really a person but a myth: he is "castrated" and
feminine and yet exceedingly dangerous and over-sexed, a symbol
at once of the id and of the super-ego. The Negro, according to
one psychoanalytic interpretation, represents the nocturnal, sexual
father, whom the son wishes to castrate—hence the castrative
aspects of lynching. Anti-Negro man-hunts resemble the hunting
of animals in groups, both phenomena being derived from the
banding together of the sons against the primal father.

These observations may or may not adequately characterize the
experience of an individual psyche who is participating in the
sociocultural process of racial antagonisms. But even if they do
realistically describe the individual experience, they do not explain the social phenomenon at all. It is all too frequently assumed
that a sociocultural phenomenon has been explained when one

---

* Even as recently as the summer of 1948, more than one psychologist
solemnly suggested that international athletic contests, such as the Olympic
games then in progress, might serve to prevent wars by working off aggressive
tendencies in a peaceful manner.

has isolated and defined the psychological experiences of an individual within that sociocultural context. Thus, it is said, men may identify the Negro with the father, their rival, and then proceed to give these inner feelings overt expression in acts and attitudes of hostility toward the Negro.

What these attempts at psychological interpretations fail to do, of course, is to explain why it is that the Negro represents the nocturnal father in some societies but not in others; why antagonisms are directed primarily toward one minority group rather than another; why racial antagonisms are lacking altogether in some situations. The fallacy of psychological interpretations of sociocultural phenomena consists in the assumption that the subjective psychological experience correlated with the institution has brought the institution into existence. It is as if one discovered —or came to believe—that riding in an airplane was the realization of sexually motivated dreams of flying; or that flying in airplanes gave one a sense of power and mastery, and concluded therefore that the *airplane*, as an element of culture, had been explained by citing sexual dreams and a will to power. We do not deny or minimize the subjective psychological experiences of the individual at all—although we would like to see some of the psychoanalytic interpretations supported with a little more verification. These experiences are of course real. But, we would argue, they are functions of sociocultural situations; not the causes of them. Individual psychological experience has been evoked by the social phenomenon of race antagonism just as the thrill of power and mastery is evoked by the airplane; it is not the subjective experience that produces the antagonism or the airplane.

There are non-psychoanalytic psychological interpretations of racial antagonisms, also. The "frustration-aggression" hypothesis has been called upon to explain inter-racial conflicts. A people is frustrated and becomes aggressive as a consequence, choosing perhaps a minority group upon which to vent the aggressive impulse. But here again, the great variety and range of inter-racial conflicts and antagonisms is not illuminated very much by merely pronouncing the magic couplet "frustration and aggression."

One of the weakest of psychological explanations of race prejudice with which we are acquainted is that given once by the late Franz Boas. The prejudice, he said, ". . . is founded essentially . . . on the tendency of the human mind to merge the individual in the class to which he belongs, and to ascribe to him all the characteristics of his class." [12] Just how the tendency of the human mind to identify an individual with "the class *to which he belongs*" produces racial prejudice and antagonism is not quite clear although Boas assures us that it "is not difficult to understand" in the light of this tendency of the human mind.

Psychological interpretations of race prejudice and inter-racial antagonisms are misleading and unsound because these problems are sociological and cultural rather than psychological. As we have pointed out, a description of subjective psychological experience correlated with an institution does not constitute an explanation of the institution. The experience of the ego is a function of the institution, not its cause. And, the institution must be explained culturologically.

We do not wish to undertake an exhaustive culturological interpretation of race prejudice at this point. We would suggest, however, that if investigation and analysis were carried out along the following lines one would come to a much deeper and more realistic explanation of this phenomenon than any amount of psychological or psychoanalytic inquiry can produce: Race prejudice and racial antagonisms are likely to appear in sociocultural situations in which (1) one group is competing with another for the possession of desirable lands (e.g., the American Indian frontier), for jobs or other economic advantages; (2) where a minority group endeavors to preserve its own integrity as a sociocultural group within a larger population; where it resists the effort of the larger society to assimilate it in an attempt to achieve a high degree of integration. Minority groups which attempt thus to maintain their own integrity, not only on the cultural plane but also by means of endogamy, are opposing the attempts of the larger society to achieve integration through assimilation, and are likely consequently to become the object of hostility and aggression from the larger society—which incidentally tends to reinforce the efforts of the minority group to maintain *its* integrity, and so on in a vicious circle. (3) Hostility toward a foreign power or toward a minority group within a society is often an effective means of unifying a nation. In times of national emergency or crisis, therefore, a nation may attempt to achieve inner unity and solidarity by fomenting hostility toward a foreign power—an old trick—or against a minority group within its gates—also an old trick.

We turn now from culturological problems that have been commonly attacked with psychological techniques to one that has seldom been so approached, namely, the question of matrilineal and patrilineal lineages or clans. Offhand, we cannot cite any attempts to explain these sociocultural phenomena in psychological terms, to say, for example, that one people had matrilineal clans because of identification with the mother imago, whereas another people were organized into exogamous patrilineal lineages because of narcissistic impulses or what not. Such psychological interpretations would however be no more misplaced than those we have just cited. Why would one people identify itself with the mother, another with the father? This is precisely the question at issue; the psychological interpretation merely raises the question, it does not answer it. The paucity or absence of psychological interpretations of unilateral organization is probably due however to lack of interest in clans rather than a realization of the irrelevance of psychological interpretation.

Our argument concerning the relationship of man the organism to his extra-somatic cultural environment may be summarized somewhat as follows: The musical behavior of peoples—the

Viennese of 1798, the black folk of Harlem, 1940, the English before 1066, the Italians at the time of Palestrina, the Nigerians, Bantus, Chinese, Pueblo Indians, and Yakuts—varies. How are these variations to be explained? Certainly not in terms of biological differences. Everything that we know about comparative anatomy and physiology will lend no support whatever to a belief that Chinese music has one form and style because of certain biological characters of the Chinese whereas the peculiar biological traits of the Bantus, Indians, or Negroes produce their respective musical types. On the contrary, our knowledge of neuro-sensory-muscular systems supports the proposition that man may be considered a biological constant so far as his human (symbolic) behavior is concerned. We observe that musical styles vary within a society during the course of time without discovering any correlative biological variation whatever. And of course the musical style of one people may be adopted by another: *Swing Low, Sweet Chariot* did not originate in Dahomey or Cameroon. Thus we see that we cannot explain these variations of musical behavior, which we may represent by M_1, M_2, M_3, M_4 . . . M_n, in terms of the human organism, O. Variables cannot be explained in terms of a constant.

How then can these differences in musical behavior be accounted for? They are to be explained in terms of different musical traditions or cultures, C_1, C_2, C_3, C_4 . . . C_n. Let us set forth our argument in a series of formulas.

$$O \times C_1 \longrightarrow M_1$$
$$O \times C_2 \longrightarrow M_2$$
$$O \times C_3 \longrightarrow M_3$$
$$O \times C_4 \longrightarrow M_4$$

O stands for the human organism; M_1, M_2, M_3, M_4 for different types of musical behavior, i.e., neuro-sensory-muscular reactions of the human organism; and C_1, C_2, C_3, C_4, for types of musical culture. The musical behavior in any particular instance is, of course, a compound made up of two distinct elements, the actions of nerves, glands, muscles, sense organs, etc., of man on the one hand (O), and the external, extra-somatic cultural tradition (C) on the other. Since, however, the human organism appears as a constant factor in all of our equations we may eliminate it entirely from a consideration of variations of behavior. Thus we strike out the O and rewrite our equations thus:

$$C_1 \longrightarrow M_1$$
$$C_2 \longrightarrow M_2$$
$$C_3 \longrightarrow M_3$$
$$C_4 \longrightarrow M_4$$

As the musical cultural tradition varies, so will the musical behavior vary. The behavior is simply the response of the organism to a particular set of cultural stimuli. M is a function of C.

What is true of musical behavior is true also of linguistic behavior, or monetary, mathematical, architectural, philosophic, religious—in short, of any kind of human behavior. We come then to the following formula: *human* behavior is the response of the organism *man* to a class of external, extra-somatic, symbolic stimuli which we call *culture*. Variations of human behavior are functions of a cultural variable, not of a biological constant. Human behavior as we find it amongst the various peoples of the world is to be explained therefore in terms of their respective cultures rather than by appeal to "human nature" or psychological tendencies.

If human behavior is to be explained in terms of culture, how are we to account for culture?

Culture is an organization of phenomena—acts (patterns of behavior), objects (tools; things made with tools), ideas (belief, knowledge), and sentiments (attitudes, "values")—that is dependent upon the use of symbols. Culture began when man as an articulate, symbol-using primate, began. Because of its symbolic character, which has its most important expression in articulate speech, culture is easily and readily transmitted from one human organism to another. Since its elements are readily transmitted culture becomes a continuum; it flows down through the ages from one generation to another and laterally from one people to another. The culture process is also cumulative; new elements enter the stream from time to time and swell the total. The culture process is progressive in the sense that it moves toward greater control over the forces of nature, toward greater security of life for man. Culture is, therefore, a symbolic, continuous, cumulative, and progressive process.

All of this means that culture has, in a very real sense, an extra-somatic character. Although made possible only by the organisms of human beings, once in existence and under way it has a life of its own. Its behavior is determined by its own laws, not by the laws of human organisms. The culture process is to be explained in terms of the science of culture, of culturology, not in terms of psychology. Let us illustrate these propositions with a simple example.

A symbolic language would, of course, have no existence were it not for human organisms. But once the linguistic process gets under way it proceeds along its own lines, in terms of its own principles and in accordance with its own laws. The linguistic process is composed of phonetic elements. These interact with one another forming various kinds of combinations and patterns —phonetic, syntactic, grammatical, lexical, etc. The language acquires form and structure and uniformities of behavior. In other words, it develops certain principles upon which it rests and in terms of which it functions.

Now this language has an extra-somatic, non-biological, non-psychological character. It had an existence prior to the birth of any individual speaking it; it comes to each person from the out-side. It seizes upon the human organism at birth and equips it with specific linguistic patterns of behavior. Languages are trans-mitted from one generation or one people to another just as tools or ornaments are. The study of language is, therefore, *philology*, not biology or psychology. Although human organisms are pre-requisite to the linguistic process they do not form a part of it *as such*, and are therefore irrelevant to the study and interpreta-tion of it. We find no reference to nerves, glands, and sense organs in a manual on English grammar; no hopes, fears, desires, instincts or reflexes in a treatise on the Indo-European languages. Language may be treated as a closed system, as a process *sui generis*. Philology is a subdivision of culturology, not of biology or psychology.

What is true of language will hold for every other logically distinguishable portion of the culture process—technological, social, ideological—and for human culture as a whole. Culture is a continuum of interacting elements (traits), and this process of interaction has its own principles and its own laws. To intro-duce the human organism into a consideration of cultural varia-tions is therefore not only irrelevant but wrong; it involves a premise that is false. Culture must be explained in terms of cul-ture. Thus, paradoxical though it may seem, "the proper study of mankind" turns out to be not Man, after all, but Culture. The most realistic and scientifically adequate interpretation of culture is one that proceeds *as if* human beings did not exist.*

This is really not as radical or as novel as it may seem at first glance. As we have noted in a preceding chapter, scholars have been making culturological studies for decades, studies in which institutions, philosophies, or technologies are treated as classes

---

* "Hence it is both possible and permissible to study the history of a folkway, or the evolution of culture in general, without reference to indi-viduals or their organic and mental characteristics," (Geo. P. Murdock, "The Science of Culture," p. 206).

of extra-somatic, non-biological phenomena. Thus, in addition to philological investigations we have studies of the evolution of currency, geometry, architecture, astronomy, the plow, parliamentary government, the clan, jurisprudence, etc. We have such studies as the effect of the automobile upon the family, the divorce rate, mating customs, the small town country schools, the rubber industry, the blacksmith's trade, street-sweeping, tourist camps, national parks, etc.; or the influence of telescopes and microscopes upon religious and medical beliefs, etc. Culturology as a practical art of interpretation is therefore not new or revolutionary by any means.

Nor is a formulation of the philosophy of the science of culture a recent achievement. As we have already seen, it was well expressed as early as 1871 in the first chapter of E. B. Tylor's *Primitive Culture*, significantly entitled, by the way, "The Science of Culture." It was made explicit in much of Durkheim's writings, particularly *Les Règles de la Méthode Sociologique* (1895). And it has been developed in American anthropology by A. L. Kroeber, R. H. Lowie, Clark Wissler, George P. Murdock, and others.

Despite the respectable age of this point of view and notwithstanding the fact that it is the basis upon which countless culturological studies have already been made in philology, economics, sociology, history, and anthropology, it is still ignored or opposed in many quarters. As we noted in a previous chapter, many psychologists and sociologists hold to a point of view that either obscures the science of culture or actually and specifically opposes it. And, despite the fact that it was, as Kroeber has remarked,[18] the anthropologists who "discovered culture" and recognized it as a distinct class of phenomena, as a separate order of reality, there are many anthropologists who have been quite unable to grasp clearly the conception of a supra-psychological, supra-sociological science of culture and so have opposed it with more or less vigor.

Opposition to the science of culture expresses itself variously, but one theme runs fairly consistently through most if not all of it. This is the objection that it is not *culture* but *people* who do things. Again to quote Lynd's pointed and apt phrase, "Culture does not enamel its fingernails, vote, or believe in capitalism but people do." This observation is no doubt meant to express scientific realism as well as common sense. Anyone can see for himself that it is human beings that mark ballots and drop them into a box.

"Realism" of this sort is simply pathetic. As a matter of fact, it is not realism at all but anthropocentrism, an inability to interpret a chain of events except in terms of man as the prime mover. *Of course* it is people who enamel their fingernails; *of course* culture is not a disembodied soul going its way of its own sweet will; *to be sure*, it is people who wind clocks, manufacture automobiles, build skyscrapers. But the question is not the simple one of who does what from the layman's point of view. The question is, *How are the events that the layman observes to be explained from the scientist's point of view?* The layman sees one people drinking cow's milk, avoiding mothers-in-law, practicing polygyny and inhumation, and forming plurals by affixation. He notes that another group loathes milk, associates freely with mothers-in-law, practices monogamy and cremation, and forms plurals by reduplication. Now the question is not "Who drinks the milk—the people or the culture?" The culturologist knows who does the drinking quite as well as his "realistic" opponents. The question is, "Why does one people prize milk as a nutritious and tasty beverage while another regards it with loathing?"

To the culturologist the reasoning that says that one people drinks milk because "they like it," another does not because "they loathe it," is senseless; it explains nothing at all. Why does one people like, another loathe, milk? *This* is what we want to know. And the psychologist cannot give us the answer. Nor can he tell us why a people does or does not avoid mothers-in-law, practice monogamy, inhumation, the couvade, or circumcision;

use chopsticks, forks, the pentatonic scale, hats, or microscopes; form plurals by affixation—or any of the other thousands of customs known to ethnography.

The culturologist explains the behavior of a people by pointing out that it is merely the response of a particular type of primate organism to a particular set of stimuli. And he explains culture along the lines indicated earlier in this chapter. Thus, while the culturologist is quite willing to admit that it is people who "enamel their fingernails" or drink milk, he desires to point out that whether they do or not is determined not by themselves but by their culture. Scientific explanation is a quest for determinants, for cause and effect relationships, for distinctions between constants and variables, distinctions between dependent and independent variables. The culturologist is well aware that culture does not and cannot exist without human beings. Need it be said that there could be no plural forms of nouns, no geometry, no dynamos, no pinochle, if there were no human beings? And certainly there could be no mother-in-law taboos if there were no women! But, as the culturologist demonstrates, culture may be treated as if it had a life of its own, quite apart from human organisms, just as the physicist may treat a falling body as if there were no atmospheric friction. The behavior of peoples is explained as their response to their respective cultures. It is not mystical at all to treat culture as if it were independent of human beings, as Boas, Benedict and others have claimed, any more than it is mystical for the physicist to treat falling bodies as if there were no friction. It is simply the application of the point of view and the techniques of science, long familiar in physics, to the realm of culture.

It should not be necessary to point out that the thesis here set forth is not in any sense a criticism, much less a belittling, of psychology. The position of this science is as honorable as it is secure. What we have done is to distinguish between psychological and culturological interpretations of behavior and, further, to demonstrate that certain problems are to be solved with culturo-logical rather than with psychological techniques. Since human behavior is composed of two kinds of ingredients, the biological, or psychological, and the extra-somatic cultural, there are two corresponding classes of problems. In the one, we hold the biological factor constant while we study the cultural variable; in the other class we hold the cultural factor constant and study the reactions of human organisms to it. The existence of the institution of trial by jury, for example, cannot be accounted for psychologically; the explanation must be culturological. But to understand the function of this institution in the lives of men we must study their psychological reactions to it. One and the same set of events may therefore be referred to either context, the psychological or the culturological. Psychology and culturology deal therefore with biological and extra-somatic aspects respectively of one and the same set of events. Both sciences are essential to a comprehensive interpretation of human behavior. It is necessary, however, in order to avoid confusion, to know and respect the proper boundaries of each.

CHAPTER SEVEN

CULTURAL DETERMINANTS OF *MIND*

"When I fulfil my obligations as brother, husband, or citizen, when I execute my contracts, I perform duties which are defined, externally to myself and my acts, in law and in custom. Even if they conform to my own sentiments and I feel their reality subjectively, such reality is still objective, for I did not create them; I merely inherited them through my education. . . . Similarly, the church-member finds the beliefs and practices of his religious life ready-made at birth; their existence prior to his own implies their existence outside of himself. . . . Here, then, are ways of acting, thinking, and feeling that present the noteworthy property of existing outside the individual consciousness.

"These types of conduct or thought are not only external to the individual but are, moreover, endowed with coercive power, by virtue of which they impose themselves upon him, independent of his individual will . . ."—Emile Durkheim, *The Rules of Sociological Method.*

Human behavior is, as we have just seen, a compound of two separate and distinct kind of elements: psychosomatic and cultural. On the one hand we have a certain type of primate organism, man; on the other, a traditional organization of tools, ideas, beliefs, customs, attitudes, etc., that we call *culture.* The behavior of man as a human being—as distinguished from his non-symbolic, primate behavior—is an expression of the interaction of the human organism and the extra-somatic cultural tradition. Human behavior is, therefore, a function of culture as well as of a biological organism. In the preceding chapter we examined the relationship between man and culture at some length. We endeavored to show that psychological interpretations of cultures—of institutions, customs, attitudes, etc.—which have been, and still are, so popular, are unsound; that cultures cannot be explained psychologically but only culturologically. In the present chapter we shall continue our inquiry into the relationship between man and culture, but this time our focus will be upon the human organism rather than upon the external cultural tradition. If we cannot explain cultures psychologically, and, if human behavior is a product of culture as well as of nerves, glands, muscles, sense organs, etc., perhaps some of the phenomena commonly regarded as psychological are actually culturally determined. If, on the one hand, there has been a widespread tendency to regard cultures as psychologically determined, perhaps there has been a corresponding failure to recognize cultural determinants of mind. The point of view and habit of thought that sees in a custom or institution merely the expression of an innate desire, need or ability, is likely also to think of the "mind" of man as something innate in his organism, biologically determined. Just as culture is naively thought to be a simple and direct expression of "human nature," so is the "human mind" thought to be a simple and direct expression of the neuro-sensory-glandular-etcetera organization of man.

This view is, however, an illusion. Just as scientific analysis discovers a non-anthropomorphic, culturological determination of culture, and demonstrates the irrelevance of psychological explanations of cultures, so does it find that many of the elements or attributes of "the human mind" are not to be explained in terms of the action of nerves, brains, glands, sense organs, etc., but in terms of culture. This does not mean that the reactions of the human organism to cultural elements in the external world are not "psychological" or "mental"; they are. It simply means that in the *minding* of man as a human being there are non-psychosomatic, i.e., extra-somatic cultural, determinants. The "human mind" is the *reacting* of the *human organism* to external stimuli; mind is minding here as elsewhere. But this reacting, this minding, varies. The Hottentot mind, or minding, is not the same as Eskimo, or English, minding. The "human mind"—human minding—is obviously a variable. And its variations are functions of variations of the cultural factor rather than of the psycho-somatic factor, which may be regarded as a constant. The whole concept of "the human mind" is thus thrown into a new light and perspective.

In other animal species, the "mind" is a function of the bodily structure, of a particular organization of nerves, glands, sense organs, muscles, etc. Thus the mind of the gorilla differs from that of the chimpanzee; the mind of a bear differs from that of a cat or a squirrel. In each case, the minds are functions of their respective bodily structures, differences of mind are correlated with differences of bodily structure. In the case of the human species, however, this is not the case. The mind (minding) of the Chinese is not like the mind of the Sicilians or the Hopi Indians. But here the differences of mind are not due to differences of bodily structure for, from the standpoint of the human behavior of races or other groups, this may be considered as a constant. Differences of mind among different ethnic groups of human beings are due to differences of cultural tradition. Thus we have a radical and fundamental difference between the determination of mental variation among sub-human species and mental variation within the human species. For the sub-human species the formula is: $V_m = f(V_b)$—variations of mind are functions of variations of bodily structure. For the human species the formula is: $V_m = f(V_c)$—variations of human minding are functions of the extra-somatic tradition called culture.

In the realm of human behavior we are concerned of course with organisms: organizations of bones, muscles, glands, nerves, sense organs, and so on. And these organisms react to external stimuli, cultural as well as otherwise. The human mind is still the reacting of the human organism. But we now see that the specific content of the human mind in any particular expression—speaking here of peoples rather than of individuals—is determined by the extra-somatic factor of culture rather than by the neuro-logic, sensory, glandular, muscular, etc., constitution of the human organism. In other words, the Chinese mind, the French, Zulu, or Comanche mind, as a particular organization of human behavior, is explainable in cultural terms, not biological.

In the category "the human mind," therefore, in the minding of human beings, we discover cultural determinants as well as psychosomatic factors. And, furthermore, we learn that in an explanation of differences among types of the human mind, such as Eskimo, Zulu, or English, it is the cultural determinant that is significant, not the psychosomatic. A comparative, ethnographic survey of the human mind leads to a realization that many of its attributes are not due to an inborn "human nature" at all, as was formerly supposed, but to differences of external cultural stimulation.

One of the most popular formulas of interpretation of human behavior is that of "human nature." People behave as they do, have the institutions, beliefs, attitudes, games, etc., that surround them, because "it is human nature." And, incidentally, most people—however much they may be willing to admit their ignorance in other respects—usually feel that they "understand human nature." The human mind and organism are so constituted, according to this view, as to make certain kinds of response simply and directly forthcoming. One has only to know human nature to understand society and culture and to predict their course of development. The fallacy or illusion here is, of course, that what one takes for "human nature" is not *natural* at all but cultural. The tendencies, emphases, and content that one sees in the overt behavior of human beings are often not due to innate biological determination—though such determinations do of course exist—but to the stimulation of external cultural elements. Much of what is commonly called "human nature" is merely *culture* thrown against a screen of nerves, glands, sense organs, muscles, etc. We have a particularly fine example of this illusion, this mis-

taking of culture for nature, in a passage from Thomas Wolfe's
*You Can't Go Home Again:**

For what is man?

First, a child, unable to support itself on its rubbery legs,
befouled with its excrement, that howls and laughs by turns,
cries for the moon but hushes when it gets its mother's teat;
a sleeper, eater, guzzler, howler, laugher, idiot, and a chewer of
its toe; a little tender thing all blubbered with its spit, a reacher
into fires, a beloved fool.

After that, a boy, hoarse and loud before his companions,
but afraid of the dark; will beat the weaker and avoid the
stronger; worships strength and savagery, loves tales of wai
and murder, and violence done to others; joins gangs and hates
to be alone; makes heroes out of soldiers, sailors, prize fighters,
football players, cowboys, gunmen, and detectives; would
rather die than not out-try and out-dare his companions, wants
to beat them and always to win, shows his muscle and demands
that it be felt, boasts of his victories and will never own defeat.

Then the youth: goes after girls, is foul behind their backs
among the drugstore boys, hints at a hundred seductions, but
gets pimples on his face; begins to think about his clothes, becomes a fop, greases his hair, smokes cigarettes with a dissipated
air, reads novels, and writes poetry on the sly. He sees the world
now as a pair of legs and breasts; he knows hate, love, and
jealousy; he is cowardly and foolish, he cannot endure to be
alone; he lives in a crowd, thinks with the crowd, is afraid to be
marked off from his fellows by an eccentricity. He joins clubs
and is afraid of ridicule; he is bored and unhappy and wretched
most of the time. There is a great cavity in him, he is dull.

Then the man: he is busy, he is full of plans and reasons, he
has work. He gets children, buys and sells small packets of
everlasting earth, intrigues against his rivals, is exultant when he
cheats them. He wastes his little three score years and ten in

---

* New York, The Sun Dial Press, pp. 432-33. Quoted by permission of
Harper and Brothers.

spendthrift and inglorious living; from his cradle to his grave he scarcely sees the sun or moon or stars; he is unconscious of the immortal sea and earth; he talks of the future and he wastes it as it comes. If he is lucky, he saves money. At the end his fat purse buys him flunkeys to carry him where his shanks no longer can; he consumes rich food and golden wine that his wretched stomach has no hunger for; his weary and lifeless eyes look out upon the scenery of strange lands for which in youth his heart was panting. Then the slow death, prolonged by costly doctors, and finally the graduate undertakers, the perfumed carrion, the suave ushers with palms outspread to leftwards, the fast motor hearses, and the earth again.

To many, no doubt, Wolfe's characterization of man is both true and apt. This is what man really is, they feel. Others, perhaps, would disagree and say, "No, man is not as Wolfe depicts him; he is *this* sort of being." Each view may seem plausible; each can be supported with evidence. And, however much Wolfe's characterization of man may differ from that of another, both may agree that the *method of interpretation* is sound. You place man before you; you study him, analyze him, and then report your findings. Plausible and reasonable as this may seem, it is but an illusion. The Wolfes are not describing Man at all, but Culture.

This is not quibbling in any way. The distinction is real, profound, and important. What Wolfe describes as Man is merely the way the human organism responds to a certain set of cultural stimuli. In another kind of culture the organism would respond quite differently. His characterization of man would certainly not be applicable to the Zuni Pueblo Indians nor to the Pygmies of the Congo, the aborigines of Australia, or the peasant folk of Mexico. And, as a matter of fact, he all but says that it is not man's "real nature" that he is describing. Does he not suggest at least that man *is* a being who *could* "see the sun, moon and stars and be conscious of the immortal sea and earth" were it not for the culture which holds him in its grip and compels him to waste his precious life selling real estate, cheating rivals? Wolfe is describing a *culture* in terms of its effects upon the human organism.

But what difference does it make, one might ask, whether "human nature" or "culture" is the cause so long as man actually performs the acts and must suffer their consequences? What difference does it make whether a gangster murders a cashier and robs a bank because he was born and reared in a certain type of culture or because he was "by nature" murderous, vicious, and rapacious? The cashier is dead in either case, the money gone, and the police are hot on the gangster's trail. True enough; things are what they are. But it makes all the difference in the world whether the man did the killing and the robbing because it is human nature to do so, or whether his behavior was determined by the type of culture, the kind of social system, he happened to be living in. All the difference, that is, to the scientist who wishes to provide an adequate *explanation* of the behavior. And a great deal of difference to the layman, too, because of the implications inherent in the two alternatives: cultures may change—they are constantly changing in fact; but human nature, biologically defined, is virtually constant—it has undergone no appreciable change in the last 30,000 years at least.

Wolfe's description of man is a philosophy of behavior, an explanatory device. It is based on certain premises. It may be supported by much evidence, but the premises are wrong for all that, and much confusion and error flow inevitably from them.

Let us consider a few areas of behavior. Take food habits for example. Man is one but his tastes vary enormously. A food loathed by one people may be a delicacy to another. Many Chinese cannot bear the thought of eating cheese, whereas most Europeans are very fond of it, and the choicest cheeses are often those with an odor of putrefaction or ordure. Neither do the Chinese like milk—even Grade A. Some tribes will not eat chicken or eggs. Others will eat eggs but prefer rotten eggs to fresh ones.

The choicest porterhouse steak has no charms for the Hindu, nor baked ham or pork chops for the Jew. We have an aversion for worms and insects as food but many peoples eat them as delicacies. The Navajos will not eat fish. We will not eat dogs. The eating of human flesh is regarded with extreme revulsion by some peoples; to others it is the feast supreme. It would be hard indeed to name an edible substance that is regarded everywhere as food. The aversions and loathings likewise vary. What then can we attribute to "human nature?" Virtually nothing. What a people likes or loathes is not determined by the innate attractions and repulsions of the human organism. On the contrary, the preferences and aversions are produced within the human organism by a culture acting upon it from the outside. Why cultures vary in this respect is another matter; we shall turn to it later on.

Is it human nature to kiss a loved one? If it were, then the practice would be universal. But it is not. There are peoples who do not kiss at all. Some rub noses. Others merely sniff the back of the neck of children. And in some societies a parent or elder relative will spit in the face of a child; saliva is here regarded as a magical substance and this act is therefore a sort of blessing. Among some peoples adult males kiss each other. I once witnessed greetings between men in one of the isolated valleys of the Caucasus mountains. They kissed each other fervently, pushing aside a thick growth of whiskers to reach the lips. Other peoples regard kissing among adult males as unmanly. Where does human nature enter this picture? It does not enter at all. The attitude toward kissing as well as its practice is not determined by innate desires of the human organism. If this were so, kissing behavior would be uniform throughout the world as the organism is uniform. But this is not the case. Behavior varies because cultures differ. You will do, or taboo, what your culture calls for.

Human behavior varies widely at other points. Sexual jealousy is so powerful and so poignant in some societies that to doubt that it is a simple and direct expression of human nature might seem almost absurd. It is "just natural" for a lover to be jealous of a rival. If a man kills the "seducer" of his wife, a jury of his peers may let him go scot free; it was only natural that he should do this, they observe. Yet, we find societies, like the Eskimo, where wives are loaned to guests as a part of hospitality. And Dr. Margaret Mead reports that the Samoans simply cannot understand jealousy among lovers, and find our sentiments in this respect incredible or preposterous.

In some groups premarital sexual intercourse is not only permitted to girls but the practice forms an integral part of the routine of courtship. Out of these intimacies come an acquaintance, a sympathy, and an understanding that make for an enduring marriage. In other groups, brides may be subjected to chastity tests and killed if they fail to pass them. The unmarried mother is stigmatized in some societies, taken for granted in others. Attitude toward homosexuality varies likewise; in some groups it is a mark of shame and degradation, in others it is recognized and accepted. Some societies recognize and give status to a third, or intermediate, sex—the *berdache*, transvestite—in addition to man and woman. A man must avoid his mother-in-law assiduously in some societies; he must not speak to her or allow himself in her presence. In other tribes, a man must have no social intercourse with his sister. Some peoples regard polygamy with aversion, even horror. To marry one's deceased wife's unmarried sister is a crime in some societies, a sacred obligation in others.* In none of these

---

* ". . . . in modern England . . . marriage with a deceased wife's sister became equivalent to incest and the thought of such marriage was defined as 'psychic incest.' . . . Around the year 1850, when Lord Russell's bill for the repeal of the law against such marriages was being debated, countless sermons were preached and thousands of pamphlets and letters were printed protesting against repeal:

" 'It would be difficult (says Lecky) to overstate the extravagance of language employed. . . . One gentleman (Lord Hatherley), who had been Lord Chancellor of England, more than once declared that if marriage with a deceased wife's sister ever became legal "the decadence of England was inevitable," and that for his part he would rather see 300,000 Frenchmen

instances can we explain custom or institution in terms of the innate desires, sentiments, and aversions of the people concerned. It is not one set of sentiments and desires that produces monogamy here, another set polygamy there. It is the other way around; it is the institution that determines the sentiments and behavior. If you are born into a polygamous culture you will think, feel and behave polygamously. If, however, you are born into a Puritan New England culture you will look upon polygamy with marked disapproval.

There are still other aspects or expressions of the human mind that were once thought to be determined by innate psychobiological factors but which we now recognize as being largely determined by culture. Take the Oedipus complex for example. It was once thought that a boy's hostility toward his father and his love for his mother were simply expressions of his biological nature. But, as Malinowski and others have shown, these attitudes vary with type of family organization. In some societies the husband is not the head of the family, the disciplinarian. It is the mother's brother who takes this role, and the father is merely the kindly, indulgent friend and companion. The attitude of boys toward father and mother are not the same here as in the patriarchal household known to Freud. Polygynous and polyandrous households produce other orientations of attitude. In some cultures it is the sister rather than the mother who becomes the primary object of incestuous desire. The definition of incest, and consequently one's attitude toward sexual union with cross or parallel, first or second, cousins, varies with the culture as we shall see later on.

landed on the British coasts,' " (Wm. I. Thomas, *Primitive Behavior*, pp. 196-97).

Contrast this with the command, in Deuteronomy (XXV: 5-12) that a man shall marry his deceased brother's wife. Should he refuse, the woman shall disgrace him publicly, taking off his sandal "in the presence of the elders . . . and spit in his face." Note, also, that Onan was killed by the Lord for avoiding his duty to his deceased brother's widow (Genesis XXXVIII: 6-11).

One's conscience is often thought to be the most intimate, personal and private characteristic of one's ego. Here if anywhere one ought to find something that is wholly one's own, a private and unique possession. To an ordinary individual the conscience seems to be a mechanism, an inborn ability, to distinguish between right and wrong, just as he possesses a mechanism for distinguishing up from down, the vertical from the horizontal. Except, perhaps, that conscience seems deeper within one, a more intimate part of one's make-up, than semi-circular canals. After all, these canals are merely a mechanical device, whereas a conscience is an integral part of one's self, one's ego. Yet, for all the conviction that immediate experience carries, we can still be tricked by illusion. And this is exactly what has happened in the present instance. Our sense of balance, our distinction between up and down, is indeed a private faculty; it is built into our psychosomatic structure and has no origin or significance apart from it. But our conscience has a sociocultural origin; it is the operation of supra-individual cultural forces upon the individual organism. Conscience is merely our experience and our awareness of the operation of certain sociocultural forces upon us. Right and wrong are matters of sociocultural genesis; they are originated by social systems, not by individual biological organisms. Behavior that is injurious, or thought to be harmful, to the general welfare is wrong; behavior that promotes the general welfare is good. The desires inherent in an individual organism are exercised to serve its own interests. Society, in order to protect itself from the demands of the individual as well as to serve its own interests, must influence or control the behavior of its component members. It must encourage good behavior and discourage the bad. It does this by first defining the good and the bad specifically, and secondly, by identifying each good or bad with a powerful emotion, positive or negative, so that the individual is motivated to perform good deeds and to refrain from committing bad ones. So effective is this socio-psychologic mechanism that society not only succeeds in enlisting individuals in the cause of general welfare but actually causes them to work against their own interests— even to the point of sacrificing their own lives for others or for the general welfare. A part of the effectiveness of this social mechanism consists in the illusion that surrounds it: the individual is made to feel that it is he who is making the decision and taking the proper action, and, moreover, that he is perfectly "free" in making his decisions and in choosing courses of action. Actually, of course, this still small voice of conscience is but the voice of the tribe or group speaking to him from within. "What is called conscience," says Radcliffe-Brown, "is . . . the reflex in the individual of the sanctions of the society." [1] The human organism lives and moves within an ethical magnetic field, so to speak. Certain social forces, culturally defined, impinge upon the organism and move it this way and that, toward the good, away from the bad. The organism experiences these forces though he may mistake their source. He calls this experience conscience. His behavior is analogous to a pilotless aircraft controlled by radio. The plane is directed this way and that by impulses external to it. These impulses are received by a mechanism and are then transmitted to motors, rudders, etc. This receiving and behavior-controlling mechanism is analogous to conscience.

That conscience is a cultural variable rather than a psychosomatic constant is made apparent of course by a consideration of the great variation of definition of *rights* and *wrongs* among the various cultures of the world. What is right in one culture may be wrong in another. This follows from the fact that an act that will promote the general welfare in one set of circumstances may injure it in another. Thus we find great variety of ethical definition and conduct in the face of a common and uniform human organism, and must conclude therefore that the determination of right and wrong is social and cultural rather than individual and psychological. But the interpretation of *conscience*, rather than custom and mores, in terms of social and cultural forces serves to demonstrate once more that the individual is what his culture makes him. He is the utensil; the culture supplies the contents. Conscience is the instrument, the vehicle, of ethical conduct, not the cause. It is well, here as elsewhere, to distinguish cart from horse.

The unconscious also is a concept that may be defined culturo-logically as well as psychologically. Considered from a psychological point of view, "the unconscious" is the name given to a class of determinants of behavior inherent in the organism, or at least, having their locus in the organism as a consequence of the experiences it has undergone, of which the person is not aware or whose significance he does not appreciate. But there is also another class of determinants of human behavior of which the ordinary individual may be—and usually is—unaware, or at least has little or no appreciation of their significance. These are extra-somatic cultural determinants. In a general and broad sense, the whole realm of culture constitutes "an unconscious" for most laymen and for many social scientists as well. The concept of culture and an appreciation of its significance in the life of man lie beyond the ken of all but the most scientifically sophisticated. To those who believe that man makes his culture and controls its course of change, the field of cultural forces and determinants may be said to constitute an unconscious—an extra-somatic unconscious.

The unconscious character of the operation of culture in the lives of men can be demonstrated in many particular instances as well as in a general way. A moment ago we distinguished the unconscious factor in ethical behavior. The determinants of ethical behavior—why, for example, one should not play cards on Sunday —lie in the external cultural tradition. The individual, however, unaware of either the source or the purpose of the taboo, locates it in his inner self: his conscience is but the screen upon which the unconscious factors of society and culture project themselves.

Incest is defined and prohibited in order to effect exogamous unions so that mutual aid may be fostered and, consequently, life made more secure for the members of society. But of the existence and significance of these cultural factors all but a few are unconscious. To the individual, incest is simply a sin or crime that is inherently and absolutely wrong.

Or, take the rules of etiquette: A man in a certain society is not permitted to wear earrings or to use lipstick. The purpose of these restrictions is to define classes of individuals within society: a man, woman, priest, etc., is an individual who behaves positively in a certain manner and who must refrain from certain kinds of acts. By means of these definitions, prescriptions, and prohibitions, each individual is made to conform to his class and the classes are thereby kept intact. Thus, order is achieved in society, order both structurally and functionally. And, to conduct its life effectively a society must have order. But the individual seldom has any appreciation of the source and purpose of these rules; he is apt to regard them, if he thinks about them at all, as natural and right, or as capricious and irrational. Another example of the cultural unconscious.

The church is an organ of social control; it is a mechanism of integration and regulation. In this respect it has political functions just as does the State (see p. 242). It operates to preserve the integrity of society against disintegration from within and against aggression from without. It is thus an important factor in a nation's war machine; it mobilizes the citizenry to fight against foreign foes. It must also strive to harmonize conflicting class interests at home. This it does frequently by telling the poor and the oppressed to be patient, to be satisfied with their lot, not to resort to violence, etc.* In these ways the Church like the State

---

* "Religion teaches the laboring man and the artisan to carry out honestly and fairly all equitable agreements freely entered into; never to injure the property, nor to outrage the person, of an employer; never to resort to violence in defending their own cause, nor to engage in riot or disorder . . ." (Pope Leo XII's Encyclical on Condition of Labor, May 15, 1891, *The Official Catholic Year Book Anno Domini*, 1928), p. 540.

exercises political functions that are essential to the life of the society. Yet how many members of a congregation or of the clergy have any awareness of this aspect of the rituals, paraphernalia, theology, and dogma that occupy them?

The determinants of our form of the family lie so deep within our cultural unconscious that even social science has yet no adequate answer to the question why we prohibit polygamy (see p. 335). The Chinese, according to Kroeber, were long unaware that their language had tones. "This apparently simple and fundamental discovery," he says, "was not made until two thousand years after they possessed writing, and a thousand after they had scholars." [2] And they might not have made it even then had not "the learning of Sanskrit for religious purposes . . . made them phonetically self-conscious." Like the rustic who had been talking prose all his life without realizing it, the peoples of the Western world, too, have long been unconscious of much of the structure and processes of Indo-European languages.

Thus, in addition to the determinants of behavior that lie deep within the tissues of our own organisms, below the level of awareness, there is another class of determinants of which we are equally unconscious: forces and factors within the extra-somatic cultural tradition. The science of culture is endeavoring to discover, define and explain these unconscious cultural factors as psychoanalysis has undertaken to explore and make known the intra-organismal unconscious.* We may illustrate these two realms of the unconscious in the following diagram:

---

* Kroeber has a fine appreciation of the unconscious character of cultural determinants of human behavior as the section "Unconscious Factors in Language and Culture" in his *Anthropology* (1923) makes clear. But despite certain examples which he cites and which show quite clearly that the locus of the unconscious *is in the culture process*, he locates it "in the mind." Thus he says: "It is difficult to say where the creative and imitative impulses of fashion come from; which, inasmuch as the impulses obviously reside somewhere in human minds, means that they spring from the unconscious portions of the mind" (p. 127).

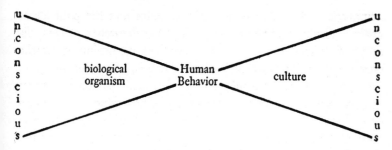

Human behavior is a function of the biological organism on the one hand, and of the extra-somatic cultural tradition or process, on the other. The individual is more or less aware of some of the determinants of his behavior in each category, the cultural and the biological. But of others he is quite unaware, or has no adequate appreciation of the role they play as determinants of his behavior. These are the realms of the unconscious: the biological and the cultural.

The nature of the relationship between the mind of the individual human organism on the one hand and the external cultural tradition on the other may be illuminated by a critical examination of a certain thesis widely held in recent and current anthropological circles in the United States. Briefly stated, this thesis asserts that man has created culture, that culture is the accumulated product of the creative acts of countless individuals, that the individual is the *fons et origo* of all cultural elements, and, finally, that the culture process is to be explained in terms of the individual.

Thus Ralph Linton writes: "... the individual ... *lies at the foundation of all social and cultural phenomena. Societies are organized groups of individuals, and cultures are, in the last analysis, nothing more than the organized and repetitive responses of a society's members. For this reason the individual is the logical starting point for any investigation of the larger configuration*" [3] (emphasis ours). "If we had the knowledge and the patience to analyze a culture retrospectively," says Goldenweiser, "*every element* of it would be found to have had its beginning in the creative act of *an individual mind.* There is, of course, *no other source* for culture to come from . . . An *analysis of culture,* if fully carried out, *leads back to the individual mind*" [4] (emphasis ours). Edward Sapir asserts that the "currency [of "any cultural element"] in a single community is . . . an instance of diffusion that has radiated out, at last analysis, from a single individual." [5] Ruth Benedict declares that "no civilization has in it any element which in the last analysis is not the contribution of an individual. Where else could any trait come from except from the behavior of a man, woman or a child?" [6] Clark Wissler said that "the inventive process resides in individual organisms; so far as we know, it is a function of the individual organism." [7] Linton asserts that "*it is the individual who is responsible,* in the last analysis, for *all additions to culture*" [8] (emphasis ours). Hallowell finds the conception of *cultural* influence unrealistic; "In the last analysis," he says, "it is *individuals* who respond to and influence one another." [9] Both Goldenweiser and Malinowski place the individual "at the beginning and the end" of the sociocultural process.[10] And, finally, we cite Sapir's categorical dictum: "It is *always the individual* that *really thinks* and *acts* and *dreams* and *revolts.*" * [11]

The import of the foregoing is clear. It is the individual who "is responsible" for culture change; it is the individual who *really* does things; every cultural element has its beginning in the creative act of an individual mind, etc., etc. It would appear from our quotations that their authors feel that they are expressing a fundamental proposition and point of view. Nearly all of them use the phrase "in the last analysis" in setting forth their position. Their premises seem to appear to them so simple and so realistic

---

* We recall at this point Georg Simmel's emphatic assertion: "It is *certain* that *in the last analysis* only individuals exist," (emphasis ours); see p. 84.

as to be virtually axiomatic: "Every cultural element originates in the mind of an individual—of a man, woman, or child. Where else could it come from?" Culture is pictured as a great structure built by countless individuals, much as a coral reef is produced by myriads of marine organisms during the course of time. And, as the coral reef is explained in terms of the activities of marine organisms, so culture may be explained by citing the "creative acts of the individual human mind."

This view seems plausible enough: as a matter of fact, it appears to be virtually self-evident. Anyone can see for himself that it is man, human individuals, who chop down trees, build houses, pass laws, write sonnets, worship gods, etc. But we have become a bit wary of the self-evident and the obvious: anyone can see for himself that it is the sun, not the earth, that moves. But, thanks to Copernicus, we now know better.

Obvious and self-evident though the proposition that culture is made by individuals may appear to be, we must reject it as a means of explaining cultural processes or traditions. As a matter of fact, we regard it as an expression of the primitive and prescientific philosophy of anthropomorphism. Man has been explaining the world he lives in by attributing its existence and nature to the action of some mind, his own or a god's, for ages on end. William James accounted for machines, instruments, and institutions by asserting that they "were flashes of genius in an individual head, of which the outer environment showed no sign." [12] To Newton "this most beautiful cosmos could only proceed from the counsel and dominion of an intelligent and powerful Being." [13] To Plato, the material world was but the expression of "ideas in the mind of God." "Let there be light," said Yahweh, "and there was light." In the mythology of ancient Egypt, everything came from the thinking and willing of the great artificer deity, Ptah.[14] Among our preliterate Keresan Pueblo Indians, Tsityostinako, or Thought-Woman, brought things to pass by acts of thought and will.[15] And today, in line with this ancient and primitive philosophic tradition, we are told that culture has issued from the mind of man—of men, women, and children—and therefore if we are to understand culture and explain its content and course of change, we must do so in terms of the individual.

It is obvious, of course, that culture has emanated from the organisms of human beings: without the human species there would be no culture. We recognize also that a generic relationship obtains between culture as a whole and the human species in its, or their, entirety; the general character of culture is an expression of the biological properties of the human species. But, when it comes to an explanation of any particular culture—and all the cultures of the world are particular, specific cultures—or to an explanation of the process of culture change in general, a consideration of the human organism, either in its collective or individual aspects, is irrelevant. The culture process is not explainable in terms of races, physical types, or of individual minds. It is to be explained in terms of culture itself. In short, the culture process is to be explained culturologically rather than biologically or psychologically.

Thus we do not account for differences between Chinese and Swedish culture by appeal to the physical, somatological, and innate psychological differences between the Chinese and the Swedish peoples. We know of no differences between cultural traditions, no specific feature of the culture process, that can be explained in terms of innate biological properties, physical or mental. On the other hand, we can explain the human behavior of Chinese and Swedish peoples as biological organisms in terms of their respective cultures.

The proposition just enunciated is generally accepted in the social sciences today. We no longer subscribe to racial explanations of culture. But the thesis that the sociocultural process is explainable in terms of individuals rests upon the same premise, namely, that biological factors are relevant to interpretations of the culture process. Thus, it is admitted that the biological factor is extraneous to an interpretation of the culture process when taken in its collective (i.e., racial) aspect, but, many scholars contend, it is not only relevant but fundamental when taken in its individual aspect. We regard this reasoning as unsound; a single individual organism is as irrelevant to an interpretation of the culture process as a group of individuals.

It might be well at this point to draw a distinction between two fundamentally different propositions. The individual himself is not irrelevant to the actual culture process. On the contrary, he is an integral and in one sense a fundamental part of it. Individuals do indeed enamel their fingernails, vote, and believe in capitalism as Lynd has observed. But *the individual is irrelevant to an explanation of the culture process*. We cannot explain the culture trait or process of enameling nails in terms of innate desire, will, or caprice. We can however explain the behavior of the individual in terms of the culture that embraces him. *The* individual, the average, typical individual of a group, may be regarded as a constant so far as *human*, symbolic behavior is concerned. The typical Crow Indian organism may be regarded as biologically equivalent to the typical English, Zulu, or Eskimo organism so far as his capacities and inclinations for human behavior are concerned. The alternative to this proposition is acceptance of a racial determinant of human behavior and culture. In the process of interaction between the human organism on the one hand and the extra-somatic cultural tradition on the other, the cultural factor is the variable, the biological factor the constant; it is the cultural factor that determines the variations in the resulting behavior. The human behavior of the individual organism is therefore a function of his culture. The individual becomes then the locus of the culture process and the vehicle of its expression. Thus we arrive at a culturological conception of individuality to add to those of anatomy, physiology, and psychology.

Since the earliest days of human history every member of the human species has been introduced at birth into a cultural environment of beliefs, customs, instruments, expressions of art, etc., as well as a natural habitat of climate, topography, flora and fauna. This cultural environment is a continuum, a tradition; it descends lineally from one generation to another, and it may diffuse laterally from one people to another. Culture is an elaborate mechanism whose function is to make life secure and continuous for groups of human beings. In order to perform these functions, culture must harness energy in one form or another and put it to work. Culture is, therefore, a thermodynamic system in a mechanical sense. Culture grows in all its aspects—ideological, sociological, and technological—when and as the amount of energy harnessed per capita per year is increased, and as the means of expending this energy are improved. Culture is thus a dynamic system capable of growth. A cultural tradition is a stream of interacting cultural elements—of instruments, beliefs, customs, etc. In this interactive process, each element impinges upon others and is in turn acted upon by them. The process is a competitive one; instruments, customs, and beliefs may become obsolete and be eliminated from the stream: stone axes give way to metal ones; science replaces myth and magic; tribe and clan become obsolete at a certain stage of social evolution and the state takes their place. New elements are incorporated into the cultural stream from time to time: metals, the wheel, beliefs consequent upon the use of the microscope, etc., enter the cultural tradition at certain stages of its development. New combinations and syntheses of cultural elements—i.e., inventions and discoveries—are continually being formed in this interactive process: the invention of the steam engine, the "discovery" of the Periodic System of the elements, the formulation of the laws of thermodynamics, etc., are new combinations or syntheses of cultural elements. A cultural tradition is therefore a dynamic system (powered by natural forces which it harnesses) that behaves and grows in terms of its own principles and laws. It may therefore be explained on its own level, in culturological terms rather than with the concepts of psychology, biology, chemistry or physics. It may be regarded as a system *sui generis*.

In relation to the process of culture change and growth the biological factor of man may be regarded as a constant and hence irrelevant to an explanation of the culture process. Relative to an explanation of the difference between the culture of the Swedes and that of the Chinese or Zulus, the biological factor—such things as skin, hair, or eye color, stature, innate abilities, etc.—may, as we have noted, be regarded as irrelevant. It is irrelevant also to an explanation of the differences between the culture of England in A.D. 1200 and that of A.D. 1900. We see, then, that to the problem of interpretation of the culture process, the biological factor of man is irrelevant. The culture process is explainable culturologically, not biologically or psychologically.

Let us now consider *the individual* in relation to the culture process. As we have noted, every individual is born into a culture that existed prior to his birth. This culture seizes upon him at birth and as he grows and matures equips him with language, customs, beliefs, instruments, etc. In short, it is culture that provides him with the *form* and *content* of his behavior as a human being. Thus, Crow Indian behavior is the response of the organism *Homo sapiens* to a particular organization of stimuli that we call "Crow culture." Similarly, American, Eskimo, and Zulu behaviors are the responses of the same kind of organism to other cultural traditions. *The individual* in each case is merely an organization of cultural forces and elements that have impinged upon him from the outside and which find their overt expression through him. So conceived, the individual is but the expression of a supra-biological cultural tradition in somatic form.

We turn now to the role of the individual in the process of culture growth, and specifically to the propositions that, "in the last analysis," it is the individual who "is responsible for all addi-

tions to culture"; that "every culture element is to be traced back
to the creative act of an individual mind"; that it is always the
individual who really thinks, acts, dreams, and revolts; and that
the individual is "the logical starting point for any investigation
of the larger configurations" such as society and culture.

To be sure culture is dependent upon the human species and
could not exist without it. It is true also that the human species
is composed of discrete physical entities that we call individuals.
But the scholars that we have just quoted are doing more than to
give utterance to these obvious and trite commonplaces. They are
asserting that the individual is a prime mover, a determinant;
that he is the cause, culture the effect; that it is the individual
who "is responsible" for change in the culture process; and that,
therefore, an explanation of "the larger configuration" of culture must lie in a consideration of the individual. And it is this
proposition that we reject—and reverse: it is the individual who
is explained in terms of his culture, not the other way around.

Let us consider inventions and discoveries, or any significant
advance in the arts, science, or philosophy. To say that they are
the achievements of certain individuals is merely to locate them,
not to explain them. To say that the calculus was invented by
Newton and Leibnitz is to identify these events historically or
biographically but it does not explain them as events in a culture
process. Why did these events take place when and where they
did? We wish to know this too as well as what particular person
made the invention or discovery. Merely to say "the individual" is
no answer to this question. Nor is such a reply improved by limit-
ing the individuals to persons of exceptional native ability. There
were individuals of this category in the Middle Ages and in the
Bronze Age and, in the time of Newton, they were sprinkled
through the populations of Tibet, Bechuanaland, and the Andean
Highlands. Why was not the calculus invented at other times and
in other lands?

An invention, discovery, or other significant cultural advance is an event in a culture process. It is a new combination or synthesis of elements in the interactive stream of culture. It is the outcome of antecedent and concomitant cultural forces and elements. The Laws of Motion, formulated by Newton, were the synthesis of cultural elements historically identified with the persons of Kepler, Brahe, Galileo, and others. The occurrence of their formulation took place where and when it did because the circumstances of culture growth and history brought together the elements requisite to this synthesis at a particular time and place. We can trace the growth of these elements through time and place. Thus we explain the occurrence of this significant event culturologically. And, moreover, we explain the behavior of Newton by showing that the formulation of these laws was the response of his organism to certain cultural stimuli. We know virtually nothing about his nervous system directly; we make inferences concerning it on the basis of the effect of cultural stimuli upon him. In short, we know his mentality only through his culture. But Newton was also much concerned with theology and Biblical interpretation, which again is explained by the fact that he was born into a powerful theological "gravitational field" as well as a scientific one and that he felt the "pull" of the one as he did the other. In another age or culture, Newton would have devoted himself to such things as designing fish traps, hepatoscopy, or the elaboration of a theory of totemism. But when a certain concatenation of cultural forces and elements occurs at a given time and place they will become synthesized in the neuro-sensory-muscular-etc. system of one individual or another.

Nothing demonstrates more clearly the nature of the culture process and its expression in significant episodes of cultural advance, and at the same time the irrelevance of the individual to an explanation of this process, than the phenomena of multiple and simultaneous, but independent, inventions and discoveries. Time after time, in the history of science, mathematics and technology, an important invention or discovery has been made by anywhere from two to ten persons simultaneously and independently.* To explain phenomena of this sort by invoking "coincidence," "fortuitous clusterings of genius," etc., as William James and others have done, is empty and sterile. A culturological interpretation, however, readily makes them intelligible: when growing and converging lines of cultural development reach a certain point, fusion and synthesis will take place. If culture is advancing on a wide front, these syntheses will find two or more independent and approximately simultaneous expressions. The invention or discovery is explained therefore in terms of a growing and interactive culture process; the individual inventors or dis-

---

* The following instances of multiple, simultaneous but independent inventions or discoveries are taken from the list compiled by Wm. F. Ogburn and published in his *Social Change*, pp. 90-102. Examples could be multiplied almost indefinitely.

Theory of planetary perturbations: Lagrange, 1808; Laplace, 1808.

Discovery of planet Neptune: Adams, 1845; Leverrier, 1845.

Discovery of sun spots: Galileo, 1611; Fabricus, 1611; Scheiner, 1611; and Harriott, 1611.

First measurement of parallax of star: Bessel, 1838; Struve, 1838; Henderson, 1838.

Introduction of decimal point: Bürgi, 1592; Pitiscus, 1608-12; Kepler, 1616; and Napier, 1616-17.

Discovery of oxygen: Scheele, 1774; Priestley, 1774.

The Periodic Law: De Chancourtois, 1864, Newlands, 1864; Lothar Meyer, 1864. Law of Periodicity: L. Meyer, 1869, Mendeleeff, 1869.

Telescope: Lippershey, 1608; Della Porta, 1558; Digges, 1571; Johannides, Metius, 1608; Drebbel, Fontana, Janssen, 1608; and Galileo, 1609.

Law of Conservation of Energy: Mayer, 1843; Joule, 1847; Helmholz, 1847; Colding, 1847; and Thomson, 1847.

Telegraph: Henry, 1831; Morse, 1837; Cooke-Wheatstone, 1837; and Steinheil, 1837.

Cellular basis of both animal and vegetable tissue: claimed by Schwann, Henle, Turpin, Dumortier, Purkinje, Muller, and Valentin, all at about the same time: 1839.

Solution of the problem of respiration: by Priestley, Scheele, Lavoisier, Spallanzani, and Davy, all in 1777.

Sulphuric ether as an anaesthetic: Long, 1842; Robinson, 1846; Liston, 1846; Morton, 1846; and Jackson, 1846.

Self-exciting dynamo: claimed by Hjorth, 1866-67; Varley, 1866-67; Siemens, 1866-67; Wheatstone, 1866-67; Ladd, 1866; Wilde, 1863-67.

coverers are merely the loci and the vehicles of expression of this process.

To return now to Sapir's dictum that "it is always the individual who really thinks and acts and dreams and revolts." This statement does not merely distort the picture of human behavior; it inverts it. If he had said it is always the individual that *sleeps* and *yawns* and *hears* and *breathes*, we would offer no objection, for these activities *are* functions of individual organisms; there is no communal or group mechanism of yawning or breathing. But to say it is the individual who *does* such things as *human* thinking, feeling and acting is misleading to say the least; it implies a premise that is unwarranted. An individual can independently as an organism, yawn, sleep, and breathe.* But no one can think, act and feel as a human being as an independent, autonomous organism; he can do so only as a part of a sociocultural system. A question of technical terminology is involved here. It may be argued that the words *think, feel, dream,* etc., are properly applicable to neuro-sensory-muscular-etcetera systems only. If this ruling be accepted, then it is true of course that it is always the individual organism that thinks, feels, and acts. But it was not to set forth this tautology that Sapir took such pains and emphasis of expression. It was his purpose to present the individual as a prime mover, as an initiator and determinant of a process. And it is this proposition that we reject.

We may indeed say that thinking, feeling, and acting are functions of individual biological organisms. There is no communal nervous system, no group brain, of course. But, human thinking, feeling, and acting cannot be accounted for in terms

---

* Yawning, breathing, etc., although functions of an individual and autonomous organism, may be modified, of course, by cultural forces. It is interesting to note that Sapir, who has insisted so vehemently upon the autonomy of the individual in thinking, feeling and acting, should have taken pains, in another connection, to point out that *breathing* may function within and be modified by a sociocultural process ("The Unconscious Patterning of Behavior in Society," in *The Unconscious*, E. S. Dummer, ed., New York, 1927), pp. 117-18.

of biological organisms, by saying that the individual *does* these things. Spitting, yawning, scratching, etc., are intelligible as functions of individual organisms. But believing in ghosts, dreaming of the Blessed Virgin, avoiding one's mother-in-law, scalping a vanquished foe, *as events or processes*, cannot be made intelligible merely by saying that it is the individual who does these things. In human thinking, feeling, and acting the individual is merely responding to stimuli, to cultural elements. But we cannot explain the form and content of the response merely by citing the biological organism that does the responding. Whether a person believes that a fever has been caused by bacteria or the violation of a taboo is a matter that is not made intelligible by invoking the individual organism who "always does" the believing. The organism is the same in both cases.

Thus we are left in the position where we have designated certain psycho-biological processes "thinking," "feeling," or "acting," but where we cannot explain these processes at all merely by considering them as individual phenomena. "It is always the individual who thinks, etc.," tells us, therefore, nothing of any significance. *What* does the individual think, and *why* does he think thus and so? This is what we want to know, and the conception of the individual as a prime mover, as an initiator or determinant of the culture process, as one who "is responsible" for all culture change, etc., will not give us the answer. On the contrary, it will effectively obscure or conceal it.

The events or processes that we technically designate "thinking, feeling, and acting" are, in so far as they are on the human, symbolic level, functions of sociocultural systems. They are, as a matter of fact, sociocultural processes. Note that we have said that these *events* and *processes* are functions of sociocultural systems. We have not said that "thinking," "feeling," and "acting" are sociocultural processes. An event is what it is—an event. When we label an event "thinking" we refer it to a neurologic context and to that kind of context only. But the very same event that is

called "thinking" and thus referred to a neurologic context may
also be referred to another context, a sociocultural context. Thus,
believing in witches or bacteria as the cause of an illness is an
event or process that can be referred to a psychologic context or
to a culturologic context; it may be considered as a function of a
nervous system or of a sociocultural system. But, although it is
perfectly true that we can have no belief in witches apart from
a nervous system, we learn virtually nothing about such a belief
as an event, act, or process from a consideration of its neurologic
aspect.

A belief in witches or bacteria as an event or process is to be
explained in sociocultural terms rather than with neurologic concepts. The *believing* is the response of a human organism to a
cultural stimulus. But *what* the organism believes is determined
not by itself but by its culture. And the cultural element that
serves as stimulus is not to be explained in terms of individual
neurologic processes but in terms of other cultural elements and
processes. Thus to say that believing in witches or bacteria is
something that an individual *does* is either an empty tautology—
"believing" being *by definition* an individual biological affair—
or it implies a premise that is false, namely, that it is the individual who initiates and determines the belief. The individual had
nothing to do with the origin of the belief; it was in the cultural
tradition of his people before he was born. He did not originate
it; it came to him from the outside. A belief in witches is the outgrowth of antecedent ideas and beliefs that we can trace back to
the Old Stone Age. The belief in bacteria also is a synthesis of
cultural elements, of concepts, microscopes, etc. Thus, the specific
act or process of believing that witches or bacteria cause illness
has been determined not by an individual organism at all but by
a sociocultural system. The event is something that the culture
has done to the individual rather than the other way around. If
it be argued that some time, somewhere, there must have been a
single individual who was the first person in history to believe

that illness is caused by bacteria rather than by witches, it must be pointed out that this event, too, is merely a synthesis of cultural elements that have come to the individual from his circumambient cultural tradition.

To take this view of the relationship between the individual and the culture process is not to regard the former, as an organism, as a purely passive thing. The individual does not receive cultural material from the outside in a purely passive way, like a cup into which coffee is poured, nor does it reflect this material like a perfect mirror does an image. The human organism is a dynamic system. It not only receives cultural elements from the outside, it acts upon them. It is by virtue of the action of the neuro-sensory-glandular-etcetera system upon cultural elements that they are made to act and react upon one another, to form new combinations and syntheses. We do not therefore minimize the dynamic nature of the individual as an active as well as a reactive organism. We are merely saying that a consideration of the dynamic character of this organism does not help us to explain the form and content of its reactions and responses. The organism does the reacting, of course. But, in human behavior, the specific nature of its reactions is determined not by the organism but by cultural elements serving as stimuli.

Neither does our point of view regard all individuals as alike. On the contrary, we recognize that no two individuals are identical biologically. Since human organisms are the mediums of expression of the culture process, it follows that variations of cultural expression will be produced by variations of individual biological structure. But not all variations of expression of the culture process are due to individual biological variation by any means. The culture process is itself inherently variable. No two cultural elements—no two axes or fetiches, no two expressions of sentiment or attitude—are identically alike either. Some of the variation of expression of the culture process is due therefore to variation of cultural stimuli. Furthermore, it is a striking and significant fact that, within a fairly uniform cultural environment, the most diverse physical types—the tall and the short, fat and thin, lazy and energetic, endomorphs and ectomorphs, etc.—react in a highly uniform manner in such respects as language and dialect, attitudes, beliefs, food habits, rituals of social intercourse, and so on. Thus a consideration of individual biological variation only serves to make clearer and more emphatic the dominance of the cultural factor in the determination of human behavior.

The conception of the individual as a prime mover, as a First Cause, as the initiator and determinant of the sociocultural process, finds free and full expression in one of our theories of government. The basic premise of democracy as a theory of government is that the people rule. That is, the citizenry as individuals want certain things and oppose others; they reflect, weigh and consider and finally make a decision which they express at the polls. The men put into office by this process, having received the mandates of the electorate, set about to do the people's will. Thus, we have, according to this view, a cause and effect sequence from lowliest citizen to the highest executive. It is always the individual who votes, etc., to paraphrase Sapir.

This picture of the political process is a gross distortion as was the general proposition about the individual always thinking, acting, and revolting. The theory of democracy as outlined above is a fiction, an illusion. And, of course, it is based upon the anthropocentric premise that it is man who, like God, says let there be this or that, and it is done.

A democratic nation is a social organism. Its life is regulated by a mechanism of integration and control that is the State in its formal aspects and the "political machine" in its non-institutionalized or at least extra-legal aspect. This mechanism coordinates the various segments and processes of the body politic, and negotiates relations with other nations. The life of the nation is thus regulated and controlled by a relatively small segment. The

electorate is permitted to say "yes" or "no" with reference to a
number of candidates whom they have had no hand in choosing,
and of whom, for the most part, they have never heard. The
"choices" of the voters are and can be little if anything more than
responses to outside cultural stimulation—i.e., campaign propaganda and "news" selected and disseminated by agencies over
which "the people" have no control. To be sure, it is always the
individual who drops his pasteboard in the ballot box or pulls
the lever on the voting machine. But what can he do but respond
to sociocultural influences that play upon him from the outside?
The picture of free will and choice is an illusion.* Certain regions
always go Democratic or Republican. In other regions, other
political magnetic fields, the sociocultural forces vary and fluctu-
ate, drawing a preponderance of voter iron filings toward one
pole or another, or leaving them evenly divided between currents
of equal intensity. It is "always the individual who votes" because
voting, like thinking, is by definition a function of an individual
organism. But one can come to no adequate understanding of the
political governmental process by a consideration of the individual. We can, however, illuminate the behavior of the individual
by interpreting it as an event in a sociocultural process. The
voter reacts, responds to cultural stimuli which move him this
way or that; he does not rule. The administration and control of
the nation by the relatively small integrative and regulative
mechanism is facilitated, however, by the popular illusion that the

---

* Any response of the human organism is the resultant of countless antecedent and concomitant events that we may term "causes." The human
organism is constantly organizing and synthesizing these causative factors on
the one hand, and expressing the resultant behavior overtly on the other.
When causative factors for and against a given course of action are evenly
balanced, we call this "indecision": "I can't make up my mind whether to
play golf or to mow the lawn." When one set of causative factors outweighs
another, we call it "choice" or "decision": I decide to play golf. "Free will
and choice" is merely the way in which we experience this preponderance of
one factor or set of factors over another. Not realizing what lies back of this
experience we can believe that it is our own doing and hence call it choice
and Free Will.

people rule. As long as the electorate believes that it does the governing, i.e., as long as its members are unaware of the genesis of the social forces that impinge upon them individually from the outside, just so long will the actual governing mechanism have a freer hand. And, if misfortune overtakes the nation, the illusion of democracy lays the blame upon the people, which is also an advantage to the actual governing mechanism.

To say, however, that this premise of democracy is an anthropocentric illusion is not to deny significance to the electoral process by any means. Illusions are as real as anything else and may be quite as significant. Voting is a process by means of which certain types of social organisms (nations) conduct their lives. Nations like individuals are occasionally confronted with the necessity of choosing between alternatives; shall it follow this course or that? Voting is a means of measuring the factors or forces relevant to the choice between alternative courses of action. The role of voting in the democratic body politic might be likened to the determination of a choice in an individual: shall he eat or sleep or follow some other course of action? A wise choice would depend upon an assessment of the needs and resources of the individual. So it is with nations: should a nation do this or that? A wise choice will depend upon a realistic appraisal of the weight and force of the various factors involved. The electoral process can be an attempt to weigh and to measure these factors. Or, an election may serve merely to measure the effect of the influence exerted by the government by means of propaganda upon the citizenry of the nation. In any event, an election is a measuring device, a yardstick or barometer. A majority vote indicates the preponderance of one factor, or set of factors, over another in a given situation. A tie vote indicates an equivalence of magnitude of these factors. It goes without saying that a nation that can make these measurements only at fixed times and intervals is unable to derive full advantage from the electoral process. It may be unable to make a measurement, take a reading, at a time when one is urgently needed. And on the other hand, it may be required to go through the cumbersome and expensive ritual of taking a reading—holding a national election—when none is needed.

If democracies work under the illusion that the people rule, the "dictatorship of the proletariat" is probably an even greater illusion, assuming of course that a considerable number of people do actually take this formula at its face value. A dictatorship is a more highly integrated form of government than a democracy and consequently the political mechanism of integration and control is a smaller segment of the social organism than is the corresponding mechanism in a democracy. Hence, "the people" do even less ruling in a dictatorship than in a democracy. A dictatorship *without disguise* may however be more responsive to popular will than the *de facto* governing mechanism in a democracy, because in the former case, the dictator will obviously be held responsible for errors or shortcomings of the government; but if "the people rule" responsibility must rest ultimately upon them rather than upon the actual governing mechanism. But a "dictatorship *of the proletariat*" is a delusion. It, too, declares that "the people" rule; not *all* the people, but only a particular class —a "chosen people." The course of social evolution in recent years has shown how unrealistic this slogan is. "The dictatorship of the proletariat" is both a logical and a sociological contradiction of terms.

"It is always the individual who really revolts" (Sapir). But to explain profound political or social change by pointing to a Revolutionist is as naive as it is futile. What produced the Revolutionist? One might as well "explain" a shotgun by pointing to the puff of smoke issuing from its muzzle. If great social convulsions were caused by revolutionists, and if a revolutionist is a psycho-biological phenomenon, then we ought to find them distributed uniformly throughout the human species in time and place like other biological events such as the birth of twins. But we do not; there are great areas and long periods of time when no revolutionists appear at all.

In cultures that have attained a high degree of integration and a stable equilibrium such as those of many primitive peoples, we find no reformers or revolutionists at all. People are satisfied and desire only to continue life undisturbed. In cultures which contain disharmonious or conflicting elements, however, we find reformers, revolutionists and reactionaries. The human organisms are the same in both cases. Revolutions are not the product of an inborn desire for radical change expressed in fiery declamations from the soap-box. A revolutionist is a human organism that is held and wielded by certain cultural elements and forces that are moving in the direction of profound change. Arkwright, Newton, Darwin, Jefferson, Lobachewsky, Lenin, Watt, were revolutionists as well as those nameless men and women who served as the biological media for such cultural advances as agriculture, metallurgy, writing, and coinage. By the same token, a reactionary is a person held firmly in the "magnetic field" of cultural elements about to be vanquished or rendered obsolete in the competitive interaction of the culture process. And the reformer or "Liberal" is one who feels the pull of both sets of forces, those striving to preserve the obsolete, and those struggling to destroy the old in order to create the new. They deplore the evils of the old system and urge reforms. But, held fast by both sets of forces, they can neither relinquish the past nor give themselves up to revolutionary advance. They wish to keep the old system but without its inherent defects. They desire the new but without the trauma of birth. They lie becalmed midway between the poles of the magnet. They have neither a positive nor a negative charge; they are the human neutrons of the culture process.

One might think that in *dreaming*, if anywhere, one might find an activity that "the individual always really does" in the Sapirean manner. Here as in *thinking, dreaming* is a word that labels a neuro-sensory-glandular-etcetera process; there is no group mechanism that dreams. But what the individual dreams is determined in part by his culture—and to a greater extent than is commonly supposed. As the scientific interpretation of dreams matures, more and more cultural determinants are disclosed: tensions arising from forms of social organization, the family and kinship groups, rivalries in quests of recognition and power, etc., all of which are culturally defined and vary from one cultural system to another. In some cultures visions become standardized. Among Plains tribes of North America the vision by means of which a youth acquired "power" was a stereotype: a spirit would appear to the youth, address him as "son," tell him that he had heard his pleas for help, that he was going to adopt and aid him, etc. Then the spirit would give the youth power to do something—to hunt, kill enemies in battle, control weather, or heal the sick—instruct him in a song, show him how to paint his face and how to make and use a medicine-bundle, impose a taboo upon him, and depart. Similarly saints and mystics of Europe used to have stereotyped dreams or visions of Christ or the Blessed Virgin. As Tylor once remarked, "The South African who believes in a God with a crooked leg sees him with a crooked leg in dreams and visions." There is indeed very little individuality in much of our dream and vision experience. Again to quote Tylor: "Want of originality seems one of the most remarkable features in the visions of mystics . . . When the devil with horns, hoofs and tail had once become a fixed image in the popular mind [i.e., in the cultural tradition], of course men saw him [in visions] in this conventional shape." [16] It is always the individual that does the dreaming— which merely defines the word in neurologic terms. But it is the culture that gives the dream much of its form and content as well as providing the initial stimulus in many instances. The event or process that we label "dreaming" is, like the events called "thinking," "feeling," and "acting," a function of a system in which the individual is but a component part: a sociocultural system.

Thus, the whole concept of the individual, the individual human organism, is profoundly altered by culturological interpretation. Instead of regarding the individual as a First Cause, as a prime mover, as the initiator and determinant of the culture process, as one who creates culture by acts of mind,* as one who is responsible for all additions to culture, etc., etc., we now see him as a component part, and a tiny and relatively insignificant part at that, of a vast sociocultural system that embraces innumerable individuals at any one time and extends back into the remote past as well. We see culture as a vast continuum, a stream of cultural elements—of language, tools, utensils, beliefs, customs, and attitudes—that flows down through time. Culture was of course brought into existence by man—by countless human individuals—and it could not continue without them. But, we do not need to consider man at all—as a species, race or individual —*in an explanation* of culture change. For purposes of scientific interpretation, the culture process *may be regarded* as a thing *sui generis*; culture is explainable in terms of culture. In this great sociocultural system, and from the standpoint of an interpretation of this system, the individual is (1) a catalytic agent that makes the interactive culture process possible, and (2) a medium of expression of the culture process.

---

* In a recent publication we find a fine example of this: "There is present in an Indian's mind the idea of a dance . . . This idea influences his body so that he behaves in a certain way. The result of this behavioral activity is the pattern of the dance . . ." (W. W. Taylor, *A Study of Archeology*, Memoir 69, American Anthropological Association, 1948), pp. 101-102. The view that culture consists of "ideas in the mind" is still widely held in American ethnology today.

The culturological conception of the individual does not and cannot deprive psychology of anything that properly belongs to it. The individual, as a biological organism, is a dynamic, active and reactive system and may be studied and interpreted as such. This is the business of the neuro-anatomist, the physiologist, the psychologist, etc., *not* of the student of culture. The fact that language may be interpreted philologically, or culture treated culturologically, in no way prevents one from interpreting biological organisms psychologically.

The question at issue is, of course, how is culture to be interpreted, psychologically or culturologically? The conception of the individual as the creator and determinant of the culture process offers a type of interpretation that we find unacceptable. It is anthropomorphic as well as irrelevantly psychologic.

It is not, however, as if we were deploring a Ptolemy before Copernicus; we are, so to speak, deploring a continuation of the Ptolemaic tradition generations *after* Copernicus. The nature of the articulation of the individual human organism with the culture process was recognized and pointed out decades ago by Adolph Bastian when he said that the individual "is nothing, at best an idiot; only through spoken intercourse in society does he become conscious of thought, is his nature realized. The thought of society, social thought, is the primary result and the thought of the individual is won by later analysis from it." [17] And the Polish sociologist, Gumplowicz, argued that "the great error of individualistic psychology is the supposition that man thinks . . . it is not man himself who thinks but his social community . . . he cannot think ought else than what the influences of his social environment concentrating upon his brain necessitate." [18] Emile Durkheim and his co-workers, too, showed clearly how, on the one hand, culture is an extra-somatic tradition that can be explained in terms of its own interactive elements and processes and how, on the other hand, the individual organism is influenced, his behavior given form and content, by the action of the external culture upon him. And, in more recent times in America, the work of Wissler, Kroeber, Lowie, and others has continued the tradition of a culturological interpretation of culture.

But anthropomorphism dies hard. The death is especially slow and difficult when anthropomorphism is mistaken for the soundest realism, as it is by those who actually see people, individual men and women, voting, enameling their fingernails, building ships, inventing machines, writing sonnets, composing symphonies, etc. "Where else," they ask, "could new cultural elements come from but from the creative act of some individual human mind—from a man, woman, or child?"

A culturological conception of *the individual* is also a culturological interpretation of mind, of *human* minding. We still retain the use of the words *mind, thinking, feeling,* etc., in their traditional psychological sense: that is, they designate biologic—neuro-sensory-glandular-etcetera—processes. But we realize that we cannot by any means give a full account of these acts of human thinking and feeling in terms of individual organisms. The individual does the thinking and feeling—by definition. But, as we have previously noted, *what* he thinks and feels is determined not by himself but by the sociocultural system into which the accident of birth has placed him. A sociocultural system is a vast network of relations, of interactions of concept, tools, customs, beliefs, etc. Thus, a belief in witchcraft is an organization of beliefs and attitudes that has grown up in conjunction with activities of medicine, offense and defense, and subsistence, carried on by means of certain technologic tools and implements. The beliefs and attitudes of witchcraft find expression in turn in certain rituals and paraphernalia. The culture complex called "witchcraft" is therefore something that is to be explained culturologically. It is found in some cultures but not in others. When it

exists, it varies from one culture to another. The culture complex
has to be explained, therefore, in terms of cultural elements and
cultural processes.

An individual, born into a sociocultural system that contains
the complex called *witchcraft*, will behave in a certain way; he
will think, feel, and act as his culture directs and prescribes.
He will suspect certain persons of the black art and fear them; he
will take certain precautions to safeguard himself from them; and
he will occupy himself with the detection, punishment or eradica-
tion of witches, all in a manner prescribed by his culture. What
meaning could be attached to the assertion that "it is always the
individual who believes in, fears, and contends with, witches?"
Simply that the individual organism responds to certain cultural
elements as external stimuli. But we are able to give an account
of his believing, fearing, and contending, not by a consideration
of the individual but of the organization of cultural elements, the
cultural system, that determines his believing, fearing, etc. It
would be more realistic to say that his thinking and feeling are
things that the culture *does to* the individual than to say that
they are things that *he does*. The individual's thinking, feeling,
and behaving as a human being is merely his participation in a
sociocultural process. His thinking, feeling and overt behavior are
expressions of a system of culture, of a cultural process, through
the medium of his organism.

And so it is with the human mind as a whole. *Minding* is
merely the individual biologic aspect of a sociocultural process.
The minding in its form and content is determined by the culture.
The individual mind is a function of the cultural system that
embraces it. What it does, what it believes, thinks and feels,
are determined not by the individual but by the circumambient
culture. The individual human mind can be made intelligible
only by a consideration of the culture of which it is but a reflex.

But we cannot explain the *culture* in terms of the *individual mind*; cultural systems can only be explained in cultural terms.

The problem of distinguishing determinants that confronts the student of human behavior is paralleled by a like problem in biology: does the determination of a multi-cellular system lie in the *individual cells*, or is the behavior of the individual cell a function of the organism, or system, as a whole? Many biologists argue that the system is determined by properties inherent in the *individual cell*, just as many students of human behavior insist that *society* and *culture* are determined by *individuals*. Thus, Alexander B. Novicoff quotes L. V. Heilbrun, *An Outline of General Physiology*, pp. 3-4 (Philadelphia, 1943), to the effect that "the ultimate mechanism responsible for any form of vital activity lies *inherent in an individual cell*" (emphasis ours). But Novicoff, citing the work of Coghill, Lashley, Goldstein and others, argues that the behavior of the cell is determined by *its position within the system*. Thus, "if ectoderm cells which normally form belly skin were removed from a salamander embryo and transplanted over the mouth organizer of a frog embryo, they would develop into salamander structures—of the mouth; they would form teeth and not belly skin." [19]

Similarly, would not everyone admit that a baby transplanted during its first year of life from a Swedish family and community to a Chinese cultural milieu would learn Chinese rather than Swedish? And would not this baby acquire his other patterns of behavior, sentiments, and attitudes from the sociocultural system to which he had been transplanted? What, indeed, could be plainer than the fact that the individual in his behavior *as a human being*, as distinguished from mere primate or animal, is a function of the sociocultural system of which he is a part? *

As we have already indicated by quotations from Bastian and

---

* "Before Clerk Maxwell," Einstein writes, "people conceived of physical reality . . . as material points. . . . After Maxwell they conceived physical reality as represented by continuous fields . . ." (1934, p. 65). Before, or

Gumplowicz, many scholars of a generation or so ago clearly
understood the relationship between the individual human organism and culture. They realized full well that the individual mind
—the minding of an individual organism—was a function of a
sociocultural system. Some of them, therefore, like Gumplowicz,
expressed this fact by saying that it is not the individual who
thinks, feels, etc., but his society or culture. Others, like Durkheim, spoke of a "collective consciousness." Thus the concept of
a "group mind" emerged and crystallized. This concept was
criticized and rejected by those who could not free themselves
from an anthropocentric point of view, and who could not understand cultural systems and their role as determinants of human
behavior. How, they asked, can society think, feel, etc.; there is
no collective sensorium, no group brain. Thus, a profound insight
and a realistic understanding were defeated by inappropriate
terminology: a psychological term—"group mind"—was used to
designate a culturological process. What those of the "group
mind" school meant, of course, was that "the form and content
of an individual's mind is determined by his culture, that cultures express themselves through the media of individual organisms." What they *said*, however, was "it is not the individual
but the group who thinks." This was rejected not only as false
psychologically but as mystical as well.

Another defect of the "group mind" theorists was that they
did not properly locate and define the supra-individual deter-

outside of, the science of culture, we may say, students conceive of human
cultural reality as a series of material points, i.e., individuals. After, or within,
the science of culture, human reality is seen to consist of a network of sociocultural relations, with the individual a function of the system as a whole.
Karl Marx saw this clearly over a hundred years ago when he wrote, in the
Sixth Thesis on Feuerbach: "The essence of man is no abstraction inherent
in each separate individual. In its reality it is the *ensemble of social relations*"
(emphasis ours). As the science of culture grows and extends its influence
among students of human behavior, this view, this understanding, will become
commonplace.

minant of minding. They located it in the group. Group and *in-dividual* are of course complementary terms; one can be interpreted in terms of the other. A group mind could therefore be reduced to a number of individual minds and, by so doing, the force and significance of "the group mind" concept would be lost.

The "group mind" school was perfectly sound in its assertion that it is not the individual who determines the form and content of his minding. But, lacking the concept of culture, they erred in locating the supra-individual determinant in the group. It is not the group, but culture that is the determinant. And, unlike group, culture cannot be explained in terms of individuals. On the contrary, groups—their structures and processes—are functions of culture just as individual minds are in their form and content. Technically it is as wrong today to say that it is culture that thinks as it was formerly to say that it is the group that thinks. *Thinking* is the name of a neurologic process and none other. But the advance made in the scientific interpretation of human behavior by the "group mind" school was real and important. Their error was not in going too far but in not going far enough. They saw clearly the inadequacy of an individual psychological interpretation. But science had not advanced far enough at that time to elevate them above the sociological level to that of culturology. Today, thanks to the expansion of the scope of science, we have the concept of culture. We appreciate the necessity of regarding culture as an autonomous process for the purpose of scientific interpretation. We realize that cultural systems can be explained only in terms of culturological principles and laws. And we understand the relationship between the human organism—either as a species, race, or individual—and culture. In view of this understanding, the old-fashioned psychologistic, anthropomorphic interpretation of culture as something that is produced by "creative acts of the individual mind," that it is the individual who "is always responsible for additions to culture," that "it is always the individual who really thinks and acts," etc., is definitely out of place in modern ethnological theory. We more than suspect that this emphasis upon individualism has been outgrown in psychology, that social psychology of the present day would regard this conception of the individual as a creator of culture as being as unrealistic as we do. Its perpetuation in anthropological circles today is therefore to be deplored all the more.

If a growing understanding of the relationship between man and culture means, on the one hand, a decline of the anthropocentric view of man as the creator of culture, it fosters, on the other hand, an appreciation of the role of culture in the minding of man. The human mind is no longer merely an individual biological phenomenon. Nor is a "group mind" a proper definition of the situation. It is a question of individual organism on the one hand and an extra-somatic cultural tradition or system on the other. Whereas in the case of the lower animals, or in the non-symbolic, non-human behavior of *Homo sapiens*, the individual biological organism is significant as a determinant of the individual's behavior, in the case of *human* behavior, of the human mind, the organism as such is not significant; it is not stature, skin color, cephalic index, cortical activity, or glandular secretion that determines whether a person will speak Chinese, believe in witches, have an aversion for milk, or regard cows as sacred. These things are determined by one's culture. An understanding of the human mind, therefore, calls for an appreciation of the role of cultural factors as determinants of thinking, feeling and acting. The mind of the individual—the average, typical, normal individual—is as its own culture has made it. To understand the mind one must understand culture as well; human "mental processes" are but the psychosomatic form of expression of an extra-somatic culture process. The student of human minding must therefore be culturologist as well as psychologist. To be sure, within a single and fairly uniform culture, the cultural factor may be regarded as approximately a constant. But, ever here, it would be well, first of all, to be aware of this constant, and, secondly, to realize that it is cultural in nature and genesis, and that, from the standpoint of the individual organism, it is just as external and foreign to it as are the elements and processes of meteorology.

CHAPTER EIGHT

GENIUS: ITS CAUSES AND INCIDENCE

"Geniuses are the indicators of the realization of coherent pattern growths of cultural value . . ."—A. L. Kroeber, *Configurations of Culture Growth.*

*T*he significance of *the genius* in history has been discussed so many times in the last seventy-five years that one should not go over the well-trodden ground again without a special warrant for doing so. The expansion of the scope of science in general and the recent development of the science of culture in particular are here cited and offered as our excuse for embarking once again upon this perennial debate.

Briefly stated, the problem is this: are epoch-making social and historical events to be explained in terms of men of genius, or are great men explainable in terms of social processes and historical trends? Or, do both, the great man and his social matrix, combine to produce the event or trend, and if so in what proportions?

Most of those who have wrestled with this problem have championed *either* the great man or society as the motive force, as the cause, the other being regarded as the effect; few have been willing to give equal, or even approximately equal, weight to each factor. Let it be said at once that we have no intention of being "impartial" and of taking the latter course. We are convinced that the great man is best understood as an effect or manifestation rather than as a prime mover. And we believe we have a new technique for demonstrating this, or at least a refinement upon

190

techniques employed for this purpose in the past. But before we introduce our technique, let us turn briefly to the history of this problem.

It has, of course, long been the fashion to interpret great events as the work of great men. From the time of the Pharaohs, rulers have boasted of their deeds and accomplishments, and before that, no doubt, tribal chieftains made similar claims. Bards and troubadors once sang of the exploits of heroes, and modern historians have tended to write in the same vein: History is a record of the deeds of Great Men, good and bad. When we turn from the political events of history to great works of art, new philosophies or religions, significant discoveries in science, and epoch-making inventions, we find the same type of interpretation: these advances and achievements are the work of geniuses, of men like Michelangelo, Kant, Beethoven, Newton, and Edison.

In 1869 a distinguished British man of science, Francis Galton, F.R.S., gave formal and authoritative expression to the Great Man theory in his *Hereditary Genius*. Great events and great periods in history, he argued, are due to men of genius; the greater the period, the more numerous the men of genius. A man of true genius will assuredly come to the fore and make himself known and felt despite any opposition or handicap that social conditions may place in his way. Galton compares the United States with England to demonstrate this point. Class distinctions are less rigid in America, he reasons, and it is therefore easier for one to overcome the disadvantages of low social status there than in England. Yet, he says, there are no more men of genius per million in America than in England; on the contrary, there are less. Therefore, he concludes, we may assume that if genius *is* present it will assert itself and find expression and recognition.[1]

Galton carried his reasoning still further. Since the correlation between inborn ability and fame is so close, we can evaluate and compare races by counting the men of genius per thousand or million. Proceeding on this basis, Galton finds that the Athenians of the time of Pericles were two grades higher than the English, who in turn were two grades higher than the African Negro.[2]

The scientific prestige of Galton and the scholarly character of his work did much no doubt to confirm many in their belief not only that civilization has been the work of geniuses but that certain races are more richly endowed than others. In short, Galton provided a simple, scholarly, "scientific"—it was supported with statistics!—and authoritative theory with which one could explain the histories of nations and the development of civilization.

One of the first of modern scholars to challenge the Great Man theory was Herbert Spencer. In *The Study of Sociology* (1873) he offered a cogent argument against the interpretation of important social events by invoking genius or Great Men. Before the Great Man can make society, he insisted, society must make him. Not only does Spencer indicate the nature and extent of society's influence upon every individual, great and small, he brands the Great Man theory as a form of anthropomorphism popular alike among savage tribes and civilized societies.[3]

William James took sharp and and vigorous issue with Spencer in an address, "Great Men, Great Thoughts and the Environment," published in the Atlantic Monthly in 1880. Great events and epochs in history are the work of Great Men, he insists. A single important event may be produced by a single, or at most a few, geniuses. But for a great epoch many are required. "For a community to get vibrating through and through with active life," he says, "many geniuses coming together and in rapid succession are required. This is why great epochs are so rare—why the sudden bloom of a Greece, an early Rome, a Renaissance, is such a mystery. Blow must follow blow so fast that no cooling can occur in the intervals. Then the mass of the nation grows incandescent, and may continue to glow by pure inertia long after the originators of its internal movement have passed away. We often hear surprise expressed that in these high tides of human affairs not only the people should be filled with stronger life, but that individual geniuses should seem so exceptionally abundant. This mystery is just about as deep as the time-honored conundrum as to why great rivers flow by great towns." [4]

James admits that the great man's environment may condition his behavior or affect the consequences of his behavior, but he denies emphatically that the social environment can *produce* him. "If anything is humanly certain," he insists, "it is that the great man's society, properly so called, does *not* make him before he can remake it." [5]

This point of view so adroitly expressed by James is, of course, widely held today. Every great event is regarded as the work of one or a few outstanding individuals. The fate of a whole nation may rest in a single pair of hands. It was a common thing a few years ago to hear that World War II had been caused by one person, and since V-E day we have tried and hanged a number of men for having brought the war about. Nor is this view confined to the man in the street or even to statesmen in high places. Many scholars and men of science subscribe to it also. Thus a prominent American anthropologist, Edgar Lee Hewett, has recently attributed almost every great historical epoch, from Xerxes to Hitler, to the genius, pathologic or otherwise, of a single individual: all great "irruptions" of history have been "one man affairs," he says. E. A. Hooton speaks of "men like Hitler and Mussolini [who] impose their evil will upon stupid and suggestible masses." Lawrence K. Frank says that "as long as we are at the mercy of the warped, distorted personalities who seek power and prestige . . . at whatever cost to others, we are helpless." The distinguished physicist, Robert A. Millikan, can see no way by which science can prevent the destruction of civilization by man's wickedness or folly: "I see no prospect," he says, "of our ever being able to turn some new type of ray upon a dictator filled with lust of power and conquest and thus transform him into a humanitarian." In a different context, Goldenweiser says that history "abounds in examples of periods of precipitated change

due to the emergence of . . . dominant personalities." Franz
Boas speaks of African "Negro rulers whose genius for organization
has enabled them to establish flourishing empires." Clark Wissler
supposes that "long ago . . . there arose a genius for empire
building which set a pattern" that endured for thousands of years.
And Ralph Linton more conservatively admits that the "individual is dominated and shaped by his social environment but he
is not obliterated by it. Under favorable conditions," he says, "he
can even change and mold it." [6] A great man could therefore
presumably work great change.

Thus we have two opposing views. On the one hand, great
events or great epochs of history, important advances in philosophy, art, and science, are interpreted as the handiwork of exceptionally gifted persons. On the other, it is argued that the
genius is conditioned by his social environment if not produced
by it. Both views seem plausible and tenable. Each side is able
to advance reasons and marshall evidence in support of its position. If, therefore, we are to extricate ourselves from this circular
argument, we shall have either to rephrase the problem or apply
new and better techniques to its solution. Let us see what can
be done.

Galton and James make the interpretation of history seem
simple and easy: Great events and epochs are the work of men
of genius; if an era is uneventful or mediocre it is because genius
is lacking. Why has Sardinia fallen far below Sicily in greatness
and distinction when "all the material advantages are in favor
of Sardinia?" James asks. His ready answer: "Simply because no
individuals were born there with patriotism and ability enough
to inflame their countrymen with national pride, ambition, and
a thirst for independent life." [7]

But if great epochs are caused by geniuses, how are geniuses
to be accounted for? James' answer to this question is hardly
satisfying. He says in effect that we cannot explain their origin
and incidence. "The causes of production of great men," he says,

"lie in a sphere wholly inaccessible to the social philosopher. He must simply accept geniuses as data, just as Darwin accepts his spontaneous variations." It is the "invisible and unimaginable play of forces of growth within the nervous system which, irresponsibly to the environment, makes the brain peculiarly apt to function in a certain way." And, just as an individual genius appears spontaneously, so do they cluster "fortuitously around a given epoch making it great" or they are "fortuitously absent from certain places and times." [8]

This theory may seem plausible, especially since it comes from an eminent scientist and philosopher. But is it much better than the explanations astrology has to offer? One might say that the birth of individual geniuses and their clustering about certain historical epochs are governed by the stars. James' theory is of course superior to that of astrology both because it is less mystical and because it explains less. The astrologist really offers an explanation though a false one: human events are controlled by stars. But is James' answer, "chance," really an explanation? Or is it a device to conceal ignorance and helplessness, a declaration that there is and can be no better answer? Or is it an assertion that the phenomena in question are indeed statistical in nature? The scientist is not likely to be satisfied with "chance" as an answer to his queries—unless, of course, he can see how he can deal with it statistically and thus relate chance to scientific law. James shows no interest in a statistical consideration of these phenomena; he is content to leave the matter on the basis of "an invisible and unimaginable play of forces," and upon spontaneous and fortuitous events.*

Galton does not rely so squarely upon sheer chance. Genius tends to be hereditary, he reasons, and therefore when a genius

---

* A more recent writer resorts to the fortuitous appearance of genius to explain great historic events. The Reverend H. Harrington, writing in the Encyclopaedia Britannica ("Roman Catholic Church," 14th ed.), says that the Protestant revolt was "almost fortuitous. Genius defies all laws, and the greatest Protestant leader [Luther] had genius."

appears it is because he has had exceptionally gifted forebears. Certain conditions cause an increase in the number or proportion of geniuses; others bring about a decrease. If Athens was once rich in geniuses it was because certain conditions brought it about; if she fell from her former high state, that, too, was due to certain circumstances. Galton thus does not content himself, as James does, with the assertion that presence or absence of genius at certain times and places is purely fortuitous. But his explanation of the rise and fall of Athens in terms of racial ability is not very convincing. As the distinguished sociologist, C. H. Cooley, pointed out long ago in a well reasoned criticism of Galton, "both the rise and the decline of the race are ascribed to the same cause, namely immigration. Certainly, then, some reason should be given for supposing that there was a radical change in the character of the immigration: but no such reason is given." [9]

With regard to the relationship between exceptionally gifted persons and their environment, we have already noted that Galton believes that genius, like murder, will out, no matter what obstacles the environment may oppose. James admits that social environment may affect a genius, that it may help or hinder him. But, he insists, the significant factor in this environment is merely another genius or geniuses! "It is true," he writes, "that great public fermentations awaken and adopt many geniuses, who in more torpid times would have had no chance to work. But . . . there must be an exceptional concourse of genius about a time to make the fermentation begin at all." If, on the other hand, a social setting is not hospitable to a particular genius, it is because "some previous genius of a different strain has warped the community away from the sphere of his possible effectiveness. After Voltaire, no Peter the Hermit." Thus, according to James, the thing that fosters or frustrates a man of genius is not simply an environment, but another, or other, geniuses. Whether, therefore, genius finds expression and bears fruit or remains unrecognized and unknown, the cause is always "genius." We thus have a ready and easy explanation of history and social movements: the presence or absence of genius. But, unfortunately, says James, we cannot predict genius; that is a matter of the "invisible and unimaginable play of forces within the nervous system." The utmost that sociology can ever predict, he argues, "is that if a genius of a certain sort show the way, society will be sure to follow." [10] Science is not likely to be satisfied with reasoning and conclusions such as these.

We do not propose to go over the old familiar argument of individual vs. society; it is too much like the old conundrum about the priority of the egg or the chicken. Indeed, as we have seen, the Great Man vs. Society debate has been put in precisely this form, with Spencer contending that *before* the great man can affect society, society must make him, whereas James insists that the genius must come first. Obviously, some men are distinguished markedly from others, and their lives and deeds are especially significant. Obvious also is the influence of society upon exceptionally gifted persons. A *whole* is made up of parts, and *parts* comprise a whole. If this were all there is to the Great Man vs. Society controversy we should have to leave it at that and say that each factor is a function of the other. But this is *not* all there is to this problem. The growth and expansion of science has brought forth a new science that has a great deal to say on this point, namely, culturology. Psychology presents the man of genius and demonstrates his effect upon society. Sociology shows how society conditions the life of the exceptionally gifted person. Culturology explains both the great man *and* society and the relationship between them.

What *is* genius? The debate of decades has made it quite clear that he is not identical with a neuro-sensory-glandular-etc. system of exceptionally high quality. On the one hand, we do not know that every outstanding individual possesses an exceptionally fine neuro-sensory-glandular-etc. system. On the other hand, we do not know that undistinguished persons have only mediocre or inferior systems. We are not warranted, therefore, in equating "genius" with "superior organism": $G = O$, in which G represents the person of distinction, while O stands for his biologically superior organism. Nor may we use the equation $O \times S = G$, in which O is a superior organism, S, the social environment, and G the resulting genius, because, as we have seen, it can be argued both that O is a function of S and that S is a function of O. We must write our equation thus: $O \times R = G$. Here O will stand merely for an individual biological organism, not necessarily one of superior quality, G for genius, and R for a factor which we have yet to define.

How do we recognize a genius? By his deeds, of course. But how can we know that he has an exceptionally fine neuro-sensory-glandular-etc. system? By his deeds, say Galton, James, *et al.* But to say this is to admit that his innate biological superiority *is merely an inference* based upon observation of his overt behavior, and also to insist that the exceptional features of this behavior *cannot be explained in any other way* than by attributing them to superior brains, glands, etc. If one could demonstrate the biological superiority of the genius by direct examination of his nerves, glands, senses, etc., or by psychological tests that would rule out all factors not genetically acquired, instead of postulating it inferentially, then the case of the champions of genius as prime movers would receive substantial support. But this has never been done. This is not to say, of course, that one organism is as good as another, or that it is impossible to tell a biological silk purse from a sow's ear. All of the sciences of man will freely grant, if not insist upon, the biological inequality of individual human beings. Nor would anyone, I suppose, maintain that one cannot distinguish an idiot or imbecile from one of superior intelligence by observations of their behavior—at least in a high percentage of instances. But this is a far cry from the assertion that *if* a man plays a distinguished role in social life he *must* have superior germ plasm whereas if he is undistinguished he must have mediocre or inferior plasm. We are not content to derive our biology by inference, and, secondly, we can explain distinction in other terms than superior nerves and glands.

But to invoke "society" as Spencer and countless others since 1872 have done to account for distinction is not enough. Society is but an organization of individuals, and so we have one person affecting another, the ordinary man jostling his brother while the genius fosters or discourages genius, as James has argued. *Society* and *individual* are simply two aspects, opposite but inseparable poles, of the same phenomenon; we can "explain" each one in terms of the other. Thus we go around in circles, chasing our tails, getting nowhere.

The *science of culture* liberates us from this dilemma. It provides us with techniques with which we can explain both society and individual. The behavior of human beings, both individually and collectively, is determined by their biological make-up on the one hand, and by a body of extra-somatic phenomena called *culture*, on the other: $O \times C \longrightarrow B$, in which O stands for the biological factor, C for the extra-somatic, supra-biological factor of *culture*, and B, the resultant behavior.*

Individual human beings differ biologically from one another and differences in their behavior may legitimately be ascribed in part to their anatomical and physiological differences. Human beings vary as groups, too; one race, stock, or physical type, may be distinguished from another. But, so far as we know, none of the differences of behavior between *peoples*—races, tribes, nations—can be attributed to their biological differences. The biological factor may conceivably contribute something to the variation of

---

* Both organism and culture—and consequently the behavior resulting from the interaction of these two factors—are of course affected by the natural environment. But in the problem which confronts us now we are concerned only with the relationship between man and culture. The environmental factor may therefore legitimately be considered a constant and as such be omitted from our consideration.

behavior, but this contribution is so small in comparison with the influence of the cultural factor that it may be regarded as negligible. In short, the differences of behavior from one people to another are culturally, not biologically, determined. In a consideration of behavioral differences among peoples therefore we may regard the biological factor as a constant and hence eliminate it from our calculations. We may, then, rewrite our formula for the behavior of any people with reference to the behavior of others as follows: $C \longrightarrow B$, culture produces, or determines, behavior; the behavior of a people is determined by its culture. Or, $B = f(C)$: behavior is a function of culture. Variations in behavior among peoples are functions of variations in culture: $V_b = f(V_c)$. The relationship between the human biological factor in the mass and the extra-somatic cultural factor is thus made clear. Where then does *society* enter this picture?

Why does one people have one form of society whereas another has a different form? The psychologist cannot account for this difference because, as we have just seen, the psycho-biological factor is a constant. "Social process," or "social interaction," the basic concept of the sociologist, is equally inadequate. Why does one type of social process take place in one case whereas in another we find a different type of interaction? This is precisely the question at issue; "social process" is an effect, not a cause. What then is the cause? The answer is, of course, *culture.*

Culture is, as we have seen repeatedly, a class of extra-somatic, supra-biological phenomena. They have an existence prior to the birth of every individual. They are external to him and act upon him from the outside. They are traditional; they are passed down from one generation to another, and they may be borrowed, laterally, from one's contemporaries and neighbors. Culture consists of beliefs, customs, institutions, tools, utensils, etc., which lay hold of the organisms of *Homo sapiens* at birth and mold and shape them this way and that. A people has one form of social organization rather than another because *as biological organisms* they react and respond to different sets of cultural elements as stimuli. But how are we to explain culture? We need not resort to circular reasoning here. We do not explain culture in terms of "social process" and "social process" again in terms of culture, as the sociologist is wont to do. Nor do we explain individual personality in terms of culture and then turn around and explain culture in terms of personality, as many social psychologists and psychologically minded anthropologists do. We explain culture in terms of culture.

To many, no doubt, this will seem like no explanation at all. In an earlier day it may have seemed empty to explain the behavior of stars and planets in terms of stars and planets instead of the will and whim of spiritual beings. But the explanation of events in non-animistic and non-anthropomorphic terms is now well established in the physical and biological sciences. We still retain more than a vestige of anthropomorphism in the social sciences.

To explain culture in terms of culture is merely to say that cultural elements act and react upon one another, form new syntheses, eliminate some elements as obsolete, and so on. Thus a change in the process of forming plurals is a *linguistic* phenomenon, not a psychological or sociological one. Matrilineal organization is a combination of certain cultural elements; patrilineal organization, a synthesis of other elements. We discover the relationship between the manufacture of automobiles and the use of buggies directly, and so on. In short, culture may be interpreted culturologically rather than sociologically or psychologically. More than that, there are many problems that can be solved only by culturological techniques, psychological and sociological interpretations being illusory or irrelevant. Let us now return to the problem of genius.

We shall begin with a statement of premises: 1. A genius will be defined as a person who is regarded as a genius; there is no

point in saying that many a genius is born, lives and dies unrecognized. One may well say that many a person of very superior
native endowment lives and dies without full realization of his
potentialities and without achieving recognition or fame. But for
purposes of our inquiry we will confine ourselves to persons who
have been regarded as geniuses. 2. The distribution of native
ability, from those of very low capacity on the one end of the
curve to the exceptionally gifted on the other, has been uniform
throughout time, at least within the species *Homo sapiens*. We
have no reason for believing that more or less idiots or persons
of exceptional ability were born per 100,000 in one age than
another. 3. The average and range of native abilities among the
various races of the world are at least approximately the same
for all. Degree of cultural development is, of course, no index of
native ability, and the testimony of comparative anatomy, physiology and psychology will support this proposition. Let us turn
now to some of the specific problems of genius.

Why do geniuses cluster about certain epochs of history instead
of being uniformly distributed through time? James says that it
is "fortuitous," pure chance. But the laws of probability tell us
just the opposite. One cannot tell which woman will give birth
to an exceptionally gifted child or to twins. But the laws of
probability tell us how many pairs of twins we may expect in
every 100,000 births, or per year in a given population, and we
may assume that the number, or proportion, of idiots or babies
of exceptional endowments born will likewise be definite and
constant. It is precisely the factor of chance and probability that
justifies our assumption of a uniform distribution of exceptionally
gifted persons in a large population over a considerable period of
time. How, then, can we explain the fact—for it *is* a fact—that
geniuses are *not* distributed uniformly in time and place but do
cluster about certain epochs and regions?

A culturological interpretation makes this quite clear. Culture
does not grow or change at uniform rates; there are periods of

intense activity and periods of stagnation and even retrogression. A culture may exhibit little change or progress for a long period and then suddenly burst forth with vigorous activity and growth. An invention or discovery such as metallurgy, agriculture, the domestication of animals, the keystone arch, the alphabet, microscope, steam engine, etc., may inaugurate an era of rapid change and progress.

But are not inventions the work of genius? The answer is of course "Yes," if by genius you mean "someone who makes a significant discovery or invention." But this is just reasoning in a circle. Merely because a person makes a great discovery or invention it does not follow that he is possessed of exceptionally great natural endowment, and much less does it mean that he is superior to all others who have no great achievement to their credit. Therefore, to appeal to "genius" to explain the invention or discovery is an empty redundancy since genius is here defined in terms of the event, and the appeal to exceptionally great native endowment is unwarranted or at least misleading.

According to our premises we must assume that there were men in England in Neolithic times with as much natural ability as James Watt possessed. Yet no one would claim that such a man could have invented the steam engine. This is of course but a recognition of the fact that there is more to an invention or discovery than germ plasm or brain tissue, no matter how excellent they may be. An invention or discovery is a cultural, i.e., an extra-somatic, supra-biological, affair as well as a psychological act. An invention is a new synthesis of cultural elements.* In any cultural system there is constant interaction among its constituent elements: culture traits. They act and react upon one another, changing and modifying one another, forming new combinations and syntheses. Certain traits or elements become obsolete and are

---

* "An invention is not an accidental mutation of the germ plasm, but a new synthesis of the accumulated experience to which the inventor is heir by tradition only," (V. Gordon Childe, *Man Makes Himself*, p. 19).

eliminated from the stream. New elements are introduced from the outside from time to time.

Thus, in this interactive process, axes are fitted with handles, eyes are put into awls and they become needles, clay is first sun-dried then fired; tempering material is added; the wheel is adapted to the ceramic art; certain customs become synthesized into the clan, trial by jury, primogeniture, or parliamentary government; in philosophy and science old concepts are synthesized into new formulations, the work of Galileo, Kepler and Brahe is synthesized into laws of motion and gravitation in the hands of Newton; coal, copper, etc., are introduced into the stream of culture. Discoveries may of course occur by chance, as in the case of the association of pitchblende and a photographic plate in the laboratory of Röntgen. But to be significant, the chance must have the proper soil, a suitable cultural context.

An invention or discovery is a synthesis of already existing cultural elements, or the assimilation of a new element into a cultural system. The invention of the steamboat is a good example of the former; the origin of metallurgy, of the latter. The steam engine was the outcome of an age-old process of cultural accumulation and synthesis. We can trace it back through many lines, mechanical, metallurgical, and ideological, to the Old Stone Age. The boat, too, is the outgrowth of an interactive and synthesizing culture process that we can trace back to antiquity. The invention of the steamboat was, therefore, simply a merging of these two streams of cultural development. With regard to the origin of agriculture, metallurgy, non-Euclidean geometry, the germ theory of disease, etc., each of these was the organized expression of an accumulation of cultural experience. Just as the discoveries of Pasteur would have been impossible in the time of Charlemagne, so was agriculture impossible in the days of Cro-Magnon. Every invention and discovery is but a synthesis of the cultural accumulations of the past with the experiences of the present.

Two significant conclusions can now be drawn: (1) No invention or discovery can take place until the accumulation of culture has provided the elements—the materials and ideas—necessary for the synthesis, and, (2) When the requisite materials have been made available by the process of cultural growth or diffusion, and given normal conditions of cultural interaction, the invention or discovery is bound to take place.

The first of these propositions will probably be accepted more readily than the second. Almost everyone would admit that the steam engine could not have been invented in the Paleolithic Age. But many persons, resenting a determinism that they fear but do not understand, will demand, "How can you prove that someone else would have invented the steam engine, the cotton gin, etc., if Watt, Whitney, etc., had not done so?" Of course this cannot be proved, in one sense at least. Neither can one prove that it will rain in Detroit in the summer of 1973, or even that the sun will rise tomorrow. But we can adduce so much evidence in support of our claim as to make its validity seem virtually conclusive. Take for example the matter of multiple inventions and discoveries made simultaneously but independently. Kroeber discussed the significance of such phenomena in "The Superorganic" (1917). Five years later Ogburn and Thomas published a long list of simultaneous but independent inventions in an article significantly entitled "Are Inventions Inevitable?" Ogburn published this list later in *Social Change*. The evidence is voluminous and impressive. Time after time, two or more men, working quite independently, have made the same invention or discovery. In 1843, the Law of Conservation of Energy was formulated by Mayer. In 1847, it was formulated by four other men, Joule, Helmholz, Colding, and Thomson, working independently of one another and, of course, Mayer. The discovery and recognition of the cellular basis of both animal and plant tissue was made (or claimed) by no less than seven men (Schwann, Henle, Turpin, Dumortier, Purkinje, Muller, and Valentin) and all in the same, or very approximately the same, year: 1839.

Now the question is, Why in each of these instances did a number of men working independently make a notable scientific discovery or invention at almost exactly the same time? How are we to explain the fact that a great generalization like the Law of Conservation of Energy or a great discovery like the cellular basis of life, which had lain beyond the capabilities of everyone before this time, suddenly and almost overnight was achieved by not one individual or two, but by a whole handful?

William James would say that these achievements were the work of genius and that the appearance of a man of genius is fortuitous. But if the appearance of a single genius is a chance occurrence, "the unlikeliness of the concourse of genius about a time is far greater." Yet we have many such "concourses": anywhere from two to seven or more persons achieving independently the same important result. This places a heavy burden upon the theory of probability, a burden that is increased when we think of the ages of the men at the time of their noteworthy achievement. Thus, in a single year a number of geniuses of widely varying ages all light their lamps at the same time! Even if we had no other explanation at all for this phenomenon than "chance" one wonders why anyone would want to dignify this feeble gesture by calling it a scientific explanation.

Culturological theory provides a simple explanation of this remarkable "coincidence." The Law of Conservation of Energy was simply the synthesis of already existing concepts, each of which, in turn, was the outgrowth and synthesis of earlier experience. A synthesis of cultural elements requires two things: the elements in question and a process of interaction. Cultural interaction is always going on in any cultural system, although the rate of interaction may vary. A given synthesis cannot take place until the elements requisite for it are available, obviously. But, when the elements are present, the process of cultural interaction is bound to effect the synthesis. The situation is something like the chain reaction in Uranium 235. If the mass of metal is below a certain size a chain reaction is impossible. But when a certain size—the "critical size"—is reached, the chain reaction is inevitable. Prior to 1843-47, the elements requisite to the formulation of the Law of Conservation of Energy were not available. But, when they became available the interactive culture process made their synthesis so "inevitable" that it was achieved not once but five times.*

The phenomena of multiple and simultaneous, but independent, inventions and discoveries thus have an important bearing upon the question of genius and the Great Man. As we have already noted, we are justified in assuming that the birth of men of exceptional ability is fairly uniform within a large population like that of Western Europe for example. To assume that there was no one in Europe with sufficient mental ability to formulate the Law of Conservation of Energy in 1823-27, or in 1833-37, but that in 1843 one such person appeared only to be followed by four more in '47, is to put a severe strain upon the laws of chance. The culturological interpretation, however, makes very modest assumptions. It assumes that the cultural elements requisite for the synthesis that is the Law of Conservation must be on hand and available otherwise the synthesis could not be made; no one however able or intelligent can build without materials. The culturologist assumes further that these materials did not suddenly spring into being out of nothing, but that they had antecedents, that they grew out of previous cultural situations. This, too, is a reasonable and modest assumption. We know of no instance in which something has come from nothing, in cultural systems or in those of any other kind; one thing grows out of another. In short, the culturologist merely assumes the existence of a culture process, the existence of such things as languages, beliefs, tools, customs, etc., that constitute an extra-somatic, metabiological continuum, i.e., they are passed down from one

---

* ". . . there is a good deal of evidence to indicate that the accumulation or growth of culture reaches a stage where certain inventions if not inevitable are certainly to a high degree probable . . ." (Ogburn, *Social Change*, p. 343).

generation to another by mechanisms of *social* heredity. The elements of this process interact upon one another: tool upon tool, tool upon belief, belief upon custom, custom upon custom, etc. In this interactive process new combinations of elements are formed, new syntheses achieved. It goes without saying that a given synthesis cannot be achieved until the requisite elements for the synthesis are available: the steam engine could not have been invented in the Neolithic age. It is not quite so obvious, perhaps, that when the elements necessary for a given synthesis are present in a process of interaction that the synthesis *will* take place. The lay mind rebels at this notion of a deterministic process going on of itself, effecting inventions and discoveries automatically, so to speak, and inevitably. Man still likes to think of himself as the image of One who could say, "Let there be light and there was light." Let there be a law of conservation of energy and there will be such a law. But the formulation of such a law must be *man's* doing, he fondly believes, not that of some impersonal culture process that not only determines its own course and content but the behavior of man as well.

But the evidence is against such a view, however flattering and consoling it may be. When the culture process has reached a point where an invention or discovery becomes possible, that invention or discovery becomes inevitable. This language may seem intemperate and unwarranted, but this is only because we are not yet accustomed to thinking of the culture process in terms of *natural law*; we still think of it as operating to some extent at least in the realm of human free will. To say that an invention or discovery becomes inevitable at the same time that it becomes possible is merely a way of saying that it will happen when it will happen. It is significant to note that we do not recoil from or object to this point of view when we consider the weather. No one would argue that "it" could rain if the various factors and conditions necessary were not present and in conjunction. Neither would one want to argue that rain could *fail* to fall if all the factors necessary for precipitation were present and in conjunction. Nor would many be inclined to call this *fatalism*. We simply say that when certain conditions are present precipitation occurs; when these factors or conditions are not present precipitation does not take place.

And so it is with inventions and discoveries: when certain factors and conditions are present and in conjunction an invention or discovery takes place; when they are not present, the invention or discovery does not occur. Let us glance at more of the evidence.

The discovery of sun spots was made independently by at least four men in a single year: by Galileo, Fabricus, Scheiner, and Harriott, in 1611. The parallax of a star was first measured by Bessel, Struve, and Henderson, working independently, in 1838. Oxygen was discovered independently by Scheele and Priestly in 1774. The invention of the self-exciting dynamo was claimed by Hjorth, Varley, Siemens, Wheatstone, and Ladd in 1866-67, and by Wilde between 1863-67. The solution of the problem of respiration was made independently by Priestly, Scheele, Lavoisier, Spallanzani, and Davy, in a single year: 1777. Invention of the telescope and the thermometer each is claimed by eight or nine persons independently and at approximately the same time. "Even the south pole, never before trodden by the foot of human beings, was at last reached twice in one summer" [11] (Kroeber). The great work of Mendel in genetics lay unnoticed for many years. But when it was eventually re-discovered, it was done not by one man but by three—deVries, Correns, and Tschermak—and in a single year, 1900. One could go on indefinitely. When the growing, interactive culture process reaches a certain point, an invention or discovery takes place.

The simultaneity of multiple inventions or discoveries is sometimes striking and remarkable. Accusations of plagiarism are not infrequent; bitter rivalries are waged over priorities. "The right to the monopoly of the manufacture of the telephone," says Kroeber, "was long in litigation; the ultimate decision rested on an *interval of hours* between the recording of concurrent descriptions by Alexander Bell and Elisha Gray" [12] (emphasis ours).

"But an invention or discovery could not occur without a person to make it, and that person must be a genius," * we are told with some impatience or exasperation. Of course; an invention or discovery cannot take place without the activity of a human being. This goes without saying; culture does not and cannot exist without human beings. *But, we add nothing to an explanation of this culture process by including man in our calculations.* Conjugations of verbs could not take place without human organisms, but do we need to introduce metabolism and respiration into philological science? Tractors would not have replaced horses on American farms unless man had been there to effect the change. But in a statement of the relationship between tractors and horses, the human organism may be—and should be—completely disregarded.

But what about *genius?* Granting that inventions and discoveries are *cultural* events, does not a great event require a great man? Could an epoch-making invention or discovery take place without the action of a person of exceptional natural endowment?

The culturologist, like the biologist, assumes that human organisms vary both qualitatively and quantitatively. One person's feet, liver, brain, etc., may be larger or smaller than another's; one set of glands, nerves, or sense organs may function better, i.e., more efficiently or effectively, than another. In short, individual human beings differ in their natural endowments and abilities; some are superior to others. Of one thing we may be sure: all men are not equal.

Now if superior, mediocre, and inferior minds are exposed equally and uniformly to the influence of a given cultural tradition, we must conclude that significant inventions and discoveries will be made by the superior, rather than by the average or inferior,

---

* "Origination, when it is more than chance accident, is always the product of a superior mind," (E. B. Reuter and C. W. Hart, *Introduction to Sociology*, p. 221, New York, 1933, emphasis ours).

minds. Just as lightning will seek the best conductor, so will the culture process effect its syntheses in the best brains available. But the best brains *available* are not necessarily the best brains extant in society. A given cultural tradition does not affect *all* brains in a given society equally. Illiteracy cuts off a portion of the population from certain cultural influences. In Newton's day the vast majority of Englishmen were illiterate; the great and vital traditions that kindled their flame in Newton lay beyond the horizon of most men. Had Newton been reared a swineherd instead of going to Cambridge, the law of gravitation would have been formulated by someone else.

But does not the fact that the laws of motion and the calculus were synthesized in Newton's brain prove that he was a genius? At last we have come to the crucial point: are we to define a genius psychologically or culturologically?

Is a genius a person of exceptional native endowment? * Or, is he an individual in whose neuro-sensory-glandular-etc. system an important synthesis of cultural events has taken place?

To assume that a person who has made a significant achievement has superior native ability is, as we have seen, merely an inference. Can we discover outstanding natural endowment apart from distinguished achievement? Our experience with intelligence tests gives us little assurance on this score. To be sure, we can grade persons in terms of intelligence quotients. But many a person with a high I.Q. lives and dies undistinguished by any notable achievement. Tests that endeavor to measure native ability *unaffected by social or cultural influences* are not likely to discover men and women who will go down in history as "geniuses." E. T. Bell tells us in *Men of Mathematics* that the great mathematical physicist, Henri Poincaré, made such a poor showing on the Binet tests as to warrant the rating of imbecile.[13]

---

* W. B. Pillsbury and L. A. Pennington define a genius as "a person of very marked ability . . . an I.Q. of 140 or above . . . less than one percent of the population . . ." (*Handbook of General Psychology*, p. 327).

To be sure, many men in whom great cultural syntheses have taken place may well have been organisms of exceptional natural endowment as well as the neural loci of the interaction of cultural elements. This is of course to be expected: if other factors are constant, the significant cultural synthesis will take place in a nervous system of superior quality. But, of course, other factors are *not* constant. We are therefore thrown back upon the culturological definition of genius: A person in whose organism a significant synthesis of cultural elements has occurred. He may have superior brains or he may not. He may have been a person of very average natural endowment, but with superlative education and training or exceptional opportunity, or both.

A consideration of many significant inventions and discoveries does not lead to the conclusion that great ability, native or acquired, is always necessary. On the contrary, many seem to need only mediocre talents at best. What intelligence was required to invent the steamboat? Is great intelligence required to put one and one—a boat and an engine—together? An ape can do this. James Watt is listed as a genius in many a treatise on this subject. It is even misleading to say that he "invented" the steam engine. He merely added a little to the achievements of many other men —Hero (c. 130 B.C.), Battista della Porta (1601), Edward Somerset (1663), Thomas Savery (1698), Desgauliers, Papin, Newcomen, Cawley, Smeaton, *et al*—before him. The cultural process was merely carried further in the person of Watt as it has been in the organisms of many others since his day. Does it require much intelligence to discover satellites of Jupiter or sun spots when you have a telescope? Or bacteria and the cellular basis of life if you have a microscope? A telescopic or microscopic lens is a piece of glass that changes the course of light passing through it. Glass is the product of an age-old culture process going back to the burning of brick in Egypt and to sun-dried brick and daubing with mud before that.

Isotopes—elements having the same atomic number, the same chemical properties, but different atomic weights—were discovered early in the present century. In 1906, Boltwood of Yale isolated an element, ionium, from pitchblende. It was exactly like thorium except in atomic weight. Three kinds of lead, each with an atomic weight of its own, were found. J. J. Thomson found two kinds (weights) of neon. Frederick Soddy and Kasimir Fajans (working independently, be it noted) advanced an hypothesis by which these different forms might be explained. Thomson and F. W. Aston in England and K. T. Bainbridge in the United States examined the whole series of elements in a search for isotopes. They found that many elements have isotopes. The atomic weight of hydrogen—1.00778 instead of 1.0—indicated the existence of an isotope of this element but neither Aston nor Bainbridge could isolate it with the mass spectrometer. Harold C. Urey thought that separation might be effected by evaporation of liquid hydrogen. It was assumed that the light isotope would evaporate more freely, leaving a concentration of the heavy form in the residue.

As Professor Selig Hecht tells the story in his recent book, *Explaining the Atom*, "Urey interested F. G. Brickweddie at the Bureau of Standards, who proceeded to make a gallon of liquid hydrogen. Brickweddie then allowed the liquid to evaporate slowly until all but a gram (1/28 of an ounce) of liquid hydrogen was left, which he shipped to Urey." With this specimen and the mass spectrometer, Urey and G. M. Murphy isolated the heavy isotope, and "for this exciting discovery," says Hecht, "Urey was awarded the Nobel prize in 1934." [14]

Now we have no desire to minimize the importance of this discovery as a scientific achievement. And we certainly do not wish to belittle Dr. Urey's native and inborn abilities. But, we would like to ask, Was intelligence of a high order required for this discovery? What precisely did it involve? No new theory of atomic structure was advanced; on the contrary, Urey had the heritage of generations of workers at his disposal. Urey did not discover isotopes;

they had been found experimentally and explained theoretically by others. Isotopes of many elements had been isolated and identified before Urey. Techniques of isolation had been developed by Thomson, Aston, Bainbridge, and others. He did not invent the mass spectrometer; it is a descendant of the tube invented by Heinrich Geissler about 1862. He did not provide the liquid hydrogen or even manage its gradual evaporation. The idea that a light isotope would diffuse faster than a heavy one was not original; it had been tried out experimentally by Aston with positive results. What then did Urey contribute?

Again, let us repeat, we are not minimizing the inborn capacities of Dr. Urey. He may have a superlatively fine organization of nerves, glands, and sense organs. We have, however, implied that intelligence of a high order was not essential to the isolation of heavy hydrogen, and we now wish to make this implied conclusion explicit and unequivocal: it could have been achieved by a very ordinary intelligence. As a matter of fact, we believe that many a household problem—such as removing a stain from a dress or opening a recalcitrant jar of pickles—requires as much ingenuity, though perhaps not as much technical information—which is a matter of education, not native ability—as that required in the isolation of heavy hydrogen. Take a person of *average* intelligence, give him excellent technical training, put him in a well-equipped laboratory, and assuming some interest and enthusiasm on his part, how could he help but make *some* significant discovery? One cannot adventure very long with an electron microscope or a cyclotron without stumbling upon something new. And "stumbling upon" very aptly characterizes many significant advances in science. The reason that superlatively great advances in science are few is not because "genius" is rare but because great syntheses must be built upon, or grow out of, a multitude of minor ones.

There is another property or aspect of culture that has an important and significant bearing upon the problem of genius, namely, *pattern*. Nowhere is culture a mere aggregation or ag-glomeration of traits; culture elements are always organized into systems. Every culture has a certain degree of integration, of unity; it rests upon a certain basis, and is organized along certain lines or principles. Thus, a culture may be organized around the hunt-ing of seal, reindeer breeding, the cultivation of rice, or manu-facturing and trade. Military activity also may be an important factor in the organization and life of a culture. Within any given cultural system a number of sub-systems, which we may call pat-terns, can be distinguished. Painting, music, mythology, philoso-phy or science, mechanics, industrial crafts, the medical arts, and so on are such patterns.

A culture pattern in this sense is a cluster of cultural elements, or traits, organized upon the basis of a certain premise and directed by a certain principle of development. A pattern of painting or bead-work may be based upon geometric forms or it may attempt to depict natural phenomena realistically. Or, symbolic representa-tion may be developed in a certain direction. The art of divination will rest upon a certain basic assumption and will develop in a certain direction. The mechanical and industrial arts, science, and philosophy, too, will be organized as patterns and will develop as such.

Now a pattern, having a given premise, and certain principles of development, has specific potentialities and also inherent limita-tions. When these limits have been reached no further develop-ment is possible. To illustrate with a simple example: You are trying to draw a circle. When a perfect circle has been achieved you can go no further. Realistic representation of natural objects in painting and sculpture cannot be developed beyond a certain point; and symbolic representation, too, seems to have its limits. The art of divination based upon the assumption that the future can be read in the liver may be developed considerably, as the little Babylonian clay models, with various sections marked off, indicate. But hepatoscopy has its limits. The development of

geometry upon the basis of the axioms of Euclid had limits that
were inherent in the system or pattern. A certain musical pattern
reached its culmination or fulfillment apparently in the works of
Bach, Mozart, and Beethoven. Gothic art as a pattern was inherently limited. Ptolemy carried the development of a certain
type of astronomic system about as far as was possible. All cultural development takes place within organized forms, or patterns.
Now, as Kroeber has pointed out repeatedly in *Configurations of
Culture Growth*, when a pattern has reached the limits of its
potentialities no further development is possible. The alternatives
then are slavish repetition of old patterns or the revolutionary
overthrow of the old and the formation of new patterns. In some
instances, such as in ancient Egypt, we find monotonous and endless repetition of old forms; or, we see a nation like the United
States adopting architectural styles from ancient Greece or the
Middle Ages. But the history of culture abounds, of course, in
examples of the growth, culmination or fulfillment of patterns
and of their replacement by new patterns. New, non-Euclidean
systems of geometry are constructed. New forms emerge in the
industrial and esthetic arts. New patterns are constructed on new
premises in philosophy and science.

This phenomenon of culture pattern has an important bearing
upon the problem of genius. The development of a pattern is the
labor of countless persons and of many generations or even
centuries. But the pattern finds its culmination, its fulfillment, in
the work of a few men—the Newtons, Darwins, Bachs, Beetho-
vens, Kants, etc. Men working both before and after the time of
fulfillment of the pattern have less, usually much less, chance of
winning distinction. The men whose accident of birth has placed
them somewhere along the slope of the pyramid of the developing
pattern have no chance to win the sort of achievement and fame
given to those whose births place them at the peak. A Bach or a
Beethoven born a century or two earlier would have been a mere
contributor to a pattern of development rather than the vehicle

of its culmination. But a pattern of thought, long in the process of development, will receive its fulfillment in the lives and work of a few persons.

Men and women who come after the culmination of a culture pattern also have little chance of winning distinction—except as wreckers of the old and perhaps as builders of the new. A pattern of growth in physical theory reached its culmination in the work of Newton. So finished and complete was this pattern at Newton's death that it held physicists and astronomers within its forms for over two hundred years. As Lagrange once remarked, Newton was not only the greatest genius that ever lived but the most fortunate as well, "for we cannot find more than once a system of the world to establish." [15] To be born in the wake of Newton was to find one's self with no more worlds to conquer.

It is plain, then, that culture patterns are significant determinants of genius. The culture process is not an even and uniform flow. There are initial stages of development, periods of steady growth, peaks of culmination, plateaus of continuity and repetition, revolutionary upheavals and innovations, disruption, disintegration, and decline. Whether an individual of exceptional natural endowment achieves the distinction of genius or not depends therefore very much upon the accidental time of his birth. Should chance place him somewhere along the slope of a developing pattern his chances of distinction will be relatively slight. Or, if he should be born after the culmination has been reached and passed, his chances for distinguished achievement and fame would also be meager. But should he chance to be born at the time and place where streams of culture are converging and fusing into a final and complete synthesis, then his chances will be relatively great.*

---

* Even so, there is apt to be room for but one genius only. It was Darwin, not Wallace, who won recognition and fame—became the capstone of the edifice—even though the latter had worked out the same theory and at the same time.

To become a genius it is necessary to be born at precisely the right time.

The cultural milieu into which an individual is thrust at birth also has much to do with the likelihood of his achieving recognition as a genius. If he is born and reared in a frontier culture where life is hard and hazardous, where a keen eye and a quick trigger finger are prized, where hard drinking and harder fighting are manly virtues, and where a square dance to a squeaky fiddle is the highest form of art, he is not likely to achieve fame as a poet, composer, sculptor, philosopher, or scientist. He may possess superb natural endowment, he may excel all others in tracking a bear, roping a steer, or in "calling" a dance, but the accolade of "genius" is not accorded to primacy in these fields. Should, however, an individual be born into a cultural milieu in which a rich and vigorous tradition of music, painting, science or philosophy flourished, he could readily become a genius if of exceptional natural ability, or a distinguished person if of a little more than average talent. As Cooley observed, in his critique of Galton, "it is as difficult for an American brought up in the western part of our country [in 1897] to become a good painter as it is for a Parisian to become a good base-ball player, and for similar reasons." [16] The production and incidence of genius are thus seen to be functions of the cultural setting. Whether a genius is realized or not depends upon the soil and climate of the cultural habitat.

We now come to another interesting point: namely, the relationship between the rate of cultural advance and the factor of human ability. Here we have, on the one hand, a supra-biological process: the evolution of culture, a temporal-formal sequence of extra-somatic events. On the other, we have the neuro-sensory-muscular-glandular-etc. process. The culture process can, as we have seen, be studied, analyzed, and explained in terms of itself, independently of the human organism. This does not mean of course that man has "nothing to do" with the culture process; in one sense he has everything to do with it. It is man who brings culture into existence and makes its continuity possible. But it does not follow from this that we must reckon with the human organism in an analysis of culture change. To interpret the culture process without taking the human organism into account is merely to regard the biological factor in the man-culture equation as a constant. But, suppose the biological factor were not constant, how would its variations affect the culture process? Let us examine this problem in terms of the magnitude of abilities only, not their qualitative variations.

Let us consider populations of 100,000,000 persons each. Let us assume also that ability is distributed normally rather than skewed. Then if all members of society are stimulated equally by their culture, the rate of cultural advance, through invention and discovery, will increase if (1) the average ability is increased, or (2) the range of ability is extended in the direction of superior minds, other factors remaining constant. In other words, if the biological factor of mental ability is increased, either by an elevation of the average or by an extension of the range, the rate of cultural advance will increase. The acceleration will of course be greater if both average and range are increased instead of one only. This means that the probability of an invention or discovery taking place at a certain time will vary as the average or range of mental ability of the population varies, other factors remaining constant. Thus, in a given cultural situation a certain invention or discovery —a steam engine, the alphabet, the cellular basis of life—would be more likely to occur in a population with a high average of intelligence than a low one, in a society with a high "ceiling" than in one with a low one.

We see then that a relationship can be established between the extra-somatic cultural tradition and the biological factor of mental ability which we can express thus: $C \times B = P$, in which C stands for the cultural tradition, B for the biological factor of mental ability. and P for the probability of a certain invention or discovery taking place. The probability is increased if either C or B is increased while the other factor remains constant. But—and here is a very interesting point, and one not widely appreciated— in any actual historical situation, the factor of mental ability is virtually constant for a considerable period of time. The cultural factor, however, may, and in many cases will, not be a constant. In the cumulative, interactive stream of culture, the likelihood of a given invention or discovery increases day by day. With the accumulation of facts and the growth of theory, certain syntheses are bound to occur. Thus, if the mental ability requisite to a given invention or discovery is not present at a given time, the growth and advance of the culture process will bring the possibility of the neurological synthesis within the range of the capacities of the population eventually. This means that if men of great ability are not available, the advancing culture process will in time bring the possibility of a significant invention or discovery within the range of men with much less ability. Incidents of this sort have no doubt occurred many times in the past. We believe we are warranted, on the basis of our premises and analysis, in making the assertion that all of the great discoveries or inventions that have ever occurred could have been achieved without one single "genius," i.e., without the aid of anyone above the present average of intelligence. In short, that our civilization could have been achieved by a race whose *maximum* intelligence was equivalent to our average. It would merely have taken longer, that is all, longer for the cultural process to reach the point where syntheses become possible to human nervous systems.

Actually, however, we have good reasons for believing that the factor of mental ability has remained fairly constant throughout the last hundred thousand years or so. At any rate, we have no evidence of a significant increase in mental ability during this time.*

---

* There is some evidence, however, that would point to a decline in the level of intelligence in Western Europe during the Christian era. At least,

Further consideration of our formula, $C \times B = P$, will illuminate other aspects of culture history also. As Morgan, Kroeber, Ogburn and others have repeatedly noted, significant inventions and discoveries were few and far between in the remote past. This was not due to a lack of persons of high mental ability but to a meagerness of cultural materials and resources. As the stream of culture grows through accumulation, assimilation and synthesis, the rate of cultural advance increases. Thus, inventions and discoveries were much more numerous and frequent in the great urban, metallurgical and literate cultures of 5,000 to 2,000 B.C. than in the period 90,000 to 87,000 B.C., and they are much more frequent today than in any earlier time. Since invention and discovery are functions of cultural milieus as well as of mental ability, it follows that men of exceptional intelligence were relatively more important and significant in the days of savagery than of civilization. Because the cultural resources were more meager, the difficulty of invention was greater. Thus, paradoxical though it may appear, the Old Stone Age might be called the Age of Genius, or Intelligence, rather than the present time because the role of native ability was relatively more important.* The foundations of

---

Darwin and Lyell cite the large scale and long continued extermination of independent minds and courageous spirits by the Holy Inquisition, as evidence of deterioration.

Speaking of the Inquisition Darwin wrote: "In Spain alone some of the best men—those who doubted and questioned, and without doubting there can be no progress—were eliminated during three centuries at the rate of a thousand a year. The evil which the Catholic Church has thus effected is incalculable . . ."(*The Descent of Man*, Ch. III). Lyell observes that "the institutions of a country may be so framed that individuals possessing moderate or even inferior abilities may have the best chance of surviving. Thus the Holy Inquisition . . . may for centuries carefully select from the thinking part of the population all men of genius . . . and may doom them by thousands to destruction, so as effectually to lower the general standard of intelligence," (*Principles of Geology*, Vol. II, New York, 1883), p. 495.

* The conclusion reached here is exactly opposite to a view widely held today, not only by laymen but by eminent anthropologists as well. Thus the late Edward Sapir wrote: "As the social units grow larger and larger, the probabilities of the occurrence of striking and influential personalities grow vastly. Hence it is that the determining influence of individuals is more

civilization—the rudiments of mechanics, the ceramic, textile, and metallurgical arts, the origin of agriculture and the domestication of animals, the invention of the plow, the wheel, the calendar and the alphabet, etc., etc.—were laid by anonymous men and women. As civilization advances inventions and discoveries become easier to make.*

If inventions and discoveries—in short, cultural advance—are to be explained in terms of an interactive cultural process, where

---

easily demonstrated in the higher than in the lower levels of culture" (1919, p. 443). This view ignores the epoch-making inventions of remote times and tends to recognize only the known and named heroes of recent and literate times.

It is interesting to note, however, that the early American anthropologist, Lewis H. Morgan, had a more realistic understanding of the developmental culture process. "Human progress, from first to last," he wrote, "has been in a ratio not rigorously but essentially geometrical. This is plain on the face of the facts; and it could not, theoretically, have occurred in any other way. *Every item of absolute knowledge gained became a factor in further acquisitions,* until the present complexity of knowledge was attained. Consequently, while progress was slowest in time in the first period, and most rapid in the last, the relative amount may have been greatest in the first, when the achievements of either period are considered in their relations to the sum. It may be suggested, as not improbable of ultimate recognition, that the progress of mankind in the period of savagery, in its relations to the sum of human progress, was greater in degree than it was afterwards in the three sub-periods of barbarism; and that the progress made in the whole period of barbarism was, in like manner, greater in degree than it has been since in the entire period of civilization" (*Ancient Society,* p. 38). This was written, it should be noted, about 1875.

* In northeastern South America the Indians cultivated manioc which in some regions was the staple article of diet. There are two kinds of manioc: bitter and sweet. The bitterness of the former is due to the presence of hydrocyanic acid, a deadly poison. In some regions, because of depradations of ants, only the bitter manioc can be grown. The Indians discovered a way to remove the poisonous element by leaching the meal ground from the roots. After the acid has been volatilized, dissolved and expressed, the meal is both edible and nutritious. How the aborigines discovered that this could be done and how they perfected this technique is a matter of wonder. Ignorant of chemistry, knowing that initially the plant was deadly, and with minds full of magic, myth, and superstition, one wonders how they ever accomplished so difficult a feat. Perhaps if we had a complete record of the discovery it might, and probably would, seem simpler. Even so, we may, I think, regard it as one of the most difficult, though not of course the greatest, inventions in history.

trait impinges upon trait, effecting modifications, new combinations and syntheses, then we ought to find instances of rapid cultural change and growth in localities or regions where a high degree of social and cultural interaction takes place. This is just what we do find. Culture change is more rapid in the center of culture areas than on the periphery, more rapid in urban than in rural areas. The rate of culture change is relatively slow in isolated regions. It is significant to note, both in the New and the Old Worlds, that the regions of most rapid culture growth were located on or near narrow land bridges connecting continental land masses: Mexico, Middle America, and the Andean highlands on the one hand, and the "Fertile Crescent"—Egypt and Mesopotamia—on the other. Thus we can establish a geographic, or topological, determinant of innovation in the culture process: the rate of invention and discovery will tend to be high where the conformation of the land and the distribution of its masses foster a high degree of social and cultural interaction.

A few moments ago we were assuming, for the purpose of our discussion, that all members of a population were exposed equally to the same cultural influences. This situation tends to prevail on low levels of cultural development where stratification of society into classes does not exist. In advanced and socially stratified cultures, however, this is not the case. All Egyptians during the dynastic period were certainly not influenced equally by Egyptian culture. The majority were serfs, slaves, or laborers on public works. As such they lived in and were affected by a very different stratum of culture than the priests and rulers and their close associates. Similarly in England in the seventeenth century most of the people were wholly illiterate and hence cut off from a large part of the cultural tradition accessible to Newton. And in the United States today although most of the population are literate, they are not directly and effectively stimulated by cultural elements in strata where significant inventions, discoveries and other ad-

vances are made. We may therefore make the following generalizations: (1) As culture advances, society becomes increasingly
differentiated and stratified. (2) This means that a progressively
diminishing portion of the population is embraced by the cultural
tradition in which significant inventions and discoveries take
place. (3) This small professional class contains only a portion of
the exceptionally gifted individuals of society; others are engaged
in non-professional occupations. (4) Consequently, significant
inventions and discoveries are made by a progressively diminishing proportion of the exceptionally gifted individuals. In other
words, as culture advances and society becomes more and more
differentiated structurally and more specialized functionally, the
fewer becomes the relative number of exceptionally gifted persons
in whose systems significant cultural syntheses take place. Here,
as before, we reach the conclusion that as culture advances, the
role of exceptional ability diminishes in significance.

The decrease in relative importance of the biological factor in
the process of invention, discovery, and cultural advance may be
demonstrated in still another quarter. Franklin made a notable
achievement with meager and simple apparatus: a key and a kite.
Nowadays, colossal and costly equipment—a 200-inch telescope,
a 100-ton cyclotron—is needed for research in many fields. But
who shall use the giant machines of astronomy and physics? Is
the man of exceptional natural endowment more likely to use
them than one with less ability? Not unless he has had the requisite training; brains are not enough. And certainly the average
individual can contribute more today with a cyclotron than a
highly gifted person with only a kite and a key. In relationship to
the kite and key, Franklin was more important than a person
of the same natural endowment would be in relationship to the
telescope at Mt. Palomar or to a giant cyclotron. *As the technological factor increases in magnitude the importance of the biological factor decreases relatively.*

The role of the gifted individual in cultural advance is diminishing in importance in still another sector. Research is rapidly becoming socialized, so to speak, or institutionalized. Of course, no one ever worked and achieved great things in actual isolation. Newton had the products of predecessors at his disposal and he used to exchange ideas with contemporaries, obtain measurements and other data from them. But today research is becoming more and more an organized co-operative enterprise. Great laboratories and research teams are replacing the individual entrepreneur in science and technology. The development of the atomic bomb— in which dozens of highly trained idea men and hundreds of skilled technicians co-operated—is of course a dramatic, but highly significant, indication of the trend of the times. The Great Man is becoming less and less significant; the community of scientific and technological workers more and more so. As the eminent German scientist, Wilhelm Ostwald, observed many years ago, "at present mankind is in a state of development in which progress depends much less upon the leadership of distinguished individuals than upon the collective labor of all workers." [17] It is not the soloist that counts so much today—although public and press still have and feed an appetite for primadonnas—it is the whole symphonic orchestra.

We are now in a position to draw some final conclusions: (1) Although we freely admit that individuals differ in their natural endowments, we have no reliable way of discovering or recognizing "geniuses" save through their achievements. We may be justified in believing that exceptional inborn ability lies back of the achievement of a Bach or a Newton. But it would be unwarranted to say that all men of lesser achievement were proportionally inferior in natural ability. On the other hand, we have good reason to believe that significant syntheses of culture traits may and do take place in organisms of unexceptional quality. Therefore, we must conclude that a psychological definition of "genius" is inferential and misleading. The culturological definition is realistic: a genius is a human organism in which an important synthesis of cultural elements has taken place. But the culturological definition does more than merely correspond with the facts more closely than does the psychological conception; it calls attention to the more significant of the two factors involved in great inventions and discoveries, namely, the biological and the cultural. The psychological conception of genius can say no more than that one organism is superior to another, even though it cannot tell reliably which is which in many instances. But the psychological interpretation cannot tell whether the superior organism will actually achieve great things or die a "mute, inglorious Milton." The culturological interpretation however tells how, why and when a genius will appear; it makes clear what the elements and processes are that produce a genius, and how it all comes about. It might be noted also that the culturologist knows quite as much about the neuroanatomy of genius as the psychologist does, namely, virtually nothing.

Conclusion 2. In the operation of the man-culture process, the factor of innate mental ability may have, and probably has, increased since man acquired the faculty of articulate speech. It seems at least reasonable to suppose—although hardly a foregone conclusion—that Homo sapiens has a higher native intelligence than that possessed by Pithecanthropus erectus. Thus in the man-culture equation over a period of a million years, we may assume some absolute increase in magnitude of the biological factor. But, during the last hundred, or even the last fifty thousand years, we have no evidence of an appreciable increase in mental ability. The great bulk of cultural development however has taken place during this time. Since a significant invention or discovery is a function of organism and culture, working together, the role of the former, and consequently of the exceptionally endowed individual, has diminished relative to the cultural factor as culture has developed and advanced. This is due not only to the increase in magnitude of the cultural factor, both absolutely and relatively, but also to the fact that differentiation of social structure, the formation of classes each with its own function, has cut off an increasing number of organisms of exceptional natural endowment from the possibility of important achievement: the illiterate peasant cannot invent the calculus no matter how excellent his cerebral cortex may be.

Conclusion 3. The rate of occurrence of inventions and discoveries at any given time is determined not only by the proportion of exceptionally gifted men and women in the population but by the number of elements in the cultural continuum and the velocity of their interaction. But the acceleration in rate of culture growth noted at various periods in human culture history is to be explained, not by an increase in the general level of intelligence or by an increase in the proportion of highly gifted individuals, but in terms of an increase in the number of culture elements or an increase in the velocity of their interaction, or both. The greater the number of traits, or the greater the velocity of their interaction, or both, the greater the number of cultural syntheses— inventions and discoveries—other factors remaining constant.

Much of our discussion thus far has dealt with outstanding achievement in science, philosophy or the arts where success is dependent upon cultural materials at hand as well as upon native ability. But how is it with history and political events? Does not the Great Man turn the tide one way or another by sheer force of his personality? Would the history of Europe between 1798 and 1815 have been what it was had it not been for Napoleon? Did not Julius Caesar change the whole course of European history? Would not the administration of law in New Orleans have been different, asks Sapir, had it not been for a certain Corsican?

We readily admit that Caesar, Napoleon and Ghengis Khan and many others have been significant factors * in the course of

---

* We say "significant factors in the course of history" rather than use the common phrase "changed the course of history." The latter phrase is an-

history. But we are not at all willing to accept the inferences that many people wish to draw from this premise. To grant that a certain individual has been outstanding in a sequence of historical events is, to many scholars, proof of his genius, his supreme ability, his force of character, his colossal greatness. History is made by men, they reason, and great changes can be brought about only by men of enormous ability. This we do not grant. An imbecile can affect the course of history as readily and as profoundly as a genius. A half-wit tampers with a switch, or a drunken switchman fails to close it; a train is wrecked, a prime minister on his way to a treaty conference is killed. The course of history is changed. Had Lenin and his colleagues been killed by a train wreck en route from Switzerland to Russia in 1917 the outcome of the Bolshevik revolution might have been profoundly different. Had Lincoln lived five years longer the Reconstruction in the South would probably have taken a different course. But it was the obscure actor, John Wilkes Booth, who "changed the course" of history.

More than this: it need not be even a half-wit who deflects the course of history; any accident from any cause can accomplish this. A rat might infect a Tsar with typhus, a squirrel might short-circuit a power line, a pig derail a train, or a stroke of lightning down a plane. Had a certain Corsican girl not chanced to meet a swarthy swain at a village festival, the genetic combination that became Napoleon would not have taken place. And a thousand and one more circumstances of sheer chance occurred between his cradle and his coronation. One recalls the statement that had Cleopatra's nose been but a half-inch longer the whole course of Roman and Egyptian history would have been different. And

---

thropomorphic in outlook, and it assumes moreover a course of events which a man can change from the outside—if he be "great" enough. It does not make sense to say that a thundershower "changes the course of the weather." The thundershower is an integral part of the meteorological process. Neither does the Great Man "change the course of history" from the outside; he is an integral part of it.

Darwin tells us in his autobiographic sketch that Captain Fitz-Roy, who was "an ardent disciple" of the mystic and physiognomist J. K. Lavater, almost refused to allow Darwin to join the expedition of the Beagle because he did not like the shape of Darwin's nose! "He doubted," wrote Darwin, "whether any one with my nose could possess sufficient energy and determination for the voyage." Had Fitz-Roy's phrenology prevailed, the whole course of the history of science would have been different. As the nursery rhyme about the chain of events set in motion by the loss of a horseshoe nail makes clear, great consequences may flow from occurrences otherwise trivial and insignificant. To have affected the course of history is, therefore, no proof of genius or colossal ability. The half-wit whose blunder kills Caesar is as significant historically as Caesar himself. To be sure, the head of a great government or political movement may be a person of enormous natural ability; societies and social movements often select superior instruments to work with. But chance and circumstance often put a mediocrity in the seat of the mighty, just as chance and accident may throw him down or destroy him.

The significance of the Great Man in history has been obscured by a failure to distinguish between history and evolution, or more precisely, between a temporal process and a temporal-formal process. As we have pointed out elsewhere,[18] many anthropologists are quite unable to make this simple distinction. The temporal process, or "history," is a chronological series of events each of which is unique. We separate these events, by conceptual analysis, from their matrix of the totality of events. The temporal-formal, or evolutionist, process is a series of events in which both time and form are equally significant: one form grows out of another in time.

The temporal process is characterized by chance and is therefore unpredictable to a high degree: no one, for example, could have predicted that Booth would kill Lincoln—or whether or not his pistol would have missed fire when he pulled the trigger. The temporal-formal process however is determinative: prediction is possible to a high degree. In the decomposition of a radioactive substance one stage determines the next and the course and rate of change can be predicted. In short, we can predict the course of evolution but not of history.

The significance of the distinction between history and evolution and its relevance to the Great Man in history is brought out nicely in the debate between Kroeber and Sapir on the "super-organic." [19] Kroeber argues that had Darwin died in infancy the advance and course of development of biological theory would have been much the same as it has been. Sapir counters by asking if the administration of law in New Orleans would have been the same today had it not been for Napoleon. Both disputants are wholly justified in their claims. Unfortunately, however, they are talking about two different things. One is dealing with a deterministic developmental process, the other with the fortuitous course of history. In the evolutionist process, the individual is, as Kroeber maintains and as the phenomena of multiple and simultaneous but independent discoveries and inventions clearly demonstrate, relatively insignificant. But, in the succession of chance occurrences that is history, the individual may be enormously significant. But it does not follow at all that he is therefore a "genius" or a person of exceptional ability. The goose who saved Rome was more significant historically than many an emperor who ruled it.

We have gone a long way since William James debated the question of genius with Herbert Spencer, John Fiske, and Grant Allen. The causes and incidence of genius no longer seem as mysterious and unpredictable as they did to James and as they have to many others since his time. The science of culture, hardly begun in James' day, has been able to illuminate and render intelligible a whole area of human experience that lies beyond the horizon of the psychologist. The problem of genius is now fairly well understood.

There is, as we have pointed out, no point in defining genius psychologically at least so far as culture history is concerned. Many a person of exceptional natural ability never achieves distinction and fame. And, on the other hand, many men of distinguished achievement have been individuals of no more than high average or even mediocre native ability. To assume that significant achievement must mean high native ability is an unwarranted inference.

Assuming that mental ability is distributed uniformly among mankind, throughout time, place, and race—and this assumption is supported by evidence from paleontology, neuroanatomy, and psychology—we may virtually rule out the biological, or psychological, factor in a consideration of the causes and incidence of genius, and work with the cultural factor alone. We would grant of course that *other factors being constant*, the individual of superior natural endowment is more likely to achieve recognition as a genius than one of lesser ability. But other factors are not constant; they are so variable, in fact, that a favorably situated individual of meager ability may have much more chance of becoming a "genius" than one of vastly superior native endowment but in a disadvantageous position culturally. All we can say then is that *in the long run*, not in any particular instance, the genius is more likely to be one of superior than of average native ability.

A genius—one who achieves recognition as a genius—is a person in whom a significant synthesis of cultural elements has taken place. In other words, he is a function of his culture. If the number of elements is small, the current slow, and streams isolated, geniuses will be few and far between. If the cultural tradition is rich and varied, the current quick and the rate of interaction rapid, geniuses will be frequent and abundant. Genius occurs readily at peaks of cultural development, rarely on the slopes or plateaus. One soil or climate will foster and bring forth genius, another will not. The "mystery" of why geniuses "seem so exceptionally abundant" in the "high tides of human affairs" is as James said "about as deep as the time honored conundrum as to why great rivers flow by great towns." He is quite right so far as the depth of the mystery is concerned but, unfortunately, he has put the cart before the horse—or the towns before the rivers. It is not the abundance of "geniuses" that produces "the high tides of human affairs" (i.e., periods of florescence in cultural development), but the other way around: it is the great periods of cultural development that find their flower and expression in men of genius. And the eras of great development are to be explained culturologically, not psychologically.

And as for attributing "genius" to men who have "changed the course of history," we have seen that an idiot or a goose can accomplish it just as well. It is not high or low levels of ability that is significant in such contexts; it is being strategically situated in a moving constellation of events. And the least of things or circumstances may deflect its course.

To explain culture history psychologically is of course to lean on mystery, to appeal to chance, to invoke "that invisible and unimaginable play of forces within the nervous system," to account for significant events and eras. The "utmost the student of sociology can ever predict," says James, " is that if a genius . . . show the way, society will be sure to follow." The culturologist, however, by working upon the supra-psychological, supra-sociological level of culture, by explaining culture in terms of culture, really makes it intelligible. And in explaining culture he explains the causes and incidence of genius as well.

CHAPTER NINE

IKHNATON:
The Great Man *vs.* The Culture Process

"Lawgivers, statesmen, religious leaders, discoverers, inventors, therefore only seem to shape civilization. The deep-seated, blind, and intricate forces that shape culture, also mold the so-called creative leaders of society as essentially as they mold the mass of humanity. Progress, so far as it can objectively be considered as such, is something that makes itself. We do not make it."—A. L. Kroeber.[1]

I

*E*very living organism is confronted by a world external to itself. This external world is in a very real sense alien to the organism and is often inimical to it. One must come to terms with one's environment, however, in order to live, to survive. To adjust to environment is to control it to a degree, at least from the standpoint of the organism; adjustment is never wholly passive. Success in adjustment means survival, and survival means mastery, mastery of organism over external world.

It is but a step from this position to the belief, in the human species, that the external world and the events that take place there are but the realization of ideas and emotions projected from the mind of God or of man. The ideas come first, they are the original seeds, the prime movers. As they are thrust forth from the mind they take form as stars and planets, animals and plants, tools and edifices, rituals and institutions. In the beginning was the Idea. And the Idea finds expression in the Word, and the Word becomes not only flesh (John I, 14), but earth and sky and all creation. Let there be Light and there was light. The external world is but a projection of the mind of God.

This view of the cosmos and reality is world-wide. In Egypt we find it expressed in the conception of the god Ptah. In his early days Ptah was the patron of architects and craftsmen. But eventually he became the supreme mind from which all things were derived: "The world and all that is in it existed as thought in his mind; and his thoughts, like his plans for buildings and works of art, needed but to be expressed in spoken words to take concrete form as material realities." [2]

As it is with gods, so it is with men, according to the neurosymbolic tropism of the race called folk-thought. As the gods create and move their worlds with thought and words, so do men shape theirs. With incantation and ritual, with verbal formula and acts, and sometimes merely by the concentration of mind and will, they can make the rain to fall, change the course of the sun in the heavens, heal the sick, smite their enemies, cause crops to grow, regulate their mode of life, and, at last, find their way safely to the Land of the Dead.

But it is not only the external world, the world of nature, that falls thus under man's control. His own world, his society, his culture, and his history are even more subject to his will, for are they not obviously made by him, and is it not plain that they are merely the expressions of his thought and wish? So runs the tropism of folk-thought.

But all men are not equal, even on the level of primitive society. Some are better shamans than others; they have more "power." On higher cultural levels we find chiefs and priests; then kings and emperors, popes and potentates. The god Ptah in the persons of artists, scientists, lawgivers, rulers, generals, prophets, and inventors spews out new tools and devices, new codes and institutions, new ways of life. Cultural advance is but the work of a relatively few gifted individuals. And as culture advances, the exceptional person increases in stature; great cultures can be built only by Great Men. Like Yahweh who made the light merely by calling for it, the Great Men make society and history by exercising their inherent genius. Thus the verbal tropism.

II

In Egypt in the fourteenth century before the Christian era some remarkable events took place. Monotheism came to the fore and waged war on the old polytheism. All gods were abolished save one, and he was made Lord of all. Temples were closed, their priests driven out, their lands and revenues confiscated. A new capital was built. The government was reorganized. A marked change in art occurred. The whole regime of Egypt changed its aspect, and, it has been claimed, the events which took place then have profoundly affected our lives today. How did all this come about? What caused this upheaval that shook Egypt to its foundations and extended its influence even to us today? One of the answers has been: Ikhnaton. This genius, through his vision and insight, caught a glimpse of a new philosophy and a new way of life, and through sheer will and determination transformed the nation at his feet. At least, so we have been told.

Needless to say, not all students of Egyptian history have relied upon so simple an explanation. There are many, especially in recent years, who have a live appreciation of the significance of cultural forces in the historic process. We shall take note of their work later.

Social science is frequently absolved from its sins of sterility and impotence by sympathetic friends who point out that the scientist in the social field does not have laboratories at his command like the physicist and hence cannot be expected to produce theories that can withstand the tests these techniques can administer. But this exoneration is fallacious and misleading. It is true of course that the social scientist does not have laboratories— like the physicist. But he does have laboratories in another, and in a very real, sense. History and ethnography provide the social scientist with the equivalent of the laboratories of the physicist. How does the human organism respond to polyandry, to mothers-in-law, money, spectroscopes, holy water, governmental regulation of prices; how will men live in desert, tundra, or jungle; what will be the effect of technological advance on social life and philosophy? Answers to these and thousands of similar questions may be obtained by studies of the infinitely varied circumstances and conditions under which man has lived on this planet during the last million years. If the social scientist could set up his experiments as the physicist or rat psychologist does, it would be difficult to imagine a requirement that has not been met by some tribe, some culture, at some time and place. The meager yield of social science is not due to lack of laboratories but rather from not knowing how to use the resources at its disposal.

Ancient Egypt is an excellent laboratory in which the social scientist can test many theories. It was quite isolated, being cut off from its neighbors by deserts, mountains, and the sea. It was therefore relatively undisturbed by outside influence. We have a fairly good record, both archeologic and documentary, of history and cultural development of Egypt for tens of centuries. The land was richly endowed—as contrasted, let us say, with Australia —and so we can observe the growth of culture from a fairly primitive level to one of the greatest civilizations of the ancient world. Here we have laid out before us, on a stage of adequate size and against a background of millenia, a culture process at work. We can take note of the materials employed, the resources both natural and cultural. We can follow the changes one by one. We can trace the development step by step. We can see how one factor influenced others. We can count and evaluate. In short, we can do about all that a physical scientist can do in his laboratory —except repeat the experiment. We have, then, in Egypt a proving ground in which to test many theories of social science.

We may distinguish two main types of historical interpretations:

the *psychological* and the *culturological*. Especially prominent in the psychological interpretation is the explanation of historic events in terms of the personalities of outstanding individuals, but it resorts also to the "temperaments" of peoples or races, and even to such things as "the spirit of the times." The culturological type of interpretation explains history in terms of *cultural* forces and processes, in terms of the behavior, not of the human psyche, but of technologies, institutions, and philosophies. Let us then go to our laboratory and use it to evaluate the theories which undertake to explain the great philosophic and political events that took place during the life of Ikhnaton. We shall examine first the psychological interpretation.

III

The great religious and political revolution which gripped Egypt about 1380 B.C. has been pictured as the work of *one man*: Ikhnaton. "Until Ikhnaton," says Breasted, "the history of the world had been but the irresistible drift of tradition. All men had been but drops of water in the great current. *Ikhnaton was the first individual in history*." And, says Breasted, Ikhnaton accomplished this revolution by imposing his own ideas, ideas born in his own mind, upon the external world: "*Consciously and deliberately, by intellectual process* he gained his position, and then placed himself squarely in the face of tradition and swept it aside" [3] (emphasis ours).

But ideas alone were not enough; will power and energy were required too. Ikhnaton possessed these qualities also, we are told. "He possessed unlimited personal force of character." He "was fully convinced that he might entirely recast the world of religion, thought, art, and life by the invincible purpose he held . . . Everything bears the stamp of his individuality. The men about him must have been irresistibly swayed by his unbending will . . . The court officials blindly followed their young king, and to every word which he spoke they listened attentively." H. R. Hall interprets Egyptian history in terms of the waxing and waning of intelligence which reached its "acme under the supremely intelligent" Ikhnaton. "His reign was the earliest age of the rule of ideas, irrespective of the condition and willingness of the people" (Breasted). The revolution of Ikhnaton "can only be ascribed to the individual genius of a very exceptional man" (Gardiner). Alexandre Moret asserts that "Amenophis IV [Ikhnaton] was the man who turned aside the natural course of events." [4]

To E. A. Wallis Budge, Ikhnaton was "a religious fanatic, intolerant, arrogant and obstinate, but earnest and sincere." No one, he says, "but a half-insane man would have been so blind to facts as to attempt to overthrow Amen and his worship." James Baikie saw him as a man with a "remorselessly clear mind," but exceedingly intolerant. "Seeing clearly," he writes, "that the universality of his god meant monotheism, he saw also that with his rigid devotion to truth there could be no room for tolerance of the easy-going old cults of the other gods." In short, the great upheaval in Egypt was brought about by a man's passion for truth and his devotion to logic. Geo. Steindorff and K. C. Seele regard Ikhnaton as "probably the most fascinating personality who ever sat on the throne of the pharaohs." He had a "mystical temperament" and "an extraordinarily single-minded character." When once "embarked on a purpose he held to it with tenacity and carried it through unwaveringly with nothing short of fanaticism." J. D. S. Pendlebury who rejects Breasted's view that Ikhnaton was "the first individual in history," regards him, nevertheless, as an "extraordinary character," the "first rebel . . . whom we know, the first man with *ideas of his own* . . ." [5] (emphasis ours).

Ikhnaton revolutionized not only theology but art as well, we are told. The new era in painting and sculpture that is associated with his reign was initiated and directed by Ikhnaton himself: "It is evident that the artists of Ikhnaton's court were taught by him to make the chisel and the brush tell the story of what they actually saw." Breasted believes that the remarkable hymn to Aton "was probably written by the king himself." [6]

So remarkable a person does Ikhnaton appear to some observers that they cannot believe him to be a normal man. "Ikhnaton pursued his aims with [such] fatuous blindness and feverish fanaticism" that Breasted feels that "there is something hectic and abnormal in this extraordinary man, suggesting a mind which may even have been diseased." Weigall believes that Ikhnaton was an epileptic, subject to hallucinations.[7]

There is of course some evidence to support the theory that Ikhnaton was abnormal. In the art of the day, which is said to be characterized by naturalism and realism, he is not infrequently depicted as misshapen and abnormal.

"The King preaches the return to nature, makes the artist work from the living model, and allows a plaster cast of his face to be taken (specimens have been found), to make sure that his features are correctly reproduced . . . The sculptors faithfully reproduce the prominent lower jaw and the long, bulging skull, even when these deformities have been further aggravated by disease." [8]

In his later years, Ikhnaton is depicted, according to Moret, as "rounded and effeminate—a hermaphrodite figure, with prominent breasts, wide hips, and thighs too much curved, which makes one suspect a morbid nature, with some pathological flaw." [9]

Some writers have attempted to account for the remarkable and unusual character of Ikhnaton in terms of race as well as of psychology; they have maintained that he was not a full-blooded Egyptian. Thus, Weigall reminds us that "it must always be remembered that the king had much foreign blood in his veins." This helped him to stand out amongst the "superstitious Egyptians [who were] ever lacking in originality." Moret, too, comments on "the mixture of Aryan blood . . . further complicated by the Syrian descent of Tïi" in Ikhnaton's racial background.[10]

Here, then, we have an explanation of Egyptian history for this period. A phenomenal person appears on the scene, a man with so much genius and power of will as to go beyond the boundaries of the normal, and by himself to transform the religion, social organization, and the art of a great nation. Here we have a theory to be tested in our "laboratory."

IV

Before turning to our laboratory proper, namely, the culture history of Egypt as we know it through archeological research and documentary studies, let us consider briefly what we know about the evolution of culture in general and the nature of societies like that of ancient Egypt in particular.

Man began his career as an anthropoid who was just learning to talk. He was distinguished from all other animal species by the faculty of articulate speech. It was this faculty which transformed the discontinuous, non-accumulative, non-progressive process of tool-using among the anthropoids into a continuous, cumulative and progressive process in the human species. Articulate speech transformed, also, the social organization of this gifted primate, and by the inauguration of co-operation as a way of life and security, opened the door to virtually unlimited social evolution. And, finally, language and speech made it possible for man to accumulate experience and knowledge in a form that made easy transmission and maximum use possible.

As we have already seen, it was the ability to use symbols—of which articulate speech is the most important and characteristic form of expression—that made the origin and subsequent growth of culture possible. But symbols did not provide the motive power for cultural advance. This could only come from energy, energy in the sense in which the physicist uses this term. All life is a matter of energy transformations. Organisms enable themselves to live by capturing free energy from non-living systems and by incorporating it into their own living systems. Culture is man's peculiar means of harnessing energy and of putting it to work in order to make human life secure. Culture grows and develops as ways of harnessing more energy per capita per year are found and as the means of making the expenditure of this energy more effective are improved. Animal husbandry, agriculture, water power, and the use of fuels in engines, together with countless inventions and improvements of tools and mechanical devices, mark the growth of culture as it is carried forward by technological advance.

The evolution of society is marked by two great stages: primitive or tribal, and civil or national. The tribe and clan are character-istics of primitive society (although the clan is by no means universal); the political state characterizes civil society. Primitive society is based upon kinship ties; civil society upon property relationships and territorial distinctions. Primitive society was relatively homogeneous structurally; civil society, more diversified.*

The transition from primitive to civil society was brought about by technological advance, specifically, by the development of agriculture, supplemented—though not everywhere—by the domestication of animals. The maturation of the agricultural arts produced the following chain of sequences: increased food supply, increase in population, increase in population density and in size of political groupings, diversion of human labor from food-producing to specialized arts and crafts, a new type of exchange and distribution of goods, money and markets, economic classes, and so on.

The differentiation of structure, the specialization of function, of civil society required a special mechanism to co-ordinate the

---

* See Lewis H. Morgan, *Ancient Society*, (New York, 1877), p. 6, for the classic statement of this thesis. Of this distinction A. R. Radcliffe-Brown writes: "Indeed we may agree with Morgan that the passage from lower forms of civilization to higher forms such as our own was essentially a passage from society based on kinship to the state based on political organization," "Some Problems of Bantu Sociology," (Bantu Studies, October, 1922), pp. 40-41.

various segments and classes of society and to integrate them into a coherent and effective whole. Such an integrative mechanism was produced. It was the "State-Church," i.e., a mechanism having temporal and ecclesiastical aspects.

The function of the state-church is to preserve the integrity of society against dissolution from within and against destruction from outside forces. In other words, this integrative mechanism must co-ordinate the various elements of society—occupational groups, social strata and classes—and relate them to one another harmoniously, on the one hand, and on the other, the life of the society must be made secure against the aggression of its neighbors. This integrative mechanism has a variety of forms. Church and state, priest and king, may be distinct or they may be one, structurally. And, of course, there are many degrees of overlapping or distinction. But everywhere in civil society—whether it be among the Maya or Inca of the New World, or in Mesopotamia, India, or China in the Old—we find this fundamental mechanism of co-ordination, integration, and regulation. And it always presents these two aspects: temporal and ecclesiastical. Thus we find it in ancient Egypt.

But one further observation before we turn to the culture history of Egypt itself: In civil societies where the temporal and ecclesiastical aspects of the integrative mechanism are structurally distinct there is always rivalry, a rivalry which not infrequently becomes a bitter struggle for power. This is not surprising, of course. Both church and state are engaged in the same tasks, both have the same function so far as the social organism is concerned, namely, integration, co-ordination, regulation. As Franklin D. Roosevelt once shrewdly observed: "That human agency which we call government is seeking through social and economic means the same goal which the churches are seeking through social and spiritual means." [11] The basis for rivalry is therefore plain. Each has its own "vested interest"; each tries to increase its power. The result is often a bitter struggle. We think offhand of the contest

between Henry VIII of England and the Roman Church, and of
the Church vs. State struggle throughout many centuries of European history. We recall Thomas Jefferson's diatribes against the
priests and churches and the efforts, not only to separate church
from state in America, but to render the former powerless. We
recall that Pius IX in his so-called Syllabus of Errors "claimed the
complete independence of the Church from state control; up-
held the necessity of a continuance of the temporal power of the
Roman See."

The position of the Roman Church on this issue has been well
set forth by Reverend H. Harrington as follows:

"Christendom is one society, and in that society the spiritual
authority is paramount because of its greater dignity, and the far
greater importance of its work. In any difficulties between spiritual
and temporal rulers the spiritual must be the judges, for without
treason to Christ they may not permit anything earthly however
important to interfere with the work of salvation. If therefore
the rulers of the church, even mistakenly, judge that this work is
hampered by some temporal policy, loyal Christians must abide
by the decision." [12]

There are numerous examples of political action taken by the
church in direct opposition to the state. To mention but a few:
Innocent III annulled the Magna Charta; Innocent X pronounced
the Treaty of Westphalia null and void; Pius IX condemned the
Austrian constitution of 1868; until 1904, Catholics in Italy were
prohibited by the Church from taking part in any parliamentary
election.

In Mexico in recent years we have witnessed a bitter struggle
between church and state. The issue has, of course, been couched
in religious terms. But everyone who understands the situation
knows that it is a question of who is to rule Mexico, the ultra-
montane clerical politicians or the temporal, national political
machine.

Finally, we may note the case of Russia. Under the Czars

church and state worked hand in hand. The church held vast
estates and other properties and received a grant of millions of
rubles from the state treasury every year. When the Bolsheviks
came to power they at once stripped the church of its *political*
functions. It is significant to note that not until this was done
was there any great outcry against "*religious* persecution" in
Russia. Under the Czars religious freedom hardly existed. There
were periodic pogroms in which thousands of persons of an alien
faith were done to death. Under the Soviets there was more
religious freedom—freedom for all faiths, freedom to believe and
to worship as one pleased—than there ever had been under the
old regime. Why then the great outcry from the clergy—Catholic,
Protestant, and Jewish alike? The answer is plain: the political
functions of the church had been done away with and their sources
of income virtually shut off.* The Bolsheviki had tried to abolish
the ecclesiastical arm of the integrative mechanism of the new
society. It is interesting to note, however, that the church has
been brought back to Russia in recent years and established once
again as an integrative mechanism. The church today is "the most
powerful unifying thing in Soviet civil life," the Metropolitan
Benjamin, titular head of the Russian Orthodox church in
America, said recently while on his way to Moscow. It is interesting to note that "Godless, anti-religious, Marxist" Russia conforms
to the pattern common to all nationalist states: the integrative
mechanism, the central nervous system, has its spiritual, as well as
its temporal, side.

V

Let us turn now to the culture history of Egypt and trace
the relationship between church and state, priest and king,
through the centuries.

---

* During a tour of Soviet Russia in 1929, I visited open churches of many
faiths. But, as a member of the clergy once complained to me: "We can't
live on kopeks!"

In the Old Kingdom (2800-2250 B.C.) we find the state, the Pharaoh, playing the leading role. To quote Breasted:

> . . . there arose at the beginning of the nation's history a state form of religion, in which the Pharaoh played the supreme role. In theory, therefore, it was he alone who worshipped the gods; in fact, however, he was of necessity represented in each of the many temples of the land by a high priest.[13]

The various temples and their respective priesthoods were supported by the produce from their endowments in land and by contributions from the royal revenues. It was the business of priests, in addition to their religious and ceremonial duties, to administer these lands and to collect revenue from them upon which they lived.

A few centuries later, during the Middle Kingdom, or the Feudal Age, we find that although the temples had increased somewhat in size, "the official cult was not materially altered, and there was still no large class of priests." [14]

But the basis for a rise to power of the priesthoods had long existed in their possession of lands which were under their control and whose produce was appropriated by them. In addition to this they received frequent contributions from the royal treasury. The temples were, of course, not subject to taxation. They were, therefore, in a favorable position to increase their wealth through accumulation and expansion, and to grow in political power as their wealth accumulated.

Under the Empire, First Period (beginning with Ahmose I, who completed the expulsion of the Hyksos about 1546 B.C.), the priesthoods had grown to considerable power and affluence. Says Breasted:

> As a natural consequence of the great wealth of the temples under the Empire, the priesthood becomes a profession, no longer merely an incidental office held by a layman, as in the Old and Middle Kingdoms. As the priests increase in numbers

they gain more and more political power; while the growing wealth of the temples demands for its proper administration a veritable army of temple officials of all sorts, who were unknown to the old days of simplicity.[15]

Not only were the temples becoming wealthier and the priesthoods more powerful, they were becoming unified as well:

Heretofore the priests of the various sanctuaries had never been united by any official ties, but existed only in individual and entirely separated communities without interrelation. All these priestly bodies were now united in a great sacerdotal organization embracing the whole land. The head of the state temple at Thebes, the High Priest of Amon, was the supreme head of this greater body also and his power was thereby increased far beyond that of his older rivals . . .[16]

Thus we find the priesthoods becoming wealthy, powerful, and organized. They are approaching the time when they will be able to threaten the supremacy of the Pharaoh himself, as we shall see.

We get some notion of the growing political power of the priesthoods from an incident that occurred during the feud of the Thutmosids. During the declining years of Thutmose I, one of his sons, born to the King by an obscure concubine, Thutmose III, was put upon the throne "by a highly dramatic coup d'etat" of the priests of Amon and in the temple of that god. In the struggles for the throne which followed, between Thutmose III and his half-brother Thutmose II, and between Thutmose III and his half-sister wife, Hatshepsut, the priests played an important part. Originally kept in the background by Thutmose III, Hatshepsut was eventually elevated to a position of supremacy by a group the most powerful member of which was Hapuseneb, who was both High Priest of Amon and vizier. "He thus united in his person all the power of the administrative government with that of the strong priestly party." [17]

These events took place about a century before the time of

Ikhnaton. During the reign of Amenhotep III, the father of Ikhnaton, one of the High Priests of Amon, Ptahmose by name, was
also one of the two grand viziers of the kingdom. Another held
the office of chief treasurer. During this reign also the priests of
Amon acquired some, if not complete control over the gold produced in the Sudan. In the use of spells used in mortuary rites
(hīke), the priests "were provided with a means of acquiring
wealth and influence which they did not fail to utilize to the
utmost." [18]

Thus we observe the growing power of the priesthoods. They
held the most important offices in the realm next to that of the
king himself. To have been chief treasurer of the kingdom must
have placed great power in the hands of the High Priests of Amon,
a power that was augmented by control over the gold supply
from the Sudanese mines. These priests could make and unmake
kings. They had but one more step to take: to seize the throne
for themselves. Breasted believes that Ikhnaton's father "had
evidently made some attempt to shake off the priestly hand that
lay so heavily on the sceptre, for he had succeeded Ptahmose by
a vizier who was not a High Priest of Amon." And Peet feels
that "it is not impossible that the increased power of the priesthood . . . was a circumstance which precipitated, if it did not
actually cause, the religious revolution of Ikhnaton." It was upon
this stage that Amenhotep IV was thrust at birth.[19]

VI

Amenhotep IV was born about 1409 B.C., the son of
Amenhotep III and his Queen Tiy. Estimates of his age at the
time he ascended the throne as coregent with his father vary
from nine to twenty-four years. For the first years of his reign,
according to those who believe he ascended to the throne as a
child, the affairs of state were managed by his mother. "To all
intents and purposes, Ti ruled Egypt for several years after her
husband's death," according to Wallis Budge, "and the boy king

did for a time at least what his mother told him." Glanville also believes that "Tiy clearly controlled him to some extent until he left Thebes." Although Amenhotep III did not die until about the tenth year of Ikhnaton's reign, he was in bad health during this period and seems to have had little to do with the government. The fact that his name was chiselled out of inscriptions in the sixth year of Ikhnaton's reign would seem to support this view.[20]

Very early in the reign of Amenhotep IV the worship of a supreme god, Aton, was inaugurated. Aton was none other than the old sun-god, Re, in a new role. Other gods were tolerated for a while, but with the growing resentment of the priesthoods, particularly that of Amon, Amenhotep IV built a new city-capital, Akhetaten, for his god, changed his name to Ikhnaton,* closed the temples of the other gods, dispossessed the priesthoods, confiscated their lands and revenues, and set to work to establish his new regime, both religious and political. All this had taken place by the sixth year of his reign.

Ikhnaton's reign was full of troubles as may well be imagined. Not only did he have a bitter struggle with powerful priesthoods on his hands, but by closing the temples he incurred the resentment and opposition of numerous other classes as well, such as tradesmen, artisans, actors, scribes, and even shepherds and peasants, who had a vested occupational interest in the old order. To be sure, the Heretic King had a group of loyal followers, whom he rewarded handsomely for their loyalty and support. Occupied as he was with a revolution at home, Ikhnaton had little or no time for affairs abroad. As a consequence, revolts flared up among Egypt's vassals in Asia, the Hittites in particular becoming defiant and aggressive. In the twelfth year of his reign, Ikhnaton's

* Amenhotep, "Amon is satisfied" (Peet) gives way to Ikhnaton, "It is well with the Aten, or Disk" (Pendlebury, Peet), or "He Who is Beneficial to Aton" (Steindorff and Seele); the old god gives way to the new in this change of names.

mother, Tiy, who resided in Thebes, visited Akhetaten, at which time she may have urged action against the revolting vassals and a moderation of policy at home, perhaps even a compromise with the priests of Aton. At any rate, we find Ikhnaton making a feeble gesture against the rebels abroad and initiating conciliatory measures at home. Smenkhkara, the "beloved" of Ikhnaton and now coregent with him, was sent to Thebes to effect a reconciliation with the priests of Amon.[21] But dissension now broke out in the king's own household. Although Ikhnaton seems to have been willing to compromise, Nefertiti, his wife, was not. At any rate, she fell into disgrace, or was estranged from her husband, and retired with some powerful followers to the north end of the city where she built a palace for herself. The political structure was disintegrating at home and abroad.

Ikhnaton died about 1369 B.C. at Akhetaten; Smenkhkara, the coregent, died at almost the same time in Thebes. Tutankhaten, a boy of nine, ascended the throne. By now the priestly party was growing rapidly in strength. The new king soon realized that he could stay on the throne only if he "came to terms with the supporters of the traditional faith," i.e., the priests. He was obliged to abandon his capital at Akhetaten and move his court to Thebes. He was compelled to abandon the heresy of Ikhnaton and to "acknowledge himself officially as an adherent of . . . Amun." Accordingly, he changed his name to Tutankhamun, "Beautiful in Life is Amun." In a manifesto he tells of his devotion to "his father Amun" and of his benefactions to his priests. He "made monuments for all the gods, fashioning their statues of pure djam-gold, restoring their sanctuaries . . . providing them with perpetual endowments, investing them with divine offerings for the daily service, and supplying their provisions on earth." [22] The triumph of the priests was virtually complete.

Tutankhamun reigned but nine years and was followed by Eye, a member of Ikhnaton's court. He too lasted but a short time.

Egypt was now in a state of anarchy. Even Thebes became a prey to plundering bands. Thus ended the Eighteenth Dynasty.

Out of this chaos and confusion law and order eventually emerged organized around a man who had been an important figure in Egyptian government for years. This man was Harmhab. He had been commander in chief of the army under Ikhnaton and Tutankhamun, and as deputy of the king he had attained a position in the empire second only to the king himself. Despite this fact, however, Harmhab was never converted to the Aton religion. He did not go to Akhetaten with his king but remained in Memphis where he had his residence. "He remained loyal to the old gods especially to the patron divinity of his native city and to Amun." [23] He was thus acceptable to the priests of Amon. With their backing and that of the army which was already under his control he ascended the throne. The ceremony of installation was in fact carried out by the priests of Amon themselves.[24] Some writers assert that he legalized his new position by marrying the sister of Nefertiti, but Alexander Scharff says that it "is certain" that this was not the case, that this assumption was born of an error of translation.[25]

Having come into power with priestly backing it is not surprising to see Harmhab busying himself with the restoration begun by Tutankhamun. As a matter of fact, as soon as his government was in working order he set about energetically to restore the temples and their priesthoods to their former condition of wealth and power:

He restored the temples from the pools of the Delta marshes to Nubia. He shaped all their images in number more than before, increasing the beauty in that which he made . . . He raised up their temples; he fashioned a hundred images with all their bodies correct and with all splendid costly stones. He sought the precincts of the gods which were in the districts in this land; he furnished them as they had been since the time of the first beginning. He established for them daily offerings every day. All the vessels of their temples were wrought of silver and gold. He equipped them with priests and with ritual priests and with the choicest of the army. He transferred to them lands and cattle, supplied with all equipment.[26]

Harmhab attempted to obliterate all traces of the era of heresy. He had the names of Ikhnaton, Tutankhamun, and Eye hacked from the monuments and his own put in their place. He considered himself the direct successor to Amenhotep III, as if Ikhnaton and his followers had never existed.

At Thebes, Harmhab razed the temple of Aton and used the materials to enlarge the temple of Amon. Aton's temple at Akhetaten was likewise despoiled to obtain building materials. Ikhnaton's "tomb was wrecked and its reliefs chiselled out; while the tombs of his nobles there were violated in the same way. Every effort was made to annihilate all trace of the reign of such a man; and when in legal procedure it was necessary to cite documents or enactments from his reign he was designated as 'that criminal of Akhetaton'." The prosperity and power of the priesthoods under Harmhab is well indicated by the words of Neferhotep, the priest of Amon:

"How bountiful are the possessions of him who knows the gifts of that god (Amon), the king of gods. Wise is he who knows him, favoured is he who serves him, there is protection for him who follows him." [27] Neferhotep "was at the moment receiving the richest tokens of the king's favour."

As Breasted observes, the triumph of Amon was now complete.

VII

We may now follow the course of the relationship between church and state in Egypt for a few more centuries.

The Nineteenth Dynasty began with wars of reconquest in Asia, followed by campaigns in Israel and against the Libyans.

With the death of Merenptah, son of Ramesses II, the land fell again into virtual anarchy from which it emerged in 1200 B.C. under Sethnakt, founder of the Twentieth Dynasty. Sethnakt came to the throne backed by the priesthoods, "these wealthiest and most powerful communities in Egypt." Ramesses III, Sethnakt's successor, was completely in the grip of the priests. The temples, says Breasted, "were fast becoming a grave political and economic menace." But Ramesses could do naught else but pour the wealth of the royal house into the sacred coffers with the most lavish liberality.[28]

We get a fair notion of the wealth and power of the priesthoods of the time of Ramesses III (1198-1167 B.C.) from an inventory in the Papyrus Harris which covers almost all of the temples of Egypt:

> . . . they possessed over one hundred and seven thousand slaves; . . . in all likelihood one person in every fifty was a slave of some temple. The temples thus owned two percent of the population. In lands we find the sacred endowments amounting to nearly three quarters of a million acres, that is, nearly one seventh, or over fourteen and a half percent of the cultivable land of the country . . . They owned nearly a half million head of . . . cattle; their combined fleets numbered eighty eight vessels, some fifty three workshops and shipyards . . . while in Syria, Kush and Egypt they owned in all one hundred and sixty nine towns. When we remember that all this vast property in a land of less than ten thousand square miles and some five or six million inhabitants was entirely exempt from taxation * it will be seen that the economic equilibrium of the state was endangered.[29]

Among the priesthoods, that of the god of Amon stood out as by far the richest and most powerful of all. Their estates and revenues were second only to those of the king. "The political

---

* This may be an overstatement; see Edgerton, 1947, p. 157.

power wielded by a community of priests who controlled such
vast wealth," says Breasted, "was from now on a force which no
Pharaoh could ignore. Without compromising with it and continually conciliating it, no Pharaoh could have ruled long." [30]

Sometimes the royal treasury stood empty while the temples
were loaded down with wealth. We read of workmen during the
reign of Ramesses III starving as they labored on some public
works until in desperation they gather before the office of their
master demanding their rations of grain. "Thus while the poor in
the employ of the state were starving at the door of an empty
treasury, the store-houses of the gods were groaning with
plenty." [31]

At the coronation of Ramesses IV, a "detailed list of all the
benefactions conferred . . . [by Ramesses III] on each and every
large and small temple of the land" was published. "In this
manner the new king contrived to confirm the clergy in their
holdings of property and to gain their influential good will for
his own reign . . . As the authority of the state grew weaker
. . . the power and prestige of Amun and his priesthood expanded
proportionately. All important public and private affairs were
regulated and decided either by the priesthood or by an oracle
which operated . . . in the imperial temple . . ." As Breasted
puts it, "the state was rapidly moving toward a condition in which
its chief function should be religious and sacerdotal, and the assumption of royal power by the High Priest of Amon but a very
natural and easy transition." [32]

It was not long until this transition did indeed take place. In
the reign of Ramesses XI, a man named Hrihor was appointed
high priest of Amon at Karnak. Next he became viceroy of Nubia
and commander in chief of the army. A little later he assumed the
vizierate of Upper Egypt. He now "had united under his personal
control all the highest spiritual, military, and civil functions of
the state. It was but a single step more to put aside the impotent
Ramesses XI and ascend the throne in his place. By this act of

usurpation (1085 B.C.), the secular state of the pharaonic empire was ushered to its grave and an ecclesiastical state was erected in its place, in which the chief god of Thebes exercised the authority through the medium of his priesthood." [33] The triumph of the priests was now complete.

VIII

No matter how individualistic Ikhnaton might have been, no matter how enormous his intellect and indomitable his will, he had his setting in a great nation, in a rich and mature culture, and we may assume that it affected his life as he is supposed to have so profoundly changed the world about him. Let us, therefore, turn to an examination of the relationship between Ikhnaton and the culture history of Egypt.

It is plain at the outset that the events which mark the reign of Ikhnaton are not novel by any means. Far from it; they are merely part of a process that had been going on for centuries before Ikhnaton was born, namely, the philosophic trend toward monotheism and the age-old rivalry between king and priest. This culture process receives more emphatic and dramatic expression during the lifetime of Ikhnaton, no doubt, but there is nothing original in it whatever.

Religious philosophy in Egypt had been moving in the direction of monotheism for centuries before Ikhnaton was born. We find in religious philosophy a reflection of the real world; the theology of a people will echo a dominant note in their terrestrial mode of life. A pastoral culture may find its image in a Good Shepherd and his flock; an era of cathedral building sees God as a Great Architect; an age of commerce finds Him with a ledger, jotting down moral debits and credits; emphasis upon the profit system and the high-pressure salesmanship that is required to make it function, picture Jesus as a super-salesman; * and, in an age of

---

* See Bruce Barton, *The Man Nobody Knows*, wherein Jesus is pictured as "a joyous, ripping good fellow, the perfect image of a 'go-getter' from the

science, God "is a god of law and order" (Millikan), a Great
Scientist moving about in his cosmic laboratory, his experiments
to perform.*

In ancient Egypt, theological thinking was, as Breasted has
so well said, "brought into close and sensitive relationship with
political conditions." [34] In the very early period, there were
numerous deities, many of which were *local* gods, or patrons of
little kingdoms. As the political unification of Egypt progressed,
a few of the greater gods emerged as *national* deities. As the nation
became more and more integrated under the rule of a powerful
single head, there was a tendency for one god to become supreme.
The ascendancy of Re, the sun-god, became marked during the
Fifth Dynasty and by the rise of the Twelfth Dynasty his supremacy was unquestioned. Other priesthoods,

. . . desirous of securing for their own, perhaps purely local
deity, a share of the sun-god's glory, gradually discovered that
their god was but a form and name of Re; and some of them
went so far that their theologizing found practical expression
in the god's name. Thus, for example, the priests of Sobk, a
crocodile god, who had no connection with the sun-god in the
beginning, now called him Sobk-Re. In like manner, Amon,
hitherto an obscure local god of Thebes, who had attained some
prominence by the political rise of the city, was from now on a
solar god, and was commonly called by his priest Amon-Re.
There were in this movement the beginnings of a tendency
toward a pantheistic solar monotheism, which we shall yet trace
to its remarkable culmination.[35]

The concept of Maat was developed from the designation of
personal qualities, or something practiced by individuals, to some-

---

Jazztown Rotary Club," (Beard, *The Rise of American Civilization*, II, one
vol. ed., New York, 1930), p. 729.
* Cf. *Living Philosophies* (New York, 1931), p. 44. Millikan's god seems
to bear a considerable likeness to a certain American Nobel prize-winner
physicist.

thing of national dimensions—a "spirit and method of a national guidance and control of human affairs . . . suffused with moral conviction. There was thus created for the first time a realm of universal values, and in conceiving the divine ruler of such a realm the Egyptians were moving on the road towards monotheism." [36]

But the conception of a supreme deity whose rule extended to the farthest reaches of the earth and embraced all lands and peoples was impossible so long as Egypt's power remained confined to the Nile valley. In the Pyramid Age the sun-god ruled only Egypt, and in the hymns of the day we find him standing guard at her frontiers, "where he builds the gates which restrain all outsiders from entering his inviolable domain." It is otherwise after Egypt's conquests abroad and the era of empire. Then the supreme god of Egypt became the Lord of the Universe. As Breasted has so succinctly put it: "Monotheism is but imperialism in religion." [37]

Thus we see that for centuries on end before the reign of Ikhnaton, religious philosophy in Egypt had been developing in the direction of monotheism as the political unification and imperial expansion of Egypt proceeded. And, as we have already seen, the rivalry between church and state, between priest and king, was already old before Amenhotep IV was born.

What then did Ikhnaton originate? The answer must be, "Virtually nothing." The trend toward monotheism was already there, and it was not until the latter years of his reign that Ikhnaton took the last logical step and attempted to abolish all other gods but Aton. As Breasted says, "this whole monotheistic movement is the culmination of the ancient recognition of a moral order by the Egyptian thinkers of the Pyramid Age and their creation of a realm of universal ethical values." Aton, the Disk god, was of sufficient importance during the reign of Ikhnaton's father to have a temple erected in his honor at Thebes. Even "the full name of the new deity, 'Re-Horus-of-the-Horizon who rejoices in his name of Shu who is the Disk' is to be ascribed not

to Akhenaten but to his father or even to some earlier king."
Indeed, the "most striking fact" pertaining to the various names
of the new deity "is that they embody a distinct attempt at continuity with the sun worship of past ages." The Hymn to Aton,
which was composed by Ikhnaton himself, according to the belief
of many authors (who, however, may know full well that the
addresses of modern heads of state are frequently written by
others), was remarkable but unoriginal, according to Peet. Two
architects of Amenhotep III, he writes, had already dedicated a
hymn to the sun-god which was "a very close anticipation of Ikhnaton's hymn to the disk . . . ; the ideas . . . [expressed in the
latter] are not at all new, nor indeed are the phrases in which these
ideas are embodied." Nor was Ikhnaton the first to erase the names
of his rivals from public monuments; this was done freely in the
feud of the Thutmosids.[38]

The struggle with the priesthoods was also acute when Ikhnaton
ascended the throne. We have already seen that the priests of
Amon held powerful offices under his father, Amenhotep III,
threatening the security of the throne. And Breasted says of them:
They were rich and powerful when Ikhnaton ascended the throne.
"They had installed Thutmose III as king, and could they have
supplanted with one of their own tools the young dreamer [Ikh-
naton] who now held the throne they would of course have done
so at the first opportunity." Moret, too, sees the drastic steps
taken by Ikhnaton as an attempt to "break the power of the
priests of Amon lest they should dethrone the kings." [39]

With the throne in danger of being captured by the priests, is
it necessary to assume that it was a new philosophy germinating
in the mind of an adolescent genius that precipitated the move
against the priests and temples—especially when this philosophy
was not new? Would it not be more reasonable to assume that
it was a bold and drastic step taken by the temporal government
in self-defense, in self-preservation? To close the temples and
confiscate their lands and revenues would be a doubly effective

political move: it would strengthen the throne at the same time that it weakened its rivals. It is significant to note that it was not a priesthood of the new god Aton who succeeded to the estates of Amon. Ikhnaton was himself the First Prophet of Aton, and as such assumed control of the vast wealth of his god. "This appropriation of the property of the temples," observes Moret, "shows us what lay beneath the religious revolution, the economic and political objects of the rupture." [40] It was probably not the first time that struggles for terrestrial power were carried on in terms of celestial ideology; it certainly has not been the last. The break between Ikhnaton and the priests was therefore but the culmination of centuries of rivalry and competition between palace and temple. With the growing power of the priests a drastic move was necessary if the king was to retain his independence. For the temporal government it was do or die. The maturing philosophy of monotheism provided an excellent pretext and a weapon. But it was merely the means employed; it was not the cause.

The position taken by some writers on this issue is rather curious. Thus, as we have already seen, Peet believes that "the increased power of the priesthood . . . was a circumstance which precipitated, *if it did not actually cause*, the religious revolution of Ikhnaton" [41] (emphasis ours). On the very next page, however, he says that it is "only an inference" to explain the revolution as a struggle between priests and king. Yet he accepts Ikhnaton's "peculiar genius"—about which we know absolutely nothing directly—as one of the causes of the revolution! In another essay, also, Peet discounts the political aspect of the revolution and portrays Ikhnaton as a theologian.[42] He explains the failure of Ikhnaton's revolution in terms of a conflict of philosophies rather than as a clash of political forces.[43] But *why* did the Aton religion fail? Why could it not win out over older beliefs? This is something that Peet's theory does not explain. Wallis Budge says that Ikhnaton failed "because his religion did not appeal to the tradition and religious instincts and susceptibilities [whatever they are, L.A.W.] that already existed among the Egyptians." [44] But is not this begging the very question at issue? Why did Ikhnaton's religion fail to appeal to the Egyptians? To say that a theological revolution failed because the new creed could win no converts is merely to say that it failed. It is like saying that a fire went out because it quit burning.

Thus we see that those who interpret the revolution of Iknaton's reign as a philosophical, or theological, affair account for political events in terms of rival philosophies, but they do not explain the philosophies. Our theory does both. It explains the struggle between Ikhnaton and the priests in terms of the structure of civil societies and the function of the State-Church as an integrative and regulative mechanism. And it explains the philosophies as instruments used by priests and king in this struggle. The philosophy of Ikhnaton failed because the political and economic power of the priesthoods was greater than that of the Pharaoh's party.

In this connection we may consider the close relationship between Queen Hatshepsut and Senenmut. Steindorff and Seele wonder what it was that caused Hatshepsut to heap honors and favors upon this man. The "manner [in which] he forged the bonds which brought him in close relations with his royal mistress . . . is a closed page of history" [45] they say. We suggest that our theory may be illuminating here also. Hatshepsut was not only a usurper, she was a woman and as such should not ascend the throne of god-men. Senenmut "had in early youth entered service in the temple of Amun at Karnak and before long had successively occupied a series of important posts." In short, he was an adroit and successful priestly politician and a powerful member of the priestly party. Hatshepsut needed help to seize and hold the throne. Senenmut brought to her side the aid of a powerful priesthood. Hatshepsut richly rewarded him for his support. In the light of our theory, the relationship between them does not seem obscure at all but rather obvious.

Priests and kings serve their own respective interests—as does every other class in society. When their interests diverge they fight each other, as in the case of Ikhnaton or Henry VIII. When, however, each can serve his own interest by helping the other, they will co-operate, as in the case of Hatshepsut and Senenmut.

IX

What part did Ikhnaton himself play in the stirring events of his reign? As we have already seen, numerous authors tell us that this young genius, virtually single-handed, initiated this revolution and carried it forward by his zeal and his indomitable will. But what is this but inference? What do we *know* directly about Ikhnaton's actions and what may be reasonably inferred from known facts?

In the first place, if we take Elliot Smith's estimate of his age at the time of his death, based upon an examination of his supposed skeletal remains, Ikhnaton was but a boy of nine, or at the most thirteen, when he ascended the throne. The "revolution" would have been well under way, therefore, when he was fifteen or nineteen. It has seemed so incredible that a youth could have accomplished all this "despite the precocity of youth in the east," that, as Professor Peet has observed, "archaeologists one and all fought shy of accepting so great an improbability." [46] They therefore put pressure upon Elliot Smith to raise his estimate of Ikhnaton's age. He did increase it from twenty-six to thirty but "he was not prepared to go further" at that time. More recently, however, he has been persuaded that Ikhnaton suffered from *Dystocia*, "one of the principal symptoms of which is the failure of the bones to knit properly . . . ossification ceases to be a test of age." [47] The archeologists may now have Ikhnaton as old as they wish!

The view that Ikhnaton *must* have been more than a boy during the early years of his reign *because* tremendously important events took place at that time is a curious one to take. Must the life of a great nation stand still, must history mark time, until boy kings grow up? It is rather generally admitted that Tutankhamun was but a boy of nine when he ascended the throne. Newberry believes that Ay "must have been the dominating personality in Egypt's political affairs" at this time. Steindorff and Seele assume that the boy king was "completely under the control of Eye," and Pendlebury believes that Nefertiti's influence upon Tutankhamun must have kept him faithful to the new religion while she lived. If we can have a boy king, with actual rule by others, in the case of Tutankhamun, why not with Ikhnaton? In this connection we may recall that Louis XIII of France ascended the throne at the age of nine years, Louis XIV at only five. Peter the Great came to the throne when he was ten; Charles XII of Sweden, at the ripe old age of fifteen.[48]

In speaking of Hatshepsut, Breasted takes it for granted that a powerful group of nobles and officials supported her and worked with her as a means of serving their own interests. He points out that "the fortunes and probably the lives of these men were identified with the success and the dominance of Hatshepsut; they therefore took good care that her position should be maintained."[49] This sounds reasonable and is in accord with everything we know about ruling cliques everywhere, from Julius Caesar to Hitler, Stalin, or Franklin Roosevelt. One man may be the titular head of the government. But without the aid and support of a powerful group of fellow politicians no one, be he king, pope, president, or dictator, can stay in office very long.

There is evidence of such a group surrounding young Ikhnaton. Breasted remarks that, idealist and dreamer though he was, "Ikhnaton understood enough of the old policy of the Pharaohs to know that he must hold his party by practical rewards." Numerous reliefs show Ikhnaton rewarding his followers with gold and honors for their allegiance. Ramose, the Vizier, is shown "loaded with gifts by the Pharaohs, as though in reward for his allegiance." One relief shows Ikhnaton, his wife and daughter showering gold upon Meryra, who had become High Priest of Aton, "on some occasion when he had been particularly successful in collecting the yearly dues of the temple . . ." "Abundant are the rewards," Meryra cries upon being installed as High Priest, "which the Aton knows to give when his heart is pleased." And another one of Ikhnaton's lieutenants says with disarming frankness: "How prosperous is he who hears thy teaching of life!" [50]

. All this sounds strangely familiar. To anyone who is familiar with the political machines of American cities and states, or to one who knows anything about the organization and conduct of ruling cliques anywhere in the world, with their community of interests and rewards for "faithful service" and support, this picture of ancient Egypt will present no mystery. Whether Ikhnaton was a dominant figure or only a figure-head is immaterial. In either case we have a dominant, ruling clique. They possess the power, they control the wealth, and they share the spoils. It is an old familiar pattern. Breasted and Weigall try to put a religious and philosophic complexion upon this tight little political machine that ruled and exploited Egypt. Weigall comments upon the rewards bestowed upon those who were intelligent enough to grasp the lofty concepts taught by Ikhnaton, and Breasted speaks of the "nucleus of men who really appreciated the ideal aspects of the king's teaching." But the anatomy of machine politics shows so clearly through its ideological vestments that both are obliged to admit that many of Ikhnaton's followers were probably more concerned with the very earthly desire for riches and honors than with a lofty view of the cosmos.[51]

X

Every effort has been made to extoll the originality and uniqueness of Ikhnaton and to emphasize his importance as an individual in the culture history of Egypt. He is but a boy when he ascends the throne, and only an adolescent when the "revolution" gets well under way. "Still, when one calls to mind the infant prodigies, the child preachers who stir an audience at an early age," Weigall writes, "one may credit a boy of eighteen or nineteen with the planning of a new city" and the founding of a new religion. Weigall does not cite any specific examples of child prodigies; perhaps he was thinking of the boy Jesus teaching the elders.[52]

Ikhnaton's anatomical and psychological peculiarities have been used to support the conception of him as a phenomenon among men. "His skull was misshapen," Weigall tells us, "and he must have been subject to occasional epileptic fits." He thinks the king must have had hallucinations, also. Some great men have been epileptic—Mohammed and Napoleon, for example. Religious leaders often have hallucinations. If, therefore, Ikhnaton was an epileptic and had hallucinations, it would indicate that he was a most unusual phenomenon—at least so it was reasoned, apparently.[53]

But what basis is there for Weigall's suppositions? Neither epilepsy nor hallucinations can be inferred from the sculptures and reliefs nor from the supposed mummy of Ikhnaton, and we know of no evidence of these traits from contemporary records.

There is, however, some evidence that indicates or at least strongly suggests that Ikhnaton was pathological in some respects, but this evidence is confused, self-contradictory at points, and certainly inconclusive.

The statues and reliefs, according to Moret, depict Ikhnaton as "a stripling of medium height, with slender bones and delicate modelling" at the time of his ascension to the throne. Later, however, he "became rounded and effeminate—a hermaphrodite figure with prominent breasts, wide hips and thighs too much curved, which makes one suspect a morbid nature, with some pathological flaw." Sir Marc A. Ruffer speaks of "the pathological obesity" of Ikhnaton, although his face, neck and legs were thin. "Where the king is represented distributing collars of gold," says this author, "his abdomen actually hangs over the edge of the balcony, a most realistic piece of portraiture." But in balcony scenes reproduced in Breasted's *A History of Egypt* (Fig. 139) and Moret, *The Nile and Egyptian Civilization* (Fig. 63), and in other works, he is shown as a very slender man indeed. Gardiner says "the portraits represent him with . . . a deformed *emaciated* body" (emphasis ours). Thus, the evidence of representations in art is inconsistent and inconclusive.[54]

When we turn to the mummy supposed by some to be that of Ikhnaton, we find the picture so confused and full of contradictions that we are inclined to give up in despair and conclude that for the present at least the evidence is insufficient to warrant a definitive verdict of any kind. Weigall says that "there can be no doubt that the mummy found in the tomb of Queen Tiy was that of Akhnaton." Elliot Smith, the British anatomist who examined the skeletal remains believed that "we have the most positive evidence that these bones are the remains of Khouniatonou [Ikhnaton]." Other scholars, however, have, on the basis of researches since the skeleton in question was found, come to deny or to doubt that the bones are those of Ikhnaton. Thus, Kurt Sethe is convinced that certain evidence "proves" that the body cannot have been that of the heretic king: "For us it is sufficient that the body cannot in any case be that of the king in whose coffin it found a resting place." A decade later, R. Engelbach expressed his conviction that the mummy was not that of Ikhnaton; he thinks it is the remains of Smenkhkara. Derry shares Engelbach's view in this matter. Peet has expressed his doubt. And Pendlebury says that "there is every reason to suppose that it is his [i.e., Smenkhkara's] skeleton, found in the cache of Queen Ty at Thebes, which has so long passed for that of Akhenaten." [55]

The age at time of death of the person whose skeleton is under consideration has been the subject of much debate, also. Elliot Smith originally estimated the age at death at twenty-four to twenty-six years. But, as we have seen, archeologists were very unwilling to accept this estimate since it would have made Ikh-

naton but a boy when he became king and hence would have
been too young to do all that he was supposed to have done.
Under considerable pressure from the archeologists, Elliot Smith
reconsidered. He came to the conclusion that the bones showed
signs of "a rare disorder, only recently recognized by physicians,"
known as Dystocia adiposo-genitalis. "One of the effects of this
condition," he says, "is to delay the process of the consolidation
of the bones." Therefore, he concludes, the person in question
may have been as old as thirty or even thirty-six at the time of
his death. But, he cannot resist adding, the bones *still* appear to
him to be those of a man who died in his early twenties! Professor
Derry believes that the bones indicate an age of not more than
twenty-three years. Regarding the pathology of the individual,
there is flat contradiction as well as confusion. Elliot Smith, who
was the first to examine the skeleton, was convinced that he had
had hydrocephalus. A. R. Ferguson, Professor of Pathology in
the Cairo School of Medicine, who also examined the cranium,
declared, according to Elliot Smith, that "the signs of hydrocephalus were unquestionable." Derry, who examined the cranium
after further restoration of it, declared that "the conformation of
the skull does not support the statement that the person to whom
it belonged suffered from hydrocephalus . . . It is indeed *the very
reverse* of the shape produced by hydrocephalus," [56] (emphasis
ours).

In view of the evidence and conflicting testimony, we believe
we would be justified in drawing the following conclusions: 1.
We do not *know* whose skeleton was found; 2. Its age is somewhat uncertain but probably not more than twenty-five years;
and 3. The clinical diagnosis is inconclusive.

XI

Attempt has also been made to account for Ikhnaton's greatness by claiming that he was of foreign extraction. Weigall says
that "it must always be remembered that the king had much

foreign blood in his veins." Ruffer suggests that "his peculiar genius may have been due to the foreign blood in his veins." Numerous authors believe that Ikhnaton's mother, Tiy, was not an Egyptian, although Breasted says that "there is not a particle of evidence to prove her of foreign birth, as is so often claimed." [57]

Elliot Smith finds evidence of non-Egyptian ancestry in the facial skeleton. The differences between Ikhnaton and his father are "far more than individual differences, for they are racial. Amenothes III's face is cast in the Egyptian mould; but in the case of Khouniatonou, the jaw is typically Armenoid, a fact most clearly demonstrated in the form of its ascending ramus." [58]

It would not be surprising at all if Ikhnaton should prove to have "foreign blood in his veins." We know that a number of Egyptian kings before Ikhnaton had wives from Asia. But what is the significance of this foreign blood or the Armenoid jaw so far as intelligence or character, monotheism or political reform, are concerned? The answer can only be: precisely nothing.

XII

How then are the striking events which took place in Egypt between 1375 and 1358 B.C. to be explained? We can choose between two types of interpretation: the one is psychological and anthropomorphic; the other is culturological. What are their relative merits?

We have already seen that what took place during Ikhnaton's reign was but a continuation and a culmination of cultural trends that had been going on for centuries before the "Heretic King" was born. Philosophic development toward monotheism was already well advanced before Ikhnaton's birth. The rivalry between the throne and the temple, the struggle between priest and king for power, was already hoary with age in 1386 B.C. More than that, this sort of competition is a characteristic of *all* nations where the temporal and ecclesiastical aspects of the central integrative mechanism are structurally differentiated. We observe these cultural trends continuing in Egypt for centuries after Ikhnaton's death. The attempt of the throne to eliminate the ecclesiastical component of the integrative mechanism failed, as fail it must; the ecclesiastic aspect of social integration and regulation has not yet been eliminated from any nation so far, as the re-establishment of the church in the Soviet Union makes emphatically clear. The contest between church and state in Egypt continued after Ikhnaton's death with the priests growing in power as they had in the reigns before his time. The theology of monotheism collapsed for the time being but we can trace this current of thought in the centuries following Ikhnaton. In short, the stirring events of Ikhnaton's reign can be accounted for as a part of a great process of cultural change and development. And we can explain this process in terms of itself. It is composed of complexes and classes of cultural elements—philosophic, political, economic—which continually act and react upon one another, producing changes of all sorts, new combinations and syntheses, and new alignments. We can explain this culture process in ancient Egypt in exactly the same way that we can account for the changes brought about in American culture by the introduction of the automobile. We do not need to call upon great men or upon psychological forces to make them intelligible.

What does the anthropomorphic, psychological—the Great Man —interpretation have to offer?

In the first place, we must ask, What could a man, a human organism, of exceptional quality and ability have done in this or any situation except to respond to it—to work with the materials at hand, to try to cope with the problems confronting him; in short, to fit himself to the culture process that is his context? A man of superior neuro-sensory-glandular-muscular make-up might have made a better, i.e., more effective, response than one of inferior brains and physique, but the pattern of the response would have been substantially the same because it would have been determined by the same cultural situation. Furthermore, the difference between the mentality of one man and another is slight indeed when measured against the background of an age-old cultural process. So that even if Ikhnaton were an organism of exceptionally fine quality, this fact would not at all suffice to explain the events of his reign.

But we do not know that Ikhnaton was an organism of superior quality. On the contrary, virtually all that we know about him indicates that he was a diseased and hence an inferior organism. Why, then, has historian after historian explained this period of Egyptian history by pointing to the colossal genius of this man?

The answer seems to be that, as we indicated at the outset, the old, primitive, anthropomorphic type of thinking that has been so popular for so many hundreds of thousands of years has not yet been outgrown. Science, and especially social science, is still too young to have made itself felt in historical interpretation to any great extent. And the science of culture is still so new as to make its proper designation, "culturology," sound outlandish. The pathetic thing about Great Man interpretations of history is that they leave the great man unexplained. It is like the medieval explanation of fossils: produced by "stone-making forces."

What Breasted, Weigall, Moret and others have done is to create a personality for Ikhnaton and then to explain events in the culture process by citing various traits of this personality. The image of Ikhnaton is created by inference: great events took place during his reign, therefore a great mind and will must have brought them about; the struggle with the priesthoods was bitter and prolonged, therefore Ikhnaton was a man of determination and perseverance; a new era in art was inaugurated, therefore the young king was original and creative. He must have had "foreign blood in his veins" because his ideas were so novel. He must have been older than his supposed skeletal remains indicate because one so young could not have accomplished so much, and so on. We may cite a particularly striking example of this. Sir Marc A.

IKHNATON   **269**

Ruffer, who made a study of the palaeopathology of ancient Egypt,
and who consequently was intimately acquainted with the evidence indicating Ikhnaton's abnormality, nevertheless argues as
follows:

". . . a monarch who founds a monotheistic religion in the
teeth of the opposition of a most powerful priesthood, who builds
a new town where he worships his god away from old associations
and among congenial surroundings, who endows that new town
with beautiful temples, who patronizes a new form of art, and
who perhaps composed the magnificent hymn to Aton, cannot
be considered as lacking in energy, or as a degenerate, or an
effeminate person." [59] Thus, certain facts indicating pathology
are not permitted for a moment to interfere with a cherished illusion of historical interpretation. Surely the mastery of myth over
realism could go no further.

Sometimes these psychological interpretations contradict each
other. Thus Sir Marc cites Ikhnaton's "pathological obesity" as a
possible reason for the loss of Egypt's Asiatic empire. "The extreme corpulency of the king," he writes, "may have been
responsible for his politics. On account of his obesity he probably
disliked physical exertion, and this may have been the reason why
he persistently refused to lead his army to war when the outlying
provinces were threatened." But when he surveys the great achievements of the Eighteenth Dynasty, he is impressed with the
"tireless energy" that characterized its rulers, Ikhnaton as well
as Ahmose! [60]

The fact is that we know very little indeed about Ikhnaton as
a political figure and virtually nothing about his personality and
character. It is usually said that Amenhotep III was Ikhnaton's
father, but Newberry asserts that this is merely an assumption:
"This is nowhere asserted on any Egyptian inscription." Concerning the ancestry of other intimates of Ikhnaton—his wife, Nefertiti, his "beloved" coregent Smenkhkara, and his son-in-law and
successor, Tutankhamun—"nothing whatever is definitely known"

(Newberry). His age at the time of his accession has been much debated and is still uncertain. Evidence concerning his health and physical condition is so varied as to be virtually worthless. We do not know why he became estranged from his wife. We do not know how he met his death, whether from natural causes or by violence. And, finally, we do not know where he was laid to rest. If, therefore, we do not have adequate information of this sort, data on Ikhnaton as a king, a political institution, how could we expect to have any reliable information pertaining to his personality and character? Indeed, do we have any facts at all on this subject? [61]

That Ikhnaton actually lived is not questioned, and he must therefore have had a personality and a character. But these cannot be inferred or deduced from the political history of Egypt. There is sharp disagreement today concerning the personality and character of the late Franklin D. Roosevelt, about whom we have a vast amount of factual data obtained by direct observation. The same might be said of Lenin, Hitler, Wilson, or any other outstanding political figure of recent times. What then can we hope to know or understand of this remote Egyptian king as a person? Yet students without number give us the most intimate and personal details about him, and they do it with confidence and assurance. Indeed, they give the impression of drawing upon the report of an exhaustive psychiatric analysis.

The extent to which the personality and character of Ikhnaton have been created ad hoc by scholars to explain the facts of Egyptian culture history is sometimes remarkable. One gets the impression that Weigall could not have known his hero better had he been a member of Amenhotep III's household at the time of Ikhnaton's birth and had associated with him daily until his death. Weigall describes him as ". . . a quiet, studious boy, whose thoughts wandered in fair places, searching for that happiness which his physical condition had denied to him. His nature was gentle; his young heart overflowed with love. He delighted, it would seem, to walk in the gardens of the palace, to hear the birds singing, to watch the fish in the lake, to smell the flowers, to follow butterflies, to warm his small bones in the sunshine." [62] Only where one knows so little can one write so much; the absence of facts gives the imagination free rein.

Thus in the Great Man interpretation of history the known facts of the culture process are explained by the pseudo-facts of psychology, the known by the unknown. A worse error of reasoning would be hard to find—within or outside the field of scholarship.

XIII

To be sure, not all students of Egypt have interpreted the history of Ikhnaton's reign in this anthropomorphic fashion; many have seen clearly that these political and theological events were the logical expression of a cultural historical process. As a matter of fact, Breasted himself describes and documents this process very well indeed as our quotations from his works show. But he seems to have given relatively little weight to cultural historical interpretation as compared with biographic and psychiatric explanation. Let us turn now briefly to those who have emphasized, or at least have called specific attention to, the process of culture history in their interpretations of Ikhnaton.

"Up to a few years ago," writes T. E. Peet, "it was customary to believe that this entire movement was a product of the brain of Ikhnaton . . . This we now know to be incorrect . . . it [is] now necessary to see in the movement not merely the personal influence of an original genius, but also the inevitable product of the conditions of the time." [63]

James Baikie writes: "It is evident, therefore, that Atenism was not the sudden break with all the religious past of Egypt which it is often represented as being; . . . [it] had its roots deep in native soil, and could be traced as far back as you can trace anything in the history of the land." [64]

John Pendlebury declares that Ikhnaton was not "the first individual in history, as has been claimed," and points out that actually "we know less about him personally than about many of his predecessors." Also, he not only recognizes the antecedents of the new religion but suggests Minoan inspiration for the new art at Akhetaten which has so often been attributed to the genius of Ikhnaton himself. This "startling change . . . in the spirit and outlook of Egyptian art," he says, "can only be attributed to a sudden intensification of Minoan influence," occasioned by the destruction of Knossos and the collapse of the Minoan empire. H. Frankfort believes that the art of Ikhnaton may have derived some inspiration from the works of the reign of Thutmosis.[65]

We also find a live appreciation of the role of cultural forces in history in the writings of Steindorff and Seele, P. E. Newberry, S. R. K. Glanville, and others. Many of these students do, however, as we have pointed out earlier, invoke the peculiar traits of Ikhnaton's personality as a means of accounting for the remarkable events of his reign.

XIV

What we have said about Ikhnaton so far would apply to any great man who has been invoked to explain historical events. We now wish to turn to aspects of the scholars' image of the Heretic King that are peculiar to him.

When Breasted, Weigall and others create a phenomenal person to explain remarkable historical events they are, as we have seen, following a tradition that has flourished since the Old Stone Age. But they had an added reason for their exaltation of Ikhnaton. This is to be found in the religious outlook of these authors.

It would appear from their discussion of Ikhnaton's role in philosophic evolution that Breasted and Weigall believe that there *is* a God, that there is only *one* God, and it would seem, He *is* an English-speaking, Protestant deity. They appear to assume also—their assumptions are implicit rather than explicit, as is so frequently the case in philosophic or scientific discussions, and the more basic the premise the more likely it is to remain unexplicit—that mankind as a whole has been moving slowly toward a realization that there is only one God and one true faith—the one taught by Jesus Christ. As culture advanced, mankind came closer and closer to a recognition of the one true God and to sense the precepts that were eventually to be expounded by His Son.

Now, for some reason which these authors do not make clear, God—the one and only God, our God, the English-speaking, Protestant God—decided to reveal himself to this Egyptian king about 1400 B.C. Ikhnaton caught the vision, was fired by it, and thereafter devoted his whole life, with passionate zeal, to an attempt to establish the true faith. But he failed. The people were not ready for it. Or, perhaps God miscalculated and revealed Himself too soon. But though this adventure in monotheism failed all was not lost. The precious truth had been let out and truth cannot and will not die. It was somehow communicated to the Hebrews who, after some centuries of incubation, were to bring it forth again in the person of Jesus Christ.

Such is our theory about Breasted and Weigall. Let us now see what there is to support it.

Weigall believes that Ikhnaton was "the first man to whom God revealed himself . . . For the first time in the history of man the real meaning of God, as we now understand it, had been comprehended." [66] Osiris was but a mythological being. So were Ptah, Set, and Horus. Even Amon-Re was but a superstition. But the God who revealed himself to Ikhnaton was genuine; this time it was real.

Ikhnaton was, according to Breasted, a "God-intoxicated man, whose mind responded with marvellous sensitiveness and discernment to the visible evidences of God about him. He was fairly ecstatic in his sense of the beauty of the eternal and universal light . . . While to the traditional Pharaoh the state god was only the triumphant conqueror, who crushed all peoples and drove them tribute-laden before the Pharaoh's chariot, Ikhnaton saw in him the beneficent father of all men. *It was the first time in history that a discerning eye has caught this great universal truth,"* [67] (emphasis ours).

Ikhnaton devoted himself with "feverish fanaticism" to spreading the true faith, "fully convinced that he might entirely recast the world of religion." [68]

After Ikhnaton had caught the vision of the true God he became impatient with the paganism of his fellow countrymen:

> Boldly he looked to God as a child to its father; and having solved what he deemed to be the riddle of life, there was no place in his mind for aught but an open, fearless adoration of the creator . . . Akhnaton was the sworn enemy of the table-turners of his day, and the tricks of priestcraft . . . were anathema to his pure mind (Weigall).[69]

With a revolution at home on his hands it is not surprising that the king did not have sufficient means to protect Egyptian possessions abroad. But our authors have another explanation for Egypt's loss of empire at the close of the Eighteenth Dynasty. It was because (1) Ikhnaton was too engrossed in his new philosophy to concern himself with politics, and (2) like Christ, he was opposed to brute force:

> "Instead of gathering the army so sadly needed in Naharin, Amenhotep IV immersed himself heart and soul in the thought of the time, and the philosophizing theology of the priests was of more importance to him than all the provinces of Asia . . . It shows the astonishing leniency of Ikhnaton in a manner which would indicate that he was opposed to measures of force" (Breasted). So he sat "singing hymns to the Disk at Tell el-Amarna while the vast empire bequeathed to him by his fathers" went to pieces.[70]

Weigall tells us that Egypt lost her empire because it was against Ikhnaton's principles to fight. He "had the power to let loose upon

Asia an army which would silence all insult but [he] did not find such a step consistent with his principles . . . Akhnaton definitely refused to do battle believing that a resort to arms was an offence to God . . . like that greater Teacher 1300 years later . . . the Pharaoh suffered a very Agony as he realized that his principles were leading him to the loss of all his dearest possessions." [71]

The image of Ikhnaton created by Breasted and Weigall bears a considerable likeness to that of Jesus Christ, as is no doubt proper to one whose mission is to bring the true faith to mankind. He was indeed "the first prophet of history . . . like Jesus . . . a prophet both of nature and of human life" (Breasted).[72]

Our authors see in Ikhnaton the first expression of the true faith that is now ours. "The faith of the patriarchs is the lineal ancestor of the Christian faith; but the creed of Akhnaton is its isolated prototype. One might believe that Almighty God had for a moment revealed himself to Egypt, and had been more clearly, though more momentarily, interpreted there than ever He was in Syria or Palestine before the time of Christ" (Weigall).[73]

Both Breasted and Weigall call attention to similarities between Egyptian hymns to Aton and Psalms of the Hebrews. Breasted points out that about "a chapter and a half of the Book of Proverbs is largely drawn verbatim from the Wisdom of Amenemope; that is, the Hebrew version is practically a literal translation from the Egyptian." The "teachings of the Egyptian sages exerted a profound influence on Hebrew religious thinking and, having thus effected lodgment in Palestine, they had advanced through the first stage in their long transition from Egypt to us of the modern world." *

---

* Breasted, The Dawn of Conscience, p. 22. Baikie admits that the resemblance between the Egyptian hymn and the Hebrew Psalter 104 is "indeed sufficiently striking" but sees "no need to imagine that there was borrowing on the part of the later author" (The Amarna Age, p. 321). W. O. E. Oesterly, on the other hand, feels that the evidence of historical connection is "convincing" ("Egypt and Israel," pp. 244-45, in The Legacy of Egypt, S. R. K. Glanville, ed.).

Thus Ikhnaton is not merely the Great Man who moves and shapes the culture history of Egypt; he becomes the instrument of Divine Purpose. Through him did God first reveal himself to man. But the time was not yet ripe; paganism and idolatry were still too strongly entrenched. So the revelation was handed on, perhaps from Joseph to Moses, down the ages until He who came to redeem us all was born.

Breasted was once enrolled in a Protestant theological school. It is probable that Weigall was a Protestant, also. It is of some interest, therefore, to note the way in which the Roman Catholic church regards this "God-intoxicated man." Plainly, they do not like him. "With the single exception of Amenhotep IV," says the Catholic Encyclopedia, "who allowed himself to be drawn into a scheme to reform the Egyptian religion, all its kings were wise and just rulers." [74] But, after all, no ecclesiastical hierarchy is likely to approve of a temporal ruler who closes temples, drives out priests, and confiscates their wealth. The other Pharaohs, however, those who, according to this Catholic authority were "great builders, and devoted their vast resources . . . to the erection of magnificent temples . . . which they richly endowed"— these rulers he finds were "wise and just." It will be noted, too, that this writer says that Ikhnaton "allowed himself to be drawn into" the scheme to reform Egyptian religion; in other words, that the movement against the priesthoods was a political device of temporal politicians to safeguard or enhance their power. Catholic scholars do not take much stock in the theory that God revealed himself first to an Egyptian. They scout the notion that Moses may have been influenced by the teachings of Ikhnaton:

"Although Moses, learned as he was in the wisdom of the Egyptians, may have been indebted to an Egyptian model for one or two external features in his organization of Divine worship, he was, thanks to the Divine inspiration, entirely original in the establishment of the Jewish priesthood, which is based on the unique idea of Jahweh's covenant with the Chosen People." [75]

The author of the article "Egypt" in the Catholic Encyclopedia is much too sophisticated in the ways of politicians whether temporal or ecclesiastical to believe that it was Ikhnaton's supernatural vision and religious zeal that animated him. "The effort of Amenhotep IV," he writes, "to introduce the cult of his only god, Aton, was perhaps not prompted exclusively by a religious ideal, as is generally supposed." He believes the long trend toward monotheism in Egypt "must have been encouraged by the Pharaohs in their capacity rather of political than of religious rulers of the nation." [76]

Jewish scholars, too, reject the idea that Moses may have been influenced by Ikhnaton. They admit that the "concept of Divine Unity has appeared among other religious and philosophic groups," but insist that "Hebrew monotheism is unique." *

If Ikhnaton was indeed the means of the first revelation of God to man, it was apparently, as we have suggested, the Protestant deity who made himself known.

XV

The drama of Ikhnaton and monotheism is excellent material for the artist as well as for the historian and scientist. Thomas Mann uses Joseph in Egypt as the vehicle for his message to a world sick and in turmoil. Amenhotep III, the father of Ikhnaton, was the pharaoh of Egypt during the earlier part of Joseph's life, according to Harry Slochower's interpretation of Mann's novel. [77] Potiphar, the eunuch husband of Mut, was allied with the growing Aton movement; Mut, with the party of Amon. The symbolism

---

* Abraham Shusterman, "Monotheism," in The Universal Jewish Encyclopedia, Vol. VII (New York, 1942), p. 624. It will be recalled that James Baikie was unwilling to admit that Hebrew psalmists may have drawn upon Egyptian hymns. Now Baikie was a clergyman. Thus it would appear that all clerical scholars—Catholic, Protestant, and Jewish alike—are unwilling to admit any connection between their own religious faith and tradition and another; historical connections are not in keeping with divine revelation. Their bias, springing from vested interest, is of course understandable; but it is hardly conducive to sound scholarship.

of Mut's longing for Joseph and her attempt to seduce him,
Joseph's rejection of Mut and his subsequent fate, is intriguing
but does not concern us here. Ikhnaton may have been the pharaoh before whom Joseph was brought after he had interpreted his
fellow-prisoners' dreams. Mann does not identify him by name,
but describes him as follows:

> Pharao is seventeen. This hypersensitive and tender youth, a
> searcher of God, like Joseph's forefathers, and enamoured of
> a dreamy religion of love, has ascended the throne during the
> time of Joseph's imprisonment. He is an anticipating, a pre-
> mature Christian, the mythical prototype of those, who are on
> the right way, but not the right ones for that way.[78]

We can only conclude that this pharaoh was indeed Ikhnaton.
Like Breasted and Weigall, Mann sees in him the instrument of
God's revelation to man. But, because he "was not the right one
for that way," it remained for the Jews to keep the vision alive
until the coming of the Messiah, our Christ.

Sigmund Freud, too, has been captured by the engrossing
theme of Ikhnaton, Moses, and monotheism.[79] He assumes that
Moses was an Egyptian—*mose* is an ending of many Egyptian
proper names—and a devout follower of Ikhnaton. Frustrated in
his desire and attempt to monotheize the Egyptians, Moses determined to give the new theology to the Hebrews then in Egypt.
In this way the philosophy of Ikhnaton was perpetuated.

XVI

"Until Ikhnaton the history of the world had been but the
irresistible drift of tradition. All men had been but drops of water
in the great current" (Breasted). Now that our study is done we
must conclude that history is still the irresistible flow of the stream
of culture and that all men are but chips floating on that stream.
Our inquiry has shown conclusively that the events of Ikhnaton's
reign were but links in a chain that extended for centuries before

and after his lifetime. The links were more striking or emphatic no doubt, but links, nevertheless. We can come to no other conclusion than that the *general trend* of events would have been the same had Ikhnaton been but a sack of sawdust.

The Great Man theory of historical interpretation is, however, one of compelling power and appeal:

> A man Caesar is born, and for ages after we have a Roman Empire. Christ is born, and millions of minds so grow and cleave to his genius that he is confounded with virtue and the possible of a man. An institution is the lengthened shadow of one man; as Monachism of the Hermit Antony; the Reformation, of Luther; Quakerism, of Fox; Methodism, of Wesley; Abolition, of Clarkson . . . all history resolves itself very easily into the biography of a few stout and earnest persons (Emerson, *Essay on Self Reliance*).

Thus wrote the man who provided the intelligentsia of America with the verbal reflexes called "thought" for so many years. The conception is still popular. History is "explained" by citing the Great Man. But how is the Great Man accounted for? He isn't. He is either taken for granted or is said to be inexplicable. "Genius defies all laws . . ."

The Great Man theory is, of course, the quintessence of anthropomorphism. It pictures man, like God, a first cause, a prime mover: "Let there be light and there was light . . . an institution is but the lengthened shadow of one man." Man ever creates himself in God's image.

The Ikhnaton we meet in the sober studies of the scholars' pen is a sheer fictional character, no more real than Hamlet or Huckleberry Finn. We know *nothing* about him *as a person* that is certain and direct. And at every point where the Great Man theory conflicts with evidence, it is the evidence that must give way. If the ossification of bones indicates a man who died too young to have done what the Great Man did, a way must be found to delay the process of ossification. If an empire is lost, it is because the Great Man is morally opposed to the use of force; or he is too fat and lazy to lead his army. If a new city is built the Great Man becomes a dynamo of energy. This Ikhnaton is nothing but the composite personification of all the political, social, military and philosophic events of his day. As such he is no different from Whirlwind Old Man, invented by the Pueblo Indians to "explain" the spirals of dust in the hot desert air, or the John Bull who determines British foreign policy. And so it is with all Great Men, whether it be a Paul Bunyan of the folk or a George Washington of historians.

It goes without saying that men differ in their talents and abilities. Some are silk purses biologically; others are sows' ears. But it takes more than superior brains and glands to make a Great Man. Perhaps we should say exceptional rather than superior, for some Great Men have been pathological in one respect or another. Mohammed, for example, is said to have been an epileptic. It takes, then, more than exceptional natural endowment to make a Great Man; a certain concatenation of cultural forces and historical circumstances is required also. No one can be a great actor without a play, a stage, and an audience. Conversely, a man of mediocre talents may become Great if chance and circumstance place him at the focal point of a tremendously significant historical event. In the process of cultural development, a Great Man is but the neural medium through which an important synthesis of culture elements takes place. Darwin, Newton, Beethoven, and Edison were men of this type. They were the neurological loci of important cultural events. To be sure, they may have been superior organisms. But had they been reared as swineherds, Greatness would not have found them. In history, in political and social movements, the Great Man is that anatomical part of a social organism that functions as a directive, regulative or integrative mechanism. Ability—or epilepsy—or chance, or both together, may have put him in this position. The

Great Man is an instrument employed by a nation or a movement in the exercise of its functions. Torn from his context, the Great Man—an exiled Napoleon, a Kaiser sawing wood, the mutilated corpse of Mussolini, a Big Name in a "War Crimes Trial"—is but an insignificant hunk of human flesh.

The measure of a Great Man in the life of nations can be taken when we see how independent of him the behavior of a nation is. The behavior of the social organism that is Russia has remained constant for decades and even centuries: expansion toward the east, tropismatic gropings toward warm-water ports, penetration of the Balkans, Pan-Slavism. Whether a Czar or a Commissar sits in the driver's seat is immaterial; the great organism goes its own way unalterably. The same observations may be made in the case of Germany. Whether the Great Man be Wilhelm, Bismarck, or Hitler, the organism that was Germany followed a constant and uniform course: *Drang nach Oesten*, lebensraum, colonies, commercial rivalry. The reasons for this uniformity of national behavior are of course plain: the land, the people who grow upon it, the resources of the land or its lack of them, its position with reference to other nations, the trade routes of the world, etc. These remain relatively constant and consequently the behavior of the social organism remains constant. Great Men and Ideologies do more to obscure these fundamental facts than to explain them. The Great Man is the instrument, the Ideology, the rationalization, of the social organism as it struggles for survival in the international jungle of nations.

CHAPTER TEN

THE LOCUS OF MATHEMATICAL
REALITY

"He's [the Red King's] dreaming now," said Tweedledee: "and what do you think he's dreaming about?"

Alice said, "Nobody can guess that."

"Why, about you!" Tweedledee exclaimed, clapping his hands triumphantly. "And if he left off dreaming about you, where do you suppose you'd be?"

"Where I am now, of course," said Alice.

"Not you!" Tweedledee retorted contemptuously. "You'd be nowhere. Why, you're only a sort of thing in his dream!"

"If that there King was to wake," added Tweedledum, "you'd go out—bang!—just like a candle."

"I shouldn't!" Alice exclaimed indignantly. "Besides, if I'm only a sort of thing in his dream, what are you, I should like to know?"

"Ditto," said Tweedledum.

"Ditto, ditto!" cried Tweedledee.

He shouted this so loud that Alice couldn't help saying "Hush! You'll be waking him, I'm afraid, if you make so much noise."

"Well, it's no use your talking about waking him," said Tweedledum, "when you're only one of the things in his dream. You know very well you're not real."

"I am real!" said Alice, and began to cry.

"You won't make yourself a bit realler by crying," Tweedledee remarked: "there's nothing to cry about."

"If I wasn't real," Alice said—half laughing through her tears, it all seemed so ridiculous—"I shouldn't be able to cry."

"I hope you don't suppose those are *real* tears?" Tweedledum interrupted in a tone of great contempt.

Lewis Carroll—*Through the Looking Glass*

Do mathematical truths reside in the external world, there to be discovered by man, or are they man-made inventions? Does mathematical reality have an existence and a validity independent of the human species or is it merely a function of the human nervous system?

Opinion has been and still is divided on this question. Mrs. Mary Somerville (1780-1872), an Englishwoman who knew or corresponded with such men as Sir John Herschel, Laplace, Gay Lussac, W. Whewell, John Stuart Mill, Baron von Humboldt, Faraday, Cuvier, and De Candolle, and who was herself a scholar of distinction,* expressed a view widely held when she said:

"Nothing has afforded me so convincing a proof of the unity of the Deity as these purely mental conceptions of numerical and mathematical science which have been by slow degrees vouchsafed to man, and are still granted in these latter times by the Differential Calculus, now superseded by the Higher Algebra, all of which must have existed in that sublimely omniscient Mind from eternity." [1]

Lest it be thought that Mrs. Somerville was more theological than scientific in her outlook, let it be noted that she was denounced, by name and in public, from the pulpit by Dean Cockburn of York Cathedral for her support of science.[2]

In America, Edward Everett (1794-1865), a distinguished scholar (the first American to win a doctorate at Göttingen), reflected the enlightened view of his day when he declared:

"In the pure mathematics we contemplate absolute truths which existed in the divine mind before the morning stars sang together, and which will continue to exist there when the last of their radiant host shall have fallen from heaven." [3]

In our own day, a prominent British mathematician, G. H. Hardy, has expressed the same view with, however, more technicality than rhetorical flourish, in A Mathematician's Apology:

* She wrote the following works, some of which went into several editions: The Mechanism of the Heavens, 1831 (which was, it seems, a popularization of the Mécanique Céleste of Laplace); The Connection of the Physical Sciences, 1858; Molecular and Microscopic Science, 1869; Physical Geography, 1870.

"I believe that mathematical reality lies outside us, and that our function is to discover or observe it, and that the theorems which we prove, and which we describe grandiloquently as our 'creations' are simply our notes of our observations." * [4]

Taking the opposite view we find the distinguished physicist, P. W. Bridgman, asserting that "it is the merest truism, evident at once to unsophisticated observation, that mathematics is a human invention." [5] Edward Kasner and James Newman state that "we have overcome the notion that mathematical truths have an existence independent and apart from our own minds. It is even strange to us that such a notion could ever have existed." [6]

From a psychological and anthropological point of view, this latter conception is the only one that is scientifically sound and valid. There is no more reason to believe that mathematical realities have an existence independent of the human mind than to believe that mythological realities can have their being apart from man. The square root of minus one is real. So were Wotan and Osiris. So are the gods and spirits that primitive peoples believe in today. The question at issue, however, is not, Are these things real?, but, Where is the locus of their reality? It is a mistake to identify reality with the external world only. Nothing is more real than an hallucination.

Our concern here, however, is not to establish one view of mathematical reality as sound, the other illusory. What we propose to do is to present the phenomenon of mathematical behavior in such a way as to make clear, on the one hand, why the belief in the independent existence of mathematical truths has seemed so plausible and convincing for so many centuries, and,

---

* The mathematician is not, of course, the only one who is inclined to believe that his creations are discoveries of things in the external world. The theoretical physicist, too, entertains this belief. "To him who is a discoverer in this field," Einstein observes, "the products of his imagination appear so necessary and natural that he regards them, and would like to have them regarded by others, not as creations of thought but as given realities," ("On the Method of Theoretical Physics," in The World as I See It, p. 30).

on the other, to show that all of mathematics is nothing more than a particular kind of primate behavior.

Many persons would unhesitatingly subscribe to the proposition that "mathematical reality must lie either within us, or outside us." Are these not the only possibilities? As Descartes once reasoned in discussing the existence of God, "it is impossible we can have the idea or representation of anything whatever, unless there be somewhere, *either in us or out of us*, an original which comprises, in reality . . ." [7] (emphasis ours). Yet, irresistible though this reasoning may appear to be, it is, in our present problem, fallacious or at least treacherously misleading. The following propositions, though apparently precisely opposed to each other, are equally valid; one is as true as the other: 1. "Mathematical truths have an existence and a validity independent of the human mind," and 2. "Mathematical truths have no existence or validity apart from the human mind." Actually, these propositions, phrased as they are, are misleading because the term "the human mind" is used in two different senses. In the first statement, "the human mind" refers to the individual organism; in the second, to the human species. Thus both propositions can be, and actually are, true. Mathematical truths exist in the cultural tradition into which the individual is born, and so enter his mind from the outside. But apart from cultural tradition, mathematical concepts have neither existence nor meaning, and of course, cultural tradition has no existence apart from the human species. Mathematical realities thus have an existence independent of the individual mind, but are wholly dependent upon the mind of the species. Or, to put the matter in anthropological terminology: mathematics in its entirety, its "truths" and its "realities," is a part of human *culture*, nothing more. Every individual is born into a culture which already existed and which is independent of him. Culture traits have an existence outside of the individual mind and independent of it. The individual obtains his culture by learning the customs, beliefs, techniques of his group. But culture itself has, and can have, no existence apart from the human species. Mathematics, therefore—like language, institutions, tools, the arts, etc.—is the cumulative product of ages of endeavor of the human species.

The great French savant Emile Durkheim was one of the first to make this clear. He discussed it in the early pages of The Elementary Forms of the Religious Life. And in The Rules of Sociological Method especially he set forth the nature of culture and its relationship to the human mind. Others, too, have of course discussed the relationship between man and culture, but Durkheim's formulations are especially appropriate for our present discussion and we shall call upon him to speak for us from time to time.[8]

Mathematics is, of course, a part of culture. Every people inherits from its predecessors, or contemporary neighbors, along with ways of cooking, marrying, worshipping, etc., ways of counting, calculating, and whatever else mathematics does. Mathematics is, in fact, a form of behavior: the responses of a particular kind of primate organism to a set of stimuli. Whether a people counts by fives, tens, twelves or twenties; whether it has no words for cardinal numbers beyond 5, or possesses the most modern and highly developed mathematical conceptions, their mathematical behavior is determined by the mathematical culture which possesses them.

We can see now how the belief that mathematical truths and realities lie outside the human mind arose and flourished. They do lie outside the mind of each individual organism. They enter the individual mind, as Durkheim says, from the outside. They impinge upon his organism, again to quote Durkheim, just as cosmic forces do. Any mathematician can see, by observing himself as well as others, that this is so. Mathematics is not something that is secreted, like bile; it is something drunk, like wine. Hottentot boys grow up and behave, mathematically as well as otherwise, in obedience to and in conformity with the mathematical and other traits in their culture. English or American youths do the same in their respective cultures. There is not one iota of anatomical or psychological evidence to indicate that there are any significant innate, biological racial differences so far as mathematical or any other kind of human behavior is concerned. Had Newton been reared in Hottentot culture he would have calculated like a Hottentot. Men like G. H. Hardy, who know, through their own experience as well as from the observation of others, that mathematical concepts enter their minds from the outside, conclude understandably—but erroneously—that they have their origin and locus in the external world, independent of man. Erroneous, because the alternative to "outside the human mind," the individual mind, that is, is not "the external world, independent of man," but culture, the body of traditional thought and behavior of the human species.

Culture frequently plays tricks upon us and distorts our thinking. We tend to find in culture direct expressions of "human nature" on the one hand and of the external world on the other. Thus each people is disposed to believe that its own customs and beliefs are direct and faithful expressions of man's nature. It is "human nature," they think, to practice monogamy, to be jealous of one's wife, to bury the dead, drink milk, to appear in public only when clad, to call your mother's brother's children "cousin," to enjoy exclusive right to the fruit of your toil, etc., if they happen to have these particular customs. But ethnography tells us that there is the widest divergence of custom among the peoples of the world: there are peoples who loathe milk, practice polyandry, lend wives as a mark of hospitality, regard inhumation with horror, appear in public without clothing and without shame, call their mother's brother's children "son" and "daughter," and who freely place all or the greater portion of the produce of their toil at the disposal of their fellows. There is no custom or belief that can be said to express "human" nature more than any other.

Similarly it has been thought that certain conceptions of the

external world were so simple and fundamental that they immediately and faithfully expressed its structure and nature. One is
inclined to think that yellow, blue, and green are features of the
external world which any normal person would distinguish until
he learns that the Creek and Natchez Indians did not distinguish
yellow from green; they had but one term for both. Similarly,
the Choctaw, Tunica, the Keresan Pueblo Indians and many
other peoples make no terminological distinction between blue
and green.[9]

The great Newton was deceived by his culture, too. He took it
for granted that the concept of *absolute space* directly and immediately corresponded to something in the external world; space,
he thought, is something that has an existence independent of
the human mind. "I do not frame hypotheses," he said. But the
concept space is a creation of the intellect, as are other concepts.
To be sure, Newton himself did not create the hypothesis of
absolute space. It came to him from the outside, as Durkheim
properly puts it. But although it impinges upon the organism
comme les forces cosmiques, it has a different source: it is not
the cosmos but man's culture.

For centuries it was thought that the theorems of Euclid were
merely conceptual photographs, so to speak, of the external world;
that they had a validity quite independent of the human mind;
that there was something necessary and inevitable about them.
The invention of non-Euclidean geometries by Lobatchewsky,
Riemann and others has dispelled this view entirely. It is now
clear that concepts such as space, straight line, plane, etc., are
no more necessary and inevitable as a consequence of the structure of the external world than are the concepts green and yellow
—or the relationship term with which you designate your mother's
brother, for that matter.

To quote Einstein again:

"We come now to the question: what is a priori certain or
necessary, respectively in geometry (doctrine of space) or its

foundations? Formerly we thought everything; nowadays we think
—nothing. Already the distance-concept is logically arbitrary;
there need be no things that correspond to it, even approximately." [10]

Kasner and Newman say that "non-Euclidean geometry is proof
that mathematics . . . is man's own handiwork, subject only to
the limitations imposed by the laws of thought." [11]

Far from having an existence and a validity apart from the
human species, all mathematical concepts are "free inventions of
the human intellect," to use a phrase with which Einstein characterizes the concepts and fundamental principles of physics. But
because mathematical and scientific concepts have always entered
each individual mind from the outside, everyone until recently
has concluded that they came from the external world instead of
from man-made culture. But the concept of culture, as a scientific concept, is but a recent invention itself.

The cultural nature of our scientific concepts and beliefs is
clearly recognized by the Nobel prize winning physicist, Erwin
Schrödinger, in the following passage:

"Whence arises the widespread belief that the behavior of
molecules is determined by absolute causality, whence the conviction that the contrary is *unthinkable*? Simply from the *custom*,
inherited through thousands of years, of *thinking causally*, which
makes the idea of undetermined events, of absolute, primary
casualness, seem complete nonsense, a logical absurdity," [12]
(Schrödinger's emphases).

Similarly, Henri Poincaré asserts that the axioms of geometry
are mere "conventions," i.e., customs: they "are neither synthetic
a priori judgments nor experimental facts. They are *conventions* . . ." [13]

We turn now to another aspect of mathematics that is illuminated by the concept of culture. Heinrich Hertz, the discoverer
of wireless waves, once said:

"One cannot escape the feeling that these mathematical

formulas have an independent existence and an intelligence of
their own, that they are wiser than we are, wiser even than their
discoverers [sic], that we get more out of them than was originally
put into them." [14]

Here again we encounter the notion that mathematical formulas
have an existence "of their own," (i.e., independent of the human
species), and that they are "discovered," rather than man-made.
The concept of culture clarifies the entire situation. Mathematical
formulas, like other aspects of culture, do have in a sense an
"independent existence and intelligence of their own." The English language has, in a sense, "an independent existence of its
own." Not independent of the human species, of course, but independent of any individual or group of individuals, race or nation.
It has, in a sense, an "intelligence of its own." That is, it behaves,
grows and changes in accordance with principles which are inherent in the language itself, not in the human mind. As man
becomes self-conscious of language, and as the science of philology
matures, the principles of linguistic behavior are discovered and
its laws formulated.

So it is with mathematical and scientific concepts. In a very
real sense they have a life of their own. This life is the life of
culture, of cultural tradition. As Durkheim expresses it: "Collective ways of acting and thinking have a reality outside the
individuals who, at every moment of time, conform to it. These
ways of thinking and acting exist in their own right." [15] It would
be quite possible to describe completely and adequately the evolution of mathematics, physics, money, architecture, axes, plows,
language, or any other aspect of culture without ever alluding
to the human species or any portion of it. As a matter of fact,
the most effective way to study culture scientifically is to proceed
as if the human race did not exist. To be sure it is often con-
venient to refer to the nation that first coined money or to the
man who invented the calculus or the cotton gin. But it is not
necessary, nor, strictly speaking, relevant. The phonetic shifts in

Indo-European as summarized by Grimm's law have to do solely with linguistic phenomena, with sounds and their permutations, combinations and interactions. They can be dealt with adequately without any reference to the anatomical, physiological, or psychological characteristics of the primate organisms who produced them. And so it is with mathematics and physics. Concepts have a life of their own. Again to quote Durkheim, "when once born, [they] obey laws all their own. They attract each other, repel each other, unite, divide themselves and multiply . . ."[16] Ideas, like other culture traits, interact with each other, forming new syntheses and combinations. Two or three ideas coming together may form a new concept or synthesis. The laws of motion associated with Newton were syntheses of concepts associated with Galileo, Kepler and others. Certain ideas of electrical phenomena grow from the "Faraday stage," so to speak, to those of Clerk Maxwell, H. Hertz, Marconi, and modern radar. "The application of Newton's mechanics to continuously distributed masses led," says Einstein, "inevitably to the discovery and application of partial differential equations, which in their turn first provided the language for the laws of the field-theory" (emphasis ours). The theory of relativity was, as Einstein observes, "no revolutionary act, but the natural continuation of a line that can be traced through centuries." More immediately, "the theory of Clerk Maxwell and Lorentz led inevitably to the special theory of relativity."[17] Thus we see not only that any given thought-system is an outgrowth of previous experience, but that certain ideas lead inevitably to new concepts and new systems. Any tool, machine, belief, philosophy, custom or institution is but the outgrowth of previous culture traits. An understanding of the nature of culture makes clear, therefore, why Hertz felt that "mathematical formulas have an independent existence and an intelligence of their own."

His feeling that "we get more out of them than was originally put into them," arises from the fact that in the interaction of

culture traits new syntheses are formed which were not antici-
pated by "their discoverers," or which contained implications
that were not seen or appreciated until further growth made them
more explicit. Sometimes novel features of a newly formed
synthesis are not seen even by the person in whose nervous system the synthesis took place. Thus Jacques Hadamard tells us
of many occasions in which he failed utterly to see things that
"ought to have struck . . . [him] blind." He cites numerous instances in which he failed to see "obvious and immediate consequences of the ideas contained" in the work upon which he was
engaged, leaving them to be "discovered" by others later.[18]
The contradiction between the view held by Hertz, Hardy and
others that mathematical truths are discovered rather than man-
made is thus resolved by the concept of culture. They are both;
they are discovered but they are also man-made. They are the
product of the mind of the human species. But they are encountered or discovered by each individual in the mathematical
culture in which he grows up. The process of mathematical
growth is, as we have pointed out, one of interaction of mathematical elements upon one another. This process requires, of
course, a basis in the brains of men, just as a telephone conversation requires wires, receivers, transmitters, etc. But we do not
need to take the brains of men into account in an explanation of
mathematical growth and invention any more than we have to
take the telephone wires into consideration when we wish to explain the conversation it carries. Proof of this lies in the fact
of numerous inventions (or "discoveries") in mathematics made
simultaneously by two or more persons working independently.*

---

* The following data are taken from a long and varied list published in
Social Change, by Wm. F. Ogburn (New York, 1923), pp. 90-102, in which
simultaneous inventions and discoveries in the fields of chemistry, physics,
biology, mechanical invention, etc., as well as in mathematics, are listed.
Law of inverse squares: Newton, 1666; Halley, 1684.
Introduction of decimal point: Pitiscus, 1608-12; Kepler, 1616; Napier,
1616-17.

If these discoveries really were caused, or determined, by individual minds, we would have to explain them as coincidences. On the basis of the laws of chance these numerous and repeated coincidences would be nothing short of miraculous. But the culturological explanation makes the whole situation clear at once. The whole population of a certain region is embraced by a type of culture. Each individual is born into a pre-existing organization of beliefs, tools, customs and institutions. These culture traits shape and mould each person's life, give it content and direction. Mathematics is, of course, one of the streams in the total culture. It acts upon individuals in varying degree, and they respond according to their constitutions. Mathematics is the psychosomatic response to the mathematical culture.

But we have already noted that within the body of mathematical culture there is action and reaction among the various elements. Concept reacts upon concept; ideas mix, fuse, form new syntheses. This process goes on throughout the whole extent of culture although more rapidly and intensively in some regions (usually the center) than in others (the periphery). When this process of interaction and development reaches a certain point, new syntheses * are formed of themselves. These syntheses are, to be sure, real events and have location in time and place. The places are of course the brains of men. Since the cultural process has been going on rather uniformly over a wide area and

---

Logarithms: Burgi, 1620; Napier-Briggs, 1614.

Calculus: Newton, 1671; Leibnitz, 1676.

Principle of least squares: Gauss, 1809; Legendre, 1806.

A treatment of vectors without the use of co-ordinate systems: Hamilton, 1843; Grassman, 1843; and others, 1843.

Contraction hypothesis: H. A. Lorentz, 1895; Fitzgerald, 1895.

The double theta functions: Gopel, 1847; Rosenhain, 1847.

Geometry with axiom contradictory to Euclid's parallel axiom: Lobatchevsky, 1836-40; Bolyai, 1826-33; Gauss, 1829.

The rectification of the semi-cubal parabola: Van Heuraet, 1659; Neil, 1657; Fermat, 1657-59.

The geometric law of duality: Oncelet, 1838; Gergone, 1838.

* Hadamard entitles one chapter of his book "Discovery as a Synthesis."

population, the new synthesis takes place simultaneously in a number of brains at once. Because we are habitually anthropocentric in our thinking we tend to say that these men made these discoveries. And in a sense, a biological sense, they did. But if we wish to explain the discovery as an event in the growth of mathematics we must rule the individual out completely. From this standpoint, the individual did not make the discovery at all. It was something that happened to him. He was merely the place where the lightning struck. A simultaneous "discovery" by three men working "independently" simply means that cultural-mathematical lightning can and does strike in more than one place at a time. In the process of cultural growth, through invention or discovery, the individual is merely the neural locus in which the advance occurs. Man's brain is merely a catalytic agent, so to speak, in the culture process. This process cannot exist independently of neural tissue, but the function of man's nervous system is merely to make possible the interactive process and to effect syntheses of cultural elements.

To be sure individuals differ just as catalytic agents, lightning conductors or other media do. One person, one set of brains, may be a better medium for the growth of mathematical culture than another. One man's nervous system may be a better catalyst for the culture process than that of another. The mathematical cultural process is therefore more likely to select one set of brains than another as its medium of expression. But it is easy to exaggerate the role of superior brains in cultural advance. It is not merely superiority of brains that counts. There must be a juxtaposition of brains with a specific cultural tradition. If the proper cultural elements are lacking, superior brains will be of no avail. There were brains as good as Newton's in England 10,000 years before the birth of Christ, at the time of the Norman conquest, or any other period of English history. Everything that we know about fossil man, the prehistory of England, and the neuroanatomy of *Homo sapiens* will support this statement.

There were brains as good as Newton's in aboriginal America or in Darkest Africa. But the calculus was not invented in these other times and places because the requisite cultural elements were lacking. Contrariwise, when the cultural elements are present, the discovery or invention becomes so inevitable that it takes place independently in two or three nervous systems at once. Had Newton been reared as a sheep herder, the mathematical culture of England would have found other brains in which to achieve its new synthesis. One man's brains may be better than another's, just as his hearing may be more acute or his feet larger. But just as a "brilliant" general is one whose armies are victorious, so a genius, mathematical or otherwise, is a person in whose nervous system an important cultural synthesis takes place; he is the neural locus of an epochal event in culture history.

The nature of the culture process and its relation to the minds of men is well illustrated by the history of the theory of evolution in biology. As is well known, this theory did not originate with Darwin. We find it in one form or another in the neural reactions of many others before Darwin was born: Buffon, Lamarck, Erasmus Darwin, and others. As a matter of fact, virtually all of the ideas which together we call Darwinism are to be found in the writings of J. C. Prichard, an English physician and anthropologist (1786-1848). These various concepts were interacting upon each other and upon current theological beliefs, competing, struggling, being modified, combined, resynthesized, etc., for decades. The time finally came, i.e., the stage of development was reached, where the theological system broke down and the rising tide of scientific interpretation inundated the land.

Here again the new synthesis of concepts found expression simultaneously in the nervous systems of two men working independently of each other: A. R. Wallace and Charles Darwin. The event had to take place when it did. If Darwin had died in infancy, the culture process would have found another neural medium of expression.

This illustration is especially interesting because we have a vivid account, in Darwin's own words, of the way in which the synthesis of ideas took place:

"In October 1838," Darwin wrote in his autobiographic sketch, "that is, fifteen months after I had begun my systematic enquiry, I *happened to read for amusement* 'Malthus on Population,' and being well prepared to appreciate the struggle for existence which everywhere goes on from long-continued observation of the habits of animals and plants, it at once struck me that under these circumstances favourable variations would tend to be preserved, and unfavourable ones to be destroyed. The result of this would be the formation of a new species. *Here then I had at last got a theory by which to work* . . ." (emphasis ours).

This is an exceedingly interesting revelation. At the time he read Malthus, Darwin's mind was filled with various ideas, (i.e., he had been moulded, shaped, animated and equipped by the cultural milieu into which he happened to have been born and reared—a significant aspect of which was independent means; had he been obliged to earn his living in a "counting house" we might have had "Hudsonism" today instead of Darwinism). These ideas reacted upon one another, competing, eliminating, strengthening, combining. Into this situation was introduced, by chance, a peculiar combination of cultural elements (ideas) which bears the name of Malthus. Instantly a reaction took place, a new synthesis was formed—"here at last he had a theory by which to work." Darwin's nervous system was merely the place where these cultural elements came together and formed a new synthesis. It was something that *happened* to Darwin rather than something he *did*.

This account of invention in the field of biology calls to mind the well-known incident of mathematical invention described so vividly by Henri Poincaré. One evening, after working very hard on a problem but without success, he writes:

". . . contrary to my custom, I drank black coffee and could not sleep. Ideas rose in crowds; I felt them collide until pairs interlocked, so to speak, making a stable combination. By the next morning I had established the existence of a class of Fuchsian functions . . . I had only to write out the results, which took but a few hours." [19]

Poincaré further illustrates the process of culture change and growth in its subjective (i.e., neural) aspect by means of an imaginative analogy. He imagines mathematical ideas as being something like "the hooked atoms of Epicurus. During complete repose of the mind, these atoms are motionless, they are, so to speak, hooked to the wall." No combinations are formed. But in mental activity, even unconscious activity, certain of the atoms "are detached from the wall and put in motion. They flash in every direction through space . . . like the molecules of a gas . . . Then their mutual impacts may produce new combinations." [20] This is merely a description of the subjective aspect of the culture process which the anthropologist would describe objectively (i.e., without reference to nervous systems). He would say that in cultural systems, traits of various kinds act and react upon one another, eliminating some, reinforcing others, forming new combinations and syntheses. The significant thing about the loci of inventions and discoveries from the anthropologist's standpoint is not quality of brains, but relative position within the culture area: inventions and discoveries are much more likely to take place at culture centers, at places where there is a great deal of cultural interaction, than on the periphery, in remote or isolated regions.

The dominating influence of the external cultural tradition upon the individual mind is sometimes felt very distinctly, but it is seldom recognized for what it really is. Thus, Goethe declared that:

"All productivity of the highest kind, every important conception, every discovery, every great thought which bears fruit, . . . is in no one's control, and is beyond every earthly power.

Such things are to be regarded as unexpected gifts from above, as pure divine products." [21]

The brothers Goncourt speak of "an unknown force, a superior will, a sort of compulsion to write, which commands the work and guides the pen; so much so that at times the book which comes forth from your hands seems not to have been born of yourself at all . . ." [22] And George Eliot declared that "in all her writings which she considered her best, there was a 'not herself' which took possession of her and made her feel 'her own personality to be merely the instrument through which the spirit acted.' " [23]

To be sure, there is a "something outside one's self," a power, a force, that lays hold of one and compels him to do thus and so. But there is nothing mysterious or mystical about it. It is not something unearthly or divine as Goethe suggested. It is simply the great tradition of culture that holds each one of us in its powerful embrace. When, as if in a river, we are caught up in a current or rapids of culture change, or swept into the vortex of cultural synthesis, we can do naught but give ourselves wholly to it. Then indeed do we feel a spirit and a power within us that we know full well is not our own. But we know whence it comes and what its nature is. It is the great and cumulative stream of human culture, flowing down to us from its sources in antiquity, carrying us upon its bosom, nourishing and sustaining us, using, but yet preserving rather than consuming, us for the culture and the generations yet to come.

If mathematical ideas enter the mind of the individual mathematician from the outside, from the stream of culture into which he was born and reared, the question arises, where did culture in general, and mathematical culture in particular, come from in the first place? How did it arise and acquire its content?

It goes without saying, of course, that mathematics did not originate with Euclid and Pythagoras—or even with the thinkers of ancient Egypt and Mesopotamia. Mathematics is a development of thought that had its beginning with the origin of man and culture a million years or so ago. To be sure, little progress was made during hundreds of thousands of years. Still, we find in mathematics today systems and concepts that were developed by primitive and preliterate peoples of the Stone Ages, survivals of which are to be found among savage tribes today. The system of counting by tens arose from using the fingers of both hands. The vigesimal system of the Maya astronomers grew out of the use of toes as well as fingers. To *calculate* is to count with *calculi*, pebbles. A *straight line* was a *stretched linen* cord, and so on.

To be sure, the first mathematical ideas to exist were brought into being by the nervous systems of individual human beings.* They were, however, exceedingly simple and rudimentary. Had it not been for the human ability to give these ideas overt expression in symbolic form and to communicate them from one person to another so that new combinations would be formed, and these new syntheses passed on from one generation to another in a continuous process of interaction and accumulation, the human species would have made no mathematical progress beyond its initial stage. This statement is supported by our studies of anthro-

---

* The question of the extent to which the form and content of mathematical thought are determined by the structure of the human mind, i.e., by the neuro-sensory-muscular-etcetera system of man, is interesting and relevant but one into which we shall not go at length here. Obviously the structure of the human organism conditions all of man's experience, mathematical and otherwise. With regard to such things as "inherent and necessary laws of thought," however, it may be remarked that normal children and many primitive peoples find nothing wrong with the notion that a body can be in two different places at the same time—not to mention the objection that is raised to the phrase "at the same time" by the theory of relativity; $3=1$ in some philosophies; an animal need not be either a mammal, A, or a non-mammal, not-A; it may be a monotreme, like the duckbill who lays eggs reptilian fashion but who suckles its young; etc. Whatever the influence of the structure and processes of the human organism upon the "laws of thought or logic" may be, it must, of course, find expression in one cultural form or another; any neurological imperative will therefore always be conditioned by convention.

poid apes. They are exceedingly intelligent and versatile. They have a fine appreciation of geometric forms, solve problems by imagination and insight, and possess not a little originality. But they cannot express their neuro-sensory-muscular concepts in overt symbolic form. They cannot communicate their ideas to one another except by gestures, i.e., by *signs* rather than *symbols*. Hence ideas cannot react upon one another within their nervous systems to produce new syntheses. Nor can these ideas be transmitted from one generation to another in a cumulative manner. Consequently, one generation of apes begins where the preceding generation began. There is neither accumulation nor progress.

Thanks to articulate speech, the human species fares better. Ideas are cast into symbolic form and given overt expression. Communication is thus made easy and versatile. Ideas now impinge upon nervous systems from the outside. These ideas react upon one another within these nervous systems. Some are eliminated; others strengthened. New combinations are formed, new syntheses achieved. These advances are in turn communicated to someone else, transmitted to the next generation. In a relatively short time, the accumulation of mathematical ideas has gone beyond the creative range of the individual human nervous system *unaided by cultural tradition.* From this time on, mathematical progress is made by the interaction of ideas already in existence rather than by the creation of new concepts by the human nervous system alone. Ages before writing was invented, individuals in all cultures were dependent upon the mathematical ideas present in their respective cultures. Thus, the mathematical behavior of an Apache Indian is the response that he makes to stimuli provided by the mathematical ideas in his culture. The same was true for Neanderthal man and the inhabitants of ancient Egypt, Mesopotamia and Greece. It is true for individuals of modern nations today.

Thus we see that mathematical ideas were produced originally by the human nervous system when man first became a human

being a million years ago. These concepts were exceedingly rudimentary, and the human nervous system, unaided by culture,
could never have gone beyond them regardless of how many
generations lived and died. It was the formation of a cultural
tradition that made progress possible. The communication of
ideas from person to person, the transmission of concepts from
one generation to another, placed in the minds of men (i.e.,
stimulated their nervous systems) ideas which through interaction formed new syntheses which were passed on in turn to
others.

We return now, in conclusion, to some of the observations of
G. H. Hardy, to show that his conception of mathematical
reality and mathematical behavior is consistent with the theory
of culture that we have presented here and is, in fact, explained
by it.

"I believe that mathematical reality lies outside us," [24] he says.
If by "us" he means "us mathematicians individually," he is quite
right. They do lie outside each one of us; they are a part of the
culture into which we are born. Hardy feels that "in some sense,
mathematical truth is part of objective reality," [25] (emphasis
ours). But he also distinguishes "mathematical reality" from
"physical reality," and insists that "pure geometries are not pictures . . . [of] the spatio-temporal reality of the physical world."
What then is the nature of mathematical reality? Hardy declares
that "there is no sort of agreement . . . among either mathematicians or philosophers" [26] on this point. Our interpretation
provides the solution. Mathematics does have objective reality.
And this reality, as Hardy insists, is not the reality of the physical
world. But there is no mystery about it. Its reality is cultural: the
sort of reality possessed by a code of etiquette, traffic regulations,
the rules of baseball, the English language or rules of grammar.

Thus we see that there is no mystery about mathematical
reality. We need not search for mathematical "truths" in the

divine mind or in the structure of the Universe. Mathematics is a kind of primate behavior as languages, musical systems and penal codes are. Mathematical concepts are man-made just as ethical values, traffic rules, and bird cages are man-made. But this does not invalidate the belief that mathematical propositions lie outside us and have an objective reality. They do lie outside us. They existed before we were born. As we grow up we find them in the world about us. But this objectivity exists only for the individual. The locus of mathematical reality is cultural tradition, i.e., the continuum of symbolic behavior. This theory illuminates also the phenomenon of novelty and progress in mathematics. Ideas interact with one another in the nervous systems of men and thus form new syntheses. If the owners of these nervous systems are aware of what has taken place they call it invention as Hadamard does, or "creation," to use Poincaré's term. If they do not understand what has happened, they call it a "discovery" and believe they have found something in the external world. Mathematical concepts are independent of the individual mind but lie wholly within the mind of the species, i.e., culture. Mathematical invention and discovery are merely two aspects of an event that takes place simultaneously in the cultural tradition and in one or more human nervous systems. Of these two factors, culture is the more significant; the determinants of mathematical evolution lie here. The human nervous system is merely the catalyst that makes the cultural process possible.

CHAPTER ELEVEN

THE DEFINITION AND PROHIBITION OF INCEST

"Again and again in the world's history, savage tribes must have had plainly before their minds the simple practical alternative between marrying-out and being killed out . . ."—E. B. Tylor [1]

*T*he subject of incest has a strange fascination for man. He was preoccupied with it long before he developed the art of writing. We find incestuous episodes in the mythologies of countless peoples. And in advanced cultures, from Sophocles to Eugene O'Neill, incest has been one of the most popular of all literary themes. Men seem never to tire of it but continue to find it ever fresh and absorbing. Incest must indeed be reckoned as one of man's major interests in life.

Yet, despite this intense and perennial concern, it is a fact that incest is but little understood even today. Men of science have been obliged all too often to admit that they are baffled and to declare that it is too mysterious, too obscure, to yield to rational interpretation, at least for the present.

One of the more common explanations of the universal prohibition of incest is that it is instinctive. Thus Robert H. Lowie once accepted "Hobhouse's view that the sentiment is instinctive." [2] To "explain" an element of behavior by saying that it is "instinctive" contributes little to our understanding of it as a rule. Sometimes it merely conceals our ignorance with a verbal curtain of pseudo-knowledge. To say that prohibitions against incest are "instinctive" is of course to declare that there is a natural, inborn and innate feeling of revulsion toward unions with close relatives. But if this were the case, why should societies enact strict laws to prevent them? Why should they legislate against something that everyone already wishes passionately to avoid? Do not, as a matter of fact, the stringent and worldwide prohibitions indicate a universal and powerful desire for sexual unions with one's relatives? Clinical evidence points in the same direction. "Freud has shown all but conclusively," writes Goldenweiser, "that incestuous tendencies represent one of the most deeply rooted impulses of the individual." [3]

There are further objections to the instinct theory. Some societies regard marriage with a first cousin as incestuous while others do not. Are we to assume that the instinct varies from tribe to tribe? Certainly when we consider our own legal definitions of incest, which vary from state to state, to claim that a biological instinct can recognize state boundary lines is somewhat grotesque. In some societies it is incestuous to marry a parallel cousin (a child of your father's brother or your mother's sister) but it is permissible, and may even be mandatory, to marry a cross cousin (a child of your father's sister or your mother's brother). We cannot see how "instinct" can account for this, either; in fact, we cannot see how instinct can distinguish a cross cousin from a parallel cousin. It is usually incestuous to marry a clansman even though no genealogical connection whatever can be discovered with him, whereas marriage with a close relative in another clan may be permissible. Plainly, the instinct theory does not help us at all, and it is not easy to find a scientist to defend it today.*

---

* In 1932, Professor Lowie abandoned the instinct theory of incest prohibitions. But he comes no closer to an explanation than to observe that "the aversion to incest is, therefore, best regarded as a primeval cultural adaptation" (Lowie, 1933) p. 67. In one of his most recent works, An Introduction to Cultural Anthropology (2nd ed., New York, 1940) he again discusses incest but goes no further than to suggest that "the horror of incest is not inborn, though it is doubtless a very ancient cultural feature" (p. 232).

Another theory, championed generations ago by Lewis H. Morgan [4] and others, and not without defenders today, is that incest was defined and prohibited because inbreeding causes biological degeneration. This theory is so plausible as to seem self-evident, but it is wrong for all that. In the first place, inbreeding as such does not cause degeneration; the testimony of biologists is conclusive on this point. To be sure, inbreeding intensifies the inheritance of traits, good or bad. If the offspring of a union of brother and sister are inferior it is because the parents were of inferior stock, not because they were brother and sister. But superior traits as well as inferior ones can be intensified by inbreeding, and plant and animal breeders frequently resort to this device to improve their strains. If the children of brother-sister or father-daughter unions in our own society are frequently feeble-minded or otherwise inferior it is because feeble-minded individuals are more likely to break the powerful incest taboo than are normal men and women and hence more likely to beget degenerate offspring. But in societies where brother-sister marriages are permitted or required, at least within the ruling family, as in ancient Egypt, aboriginal Hawaii and Incaic Peru, we may find excellence. Cleopatra was the offspring of brother-sister marriages continued through several generations and she was "not only handsome, vigorous, intellectual, but also prolific . . . as perfect a specimen of the human race as could be found in any age or class of society." [5]

But there is still another objection to the degeneration theory as a means of accounting for the origin of prohibitions against incest. A number of competent ethnographers have claimed that certain tribes are quite ignorant of the nature of the biological process of reproduction, specifically, that they are unaware of the relationship between sexual intercourse and pregnancy. Or, they may believe that coitus is prerequisite to pregnancy but not the cause of it. [6] Malinowski, for example, claims that the Trobriand Islanders denied that copulation has anything to do with pregnancy, not only among human beings but among the lower animals as well.[7] This thesis of ignorance of the facts of life among primitive peoples has been challenged by other ethnologists, and I am not prepared to adjudicate the dispute. But it may be pointed out that such ignorance should not be very surprising. Once a fact becomes well known there is a tendency to regard it as self-evident. But the relationship between coitus and pregnancy, a condition that would not be discovered until weeks or even a few months later, is anything but obvious. Furthermore, pregnancy does not always follow intercourse. And knowing primitive man's penchant for explaining so many things, the phenomena of life and death especially, in terms of supernatural forces or agents, we should not be surprised to find some tribes even today who do not understand the physiology of paternity.

At any rate, there must have been a time at which such understanding was not possessed by any members of the human race. We have no reason to believe that apes have any appreciation of these facts, and it must have taken man a long time to acquire it. There are reasons, however, as we shall show later on, for believing that incest taboos appeared in the very earliest stage of human social evolution, in all probability prior to an understanding of paternity. The reason for the prohibition of inbreeding could not therefore have been a desire to prevent deterioration of stock if the connection between copulation and the birth of children were not understood.

This thesis receives additional support from a consideration of the kinship systems of primitive peoples. In these systems a person calls many of his collateral relatives "brother" and "sister," namely, his parallel cousins of several degrees for example, and the children of his mother's and father's parallel cousins, also of several degrees. Marriage between individuals who call each other "brother" and "sister" is strictly prohibited by the incest taboo, even though they be cousins of the third or fourth degree. But marriage with a first cross-cousin may be permitted and often is required. Now these people may not understand the biology of conception and pregnancy, but they know which woman bore each child. Thus we see that the marriage rules disregard the degree of biological relationship so far as preventing inbreeding is concerned; they may prohibit marriage with a fourth parallel cousin who is called "brother" or "sister," but permit or require marriage with a first cross-cousin who is called "cousin." Obviously, the kinship terms express sociological rather than biological relationships. Obvious also is the fact that the incest taboos follow the pattern of social ties rather than those of blood.

But suppose that inbreeding did produce inferior offspring, are we to suppose that ignorant, magic-ridden savages could have established this correlation without rather refined statistical techniques? How could they have isolated the factor of inbreeding from numerous others such as genetics, nutrition, illnesses of mother and infant, etc., without some sort of medical criteria and measurements—even though crude—and without even the rudiments of statistics?

Finally, if we should grant that inbreeding does produce degeneracy, and that primitive peoples were able to recognize this fact, why did they prohibit marriage with a parallel cousin while allowing or even requiring union with a cross-cousin? Both are equally close biologically. Or, why was marriage with a clansman prohibited even though the blood tie was so remote that it could not be established genealogically with the data available to memory, while marriage with a non-clansman was permitted even though he was a close blood relative? Obviously, the degeneracy theory is as weak as the instinct hypothesis although it may be more engaging intellectually.

Sigmund Freud's theory is ingenious and appealing—in a dramatic sort of way at least. Proceeding from Darwin's conjectures concerning the primal social state of man, based upon what was then known about anthropoid apes, and utilizing W. Robertson Smith's studies of totemism and sacrifice, Freud developed the following thesis: in the earliest stage of human society, people lived in small groups each of which was dominated by a powerful male, the Father. This individual monopolized all females in the group, daughters as well as mothers. As the young males grew up and became sexually mature, the father drove them away to keep them from sharing his females with him.

"One day," says Freud in Totem and Taboo, "the expelled brothers joined forces, slew and ate the father, and thus put an end to the father horde. Together they dared and accomplished what would have remained impossible for them singly." [8] But they did not divide their father's women among themselves as they had planned. Now that he was dead their hatred and aggressiveness disappeared, and their love and respect for him came to the fore. As a consequence, they determined to give him in death the submission and obedience they had refused in life. They made therefore a solemn pact to touch none of their father's women and to seek mates elsewhere. This pledge was passed on from one generation to the next: * You must have nothing to do with the women of your father's household, i.e., of your own group, but must seek other mates. In this way the incest taboo and the institution of exogamy came into being. This part of Totem and Taboo is great drama and not without value as an interpretation of powerful psychological forces, just as Hamlet is great drama in the same sense. But as ethnology, Freud's theory would still be inadequate even if this much were verifiable. It does not even attempt to account for the many and varied forms of incest prohibition.

It is not our purpose here to survey and criticize all of the many theories that have been advanced in the past to account for the

---

* In another work, Contributions to the Theory of Sex, Freud suggests, if he does not say so outright, that the incest taboo became incorporated into the germ plasm and was consequently transmitted by means of biological heredity: "The incest barrier probably belongs to the historical acquisitions of humanity and, like other moral taboos, it must be fixed in many individuals through organic heredity," (Freud, 1938) p. 617.

definition and prohibition of incest. We may, however, briefly notice two others before we leave the subject, namely, those of E. Westermarck and Emile Durkheim.

Westermarck's thesis that "the fundamental cause of the exogamous prohibitions seems to be the remarkable absence of erotic feelings between persons living very closely together from childhood, leading to a positive feeling of aversion when the act is thought of," [9] is not in accord with the facts in the first place and would still be inadequate if it were. Propinquity does not annihilate sexual desire, and if it did there would be no need for stringent prohibitions. Secondly, incest taboos are frequently in force between persons not living in close association.

Durkheim attempts to explain the prohibition of incest as a part of his general theory of totemism.[10] The savage knew intuitively, Durkheim reasoned, that blood is a vital fluid or principle. To shed the blood of one's own totemic group would be a great sin or crime. Since blood would be shed in the initial act of intercourse, a man must eschew all women of his own totem. Thus the taboo against incest and rules of exogamy came into being. This theory is wholly inadequate ethnologically. Taboos against incest are much more widespread than totemism; the former are universal, the latter is far from being so. And the theory does not even attempt to explain the many diverse forms of the definition and prohibition of incest.

In view of repeated attempts and as many failures to account for the origin of definitions of incest and of rules regulating its prohibition, is it any wonder that many scholars, surveying decades of fruitless theories, have become discouraged and have come to feel that the problem is still too difficult to yield to scientific interpretation?

In the same work in which he presented his theory, but some pages earlier, Freud said: "Still, in the end, one is compelled to subscribe to Frazer's resigned statement, namely, that we do not know the origin of incest dread and do not even know how to guess at it." *

Professor Ralph Linton treats of the subject as follows:

> The causes which underlie such limitations on marriage, technically known as incest regulations, are very imperfectly understood. Since these regulations are of universal occurrence, it seems safe to assume that their causes are everywhere present, but biological factors can be ruled out at once. Close inbreeding is not necessarily injurious . . . Neither are purely social explanations of incest regulations altogether satisfactory, since the forms which these regulations assume are extremely varied . . . It seems possible that there are certain psychological factors involved, but these can hardly be strong enough or constant enough to account for the institutionalization of incest regulations . . . They have probably originated from a combination of all these factors . . .[11]

In other words, somewhere in the man-culture situation lie the causes of incest regulations, but where they are and why and how they are exercised are matters too obscure for description or explanation.

The late Alexander Goldenweiser, a prominent disciple of Franz Boas, never discovered the secret of the prohibition of incest. In Early Civilization he spoke of certain taboos that "are everywhere reinforced by the so-called 'horror of incest,' an emotional reaction of somewhat mysterious origin." Fifteen years later in Anthropology, his last major work, he could go no farther than to repeat these identical words.[12]

The sociologists have little to offer. Kimball Young, for example, disavows instinct as the source of incest prohibitions, but he

---

* Totem and Taboo, p. 217. Frazer's statement was: "Thus the ultimate origin of exogamy and with it the law of incest—since exogamy was devised to prevent incest—remains a problem nearly as dark as ever," (Totemism and Exogamy, Vol. I, p. 165).

advances no further explanation than to assert that "the taboo is a rather constant and expected result arising from the very nature of the social interaction between parents and children and among the children themselves" [13]—which is virtually equivalent to no explanation at all.

Dr. Clark Wissler, one of the foremost anthropologists of our day, observes:

". . . so far as we can see, the only facts sufficiently well established to serve as a starting point are that anti-incest responses of some kind are universal among mankind. As to why these are universal, we are no nearer a solution than before." [14]

These are discouraging words indeed. "Anti-incest responses" help us no more than "an instinctive horror" of incest. But in the phrase "we are no nearer a solution [now] than before," we may find a clue to a way out of the dilemma. Perhaps these theorists have been on the wrong track. Science has found itself on the wrong track countless times during its relatively brief career so far. So many, in fact, that many of the important achievements of science consist, not in the discovery of some new fact or principle, but in erecting signs which read "Blind alley. Do not enter!" Phrenology was one of these blind alleys. But until it has been explored, how can one know whether a passage is a blind alley or a corridor leading to a new world? Once it has been found to be a blind alley, however, other scientists need not and should not waste their time exploring it again. Perhaps we are confronted by blind alleys in the various theories of incest and exogamy that we have just surveyed. Wissler's admission that "we are no nearer a solution [now] than before" would lead us to think so.

Fortunately we are not in the situation of a mariner who has lost his bearings and who must try to recover his true course. We do not need to seek a new path in the hope of finding an adequate solution of the problem of incest. The solution has already been found, and that long ago.

Confusion in this field of ethnological theory has been due to circumstances such as we have just described. Theorists who have sought biological or psychological explanations of incest taboos have been on the wrong track; they have only led us into blind alleys. Those who have sought a *culturological* explanation have succeeded fully and well. The culturological point of view is younger and less widely known than the psychological or even sociological. Although it was set forth simply and adequately by the great English anthropologist, E. B. Tylor, as early as 1871, in the first chapter of *Primitive Culture*—which was significantly enough entitled "The Science of Culture"—it has not become widely known or appreciated among social scientists, even among cultural anthropologists. There are some who recognize in the new science of culture only a mystical, fatalistic metaphysic that should be shunned like the Devil. So habituated to psychological interpretations are many students of human behavior that they are unable to rise to the level of culturological interpretation. Thus, Goldenweiser looked to psychology for ethnological salvation: "It seems hardly fair to doubt that psychoanalysis will ultimately furnish a satisfactory psychological interpretation of this 'horror of incest'."[15] Professor Wm. F. Ogburn observes that:

"Incest taboos and marriage regulations may be quite fully described historically and culturally, yet there is something decidedly strange about incest and about marriage prohibitions. One's curiosity is not satisfied by the cultural facts." *

---

* *Social Change*, p. 175. What Professor Ogburn means apparently is that culturology cannot tell us *all* that we want to know about incest. This is true; psychology must be enlisted in the inquiry also. But one must insist upon a sharp and clear distinction between the psychological problem and culturological problem. Psychology cannot account for the *origin* or the *form* of the prohibitions; only culturology can do this. But for an understanding of the way the human primate organism behaves—thinks, feels, and acts—within, or with reference to, one of these cultural forms, we must go to psychology.

And even men like Lowie and Wissler, who have done excellent work along culturological lines in other areas, have relapsed to the psychological level when confronted with the problem of incest. Thus Lowie once declared that "it is not the function of the ethnologist but of the biologist and psychologist to explain why man has so deep-rooted a horror of incest." [16] And Wissler is inclined to turn over all problems of cultural origins to the psychologist, leaving to the anthropologist the study of traits after they have been launched upon their cultural careers.[17]

The science of culture has, as we have already indicated, long ago given us an adequate explanation of incest prohibitions. We find it set forth simply and succinctly in an essay by E. B. Tylor published in 1888: "On a Method of Investigating the Development of Institutions, Applied to the Laws of Marriage and Descent." "Exogamy," he wrote, "enabling a growing tribe to keep itself compact by constant unions between its spreading clans, enables it to overmatch any number of small intermarrying groups, isolated and helpless. Again and again in the world's history, savage tribes must have had plainly before their minds the simple practical alternative between marrying-out and being killed out" (p. 267).

The origin of incest taboos greatly antedates clan organization, but a sure clue to an understanding of incest prohibitions and exogamy is given by Tylor nevertheless: primitive people were confronted with a choice between "marrying-out and being killed out." The argument may be set forth as follows:

Man, like all other animal species, is engaged in a struggle for existence. Co-operation, mutual aid, may become valuable means of carrying on this struggle at many points. A number of individuals working together can do many things more efficiently and effectively than the same individuals working singly. And a co-operative group can do certain things that lone individuals cannot do at all. Mutual aid makes life more secure for both individual and group. One might expect, therefore, that in the struggle for security and survival every effort would be made to foster co-operation and to secure its benefits.

Among the lower primates there is little co-operation. To be sure, in very simple operations one ape may co-ordinate his efforts with those of another. But their co-operation is limited and rudimentary because the means of communication are crude and limited; co-operation requires communication. Monkeys and apes can communicate with one another by means of signs—vocal utterances or gestures—but the range of ideas that can be communicated in this way is very narrow indeed. Only articulate speech can make extensive and versatile exchange of ideas possible, and this is lacking among anthropoids. Such a simple form of co-operation as "you go around the house that way while I go around the other way, meeting you on the far side," is beyond the reach of the great apes. With the advent of articulate speech, however, the possibilities of communication became virtually unlimited. We can readily see its significance for social organization in general and for incest and exogamy in particular.

One might get the impression from some psychologists, the Freudians especially, perhaps, that the incestuous wish is itself instinctive, that somehow a person "just naturally" focuses his sexual desires upon a *relative* rather than upon a *non*-relative, and, among relatives, upon the closer rather than the remoter degrees of consanguinity. This view is quite as unwarranted as the theory of an "instinctive horror" of incest; an inclination toward sexual union with close relatives is no more instinctive than the social regulations devised to prevent it. A child has sexual hunger as well as food hunger. And he fixes his sex hunger upon certain individuals as he does his food hunger upon certain edible substances. He finds sexual satisfaction in persons close to him because they are close to him, not because they are his relatives. To be sure, they may be close to him because they are his relatives, but that is another matter. As a consequence of proximity and satisfaction the child fixates his sexual desires upon his immediate associates, his parents and his siblings, just as he fixates his food hungers upon familiar foods that have given satisfaction. He thus comes to have definite orientations and firm attachments in the realm of sex as in the field of nutrition. There is thus no mystery about incestuous desire; it is merely the formation and fixation of definite channels of experience and satisfaction.

We find therefore, even in sub-human primate families, a strong inclination toward inbreeding; one strives to obtain sexual satisfaction from a close associate. This tendency is carried over into human society. But here it is incompatible with the co-operative way of life that articulate speech makes possible. In the basic activities of subsistence, and defense against enemies, co-operation becomes important because life is made more secure thereby. Other factors being constant, the tribe that exploits most fully the possibilities of mutual aid will have the best chance to survive. In times of crisis, co-operation may become a matter of life or death. In providing food and maintaining an effective defense against foreign foes, co-operation becomes all-important.

But would primordial man be obliged to construct a co-operative organization for subsistence and defense from the very beginning, or could he build upon a foundation already in existence? In the evolutionary process, whether it be social or biological, we almost always find the new growing out of, or based upon, the old. And such was the case here; the new co-operative organization for food and defense was built upon a structure already present: the family. After all, virtually everyone belonged to one family or another, and the identification of the co-operative group with the sex-based family would mean that the benefits of mutual aid would be shared by all. When, therefore, certain species of anthropoids acquired articulate speech and became human beings, a new element, an *economic* factor, was introduced into an institution which had up to now rested solely upon sexual attraction between male and female. We are, of course, using the term *economic* in a rather broad sense here to include safety as well as subsistence. The human primate family had now become a corporation with nutritive and protective functions as well as sexual and incidentally reproductive functions. And life was made more secure as a consequence.

But a regime of co-operation confined to the members of a family would be correspondingly limited in its benefits. If co-operation is advantageous *within* family groups, why not between families as well? The problem was now to extend the scope of mutual aid.

In the primate order, as we have seen, the social relationships between mates, parents and children, and among siblings antedates articulate speech and co-operation. They are strong as well as primary. And, just as the earliest co-operative group was built upon these social ties, so would a subsequent extension of mutual aid have to reckon with them. At this point we run squarely against the tendency to mate with an intimate associate. Co-operation *between* families cannot be established if parent marries child; and brother, sister. A way must be found to overcome this centripetal tendency with a centrifugal force. This way was found in the definition and prohibition of incest. If persons were forbidden to marry their parents or siblings they would be compelled to marry into some other family group—or remain celibate, which is contrary to the nature of primates. The leap was taken; a way was found to unite families with one another, and social evolution as a *human* affair was launched upon its career. It would be difficult to exaggerate the significance of this step. Unless some way had been found to establish strong and enduring social ties between families, social evolution could have gone no farther on the human level than among the anthropoids.

With the definition and prohibition of incest, *families* became units in the co-operative process as well as individuals. Marriages came to be contracts first between families, later between even larger groups. The individual lost much of his initiative in courtship and choice of mates for it was now a group affair. Among many primitive peoples a youth may not even be acquainted with his bride before marriage; in some cases he may not even have seen her. Children may be betrothed in childhood or infancy—or even before they are born. To be sure, there are tribes where one can become acquainted or even intimate with his spouse before marriage, but the group character of the contract is there nevertheless. And in our own society today a marriage is still an alliance between families to a very considerable extent. Many a man has expostulated, "But I am marrying *her*, not her family!" only to discover his lack of realism later.

The widespread institutions of levirate and sororate are explainable by this theory also. In the levirate a man marries the wife or wives of his deceased brother. When a man customarily marries the unwed sister of his deceased wife the practice is called sororate. In both cases the group character of marriage is manifest. Each group of consanguinei supplies a member of the other group with a spouse. If the spouse dies, the relatives of the deceased must supply another to take his or her place. The alliance between families is important and must be continued; even death cannot part them.

The equally widespread institutions of bride-price and dowry likewise find their significance in the prohibition of incest to establish co-operation between family groups. The incest taboo necessitates marriage *between* family groups. But it cannot guarantee a continuation of the mutual aid arrangement thus established. This is where bride-price and dowry come in: they are devices for making permanent the marriage tie that the prohibition of incest has established. When a family or a group of relatives has received articles of value as bride-price or dowry, they distribute them as a rule among their various members. Should the marriage tie be broken or dissolved, they may have to return the wealth received at the time of the marriage. This is almost certain to be the case if it can be shown that the spouse whose relatives were the recipients of the bride-price or dowry was at fault. It very often happens that the relatives are reluctant to return the wealth if indeed they still have it. If it has already been consumed they will have to dig into their own pockets. It may already be earmarked for the marriage of one of their own group. In any event, the return of dowry or bride-price would be an inconvenience or a deprivation. Consequently they are likely to take a keen interest in the marriage and to try to prevent their own relative from doing anything to disrupt it.

According to our theory the prohibition of incest has at bottom an economic motivation—not that primitive peoples were aware of this motive, however, for they were not. Rules of exogamy originated as crystallizations of processes of a social system rather than as products of individual psyches. Inbreeding was prohibited and marriage between groups was made compulsory in order to obtain the maximum benefits of co-operation. If this theory be sound, we should find marriage and the family in primitive society wearing a definite economic aspect. This is, in fact, precisely what we do find. Let us turn for summary statements to two leading authorities in social anthropology. Professor Robert H. Lowie writes as follows:

> Marriage, as we cannot too often or too vehemently insist, is only to a limited extent based on sexual considerations. The primary motive, so far as the individual mates are concerned, is precisely the founding of a self-sufficient economic aggregate. A Kai [of New Guinea] does not marry because of desires he can readily gratify outside of wedlock without assuming any responsibilities; he marries because he needs a woman to make pots and to cook his meals, to manufacture nets and weed his plantations, in return for which he provides the household with game and fish and builds the dwelling.[18]

And A. R. Radcliffe-Brown makes similar observations concerning the aborigines of Australia:

The important function of the family is that it provides for the feeding and bringing up of the children. It is based on the co-operation of man and wife, the former providing the flesh food and the latter the vegetable food, so that quite apart from the question of children a man without a wife is in an unsatisfactory position since he has no one to supply him regularly with vegetable food, to provide his firewood, and so on. This economic aspect of the family is a most important one . . . I believe that in the minds of the natives themselves this aspect of marriage, i.e., its relation to subsistence, is of greatly more importance than the fact that man and wife are sexual partners.[19]

Turning to the colonial period in America we find the economic character of the family equally pronounced. According to Professor Wm. F. Ogburn:

In colonial times in America the family was a very important economic organization. Not infrequently it produced substantially all that it consumed, with the exception of such things as metal tools, utensils, salt and certain luxuries. The home was, in short, a factory. Civilization was based on a domestic system of production of which the family was the center.

The economic power of the family produced certain corresponding social conditions. In marrying, a man sought not only a mate and companion but a business partner.* Husband and wife each had specialized skills and contributed definite services to the partnership. Children were regarded, as the laws

---

* We recall Benjamin Franklin's account of his proposal to marry a girl providing her parents would give him "as much money with their daughter as would pay off my remaining debt for the printing-house." He even suggested that they "mortgage their house in the loan-office" if they did not have the cash on hand. The parents, however, thought the printing business a poor risk and declined to give both money and girl. "Therefore," says Franklin, "I was forbidden the house, and the daughter shut up," (Autobiography, Pocket Books, Inc., New York, 1940), p. 78.

of the time showed, not only as objects of affection but as
productive agents. The age of marriage, the birth rate and
the attitude toward divorce were all affected by the fact that
the home was an economic institution. Divorce or separation
not only broke a personal relationship but a business one as
well.[20]

And in our own society today, the economic basis of marriage
and the family is made clear by suits for breach of promise and
alienation of affections in which the law takes a very materialistic,
even monetary, view of love and romance.* Suits for non-support,
alimony, property settlements upon divorce, the financial obligations between parents and children, and so on, exhibit further the
economic function of the family. Marriage for many women today
means a greater economic return for unskilled labor than could
be obtained in any other occupation.

It is interesting to note, in this connection, that Freud who,
according to popular belief, "attributes everything to sex," nevertheless declares that "the motivating force of human society is
fundamentally economic." [21]

The notion that marriage is an institution brought into being
to provide individuals with a means of satisfying their sex hunger
is naive and anthropocentric. Marriage does provide an avenue of
sexual exercise and satisfaction, to be sure. But it was not sexual desire that produced the institution. Rather, it was the exigencies of

---

* One court ruling observes that "the gist of the action for alienation of
affections is the loss of consortium. 'This is a property right growing out of
the marriage relation' . . ." (Supreme Court of Connecticut, Case of Maggay
vs. Nikitko, 1933), quoted by Anthony M. Turano, "The Racket of Stolen
Love," (American Mercury, Vol. 33, p. 295, November, 1934).
    Another legal statement says that "the law generally takes the rather worldly
view that marriage is a 'valuable' consideration; a thing not only possessing
value, but one the value of which may be estimated in money, and therefore, in a sense, marriage engagements are regarded as business transactions,
entered into with a view, in part, at least, to pecuniary advantage," (Ruling
Case Law, Vol. 4, p. 143), quoted by Anthony M. Turano, "Breach of
Promise: Still a Racket," (American Mercury, Vol. 32, p. 40, May, 1934).

a social system that was striving to make full use of its resources for co-operative endeavor. Marriage, as an institution, finds its explanation in terms of sociocultural process rather than individual psychology. In primitive society there was frequently ample means of sexual exercise outside of wedlock. And in our own society the great extent of prostitution, the high incidence of venereal disease as an index of promiscuity, as well as other evidence, show that the exercise of sexual functions is not confined to one's own spouse by any means. As a matter of fact, marriage very often restricts the scope of one's sexual activity. Indeed, monogamy ideally considered is the next thing to celibacy.

Nor is love the basis of marriage and the family, however fondly this notion may be cherished. No culture could afford to use such a fickle and ephemeral sentiment as love as the basis of an important institution. Love is here today but it may be gone tomorrow. But economic needs are with us always. Absence of love is not sufficient grounds for divorce. Indeed, one may despise and loathe, hate and fear, one's mate and still be unable to obtain a divorce. Until very recently at least one state in the Union would grant no divorce at all. And certain religious faiths take the same position. Marriage and the family are society's first and fundamental way of making provision for the economic needs of the individual. And it was the definition and prohibition of incest that initiated his whole course of social development.

But to return to the definitions and prohibitions themselves. These vary, as we saw at the outset, from culture to culture. The variations are to be explained in terms of the specific circumstances under which co-operation is to take place. One set of circumstances will require one definition of incest and one form of marriage; another set will require different customs. The habitat and the technological adjustment to it, the mode of subsistence, circumstances of defense and offense, division of labor between the sexes, and degree of cultural development, are factors which condition the definition of incest and the formulation of rules to prohibit it. No people known to modern science customarily permits marriage between parent and child. Brother-sister marriage has been permitted in certain cultures such as those of ancient Egypt, Hawaii, and Peru under the Incas, but in each instance it was restricted to the ruling household. But this was not incest or "royal incest" as Lowie and Fortune call it respectively.[22] Nor was it "sanctioned incest" to use Kimball Young's phrase.[23] "Sanctioned incest" is of course a contradiction of terms; incest is by definition something criminal and prohibited. These marriages between siblings of royal families were not only not prohibited, they were required. They are examples of endogamy, as the prohibition of brother-sister marriages are examples of exogamy. Solidarity is a source of strength and effective action in society, as co-operation is a way of achieving security. And endogamy promotes solidarity as exogamy fosters size and strength of mutual aid groups.

In view of the fact that a sure clue to the reason of the origin of prohibitions of incest was set forth by Tylor as early as 1888, it is rather remarkable that we should find anthropologists and sociologists today who juggle with "anti-incest responses" and who look to psychoanalysis for ultimate understanding. As a matter of fact, we find the reasons for exogamy set forth by Saint Augustine in *The City of God* (Bk. XV), more than 1400 years before Tylor.

"For it is very reasonable and just," Augustine says, "that men, among whom concord is honorable and useful, should be bound together by various relationships, and that one man should not himself sustain many relationships, but that the various relationships should be distributed among several, and should thus serve to bind together the greatest number in the same social interests. 'Father' and 'father-in-law' are the names of two relationships. When, therefore, a man has one person for his father, another for his father-in-law, friendship extends itself to a larger number."

He comments upon the fact that Adam was both father and father-in-law to his sons and daughters:

"So too Eve his wife was both mother and mother-in-law to her children . . . while had there been two women, one the mother, the other the mother-in-law, the family affection would have had a wider field. Then the sister herself by becoming a wife sustained in her single person two relationships which, had they been distributed among individuals, one being sister, and another being wife, the family tie would have embraced a greater number of persons."

Saint Augustine does not, in these passages at least, make explicit the advantages in security of life which would accrue to the group as a consequence of exogamy. But he makes it quite clear that community of social interest and "greater numbers of persons" in the group are the reasons for the prohibition of incest.

If an understanding of incest and exogamy is as old in social philosophy as Saint Augustine and as early in anthropological science as Tylor, why is it that the subject is still so obscure and so little understood among scholars today? We have already suggested the answer: a preference for psychological rather than culturological explanations. Anthropomorphism is an inveterate habit in human thought. To explain institutions in terms of psychology—of wish, desire, aversion, imagination, fear, etc.—has long been popular. Explanations of human behavior in terms of psychological determinants preceded therefore explanations in terms of cultural determinants. But culturological problems cannot be solved by psychology. Preoccupation with psychological explanations has not only kept many scholars from finding the answer; it has prevented them from recognizing the solution when it has been reached by the science of culture. The sociological explanation, such as Kimball Young's "social interaction," is no better. As a scientific explanation it is not only inadequate; it is empty and meaningless. The sociologist's fixation upon "social interaction" keeps him, too, from appreciating a scientific interpretation of culture as a distinct class of phenomena. Even men who have made notable contributions to culturology, such as Kroeber, Lowie, and Wissler, have failed to appreciate the full significance of Tylor's early discussion of exogamy. The following incident is remarkable and revealing. A. L. Kroeber and T. T. Waterman reprinted Tylor's essay, "On the Method of Investigating the Development of Institutions," in their *Source Book in Anthropology* in 1920. But in a subsequent edition, they cut the article down apparently to conserve space, and omitted this highly significant passage!

Important contributions to science are sometimes made "before their time," that is, before the general level of scientific advance has reached a point where widespread appreciation becomes possible. There was really very little that was novel in the work of Darwin; most if not all of the ideas and facts had been presented before. But the broad front of the cultural process of biologic thought had not advanced sufficiently prior to 1859 to make a general acceptance of this point of view possible. So it is with the problem of incest. An adequate explanation has been extant for decades. But, because the problem is a culturological one, and because the science of culture is still so young and so few scholars even today are able to grasp and appreciate its nature and scope, an understanding of incest and its prohibitions is still very limited. As culturology develops and matures, however, this understanding as well as that of a host of other supra-psychological problems will become commonplace.

We do not wish to minimize the extent of this understanding today. Despite the ignorance and confusion of many scholars, there is a considerable number who do understand incest taboos. Thus Reo Fortune states that:

"A separation of affinal relationship from consanguineous relationship assures a wider recognition of social obligation, . . . Any incestuous alliance between two persons within a single consanguineous group is in so far a withdrawal of their consanguineous group from the alliance and so endangers the group's survival." [24]

Malinowski, too, has illuminated the problem of incest taboos. Instead of emphasizing, however, the positive values that would accrue from alliances formed as a consequence of compulsory exogamy, he dwells upon the disruption and discord that the unrestricted exercise of sexual appetites would introduce into a small group of relatives or close associates. "The sexual impulse," he writes, "is in general a very upsetting and socially disruptive force, [it] cannot enter into a previously existing sentiment without producing a revolutionary change in it. Sexual interest is therefore incompatible with any family relationship, whether parental or between brothers and sisters . . . If erotic passion were allowed to invade the precincts of the home it would not merely establish jealousies and competitive elements and disorganize the family but it would also subvert the most fundamental bonds of kinship on which the further development of all social relations is based . . . A society which allowed incest could not develop a stable family; it would therefore be deprived of the strongest foundations for kinship, and this in a primitive community would mean absence of social order." [25]

B. Z. Seligman expresses somewhat similar views—as well as others that are less discerning. John Gillin has a fine statement on the origin and function of incest taboos tucked away in a footnote in a monograph on the Barama River Caribs. Raymond Firth presents an illuminating "sociological" analysis of the problem in We, the Tikopia. Wm. I. Thomas sees clearly the reasons for prohibitions of incest: "the horror of incest is thus plainly of social derivation." [26]

And Freud, apart from his drama of patricide, comes close to an understanding of incest taboos and exogamy. The "incest prohibition," he says, "had . . . a strong practical foundation. Sexual need does not unite men; it separates them . . . Thus there was nothing left for the brothers [after they had killed their father],

if they wanted to live together, but to erect the incest prohibition." [27] In another work he observes that:

"The observance of this [incest] barrier is above all a demand of
cultural society, which must guard against the absorption by the
family of those interests which it needs for the production of
higher social units. Society, therefore, uses all means to loosen
those family ties in every individual." [28]

The cultural function, if not the genesis, of incest taboos and
of rules of exogamy seems to be very clearly seen and appreciated
here. It is interesting to note, too, that Freud holds substantially
the same view of the relationship between restrictions upon sexual
gratification and social evolution that has been set forth earlier in
this essay. One of the principal themes of *Civilization and Its Discontents* is "the extent to which civilization is built up on re-
nunciation of instinctual gratifications . . . This 'cultural
privation' dominates the whole field of social relations between
human beings." He sees that "the first result of culture was that
a larger number of human beings could live together in common";
that "one of culture's principal endeavors is to cement men and
women together in larger units." [29] Thus, although he proceeds
from different premises, Freud comes to essentially the same conclusion as ours.

There is, then, considerable understanding of incest and
exogamy extant in the literature today. Yet, in a comparatively
recent review of the whole problem a prominent anthropologist,
John M. Cooper, has concluded that "the desire to multiply the
social bonds [has] in all probability not been [an] important
factor" in the origin of incest prohibitions. How far he is from
an understanding of the problem is indicated by the two "chief
factors" which he cites: "(a) sex callousness, resulting from early
and intimate association . . . ; (b) the distinctly social purpose
of preserving standards of sex decency within the family and kinship circle." [30] The first factor is contrary to fact; intimacy fosters
incest rather than callousness. The second explains nothing at

all: what are standards of sex decency, why do they vary from tribe to tribe, and why is it necessary to preserve them?

The culturological theory of incest receives support from a comparison of primitive cultures with our own. The crime of incest is punished with greater severity in primitive societies than in our own, as Freud, Fortune and others have observed. Among the former the penalty of death is quite common; in our society punishment seldom exceeds ten years imprisonment and is often much less. The reason for this difference is not far to seek. In primitive societies, personal and kinship ties between individuals and families were more important than they are in highly developed cultures. The small mutual aid group was a tremendously important social unit in the struggle for security. The very survival of the group depended to a considerable extent upon alliances formed by exogamy. In advanced cultures the situation is different. Society is no longer based upon kinship ties, but upon property relationships and territorial distinctions. The political state has replaced the tribe and clan. Occupational groups and economic organization also become important bases of social life. The importance of exogamy is thus much diminished and the penalties for incest become less severe. It is not to be expected, however, that restrictions upon inbreeding will ever be removed entirely. Kinship is still an important, though relatively less important, feature of our social organization and will probably remain so indefinitely. Rules of exogamy and endogamy will therefore continue to be needed to regulate and order this aspect of our social life.

In the various interpretations, both sound and unsound, of the definition and prohibition of incest we have a neat example of a contrast between psychological explanations on the one hand and culturological explanations on the other. The problem simply does not yield to psychological solution. On the contrary, the evidence, both clinical and ethnographic, indicates that the desire

to form sexual unions with an intimate associate is both powerful
and widespread. Indeed, Freud opines that "the prohibition
against incestuous object-choice [was] perhaps the most maim-
ing wound ever inflicted . . . on the erotic life of man." [31] Psychology discloses an "incestuous wish" therefore, not a motive for
its prevention. The problem yields very readily, however, to culturological interpretation. Man, as an animal species, lives in
groups as well as individually. Relationships between individuals
in the human species are determined by the *culture* of the group
—that is, by the ideas, sentiments, tools, techniques, and behavior patterns, that are dependent upon the use of symbols and
which are handed down from one generation to another by means
of this same faculty. These culture traits constitute a continuum,
a stream of interacting elements. In this interacting process, new
combinations and syntheses are formed, some traits become
obsolete and drop out of the stream, some new ones enter it. The
stream of culture thus flows, changes, grows and develops in
accordance with laws of its own. Human behavior is but the reactions of the organism man to this stream of culture. Human
behavior—in the mass, or of a typical member of a group—is therefore culturally determined. A people has an aversion to drinking
cow's milk, avoids mothers-in-law, believes that exercise promotes health, practices divination or vaccination, eats roasted
worms or grasshoppers, etc., because their culture contains trait-
stimuli that evoke such responses. These traits cannot be accounted for psychologically.

And so it is with the definition and prohibition of incest. From
psychology we learn that the human animal tends to unite sexually
with someone close to him. The institution of exogamy is not
only *not* explained by citing this tendency; it is contrary to it.
But when we turn to the cultures that determine the relations
between members of a group and regulate their social intercourse
we readily find the reason for the definition of incest and the
origin of exogamy. The struggle for existence is as vigorous in

the human species as elsewhere. Life is made more secure, for group as well as individual, by co-operation. Articulate speech makes co-operation possible, extensive, and varied in human society. Incest was defined and exogamous rules were formulated in order to make co-operation compulsory and extensive, to the end that life be made more secure. These institutions were created by social systems, not by neuro-sensory-muscular-glandular systems. They were syntheses of culture elements formed within the interactive stream of culture traits. Variations of definition and prohibition of incest are due to the great variety of situations. In one situation, in one organization of culture traits—technological, social, philosophic, etc.—we will find one type of definition of incest and one set of rules of exogamy; in a different situation we find another definition and other rules. Incest and exogamy are thus defined in terms of the mode of life of a people—by the mode of subsistence, the means and circumstances of offense and defense, the means of communication and transportation, customs of residence, knowledge, techniques of thought, etc. And the mode of life, in all its aspects, technological, sociological, and philosophical, is culturally determined.

CHAPTER TWELVE

MAN'S CONTROL OVER CIVILIZATION:
An Anthropocentric Illusion

". . . numerous survivals of the anthropocentric bias still remain and here [in sociology], as elsewhere, they bar the way to science. It displeases man to renounce the unlimited power over the social order he has so long attributed to himself; and on the other hand, it seems to him that, if collective forces really exist, he is necessarily obliged to submit to them without being able to modify them. This makes him inclined to deny their existence. In vain have repeated experiences taught him that this omnipotence, the illusion of which he complacently entertains, has always been a cause of weakness in him; that his power over things really began only when he recognized that they have a nature of their own, and resigned himself to learning this nature from them. Rejected by all other sciences, this deplorable prejudice stubbornly maintains itself in sociology. Nothing is more urgent than to liberate our science from it, and this is the principal purpose of our efforts,"—Emile Durkheim [1]
". . . it appears like a grandiose dream to think of controlling according to the will of man the course of social evolution . . ."—Wm. F. Ogburn [2]

*T*he belief that man controls his civilization is widespread and deeply rooted. Customs and institutions, tools and machines, science, art, and philosophy are but man's creations and are therefore here only to do his bidding. It lies within man's power, therefore, to chart his course as he pleases, to mold civilization to his desires and needs. At least so he fondly believes.

Thus we find a distinguished British scientist, the late Sir James Jeans, assuring us that:

We no longer believe that human destiny is a plaything for spirits, good and evil, or for the machinations of the Devil. There is nothing to prevent our making the earth a paradise again—except ourselves. The scientific age has dawned, and we recognize that man himself is the master of his fate, the captain of his soul. He controls the course of his ship, and so, of course, is free to navigate it into fair waters or foul, or even to run it on the rocks.[3]

Mr. Stanley Field, President of the Field Museum (now the Chicago Natural History Museum), appeals to anthropologists in espousing Free Will:

But if we listen to the anthropologists, who can scientifically demonstrate that it is not color of skin, or type of hair or features, or difference of religion, that creates problems between peoples, but factors for which man is responsible and which he can control or change if he will, then we shall at least come within sight of that better world which we now realize we must achieve if we are not finally to perish as victims of our own perversity.[4]

Professor Lewis G. Westgate, in an article in Scientific Monthly, tells us that man can "take the problem of his future in hand and solve it":

The mind that can weigh the infinitely distant stars . . . track down the minute carriers of disease . . . dig the Panama Canal . . . can solve its social problems when and if it decides to do so.[5]

It would thus seem that the salvation of an earlier era has become the social reconstruction of today: we can achieve it if we will; if we fail it is because of our "perversity."

Father Wilhelm Schmidt, the leader of the Kulturkreis school of ethnology, and his disciples in America believe firmly in free will; indeed, it appears to be one of their cardinal principles.[6] And even V. Gordon Childe, whose work is for the most part infused with the spirit of scientific materialism and determinism, says, in a book significantly entitled *Man Makes Himself*, that "changes in culture . . . can be initiated, controlled, or delayed by the conscious and deliberate choice of their human authors and executors." [7]

When, however, we look for examples of man's control over culture we begin first to wonder, then to doubt. We will not begin our inquiry by asking if two World Wars in one generation are evidence of planning or perversity, or whether Germany and Japan were crushed and Soviet Russia made dominant in Eurasia in accordance with a farsighted plan or as a result of blindness and folly. We will start with something much more modest. During the last century we have witnessed attempts to control tiny and relatively insignificant segments of our culture, such as spelling, the calendar, the system of weights and measures, to name but a few. There have been repeated and heroic attempts to simplify spelling and make it more rational, to devise a more rational calendar, and to adopt an ordered system of weights and measures instead of the cumbersome, illogical agglomeration of folk measurements we now use. But what successes can we point to? Reform in spelling has been negligible. We have succeeded to a considerable extent but not wholly in eliminating the u from such words as *honor*. But to do away with silent letters, such as the *b* in *lamb*, is too big a mountain for us to move. And such spellings-and-pronunciations as *rough*, *cough*, *dough*, and *through* are much too strong to yield to our puny efforts. It usually takes a great political and social upheaval to effect a significant change in spelling or a calendrical system as the French and Bolshevik revolutions have made clear. And as for the metric system, it has found a place among the little band of esoterics in science, but yards, ounces, rods, pints, and furlongs still serve—awkwardly and inefficiently—the layman.

We begin to wonder. If we are not able to perform such tiny and insignificant feats as eliminating the b from *lamb*, or modifying our calendar system, how can we hope to construct a new social order on a worldwide scale?

Let us look about us further. Men and women are forever contending with fashions. Man perennially rebels against his attire. It is often uncomfortable, injurious to the health at times, and, some men think, the ordinary costume is unesthetic, the formal attire ridiculous. But what can he do? He must wear his coat and tie no matter how hot the weather. He is not permitted to wear pink or blue shoes. And as for "evening clothes"—he must submit to them or stay home. Man's vaunted control over civilization is not particularly conspicuous in this sector.

But if man is helpless, woman is an abject slave, in the grip of fashion. She must submit to any change, no matter how fantastic or ugly. To be sure, she may not realize that the new designs are fantastic and ugly at the time; "the latest style" can becloud a woman's judgment. But one has only to browse through an album of old snapshots to realize that beauty, grace, and charm do not dominate the course of fashion.

And as for women's skirts! First they are short; then they are long. A distinguished anthropologist, Professor A. L. Kroeber of the University of California, has made a very interesting and revealing study of the dimensions of women's dresses over a considerable period of time. He found that "the basic dimensions of modern European feminine dress alternate with fair regularity between maxima and minima which in most cases average about fifty years apart so that the full-wave length of their periodicity is around a century." [8] The rhythms are regular and uniform. Women have nothing to say about it. Even the designers and creators must conform to the curve of change. We find no control by man—or woman—here, only an inexorable and impersonal trend. When a maximum point on the curve is reached, the trend is reversed and skirts lengthen or shorten as the case may be.

Women are helpless; they can do nothing but follow the trend. When the curve ascends they must shorten their dresses; when it descends, they must lengthen them. It may seem remarkable that a great class of citizens who cannot even control the dimensions of their own skirts will nevertheless organize themselves into clubs, to administer the affairs of the world. We shall return to this point later.

Few men would undertake to repair an automobile or a radio without some understanding of its mechanism. We tend more and more nowadays to leave medicine and surgery to those who know how. Knowledge and skill are required even to make good pies or home brew. But in matters of society and culture everyone feels qualified to analyze, diagnose, and prescribe. It is one of the premises of democracy that not only do the people rule, but they have the requisite knowledge and understanding to do it effectively. In matters political, one man's view is as good as another's.

When, however, we examine the knowledge and understanding with which the affairs of the nation are administered we begin again to wonder. We find the most august authorities espousing different and even contradictory views on such subjects as inflation, the function of labor leaders, the divorce rate, the popularity of crooners, and so on. This is a picture of the anarchy of ignorance, not of wisdom.

When we turn from matters of national proportions, such as the cause of inflation, to lesser problems we are not always reassured. Does capital punishment diminish the number of murders? Does the use of alcohol affect the divorce rate? Why do people keep dogs? They are noisy, dirty, unhealthful, useless, and expensive. To say that they are kept because people like them is merely to phrase the problem in a different form. Why don't they "like" raccoons? They are cute, cleanly in their habits, and very amiable.

The fact is, we don't really know very much about the civilization we live in. Let us take one of the simplest and most elementary questions imaginable: Why does our society prohibit polygamy? Other societies permit plural mates, and Western Europe once did, also. But now we feel very strongly about it. We will put a man in a prison for years if he takes unto himself more than one wife at one time. His wives may be perfectly satisfied with the arrangement and he may have injured no one. Yet we put him in gaol.* Why? Why not have one more wife and one less schoolmarm?

There are, to be sure, ready answers to these questions: polygamy is "wrong," "immoral," "undemocratic," etc. But practices are not prohibited because they are "wrong"; they are wrong because they have been prohibited. It is not wrong to buy and sell whiskey now; it was while the Eighteenth Amendment was on the books. And as for democracy and equality, we permit a man to have two yachts if he can afford them, why not two wives?

I know of no really adequate answer to this question in such literature of social science as I am acquainted with. As a matter of fact, the question is very seldom raised. I have looked for it in a great number of treatises on sociology and anthropology written during the last quarter century without finding it. Some social scientists of the latter half of the nineteenth century tried to explain the prohibition of polygamy but we cannot accept their conclusions.

The fact is we are ignorant. We do not know the solution to such an elementary problem as singular or plural mates. And in

---

* We recall a recent instance in which a man was sent to the penitentiary for marrying some twelve women without ever bothering with the ritual of divorce. Had he been less honorable or chivalrous and lived with each woman without the formality of marriage, his "crime" would have been much less. This man served society well in a municipal railway system. His numerous wives pressed no complaint. Why did society feel it necessary to incarcerate him?

our day, we have not reached the point of asking such questions, to say nothing of answering them. As Archibald McLeish has said, "We know all the answers, but we have not yet asked the questions." Over a half-century ago the great French savant, Emile Durkheim, commented upon the immaturity of social science as follows:

> In the present state of the science we really do not even know what are the principal social institutions, such as the state, or the family; what is the right of property or contract . . . We are almost completely ignorant of the factors on which they depend . . . ; we are scarcely beginning to shed even a glimmer of light on some of these points. Yet one has only to glance through the works on sociology to see how rare is the appreciation of this ignorance and these difficulties.[9]

Despite the progress that has been made since *The Rules* was written, this statement has a certain relevance today. If the science of society and civilization is still so immature as to be unable to solve such tiny and elementary problems as the prohibition of polygamy, where are the knowledge and understanding requisite to planning a new social system, to constructing a new world order? One would not expect a savage craftsman, whose best tools are made of chipped flint, to design and build a locomotive.

Let us have a look at this civilization man thinks he controls. The first thing we notice is its antiquity. There is no part of it, whether it be technology, institutions, science or philosophy, that does not have its roots in the remote past. The lens of the new 200-inch telescope, for example, is made of glass. Glass emerged from the manufacture of faience in ancient Egypt, which in turn originated apparently as a by-product of burning bricks and pottery, which followed the use of sun-dried brick, and, earlier, mud daubs of Neolithic or even Paleolithic huts. The United Nations can be traced back to primitive tribal councils and beyond. Modern mathematics goes back to counting on one's fingers, and so on. Culture is as old as man himself. It had its beginnings a million odd years ago when man first started to use articulate speech, and it has continued and developed to the present day. Culture is a continuous, cumulative, and progressive affair.

Everyone—every individual, every generation, every group—has, since the very earliest period of human history, been born into a culture, a civilization, of some sort. It might be simple, crude and meager, or it might be highly developed. But all cultures, whatever their respective degrees of development, have technologies (tools, machines), social systems (customs, institutions), beliefs (lore, philosophy, science) and forms of art. This means that when a baby is born into a cultural milieu, he will be influenced by it. As a matter of fact, his culture will determine how he will think, feel, and act. It will determine what language he will speak, what clothes, if any, he will wear, what gods he will believe in, how he will marry, select and prepare his foods, treat the sick, and dispose of the dead. What else *could* one do but react to the culture that surrounds him from birth to death? No people makes its own culture; it inherits it ready-made from its ancestors or borrows it from its neighbors.

It is easy enough for man to believe that he has made his culture, each generation contributing its share, and that it is he who controls and directs its course through the ages. Does he not chip the arrowheads and stone-axes, build carts and dynamoes, coin money and spend it, elect presidents and depose kings, compose symphonies and carve statues, worship gods and wage war? But one cannot always rely upon the obvious. It was once obvious that the earth remained stationary while the sun moved; anyone could see that for himself. We are now approaching a point in modern thought where we are beginning to suspect that it is not man who controls culture but the other way around. The feat of

Copernicus in dispelling the geocentric illusion over four hundred years ago is being duplicated in our day by the culturologist who is dissipating the anthropocentric illusion that man controls his culture.

Although it is man who chips arrowheads, composes symphonies, etc., we cannot explain culture merely by saying that "man produced it." There is not a single question that we would want to ask about culture that can be answered by saying "Man did thus and so." We want to know why culture developed as it did; why it assumed a great variety of forms while preserving at the same time a certain uniformity, why the rate of cultural change has accelerated. We want to know why some cultures have money and slaves while others do not; why some have trial by jury, others ordeal by magic; why some have kings, others chiefs or presidents; why some use milk, others loathe it; why some permit, others prohibit, polygamy. To explain all these things by saying, "Man wanted them that way" is of course absurd. A device that explains everything explains nothing.

Before we go very far we discover that we must disregard man entirely in our efforts to explain cultural growth and cultural differences—in short, culture or civilization as a whole. Man may be regarded as a constant so far as cultural change is concerned. Man is one species and, despite differences of skin, eye, and hair color, shape of head, lips, and nose, stature, etc., which after all are superficial, he is highly uniform in such fundamental features as brain, bone, muscle, glands, and sense organs. And he has undergone no appreciable evolutionary change during the last 50,000 years at least. We may, therefore, regard man as a constant both with regard to the races extant today, and with regard to his ancestors during the last tens of thousands of years. Man has a certain structure and certain functions; he has certain desires and needs. These are related to culture, of course, but only in a general, not a specific, way. We may say that culture as a whole serves the needs of man as a species. But this does not and cannot help us at all when we try to account for the variations of specific cultures. You cannot explain variables by appeal to a constant. You cannot explain the vast range of cultural variation by invoking man, a biological constant. In England in A.D. 1500 there was one type of culture; in Japan, another. Neither culture can be explained in terms of the physical type associated with it. Culture underwent change in England between A.D. 1500 and 1900, as it did in Japan. But these changes cannot be explained by pointing to the inhabitants in each case; they did not change. Plainly, we cannot explain cultures in terms of Man.

Nor can cultural differences be explained in terms of environment. Quite apart from the difficulty of accounting for differences in musical styles, forms of writing, codes of etiquette, rules of marriage, mortuary rites, etc., in terms of environment, we soon discover that even economic, industrial, and social systems cannot be so explained. The environment of Central Europe so far as climate, flora, fauna, topography, and mineral resources are concerned has remained constant for centuries. The culture of the region, however, has varied enormously. Here again we see the fallacy of explaining the variable by appeal to a constant.

If, then, we cannot explain cultures in terms of race or physical type, or in terms of psychological processes, and if appeal to environment is equally futile, how are they to be accounted for and made intelligible to us?

There seems to be only one answer left and that is fairly plain —after one becomes used to it, at least. Cultures must be explained in terms of culture. As we have already noted, culture is a continuum. Each trait or organization of traits, each stage of development, grows out of an earlier cultural situation. The steam engine can be traced back to the origins of metallurgy and fire. International cartels have grown out of all the processes of exchange and distribution since the Old Stone Age and before. Our science, philosophy, religion, and art have developed out of earlier forms. Culture is a vast stream of tools, utensils, customs, beliefs that are constantly interacting with each other, creating new combinations and syntheses. New elements are added constantly to the stream; obsolete traits drop out. The culture of today is but the cross-section of this stream at the present moment, the resultant of the age-old process of interaction, selection, rejection, and accumulation that has preceded us. And the culture of tomorrow will be but the culture of today plus one more day's growth. The numerical coefficient of today's culture may be said to be 365,000,000 (i.e., a million years of days); that of tomorrow: 365,000,000 + 1. The culture of the present was determined by the past and the culture of the future will be but a continuation of the trend of the present. Thus, in a very real sense *culture makes itself.* At least, if one wishes to explain culture scientifically, he must proceed *as if* culture made itself, *as if* man had nothing to do with the determination of its course or content. Man must *be* there, of course, to make the existence of the culture process possible. But the nature and behavior of the process itself is self-determined. It rests upon its own principles; it is governed by its own laws.

Thus, culture makes man what he is and at the same time makes itself. An Eskimo, Bantu, Tibetan, Swede, or American is what he is, thinks, feels, and acts as he does, because his culture influences—"stimulates"—him in such a way as to evoke these responses. The Eskimo or American has had no part in producing the culture into which he was thrust at birth. It was already there; he could not escape it; he could do nothing but react to it, and that on its own terms. The English language, the Christian religion, our political institutions, our mills, mines, factories, railroads, telephones, armies, navies, race tracks, dance halls, and all the other thousands of things that comprise our civilization are here in existence today. They have weight, mass, and momentum. They cannot be made to disappear by waving a wand, nor can their structure and behavior be altered by an act of will. We must come to terms with them as we find them today.

And they will be tomorrow what their trend of development in the past dictates. We can only trot along with them, hoping to keep up.

Man has long cherished the illusion of omnipotence. It is flattering and comforting to his ego. In days gone by, man has believed that he could control the weather; countless primitive peoples have had rituals for making rain, stilling high winds, or averting storms. Many have had ceremonies by means of which the course of the sun in the heavens could be "controlled." With the advance of science, however, man's faith in his omnipotence has diminished. But he still believes that he can control his civilization.

The philosophy of science—of cause and effect relationships, of determinism—has been firmly established in the study of physical phenomena. It is well entrenched in the biological field, also. Psychology may have demonstrated the operation of the principle of cause and effect, of determinism, in mental processes, and may have dispelled the notion of free will for the *individual*. But social science is still so immature as to permit one to find refuge in a collective free will. As Professor A. L. Kroeber has recently observed:

I suspect that the resistance [to the thesis of cultural determinism] goes back to the common and deeply implanted assumption that our wills are free. As this assumption has had to yield ground elsewhere, it has taken refuge in the collective, social, and historical sphere. Since the chemists, physiologists, and psychologists have unlimbered their artillery, the personal freedom of the will is thankless terrain to maintain. Culture they have not yet attacked; so that becomes a refuge. Whatever the degree to which we have ceased to assert being free agents as individuals, in the social realm we can still claim to shape our destinies. The theologian is piping pretty small, but the social reformer very loud. We are renouncing the kingdom of heaven, but going to establish a near-millenium on earth. Our personal wills may be determined, but by collectivizing them we can still have social freedom.[10]

Primitive man could believe that he could control the weather only because he was ignorant; he knew virtually nothing of meteorology. And today, it is only our profound and comprehensive ignorance of the nature of culture that makes it possible for us to believe that we direct and control it. As man's knowledge and understanding grew in meteorology, his illusion of power and control dissipated. And as our understanding of culture increases, our illusion of control will languish and disappear. As Durkheim once observed, "as far as social facts are concerned, we still have the mentality of primitives." [11]

Needless to say, this is not the view taken by many today who look to science for our salvation. Far from expecting belief in our ability to control to diminish with the advance of social science, many people expect just the reverse. It has become the fashion these days to declare that if only our social sciences were as advanced as the physical sciences, then we could control our culture as we now control the physical forces of nature. The following quotation from a letter published in *Science* recently is a conservative statement of this point of view:

> For if, by employing the scientific method, men can come to understand and control the atom, there is reasonable likelihood that they can in the same way learn to understand and control human group behavior . . . It is quite within reasonable probability that social science can provide these techniques [i.e., for "keeping the peace"] if it is given anything like the amount of support afforded to physical science in developing the atomic bomb.[12]

In similar vein Professor Gordon W. Allport of Harvard observes that "the United States spent two billion dollars on the invention of the atomic bomb" and asks "What is there absurd in spending an equivalent sum, if necessary, on the discovery of means for its control?" [13]

The premise underlying this view is unsound. It assumes that wars are caused, or at least made possible, by ignorance and the lack of social control that goes with ignorance. It assumes that, given understanding through generous grants of funds to social scientists, wars could be prevented—the "peace could be kept." The lack of understanding and realism displayed here is pathetic. The instinct of self-preservation of a society that subsidized atom bomb inventors rather than social scientists holding views such as these is a sure one. Wars are not caused by ignorance, nor can "the peace be kept" by the findings of social scientists. Wars are struggles between social organisms—called nations—for survival, struggles for the possession and use of the resources of the earth, for fertile fields; coal, oil, and iron deposits; for uranium mines; for seaports and waterways; for markets and trade routes; for military bases. No amount of understanding will alter or remove the basis of this struggle, any more than an understanding of the ocean's tides will diminish or terminate their flow.

But the fallacy of assuming that we can increase and perfect our control over civilization through social science is even more egregious than we have indicated. To call upon science, the essence of which is acceptance of the principles of cause and effect and determinism, to support a philosophy of Free Will, is fairly close to the height of absurdity. Verily, Science has become the modern magic! The belief that man can work his will upon nature and man alike if only he had the right formulas once flourished in primitive society as magic. It is still with us today, but we now call it Science.

No amount of development of the social sciences would increase or perfect man's control over civilization by one iota. In the man-culture system, man is the dependent, culture the independent, variable. What man thinks, feels, and does is determined by his culture. And culture behaves in accordance with its own laws. A mature development of social science would only make this fact clear.

The philosophy of Free Will and omnipotence is rampant in the field of education (see p. 107). "Educators," high school principals, commencement orators, and others never seem to tire of telling the world that its salvation lies in education. An eminent anthropologist, the late Clark Wissler, looking at our civilization as he would at other cultures of mankind—of the Blackfoot Indians, the Bantu tribes of Africa, or the aborigines of Australia —finds that a faith in education and its efficacy to cure all ills is a characteristic trait of our culture. "The fact is," he says, "that we seek to solve every difficulty by education. . . . No matter what it may be, the combating of disease, the inauguration of a new public service, the appreciation of art, dress reform, or anything of that kind, we look to education to make it universal and popular." Our faith in education has, in fact, become our religion, as Dr. Wissler sees it:

"Our culture is characterized by an overruling belief in something we call education—a kind of mechanism to propitiate the intent of nature in the manifestation of culture. Our implicit faith that this formula, or method, will cause this purpose to be more happily fulfilled, is our real religion." [14]

Dr. Wissler compares our education formula with the magical formulas of primitive tribes:

We often find among peoples we choose to call less civilized, a class of men whom we designate as shamans, medicine men, conjurors, etc. . . . Where such men flourish they are called upon whenever the course of events goes wrong, sickness, famine, love, war, no matter what the nature of the trouble may be, and they always proceed in one way: i.e., recite or demonstrate a formula of some kind. They may sing it, they may dance it, or they may merely act it out—no matter, the idea is that if you go through with the correct formula the forces of nature will right the wrong. . . . In every culture formulae are used to propitiate nature in whatever form of gods or powers she is conceived, and . . . cultures differ not in this, for so far they are all alike, but as to the kinds of formulae into which they put their faith. Our great formula for bringing about the realization of our leading ideals is education. . . . It is a kind of grand over-formula by which we hope to perpetuate and perfect our culture . . .[15]

The faith of primitive man in his formulas and rituals, his medicine men and conjurors, was not shaken by a perpetual repetition of the ills they were supposed to prevent or cure. Lack of success did not prove to him that his formulas and rituals were inefficacious; it only convinced him that he needed more and better magic. And we who look to education for our "salvation" are not shaken in our faith by the spectacle of tragedy piled upon disaster. What we need, we say, is more education.

To primitive man, magic was a means, available to mankind, to exert influence upon the external world and so to shape it to his needs and desires. We think of education as an instrument with which we can transform society and mould it to our will. But education is not a force or instrument *outside* of society, but a *process within it.* It is, so to speak, a physiologic process of the social organism. Education is a means employed by society in carrying on its own activities, in striving for its own objectives. Thus, during peacetime, society educates for peace, but when the nation is at war, it educates for war. In times of peace, munitions-makers are "Merchants of Death"; in wartime, "Victory is Their Business." In peacetime, He is the Prince of Peace, but when war comes it's "Praise the Lord and pass the ammunition." It is not people who control their culture through education; it is rather the other way around: education, formal and informal, is the process of bringing each new generation under the control of a system of culture. It is unrealistic in the extreme, therefore, to think of education reforming society from the outside. No one has stated the relationship between education and society better than the great French social scientist, Emile Durkheim:

> But this is to attribute to education a power which it does not possess. It is only the image, the reflection of society. Education imitates society and reproduces it in abridged form, but it does not create it. Education is healthy when the nation itself is in a healthy state, but, not having the power of self modification, it becomes corrupted when the nation decays. If the moral milieu as it is experienced by the teachers themselves is corrupt, they cannot fail to be affected by it; how then can they impress upon those whom they train an outlook that differs from the one that they have received? Each generation is brought up by the previous generation and it is necessary therefore to reform the latter if it is to improve the one which follows it. We go around in circles. At long intervals it may well happen that someone may come along whose ideas and aspirations are in advance of those of his contemporaries, but the moral constitution of a people is not made over by these isolated individuals. No doubt it pleases us to believe that one eloquent voice is sufficient to transform the social fabric as if by magic, but, here as elsewhere, something is not produced from nothing. The strongest wills cannot create out of nothing forces which do not exist, and failures in experience always come to dispel these easy illusions. Besides, even though a pedagogical system could succeed by an incomprehensible miracle in establishing itself in antagonism to the social system, it would have no effect by reason of this very antagonism. If the collective organization (society) is maintained from which the moral state that one wishes to combat is derived, then the child cannot fail to be influenced by it from the moment he comes into contact with it. The artificial milieu of the school can only protect him for a time and then but feebly. In proportion as

the real world takes greater hold of him, it will destroy the work
of the educator. Thus education cannot reform itself unless
society itself is reformed. And in order to do that we must go
to the causes of the malady from which it suffers.[16]

The position taken here will of course be vigorously denied and
opposed. People do not give up their illusions easily. As A. L.
Kroeber has put it:

Our minds instinctively resist the first shock of the recognition
of a thing [cultural determinism] so intimately woven into us
and yet so far above and so uncontrollable by our wills. We feel
driven to deny its reality, to deny even the validity of dealing
with it as an entity; just as men at large have long and bitterly
resented admitting the existence of purely automatic forces
and system in the realm that underlies and carries and makes
possible the existence of our personalities: the realm of
nature.[17]

A common reaction—verbal reflex—to the theory of cultural
determinism is to brand it "fatalistic" or "defeatist." Long ago
William James branded as "the most pernicious and immoral of
fatalisms" the philosophy of "the contemporary sociological
school" that espoused "general laws and predetermined tendencies," and "denied the vital importance of individual initiative"
and Free Will ("I believe in free-will myself," he says).[18] And
today another student of philosophy, Dr. David Bidney, writing
in the American Anthropologist, has repeatedly called the deterministic point of view of culturology "fatalistic." The choice of
words is significant. Why is it that when one employs the principle of cause and effect in the realm of physical and chemical
phenomena no one cries "fatalism," but the instant one applies
it to human cultural phenomena this accusation leaps forth?
Why is it that an admission of our inability to control the weather

brings forth no charge of "defeatism" whereas this reproach is promptly levelled against anyone who recognizes man's inability to control the course of civilization?

The reason is fairly plain. "Fatalism" implies Free Will; "defeatism," omnipotence. When atoms, cells, or tissues behave in accordance with their nature and properties no one calls it fatalistic because no one expects freedom of choice and action of them. But when one asserts that cultural phenomena have a nature of their own and consequently must behave in terms of their nature, the response is not an acceptance of the principle of cause and effect but a charge of "fatalism." "To many educated minds," the great English anthropologist, E. B. Tylor, wrote many years ago, "there seems something presumptuous and repulsive in the view that the history of mankind is part and parcel of the history of nature, that our thoughts, wills, and actions accord with laws as definite as those which govern the motion of the waves, the combination of acids and bases, and the growth of plants . . . If law is anywhere it is everywhere." [19] We have combined "a scientific realism, based on mechanism," says Alfred North Whitehead, with "an unwavering belief in the world of men and of the higher animals as being composed of *self-determining organisms*" [20] (emphasis ours). He feels that this "radical inconsistency" is responsible for "much that is half-hearted and wavering in our civilization. It . . . enfeebles . . . [thought] by reason of the inconsistency lurking in the background."

Implicit in the charge of "fatalism" and "defeatism" is the further notion of refutation. To brand a view "fatalistic" is, to many minds, to call it false as well. "Cultural determinism is fatalistic and therefore false," is about the way the reasoning would go if it were made explicit. "*How can determinism possibly exist?*" is the question that is implied but unspoken. "Determinism is unthinkable." And so it is to one possessed by a philosophy of free will.* We find this point of view rather well expressed by Lawrence K. Frank in a recent article, "What is Social Order?"

> Perhaps the major obstacle we face today, therefore, is this essentially defeatist tradition expressed in the various conceptions of social order described earlier, as above and beyond all human control . . . In this situation, therefore, we can and we must find the courage to view social order as that which must be achieved by man himself.[21]

Of course man can "find the courage" to view social order as something "that must be achieved by himself." It does not take courage to do this, however; what is required is ignorance and hope. "Must find the courage," "must be achieved by man himself," is hardly the language of science. It is, rather, exhortation and rhetoric—of a type with which we have long been familiar: "if we will but purpose in our hearts . . ."

No doubt the first to question man's control over the weather, the first to claim that the winds will blow, the rain and snow fall, the seasons come and go, in accordance with their own nature rather than in obedience to man's wish and will expressed in spell and ritual, were accused of "fatalism" and "defeatism," if, indeed, they were not dealt with more harshly. But, in time, we have come to accept our impotence in this regard and to become reconciled to it. If it be argued that man cannot control the weather because that is a part of the external world whereas

---

* Note that we have said *possessed by*, rather than "believes in." Philosophies possess, hold, animate, guide and direct the articulate, protoplasmic mechanisms that are men. Whether a man—an average man, typical of his group—"believes in" Christ or Buddha, Genesis or Geology, Determinism or Free Will, is not a matter of his own choosing. His philosophy is merely the response of his neuro-sensory-muscular-glandular system to the streams of cultural stimuli impinging upon him from the outside. What is called "philosophizing" is merely the interaction of these cultural elements within his organism. His "choice" of philosophic beliefs is merely a neurological expression of the superior strength of some of these extra-somatic cultural forces.

culture, being man-made, is subject to his control, it must be
pointed out that the exact opposite is the case. It is precisely in
the realm of the external world that man's control is possible. He
can harness the energies of rivers, fuels, and atoms because he, as
one of the forces of nature, lies *outside* their respective systems
and can therefore act upon them. But man, as an animal organism, as a species, lies *within* the man-culture system, and there he
is the dependent, not the independent, variable; his behavior is
merely the function of his culture, not its determinant. Both
theoretically and practically, therefore, it is possible for man to
exert more control over the weather than over culture, for he
can exert *some* control over the former even now and he may increase this control in the future. But he exerts no control whatever over his culture and theoretically there is no possibility of
his ever doing so.

The usual reactions to this manifesto of cultural determinism
are as unwarranted as are the assumptions of Free Will, from
which, of course, these responses flow. After expostulating on the
theme of "fatalism" and "defeatism" the conventional protest
goes on to demand, "What is the use then of our efforts? Why
should we try to do anything to improve our lot if we have no
control over our culture? Why not just sit back and let the
evolutionary process take care of everything? Of what use could
a science of culture possibly be to us if control lies beyond our
grasp? What good is an understanding of culture if there is nothing we can do about it?"

These questions are naive and betray a lack of understanding
of what the cultural determinist—the culturologist—is trying to
say. The determinist does not assert that man is irrelevant to the
culture process. He knows full well that the contrary is the case;
that man is an absolute prerequisite to it, that without man there
could be no culture. He realizes very clearly the essential role
that man plays in the system that is man-and-culture. What the

culturologist contends is that in this system the human organism is not the determinant; that the behavior of the culture process cannot be explained in terms of this organism but only in terms of the culture itself; that the growth and changes among the Indo-European languages, for example, cannot be accounted for in terms of man's nerves, muscles, senses, or organs of speech; or in terms of his hopes, needs, fears, or imagination. Language must be explained in terms of language.

But to turn to some of the specific questions with which dissatisfaction with the philosophy of determinism is expressed. In the first place, we cannot "just sit back" and let the evolutionary process take care of all our problems. While we live we are confronted by our culture and we must come to terms with it. Even just sitting back, incubating a case of dementia praecox, is "doing something about it." So is committing suicide; as a matter of fact, suicide rates for various societies provide excellent indexes of cultural determinism. In some societies the rate is high; in others suicide is virtually non-existent. This is not because suicide determinants are more abundant in the chromosomes of some populations than of others. It is due to the fact that the cultural determinants vary: hara-kiri is something that a culture does to an organism that, of its own nature, tends to persevere in that form of motion we call "Life." It is obvious that we cannot avoid reacting to our culture.

To assume that the process of cultural evolution will take care of everything without effort on our part is of course absurd, and constitutes no part of the determinist's philosophy. Of course we must exert ourselves while we live; we cannot do otherwise. But the question is not "Who does the work, ourselves or cultural evolution?" It is obvious that the energy is expended by or through human beings. The question is, *What determines the nature, the form and content of this expression of energy in the culture process, the human organism or the extra-somatic culture?* The answer is of course fairly obvious—after a small amount of reflection. Let us consider two groups of human organisms, A and B. Group A raises taro, catches fish, carves wood, makes no pottery, speaks a Polynesian language, has chiefs but no currency, is non-literate, drinks kava, is greatly concerned with genealogy, and so on. Group B mines coal and iron, talks Welsh, imports its food from the outside, uses money, is literate, drinks ale, etc. Now the question is, Why does each group behave as it does? Is it that one group of organisms possesses traits or characteristics—genes, instincts, or psychological tendencies—that cause them to drink kava rather than ale? This is, of course, ridiculous; the one group of organisms is fundamentally like the other biologically. It is obvious that each group of organisms behaves as it does because each is reacting to a particular set of cultural stimuli. It is obvious also that a consideration of the human organism is totally irrelevant to the question. Why is one group stimulated by one set of stimuli rather than by another? This is a cultural historical question, not a biological or psychological one. So, one is not so silly as to say, "Why should we mine coal or catch fish? Let our culture do it." The question is not who mines the coal, but what is the determinant of this behavior? And, the culturologist points out the obvious: the culture is the determinant.

The reaction of many sincere, altruistic and conscientious people, upon being told that it is not they who control their culture and direct its course, is "Why then should we try to do good, to better our lot and that of mankind?" We have answered this question in part already. In the first place one cannot avoid trying to do something. As long as one accepts life and is willing to continue with it he must exert himself. "Trying" is merely the name we give to the effort exerted in the process of living. To strive for this or that, therefore, is inseparable from our lives. But what one strives for and how his effort is expressed is determined by his culture. For example, the goal of one people may be eternal life in heaven for which their terrestrial existence is but a preparation. The goal of another might be the good life "here below." One group may deny the reality of sickness; another may admit its existence and try to combat it. One group may use charms and incantations; another, clinics and laboratories. Whatever the goal and whatever the means employed to reach it, is a matter determined by the culture of the group.

But, it should be pointed out with emphasis, this is not a philosophy of defeatism or hopelessness by any means. Least of all does it declare that one's efforts do not count. The fact that one's efforts to stamp out tuberculosis are culturally determined in no way minimizes the effort or the result. A life saved is a life saved. A letter written to a congressman has an effect, too, no matter what kind or how much. A resolution on world affairs passed by a woman's club has a real function in society, although it may be a very different one from that imagined by the good ladies. The question we raise is not one of the value of effort or whether effort has consequences. Human effort is just as real as anything in the realm of the geologist. And effort is followed by consequences just as effect follows cause in physics or geology. Living human beings cannot help but exert themselves, and everything they do counts for something in one way or another. Far from wishing to deny or ignore this, we wish to emphasize it. But this is not the question raised by the culturologist, the cultural determinist. What he claims is, not that it is futile to try because what one does counts for nought, but that what one does, how he does it, and the end and purpose for which it is done is culturally determined, is determined by the culture of the group rather than by the free will of the individual or of the group. More than that, what a person or group desires is determined or at least defined by the culture, not by them. What constitutes the "good life" for any people is always culturally defined.

From the cultural determinist's point of view, human beings are merely the instruments through which cultures express themselves. A physician, saving lives each day, is an instrument through which certain cultural forces express themselves; if they were not there, or if they were different, the organism in question would not be practicing medicine or he would practice it in a different way. The gangster, evangelist, revolutionist, reformer, policeman, impoverished beggar, wealthy parasite, teacher, soldier, and shaman are likewise instruments of cultural action and expression; each is a type of primate organism grasped and wielded by a certain set of culture traits. It is only the inveterate habit of thinking anthropocentrically that makes this point of view seem strange or ridiculous.

But, granting that what we do counts even though it is culturally determined, of what use is it to develop a science of culture if we cannot control civilization or direct its course? We have a science of pathology in order to combat disease, sciences of physics and chemistry to control the external world. But if we do not control our culture and cannot ever hope to control it, of what use would a science of culture be? We might begin our reply to this question by asking, of what value is it to know the temperature of a star a million light years away? Questions such as these betray a limited understanding of science. Science is not primarily a matter of control in the sense of harnessing rivers with hydroelectric plants or constructing uranium piles. Science is a means of adjustment; control is but one aspect of adjustment. Man finds himself in a universe to which he must adjust if he is to continue to live in it. Mythology and science are means of adjustment; they are interpretations of the world in terms of which man behaves. There is, of course, a vast difference in terms of adjustment between a philosophy that interprets stars as a flock of snow birds lost in the sky, and one that measures their masses, distances, dimensions, and temperatures. This difference is a very practical one, too, in terms of the contribution that each philosophy makes to the security of life.

Our ancestors once thought they could control the weather as contemporary savages still do. They finally outgrew this illusion, even going so far as to outgrow calling the new view "fatalistic" and "defeatist." But we do not think a knowledge and an understanding of weather and climate useless. On the contrary, we are devoting more time and money to meteorology now than ever before. Here again we see the situation in terms of adjustment rather than *control*. We may not be able to control the weather but adjust to it we must. And knowledge and understanding make for more effective and satisfying adjustments. It would be advantageous if we *could* control the weather. But if we cannot, then weather prediction is the next best thing. And for prediction we must have knowledge and understanding.

So it is with culture. We cannot control its course but we can learn to predict it. As a matter of fact, we make predictions all the time and many of them are quite accurate: wheat production, traffic fatalities, freight car loadings, births, exhaustion of oil reserves, and many other matters are already within the reach of limited but nevertheless valuable prediction. If our ability to predict were greatly increased by the development and maturation of a science of culture the possibilities of a rational, effective, and humane adjustment between man and culture and between one cultural segment and another would be increased accordingly. If, for example, a science of culture could demonstrate that the trend of social evolution is toward larger political groupings, then the chances of making the futile attempt to restore or maintain the independence of small nations would be lessened. If the trend of cultural evolution is away from private property and free enterprise why strive to perpetuate them? If it could be shown that international wars will continue as long as independent, sovereign nations exist, then certain delusions now popular would find less nourishment and support. The fact is that culture has been evolving as an unconscious, blind, bloody, brutal, tropismatic process so far. It has not yet reached the point where intelligence, self-consciousness, and understanding are very conspicuous. Our ignorance is still deep-rooted and widespread. We do not understand even some of the most elementary things—the prohibition of polygamy for example. In short, we are so ignorant that we can still believe that it is we who make our culture and control its course.

This ignorance is not surprising however. It has not been very long since we gave up burning witches, cudgelling hysterics to drive out demons, and other savage practices. Even in technology, which tends to outstrip the social and ideological sectors, we have surpassed the savage at two points—fire-making and the use of the bow and arrow—only within the last century or two. Chemical matches are but a little more than a century old and the bow and arrow was used in bison hunting on the American plains in preference to the best firearms available at the time within the last hundred years. It is only yesterday, culturologically speaking, that a small portion of mankind began to emerge from a condition of savagery. For most of his career thus far man has subsisted wholly upon wild foods; less than two per cent of human history, as a matter of fact, has elapsed since the origin of agriculture. Other significant indexes: some 0.7 per cent of culture history since the beginning of metallurgy, 0.35% since the first alphabet, 0.033% since Galileo, 0.009% since the publication of Darwin's The Origin of Species, and only 0.002% since William Jennings Bryan and the Scopes trial. A mature, urbane, and rational civilization is not to be achieved in a mere million years from the anthropoid level.

It should be made clear that if an adequate understanding should come about as a consequence of a science of culture it would not have been "us" who achieved it but our culture. In the interaction of elements in the culture process, those traits less effective in providing adequate adjustment in terms of understanding and control are gradually relinquished and replaced by more effective traits. Thus, bronze axes replace stone axes, ikons and spells give way to laboratories and clinics, and finally, a science of human culture begins to challenge the primitive philosophy of omnipotence and Free Will. The new science will of course have to prove its superiority over the older view just as astronomy, chemistry, and medicine have in other sectors of experience. The success of science—the philosophy of materialism, of cause and effect, of determinism—in the physical and biological sectors of experience encourages us greatly in the belief that this point of view and these techniques of interpretation will prove effective in the social sphere also.

Our role in this process is a modest one. Neither as groups nor as individuals do we have a choice of roles or of fates. Swedes are born into their culture just as Zulus, Tibetans, and Yankees are born into theirs. And each individual is thrust by birth into some particular place in the "magnetic field" of his culture, there to be molded by the particular organization of cultural influences that play upon him. Thus he may have the belief that typhoid exists only in the mind, or is caused by witches or bacilli, thrust upon him—or "into his mind." He may be endowed with a belief in personal immortality, the efficacy of prayer, or the Periodic Law of Mindeleyev. He may be inspired to preach the only true faith to the heathen in distant lands, or to wear out his life in a genetics laboratory, or to believe that "only saps work." To be sure, the response of the human organism to cultural stimulation will vary with the quality of the organism. Some will be silk purses; others, sows' ears. The order in which an organism undergoes experiences is important, too; the influence of events a, b, c, will not be the same as a, c, b. An experience will have one effect at fifteen; quite another at fifty. There is room, therefore, for almost infinite variety of permutation and combination in the experience of individual organisms.

Man discovers his place in the cosmos slowly and accepts it with extreme reluctance. Time was when his solid earth was planted in the center, the sun and stars spread upon the vault of heaven, and men and gods together acted out the drama of life and death. It was all so compact, so familiar, so secure. Then it was that man, like God, could cry "Let there be light" and there was light. Like God, too, man was "omnipotent," if, however, to a lesser degree. With his magic formulas, his spells, prayers, charms, and rituals, mighty man could control the weather, the seasons, and even enlist the gods in the service of man. Now it is different. Man finds himself but one of innumerable animal species crawling about on an insignificant planetary speck, fighting, feeding, breeding, dying. Once the child of God, he now find himself an ex-ape. But he has acquired a new faculty, one unknown among all other species: articulate speech. As a consequence of this, a new way of life has been developed: culture. But this culture, this mass of extra-somatic tools, institutions and philosophies, has a life and laws of its own. Man is just beginning to understand this.

Man is wholly at the mercy of external forces, astronomic and geologic. As a matter of fact, it is rather disconcerting to think of how narrow is the margin within which man lives. Change the temperature, velocity, amount of water, or atmosphere of the earth but a little and life would cease. It is a curious, and from a cosmic viewpoint, momentary, concatenation of circumstances that has made life possible. Man did long rebel against his dependence upon these outside forces; to be wholly at their mercy was unendurable. As a matter of fact, man has employed his precious and unique gift of speech more to deny the facts of his existence than to improve upon them. But a certain portion of the human race has come at last to accept our dependence upon nature and to try to make the most of it.

And so it is with culture. Belief in our omnipotence has, as Durkheim says, always been a source of weakness to us. But we are now discovering the true nature of culture and we can in time reconcile ourselves to this extra-somatic order as we have to the astronomic, geologic, and meteorologic orders. To give up magic and mythology which promised much but yielded nothing—nothing but the soothing comfort of illusion—was a painful experience. But to receive and accept a science and a technology which promises less but achieves a great deal is to reach a goal most men are loathe to lose. We may believe that knowledge and understanding of culture will make for a more satisfactory life just as these traits have been of value in physics and biology. To be sure, understanding culture will not, as we have argued here, alter its course or change the "fate" that it has in store for us, any more than understanding the weather or the tides will change them. But as long as man remains an inquiring primate he will crave understanding. And a growing Science of Culture will provide him with it.

PART III ENERGY AND CIVILIZATION

Introduction

*I*n the preceding chapters we have dealt with various aspects of the culture process. We now encompass it in its entirety.

The development of human culture as a whole is here interpreted upon the culturological level. And, in addition to further demonstration, we provide, in this Part, a dynamic interpretation of culture growth in terms of its most fundamental factor, namely, energy. Cultures are dynamic systems; they require energy for their activation. The history of civilization is the story of the control over the forces of nature by cultural means. But the story of energy control may provide the epitaph of civilization, also. In its infancy or youth, culture achieved control over fire. Plants and animals were brought within the orbit of cultural control in Neolithic times through the arts of agriculture and animal husbandry. Coal and oil and water power were harnessed, and culture became of age. And now culture has succeeded in penetrating to the core of matter itself and has learned how to create energy, even as the Sun, our Father in Heaven, has created it since the dawn of time. And this advance may possibly be the last. In the symbolism of an ancient myth, it may indeed be hazardous to eat of the fruit of every tree in the garden. The mastery of terrestrial fire was tolerable, but to create energy by the transformation of matter is to play with celestial fire. Whether it can be done with impunity remains to be seen. The new Prometheus may also be the executioner.

CHAPTER THIRTEEN

ENERGY AND THE EVOLUTION OF CULTURE

"The degree of civilization of any epoch, people, or group of peoples,
is measured by ability to utilize energy for human advancement or
needs . . ."—George Grant MacCurdy, *Human Origins* [1]
". . . the history of civilization becomes the history of man's advancing control over energy . . ."—Wilhelm Ostwald, *The Modern Theory
of Energetics* [1]

*H*aving examined the culture process in a number of its
aspects, we now turn to a consideration of it as a whole.

As we have already seen, "culture" is the name of a distinct
order, or class, of phenomena, namely, those things and events
that are dependent upon the exercise of a mental ability, peculiar
to the human species, that we have termed "symbolling." To be
more specific, culture consists of material objects—tools, utensils,
ornaments, amulets, etc.—acts, beliefs, and attitudes that function
in contexts characterized by symbolling. It is an elaborate mechanism, an organization of exosomatic ways and means employed
by a particular animal species, man, in the struggle for existence
and survival.

One of the significant attributes of culture is its transmissibility
by non-biological means. Culture in all its aspects, material, social,
and ideological, is easily and readily transmitted from one individual, one generation, one age, one people, or one region, to
another by *social* mechanisms. Culture is, so to speak, a form of
social heredity. We thus view culture as a continuum, a supra-

biological, extra-somatic order of things and events, that flows down through time from one age to the next.

We have seen also, in preceding chapters, that since culture constitutes a distinct order of phenomena, it can be described and interpreted in terms of principles and laws of its own. Cultural elements act and react upon one another in their own way. We can discover the principles of behavior of various sub-classes of cultural elements and of cultural systems as a whole; and we can formulate the laws of cultural phenomena and systems.

We now propose to sketch the evolution of culture from its beginning upon an anthropoid level to the present time. We may regard the human race—man—as a one. We may likewise think of all of the various cultures, or cultural traditions, as constituting a single entity: the culture of mankind. We may, therefore, address ourselves to the task of tracing the course of the development of this culture from its source to the present day.

Let us return for a moment to a further consideration of the structure and function of the organization of things and processes, the system, that we call culture. Culture is an organized, integrated system. But we may distinguish subdivisions within, or aspects of, this system. For our purpose, we shall distinguish three sub-systems of culture, namely, technological, sociological, and ideological systems. The technological system is composed of the material, mechanical, physical, and chemical instruments, together with the techniques of their use, by means of which man, as an animal species, is articulated with his natural habitat. Here we find the tools of production, the means of subsistence, the materials of shelter, the instruments of offense and defense. The sociological system is made up of interpersonal relations expressed in patterns of behavior, collective as well as individual. In this category we find social, kinship, economic, ethical, political, military, ecclesiastical, occupational and professional, recreational, etc., systems. The ideological system is composed of ideas, beliefs, knowledge, expressed in articulate speech or other symbolic form. Mythologies and theologies, legend, literature, philosophy, science, folk wisdom and common sense knowledge, make up this category.

These three categories comprise the system of culture as a whole. They are, of course, interrelated; each reacts upon the others and is affected by them in turn. But the influence of this mutual interaction is not equal in all directions. The roles played by the several sub-systems in the culture process as a whole are not equal by any means. The primary role is played by the technological system. This is, of course, as we would expect it to be; it could not be otherwise. Man as an animal species, and consequently culture as a whole, is dependent upon the material, mechanical means of adjustment to the natural environment. Man must have food. He must be protected from the elements. And he must defend himself from his enemies. These three things he must do if he is to continue to live, and these objectives are attained only by technological means. The technological system is therefore both primary and basic in importance; all human life and culture rest and depend upon it.

Social systems are in a very real sense secondary and subsidiary to technological systems. In fact a social system may be defined realistically as the organized effort of human beings in the use of the instruments of subsistence, offense and defense, and protection. A social system is a function of a technological system. A ship, says Childe, "and the tools employed in its production symbolize a whole economic system." The technology is the independent variable, the social system the dependent variable. Social systems are therefore determined by systems of technology; as the latter change, so do the former. "The bronze axe which replaces . . . [the stone axe]," again to quote Childe, "is not only a superior implement, it also presupposes a more complex economic and social structure." [2]

Ideological, or philosophical, systems are organizations of beliefs in which human experience finds its interpretation. But experience

and interpretations thereof are powerfully conditioned by technologies. There is a type of philosophy proper to every type of
technology. The interpretation of a system of experience in which
a *coup de poing* is a characteristic feature will, as it must, reflect
this kind of experience. It would not be improper to speak of a
coup de poing type of philosophy as well as of technology. A
pastoral, agricultural, metallurgical, industrial, or military technology will each find its corresponding expression in philosophy.
One type of technology will find expression in the philosophy of
totemism, another in astrology or quantum mechanics.

But experience of the external world is not felt and interpreted
merely at the point of technological articulation; it is filtered
through the prism of social systems also. The qualities and features
of social, political, ecclesiastical, economic, military, etc., systems
are therefore reflected in philosophies.

We may view a cultural system as a series of three horizontal
strata: the technological layer on the bottom, the philosophical
on the top, the sociological stratum in between. These positions
express their respective roles in the culture process. The technological system is basic and primary. Social systems are functions of
technologies; and philosophies express technological forces and reflect social systems. The technological factor is therefore *the* determinant of a cultural system as a whole. It determines the form of
social systems, and technology and society together determine
the content and orientation of philosophy. This is not to say,
of course, that social systems do not condition the operation of
technologies, or that social and technological systems are not
affected by philosophies. They do and are. But to condition is
one thing; to determine, quite another.

We are now in possession of a key to an understanding of the
growth and development of culture: technology. A human being is
a material body; the species, a material system. The planet earth
is a material body; the cosmos, a material system. Technology

is the mechanical means of articulation of these two material systems, man and cosmos. But these systems are dynamic, not static; energy as well as matter is involved. Everything—the cosmos, man, culture—may be described in terms of matter and energy.

The Second Law of Thermodynamics tells us that the cosmos as a whole is breaking down structurally and running down dynamically; matter is becoming less organized and energy more uniformly diffused. But in a tiny sector of the cosmos, namely in living material systems, the direction of the cosmic process is reversed: matter becomes more highly organized and energy more concentrated. Life is a building up process. But in order to run counter to the cosmic current, biological organisms must draw upon free energy in non-living systems, capture it and put it to work in the maintenance of the vital process. All life is a struggle for free energy. Biological evolution is simply an expression of the thermodynamic process that moves in a direction opposite to that specified for the cosmos as a whole by the Second Law. It is a movement toward greater organization, greater differentiation of structure, increased specialization of function, higher levels of integration, and greater degrees of energy concentration.

From a zoological standpoint, culture is but a means of carrying on the life process of a particular species, *Homo sapiens*. It is a mechanism for providing man with subsistence, protection, offense and defense, social regulation, cosmic adjustment, and recreation. But to serve these needs of man energy is required. It becomes the primary function of culture, therefore, to harness and control energy so that it may be put to work in man's service. Culture thus confronts us as an elaborate thermodynamic, mechanical system. By means of technological instruments energy is harnessed and put to work. Social and philosophic systems are both adjuncts and expressions of this technologic process. The functioning of culture as a whole therefore rests upon and is determined by the

amount of energy harnessed and by the way in which it is put
to work.*

But "the way in which it is put to work" introduces another
factor besides energy. Energy by itself is meaningless. To be
significant in cultural systems, energy must be harnessed, directed,
and controlled. This is of course accomplished by technological
means, by means of tools of one kind or another. The efficiency
of technological means varies; some are better than others. The
amount of food, clothing, or other goods produced by the expenditure of a given amount of energy will be proportional to
the efficiency of the technological means with which the energy
is put to work, other factors remaining constant.

We may therefore distinguish three factors in any cultural
situation or system: (1) the amount of energy harnessed per
capita per year; (2) the efficiency of the technological means with
which energy is harnessed and put to work; and, (3) the magnitude of human need-serving goods and services produced. Assuming the factor of habitat to be a constant, the degree of cultural
development, measured in terms of amount of human need-
serving goods and services produced per capita, is determined by
the amount of energy harnessed per capita and by the efficiency
of the technological means with which it is put to work. We may
express this concisely and succinctly with the following formula:
$E \times T \longrightarrow C$, in which C represents the degree of cultural development, E the amount of energy harnessed per capita per year,
and T, the quality or efficiency of the tools employed in the
expenditure of the energy. We can now formulate the basic law
of cultural evolution: Other factors remaining constant, *culture
evolves as the amount of energy harnessed per capita per year
is increased, or as the efficiency of the instrumental means of put-*

* The functioning of any particular culture will of course be conditioned
by local environmental conditions. But in a consideration of culture as a
whole, we may average all environments together to form a constant factor
which may be excluded from our formula of cultural development.

ting the energy to work is increased. Both factors may increase simultaneously of course. We may now sketch the history of cultural development from this standpoint.

If culture is a mechanism for harnessing energy, it must find this energy somewhere; it must lay hold of natural forces in some form or other if they are to be put to work in the service of man's needs. The first source of energy exploited by the earliest cultural systems was, of course, the energy of the human organism itself. The original cultures were activated by human energy and by this source and form alone. The amount of power that an average adult man can generate is small, about $\frac{1}{10}$th of one horsepower. When women and children, the sick, aged, and feeble are considered, the average power resources of the earliest cultural systems might be reckoned at about $\frac{1}{20}$th horsepower per capita. Since the degree of cultural development—the amount of human need-serving goods and services produced per capita—is proportional to the amount of energy harnessed and put to work per capita per year, other factors remaining constant, these earliest cultures of mankind, dependent as they were upon the meager energy resources of the human body, were simple, meager, and crude, as indeed they had to be. No cultural system, activated by human energy alone, can develop very far. Some progress can of course be made by increasing the efficiency of the technological means of putting energy to work, but there is a limit to the extent of cultural advance on this basis. We can form a realistic picture of cultural development within the limits of human energy resources by looking at such modern cultures as those of the Tasmanians, Fuegians, or Andamanese; or the Paleolithic cultures of Europe.

If culture is to advance beyond the limits of maximum technological efficiency and the energy resources of the human body, it must devise new ways to harness additional amounts of energy by tapping natural resources in some new form. In some preliterate cultural systems, fire, wind or water was exploited as a source of energy, but only occasionally and to a very insignificant extent. The conquest of fire was a very early cultural achievement, but it was not until the invention of a practical steam engine that fire became important as a form of energy. Fire was important in early cultures in cooking, providing warmth, frightening wild beasts, and as a symbol, but not as a form of energy. In more advanced cultures, fire was important or essential in the ceramic and metallurgical arts, but here also it is not functioning as a form of energy: i.e., we cannot equate, or substitute, muscle power for fire in any of these contexts. There is one context, however, in which fire functions as energy in some primitive cultures: in hollowing out tree trunks in the manufacture of dugout canoes. Here fire is substituted for muscle power. And there may be a few more similar uses of fire. But, all in all, prior to the invention of the steam engine in modern times, cultural systems made very little use of fire as a form and source of energy which could be substituted for human muscle power.

Primitive peoples could float freight down a flowing stream, but until the invention of the water wheel shortly before the beginning of the Christian era, there was no other way in which moving water could be used as a source of energy for culture building. Wind was not employed as a source of energy until comparatively recent times, and it never has been an important source of power.

Thus, we see that fire, water and wind were utilized as sources of energy only to a very limited and insignificant extent during the first hundreds of thousands of years of culture history. But there is still another source of energy that was available to primitive man, and eventually we find his cultural systems harnessing it: the energy of plants and animals.

Plants are, of course, forms and magnitudes of energy. Energy from the sun is captured by the process of photosynthesis and stored up in the form of plant tissue. All animal life is dependent, in the last analysis, upon this solar energy stored up in plants. All life, therefore, is dependent upon photosynthesis.

The first men subsisted upon plants and animals as, of course, their pre-human ancestors did before them. The earliest culture systems developed techniques of hunting, fishing, trapping, collecting, gathering, etc., as means of exploiting the plant and animal resources of nature. But merely appropriating natural resources is one thing; harnessing and controlling them is quite another. After some 985,000 years of cultural development, certain plants were brought under the control of domestication and cultivation, and various animal species were brought under control through domestication. The energy resources for culture building were greatly increased as a consequence of this increase in control over the forces of nature. The yield of plant food and other useful plant materials per unit of human labor was greatly increased by the substitution of plant cultivation for wild plant gathering. Improved strains were developed through selective breeding. Cultivation, fertilization and irrigation served to increase the yield per unit of human energy, or labor. Among the plants brought under cultivation, the cereals have been especially important. Tylor has called them "the great moving power of civilization." All of the great civilizations of antiquity were brought into being by the cultivation of cereals; no great culture has ever been achieved independently of the cultivation of cereals.

The domestication of animals, too, increased the energy resources for culture building as a consequence of the increase in control over these forms of energy. Their yield in food and other useful animal products per unit of human labor was greatly increased by the substitution of domestication for hunting. In a hunting economy animals had to be killed before they could be used, and when they were consumed more had to be found and killed. By means of domestication a people could subsist upon its herds and flocks without diminishing their numbers at all; they could even be increased. Animals, like plants, were improved through selective breeding, and, in addition to supplying milk, meat, wool, and hides, some species could be used as motive power, either to carry burdens or to draw plows or vehicles. The domestication of animals thus greatly increased the amount of energy under cultural control and available for culture building.

A great advance in cultural development would be expected, therefore, as a consequence of the great increase in the amount of energy harnessed and controlled per capita per year by means of the agricultural and pastoral arts. And this is exactly what took place. The archeological record bears out our theory fully at this point. In a few thousand years after the inauguration of the arts of domestication and cultivation, the great civilizations of antiquity, of Egypt, Mesopotamia, India, China, and, in the New World, in Mexico, Middle America, and the Andean Highlands, came quickly into being. After hundreds of thousands of years of relatively slow and meager development during the Old Stone Ages, culture suddenly shot forward under the impetus of augmented energy resources achieved by agriculture and animal husbandry. Great cities, nations, and empires took the place of villages, tribes, and confederacies as a consequence of the Agricultural Revolution. Rapid progress was made, especially in the Old World, in all of the arts—industrial, esthetic and intellectual. Great engineering projects were undertaken and executed; huge architectural edifices erected. The ceramic, textile and metallurgical arts expanded and flourished. Astronomy, writing, and mathematics were developed. Beginnings were made in a rational science of medicine. Impressive works of art were produced, in relief, sculpture, and even in painting. Development and progress took place in all aspects of culture.

But culture did not advance continuously and indefinitely as a consequence of increased energy resources won by the techniques of agriculture and animal husbandry. After a period of rapid growth, the upward curve of progress levelled off onto a plateau. The peaks of cultural development in Egypt, Mesopotamia, India, and China were reached prior to 1000 B.C., in some cases considerably earlier, and from that time until the beginning of the Fuel Age, about A.D. 1800, no culture of the Old World surpassed, in any profound and comprehensive way, the highest levels achieved in the Bronze Age. This is not to say, of course, that there was no progress at all from 1,000 B.C. to A.D. 1789. There were innovations here and there and many refinements of already existing traits. But, taking cultures as wholes, and measuring them by such yardsticks as size of political unit, size of city, magnitude of architectural edifices and engineering works, density of population, production and accumulation of wealth, etc., the cultures of Europe between the disintegration of the Roman Empire and the rise of the Power Age were in general inferior to those of the ancient oriental civilizations. The reason why cultures did not continue indefinitely to advance under the impetus of an agricultural and stockraising technology is a matter that we shall consider presently.

It appears then that culture had developed about as far as it could on an agricultural and animal husbandry basis before the beginning of the Christian era, at least in the Old World; the New World lagged somewhat behind. And it is reasonable to suppose that culture never would have exceeded the peaks already achieved by this time had not some way been devised to harness additional amounts of energy per capita per year by tapping the forces of nature in a new form. A way was found, however, to do this: energy in the form of coal, and, later, oil and gas, was harnessed by means of steam and internal combustion engines. By tapping the vast deposits of coal, oil and natural gas, a tremendous increase in the amount of energy available for culture building was quickly effected. The consequences of the Fuel Revolution were in general much like those of the Agricultural Revolution: an increase in population, larger political units, bigger cities, an accumulation of wealth, a rapid development of the arts and sciences, in short, a rapid and extensive advance of culture as a whole.

But, again, after a very rapid rise, the curve of cultural development began to show some signs of levelling off. We do not wish to intimate that culture had already gone as far as it could on a Fuel basis, for we do not believe it had; we merely believe that we can detect signs of a slowing down of the advance. But before the question of how far cultural development *could* advance on a Fuel-Agricultural-Animal-Husbandry-Human-Energy basis could become anything like a matter of immediate concern, a tremendously significant technological event took place: the energy resources of atomic nuclei were harnessed. For the first time in culture history energy in a form other than solar had been harnessed. No cultural advance has as yet been effected by the utilization of this new form of energy as a source of industrial power. And before it becomes significant in this respect, another fateful question will have to be met and answered, namely, the consequences of the use of atomic energy in warfare.

Thus we trace the development of culture from anthropoid levels to the present time as a consequence of periodic increases in the amount of energy harnessed per capita per year effected by tapping new sources of power. There is, however, another technological factor involved which we have merely mentioned incidentally so far; we must now consider it more fully, namely, the role of tools in the culture process.

Energy is of course neither created nor annihilated, at least not within cultural systems; it is merely transformed. It is harnessed and it is put to work or expended. But this requires tools and machines. The amount of energy harnessed may, and the amount of human need-serving goods produced per unit of energy does, depend upon the efficiency of the tools employed. So far, we have been holding the tool factor constant and varying the energy factor. We now hold the energy factor constant and vary that of tools. We get, then, the following generalization: *the degree of* cultural development varies directly as the efficiency of the tools employed, other factors remaining constant. If, for example, one is engaged in chopping wood, the amount chopped per unit of energy expended will vary with the efficiency of the axe; the amount will increase with the improvement of axes from the Old Stone Age, through the Neolithic, Bronze, and Iron ages up to the finest axe of alloyed steel of the present day. And so it is with other instrumental means, such as saws, looms, plows, harnesses, wheeled vehicles, boats, etc. Cultural advance is effected, therefore, by an improvement of tools as well as by increases in the amount of energy harnessed.

But the efficiency of a tool cannot be increased indefinitely; there is a point beyond which improvement of any given tool is impossible. Thus, a canoe paddle can be too long or too short, too narrow or too wide, too heavy or too light, etc. We may therefore both imagine and realize a canoe paddle of such size and shape as to make any alteration of either result in a decrease of efficiency. Similarly, we may improve bows and arrows, hoes, plows, saws, etc., up to but not beyond a certain point. Perfection, as a practical matter, is either reached or at least closely approximated. No significant improvement has been made in violins in decades. The steam locomotive has apparently come close to its limits of size and speed. To be sure, improvements may be continued for a time by the use of new materials or alloys and by the application of new mechanical principles. But even so, the improvement of any tool or machine approaches closely, if it does not reach, a limit. We cannot expect locomotives or ocean liners a mile long; they would fall apart of their own weight.

In the culture process therefore, we find that progress and development are effected by the improvement of the mechanical means with which energy is harnessed and put to work as well as by increasing the amounts of energy employed. But this does not mean that the tool and energy factors are of equal weight and significance. The energy factor is the primary and basic one; it is the prime mover, the active agent. Tools are merely the means that serve this power. The energy factor may be increased indefinitely; the efficiency of the tool only within limits. With a given amount of energy, cultural development can progress only so far: to the limits of the efficiency of the tools. When these limits have been reached, no further increases in efficiency can make up for a lack of increase in amount of energy harnessed. But increases in the amount of energy harnessed result in technological progress all along the line, in the invention of new tools and in the improvement of old ones should further improvement be possible. We see, therefore, that important though the tool factor may be, it is merely secondary to the primary and basic factor of energy. And, since increases of energy foster improvement of tools, one may say that it is energy that, at bottom, carries the culture process onward and upward. The general statement that, the environmental factor being constant, the degree of cultural development is proportional to the amount of energy harnessed per capita per year is therefore sound and illuminating.

We turn now to a consideration of social systems in the process of cultural development. A social system is, as we have seen it must be, closely related to its underlying technological system. If a people are nomadic hunters—i.e., use certain technological instruments in certain ways in order to obtain food, furs, hides, and other need-serving materials—they will have one type of social system. If they lead a sedentary life, feeding upon rich beds of shellfish, or if they are pastoralists or intensive agriculturalists, or maritime traders, or industrialists, etc., they will have other types of social systems. The process of military offense and defense and the technological means with which it is exercised also acts as a determinant of social organization, sometimes a very powerful one. Thus we see that the social system of a people is at bottom determined by the use of the technological means of subsistence and of offense and defense. Those social institutions not directly related to the technology are related indirectly; they serve to co-ordinate the various sectors of society with one another and to integrate them into a coherent whole.

The social systems of primitive peoples vary tremendously in detail because the specific circumstances of natural habitat and technology vary. But all social systems resting upon a human energy (i.e., pre-pastoral, pre-agricultural) basis belong to a common type. They are all relatively small and manifest a minimum of structural differentiation and specialization of function. We find no highly developed societies upon the primitive foundation of a technology powered by human energy alone.

The societies of pastoralists and agriculturalists in the early stages of these technological developments are likewise relatively simple, undifferentiated systems. As a matter of fact we may characterize all human social systems up to a certain point in the development of the agricultural, or farming-and-animal-husbandry, technology as *primitive society*: tribes based upon kinship ties, free access to the resources of nature for all, relatively little social differentiation and specialization, and a high degree of social equality. When, however, a certain point in the development of agriculture was reached, a profound change in social systems took place. This was the *social* aspect of the Agricultural Revolution. Let us trace the course of this social revolution in its main outlines at least.

Agriculture and animal husbandry are means of producing more food and other useful materials per unit of human energy than can be obtained by hunting, fishing, or gathering. When agriculture is combined with stock raising the energy resources for culture building are of course greater than when the cultivation of plants alone is practiced. Not only do flocks and herds supply meat, milk, wool or hides, but their muscle power may be used to carry burdens, draw plows and carts, etc. All of the great civilizations of the Old World grew up on the basis of agriculture and animal husbandry. Since, however, it is the cultivation of cereals that is the basic factor in the new agriculture-and-animal-husbandry technology, we may for the sake of brevity speak of "the social consequences of a developing agricultural technology."

As the agricultural arts developed and matured, as plants were improved through selective breeding, as new techniques of cultivation, irrigation, drainage, rotation of crops, fertilization, etc., were introduced and improved, the amount of food produced increased. As the food supply was enlarged the population increased. Small tribes grew into large tribes and these into nations and empires; villages grew into towns and towns into cities.

Not only was *more food* produced by agricultural techniques than by hunting, fishing, and gathering, but more food per capita, more per unit of human labor expended. And, as the agricultural arts developed, the productivity of human labor in this field increased. It gradually became possible for a portion of the population to produce food for all. This meant that a portion of the population could be diverted from agriculture and turned into other channels, such as the industrial and esthetic arts. As the agricultural technology advanced, more and more of the population could thus be withdrawn from the fields and put to work at other tasks and occupations. Society thus became divided along occupational lines, differentiated structurally and specialized functionally. This led to further social developments as we shall see in a moment.

The mere increase in population had important consequences in another direction also. Tribes and clans were organized upon a basis of kinship ties; social relations were largely exercised in this form. This mechanism worked very well as long as the social units were relatively small; a clan or tribe could be effective as a mechanism of social organization and intercourse as long as its members were not exceedingly numerous, as long as social relations could be *personal*. But when, under the impetus of a developing agricultural technology and an increasing food supply, clan and tribal units grew to huge size, they tended to fall apart of their own weight. Primitive society tended therefore to disintegrate as a consequence of sheer increase of numbers. A new type of social organization was therefore required if chaos was to be averted. This new organization was found in the State. This was another consequence of the Agricultural Revolution.

The developing agricultural technology brought about a profound change in economic organization, also. In tribal society production, exchange, and consumption of wealth took place upon a personal, kinship basis; the economic organization was virtually identified with the kinship system. This type of economic organization worked well in a small society with a minimum of division of labor and with little differentiation of social structure along occupational lines. But as society became extensively differentiated, as a consequence of the increase in productivity of human labor in agriculture, a new type of economic system was required; a way of relating classes economically to one another must be devised. This can be done either in a feudal or a monetary-market system. In either case, however, we have a system in which property relations form the basis of social relations rather than the reverse, as was the case in tribal, kinship, society.

On preliterate cultural levels there was of course some fighting between tribal groups. Competition for favored hunting and fishing grounds or other natural resources, vengeance for real or fancied (e.g., magical) injuries, led to a certain amount of intertribal conflict. But the factors necessary for large scale and systematic and sustained warfare were lacking. These were supplied, however, as a consequence of the Agricultural Revolution. A high degree of development of the agricultural, metallurgical, ceramic, and other arts resulted in the production and accumulation of vast amounts of wealth. A rich nation's possessions together with the natural and human resources that made the wealth possible would constitute a rich prize to any people who could conquer it. Warfare became a profitable occupation. Thus we find, especially in Mesopotamia, a condition of almost chronic warfare: nations contending with one another for rich, fertile river valleys, the treasures of palace and temple, one nation conquering and looting another, new empires rising upon the ruins of old.

The social consequences of systematic and chronic warfare are significant: the formation of a professional military class, which in collaboration with political rulers and sometimes even autonomously, may become a powerful political force; the reduction of peoples of conquered nations to the status of slavery or serfdom; and the subordination of the masses at home to the imperatives of prolonged military conflict. Thus warfare tended powerfully to divide society into two major social classes: a relatively small ruling group who organized and directed the campaigns and to whom the overwhelming proportion of the wealth taken as booty went, and a large class who provided the "sinews of war"—the peasants, serfs, the common soldiers, etc. There was often but little difference between the lot of the masses at home and that of the masses of the vanquished nation after conquest and subjugation had been accomplished.

Warfare was not, however, the only means, or social process, that operated to divide societies of the post-Agricultural Revolutionary era into a small, wealthy, powerful, ruling class on the one hand, and a large class of peasants, serfs, or slaves on the other. The peaceful process of commerce, and especially the use of money, operated also to bring about the same end. Trade and commerce are means of concentrating wealth. In this competitive process the big merchants grew at the expense of the small ones. Wealth tended to gravitate into a few hands. Money lending is a particularly rapid and effective means of making the poor poorer and the wealthy richer. When interest rates range from say thirty to one hundred percent or even more, as they did in ancient times, the small borrowers rapidly sink into economic bondage to the money-lenders. It was not at all uncommon in Greece before the reforms of Solon or Kleisthenes for a small farmer to sell his children into slavery in order to pay merely the interest on his loan, let alone the principal. Taxes levied by the ruling class through the mechanism of the state and exorbitant rents levied upon small tenants by large landlords also tended to reduce the masses to a condition of economic bondage and impotence.

Thus we see that the social, political and economic effects of the technological revolution in agriculture were: the dissolution of the old social system of primitive society, the obsolescence of tribe and clan; the division of society into various occupational groups—guilds of artisans and craftsmen; the division of society horizontally into two major classes: a small, powerful, wealthy, ruling class and a large class, governed and exploited by the ruling class and held in bondage in one form or another by them. Civil society based upon property relations took the place of primitive society based upon kinship; the State replaced tribe and clan. The technological revolution in agriculture precipitated and carried through a revolution in the social, political, and economic sectors of culture. As the amount of energy harnessed and put to work per capita per year was increased by the development of the agricultural technology, society became more and more differentiated structurally and increasingly specialized functionally. Concomitant with this trend was the emergence of a special social mechanism of co-ordination of functions and correlation of structures, a mechanism of integration and regulation. This political mechanism had two aspects, secular and ecclesiastic, sometimes closely related, sometimes distinct, but always present. We call this special mechanism of co-ordination, integration and regulation the State-Church. The evolution of civil society from the early metallurgical era to the present day, passing through a variety of forms of the state and class relations, is a story that we shall turn to presently. At this point we wish to return to a matter touched upon earlier.

If culture evolves when and as the amount of energy harnessed per capita per year increases, why did not culture continue to advance indefinitely as a consequence of the technological revolu-

tion in agriculture? As we have already seen, it did not. On the
contrary, after attaining certain levels it ceased to advance and
thereafter continued on a plateau until a new and powerful
impetus came from the Fuel Revolution. Yet, agriculture as a
technological process, as a mechanism of harnessing solar energy,
was not developed to its technological limits by any means; it
has not even yet reached those limits or even approached them
very closely according to agronomists. Why, then, did technological progress in agriculture eventually slow down and virtually
stop after so rapid a rise?

The answer seems to lie in the relationship between socio-
economic system and technological system established by the
Agricultural Revolution. As we have noted, every social system
rests upon and is determined by a technological system. But every
technological system functions *within* a social system and is therefore *conditioned* by it. The social system created by the Agricultural Revolution affected the technological process so as
eventually to "contain it" and to bring further progress in culture
as a whole virtually to a standstill. This is how it was done.

The social system of civil society was, as we have seen, divided
into a ruling class and an exploited class. The latter produced the
wealth; the former appropriated so large a portion of it as to leave
the latter with but minimum means of subsistence. No advantage
would accrue to the producing class if they enlarged their production through increased efficiency; the increment would only be
appropriated by the ruling class. On the other hand, the ruling
class were not likely to resort to a long range plan to improve
the techniques of agricultural production. If they needed more
than they were obtaining at the moment the need was immediate
and a long range plan would have been of no use. They would
therefore resort to greater exactions from the producing class. But
in many, if not most, instances, it would seem, the ruling class
had ample for their needs. As a matter of fact, a great deal of
evidence indicates that one of the problems they had to contend

with was that of overproduction rather than of insufficiency. Thus we see, especially in Egypt but also in Mesopotamia and elsewhere, the ruling class engaging in "conspicuous waste and consumption" and that on a grand scale. Palaces and temples were loaded with wealth and vast treasures were deposited with the dead in tombs. In addition to this, great public works programs— pyramids, monuments, temples, tombs and palaces—were continually being built. It would appear that the ruling class was frequently confronted with the problem of over-production and the threat of technological unemployment or a surplus of population among the lower classes. Their great public works programs, the wholesale disposition of wealth in mortuary customs, etc., enabled them to solve both these problems with one stroke. Thus the social system tended to act as a damper on further increase in technological progress once a certain stage of development had been reached. In addition to the factors mentioned above, Childe has pointed out that the social system operated not only to concentrate wealth in the hands of the ruling minority but effectively prevented the fruits of technological progress from being distributed among the masses of the population. There was, consequently, no chance for the technology of production to expand quantitatively or to improve qualitatively.

We see, then, that the new agricultural technology resulted in a tremendous growth of culture in its initial stages. But in effecting this advance a social system was created that eventually curbed and contained the technological system in such a way as to bring progress virtually to a stop, despite the fact that the *technological* limits of agricultural development had not been even closely approximated. We may reasonably conclude, therefore, that human culture would never have gone substantially beyond the peaks achieved prior to the beginning of the Christian era had not the amount of energy harnessed per capita per year been considerably enlarged by tapping the forces of nature in a new form.

The Fuel Revolution was the culmination and synthesis of a number of streams of cultural elements that had been in progress of development for some time just as the Agricultural Revolution was the organized florescence of trends of earlier ages. And, like its predecessor, the Fuel Revolution brought about great social, political and economic changes as a consequence of greatly augmenting the energy resources for culture building by harnessing solar energy in a new form, this time in coal, oil and natural gas.

As in the case of the Agricultural Revolution, the new fuel technology resulted in a great increase in population. The population of Europe prior to the Coal Age grew only from 100,000,000 in 1650 to 187,000,000 in 1800. From 1800 to 1900, however, it increased to over 400,000,000. The population of England, to cite the country in which the Industrial Revolution got under way and in which it developed to a very great extent, increased 50 percent between 1700 and 1800. But during the nineteenth century, it increased 260 percent. In the two centuries prior to 1850, the populatio nof Japan increased but 41 percent. In the fifty years following 1872—about the time industrialization began—however, the population increased over 80 percent. Urban development was powerfully stimulated and accelerated by the new technology as it had been by the developing agricultural technology in the Bronze Age. The European feudal system—a rural, aristocratic, agricultural production for use economy—was rendered obsolete and replaced by an urban, parliamentary, industrial, production-for-sale-at-a-profit economy. Social structure became ever more differentiated and functions more specialized. The productivity of human labor increased as technology advanced. Farm populations decreased relatively and in some instances absolutely.

Changes occurred in the class structure of society also. The basic dichotomy—a minority ruling class and the majority of the population in a position of subordination and exploitation—remained, but the composition of these classes underwent radical change. Industrial lords and financial barons replaced the landed aristocracy of feudalism as the dominant element in the ruling class, and an urban, industrial proletariat took the place of serfs, peasants, or slaves as the basic element in the subordinate class. Industrial strife took the place of peasant revolts and uprisings of slaves and serfs of earlier days. And, in a new form, the State-Church functioned as a co-ordinative and regulative mechanism to maintain the integrity of society by containing these class antagonisms and by mobilizing the resources of society for offense and defense.

We may pause at this point to take note of an interesting feature of the process of cultural evolution: *as culture evolves the rate of growth is accelerated.* As we have already seen, the rate of growth in late Neolithic and early Bronze times was much greater than in the Paleolithic and Eolithic Ages. The Agricultural Revolution required but a few thousand years to run its course. But the Fuel Revolution is only a century and a half or two centuries old at most, and already greater changes have been effected by it perhaps than by all earlier ages put together. The change is so rapid and we are so much in the midst of it that it is difficult to grasp the situation and to realize the profound and radical nature of the revolution, social and political as well as technological, through which we are passing. Twenty-seven years ago in *New Viewpoints in American History*, Professor A. M. Schlesinger compared the culture of the United States of Lincoln's day with that of Benjamin Franklin's on the one hand, and with the culture of 1922 on the other. He remarked that the daily life with which Lincoln was familiar was in most respects like that known to George Washington and Franklin. But our culture in 1922 would have been strange and bewildering to Lincoln had he returned to the American scene:

Buildings more than three or four stories high would be new. The plate-glass show windows of the stores, the electric street-lighting, the moving-picture theaters, the electric elevators in

the buildings and especially the big department stores would be
things in his day unknown. The smooth-paved streets and
cement sidewalks would be new to him. The fast-moving electric street-cars and motor vehicles would fill him with wonder.
Even a boy on a bicycle would be a curiosity. Entering the
White House, someone would have to explain to him such
commonplaces of modern life as sanitary plumbing, steam heat-
ing, friction matches, telephones, electric lights, the Victrola,
and even the fountain pen. In Lincoln's day, plumbing was in
its beginnings, coal-oil lamps and gas-jets were coming into
use, and the steel pen had only recently superseded the quill
pen. The steel rail, the steel bridge, high-powered locomotives,
refrigerator cars, artificial ice, the cream separator, the twine
binder, the caterpillar tractor, money orders, the parcels post,
rural free delivery, the cable, the wireless, gasoline engines, re-
peating rifles, dynamite, submarines, airplanes—these and
hundreds of other inventions now in common use were all alike
unknown.[3]

But consider the changes that have taken place—in transportation, medicine, communication, and in technology in general—
since Schlesinger wrote in 1922! In warfare perhaps better than in
other areas of our culture, is the dizzying rate of technological
progress made dramatically apparent. The technology of the first
World War looks quaint today, and some of the weapons and
techniques introduced for the first time in World War II are
already obsolete. One hardly dares to picture the next great military conflict; novelties already unveiled and others only intimated
suggest all too vividly the distance that technological progress has
gone since the days of Pearl Harbor. And behind the scenes in
the theater of Mars are the great research laboratories and proving grounds, working under forced draft to develop and perfect
new tools and techniques in all phases of our technology. The
rate of cultural advance is now greater than ever before. "Our
life," wrote the distinguished physicist, Arthur Holly Compton in

1940, "differs from that of two generations ago more than American life of that day differed from the civilized life at the dawn of written history." [4] And, since Compton wrote these words, a profound and awful revolution—perhaps the most significant in all human history—has taken place: the harnessing of atomic energy.

But, even as in the case of the Agricultural Revolution and its aftermath, so in the Power Age the social system created by the new fuel technology came eventually to act as a brake upon further cultural advance. The price and profit system stimulated production and technological progress as long as the output could find a market. But, like the socio-economic system of the Bronze Age, the new commercialism of the Fuel era had its inherent limitations. No industrial nation had or could have purchasing power sufficient to keep and absorb its own output; the very basis of the industrial profit system was an excess in value of product over the cost of production in terms of wages paid to the industrial workers. Export of surplus was therefore essential; "we must export or die" is a cry of desperation heard from more than one nation in recent years. For a time new markets could be found abroad. But as the output of industrial nations increased with advances in technology, and as non-European nations such as Japan became industrialized and hence competitors for foreign markets, the international profit system began to bog down. The world market diminished as the industrial output increased. When goods could no longer be sold profitably abroad, production was curtailed at home. Entrepreneurs are disinclined to produce goods that cannot be sold at a profit. Factories, mills and mines were closed. Millions of workers were thrown out of employment. Surplus goods were destroyed, agricultural production reduced. The awful plague of overproduction and unemployment, "starvation in the midst of plenty," settled upon the land. The social system was strangling the great technological machine of industry and paralyzing the body politic as a whole. The alternatives were stagnation and death or war and revolution. If the social system were able to contain the Fuel technology and the commercial rivalries and class conflicts engendered by it, society would become stabilized in a more or less stagnant form of industrial feudalism. Should, however, the forces inherent in the new technology be able to surmount and overcome the restrictions of the price and parliamentary system, then culture could advance toward higher levels.

There is evidence aplenty that culture, powered by the mighty forces of Fuel technology, is embarking upon the latter course. The first phase of the second great Cultural Revolution—the Industrial Revolution—has run its course and we are now entered upon the second phase, that of social, political and economic revolution. And, as in the past, war is proving to be an effective means of profound political change. The system of free and individual enterprise in business and commerce is now virtually extinct. The gold standard is merely a memory of an era that is closed. The parliamentary system of government, a device designed to permit the greatest freedom for the growth of industrial and financial enterprise, is practically obsolete also. Private right is no longer significant chiefly as a means of freedom for growth as it was in the early days of commercialism. It now leads toward competitive rivalry, internecine strife, chaos, and paralysis. Concentrations of power without public responsibility among those who own or control vast wealth, or in the ranks of organized labor, are no longer compatible with the degree of unity, integrity and strength that a nation must have if it is to compete successfully with its rivals in the international arena. The exigencies of national survival require the subordination of private right to general welfare, of part to whole. In short, the State, as the integrative and regulative mechanism of civil society, is destined to acquire ever greater power and to wield more and more control. Social evolution is moving inexorably toward higher levels of integration, toward greater concentrations of political power and control.

On the international level, too, an interesting trend of social evolution can be discerned: movement toward ever larger and larger political units. The Agricultural technology replaced villages with cities, tribes with nations and empires. The modern Fuel technology also is working toward larger political groupings, fewer concentrations of political power. The relatively recent trend toward amalgamation can be seen in the unification of Germany and Italy in the nineteenth century. The Treaty of Versailles attempted, with the "Balkanization of Europe," to oppose the age-old trend of social evolution by breaking the continent up into little pieces. One of the conspicuous and significant aspects of the Second World War in its initial phase was a movement toward the unification of Europe. A half-dozen or so World Powers engaged in the First World War; only two great powers emerged from the second. The competition for power narrows as contestants are eliminated. The logical conclusion is, however, not simply the domination of the world by a single nation—this would be but a transitional stage—but a single political organization that will embrace the entire planet and the whole human race. Toward such a denouement is our mighty Power technology rapidly moving us.

But a new and ominous element has recently entered the picture: nuclear atomic energy for military purposes. Here again the significance of this new factor derives from the fact that a new source of energy has been harnessed and in awful form. Once more we are upon the threshold of a technological revolution. But the consequences of this new technological advance may possibly differ radically from those of the Agricultural and the Fuel Revolutions. New technologies in the past have rendered old social systems obsolete but they have replaced them with new systems. The new nuclear technology however threatens to destroy civilization itself, or at least to cripple it to such an extent that it might require a century, a thousand, or ten thousand, years to regain its present status. At least this is what eminent scientists and military men tell us; as laymen we are in a child's world of ignorance, with almost all the significant facts kept beyond our reach. The destruction of a few score of centers of science and industry in Europe and the United States would just about do for Western civilization and, authorities assure us that this is well within the realm of possibility, not to say probability. The hope of the future therefore, and the salvation of mankind and civilization would seem to lie in the emergence from the next war of a victor—not merely a survivor—and one with sufficient power and resources to organize the whole planet and the entire human species within a single social system.

We have thus presented a sketch of the evolution of the culture of mankind from the horizon of our prehuman forebears to the present time. It is a fascinating story of adventure and progress; of a species lifting itself up by its cultural bootstraps from the status of a mere animal to a radically new way of life, a way destined to win mastery over most other species and to exert a powerful and extensive control over the natural habitat. The origin of culture elevated the evolutionary process to a new plane. No longer was it necessary for the human animal to acquire new powers and techniques through the slow process of biological change; he now had an extra-somatic mechanism of adjustment and control that could grow freely of itself. Moreover, advances in one stream of cultural development could diffuse readily to other traditions so that all might share in the progress of each. Thus the story of man becomes an account of his culture.

Technology is the hero of our piece. This is a world of rocks and rivers, sticks and steel, of sun, air and starlight, of galaxies, atoms and molecules. Man is but a particular kind of material body who must do certain things to maintain his status in a cosmic material system. The means of adjustment and control, of security and survival, are of course technological. Culture thus becomes primarily a mechanism for harnessing energy and of putting it to work in the service of man, and, secondarily, of channelling and regulating his behavior not directly concerned with subsistence and offense and defense. Social systems are therefore determined by technological systems, and philosophies and the arts express experience as it is defined by technology and refracted by social systems. Cultural systems like those of the biological level are capable of growth. That is, the power to capture any energy is also the ability to harness more and still more of it. Thus cultural systems, like biological organisms, develop, multiply, and extend themselves. The sun is the prime mover; culture, a thermodynamic system operated by it. At least, solar energy has activated all cultural systems of history up to now, and it will continue to do so after terrestrial supplies of fissionable fuels have been exhausted—if civilization should survive and reach this point. But technology is still the leading character in our play, even though it may turn out to be a villain instead of the hero. Technology builds but it may also destroy. The belief and faith that civilization, won at such great cost in pain and labor, simply cannot go down in destruction because such an end would be too monstrous and senseless, is but a naive and anthropocentric whimper. The cosmos does little know nor will it long remember what man has done here on this tiny planet. The eventual extinction of the human race—for come it will sometime—will not be the first time that a species has died out. Nor will it be an event of very great terrestrial significance.

But man may survive the coming holocaust of radioactivity even though his culture is tumbled to the level of Neolithic times, only to begin the long climb over again, this time perhaps by a somewhat different route; culture too may be able to profit from experience. But culture may not destroy or even critically wound itself with its new powers. Destruction is no more inevitable than salvation. Great though the devastation may—and will—be in the next test of strength in the international arena, the creative powers of the new technology may be sufficiently great to rise up from the ruins and to enclose the whole world in a single political embrace. Then and only then will the curse of war be lifted and the way made free and open for a fuller and richer life.

Our sketch of the evolution of culture is, it will be noted, wholly culturological. It does not resort to race, physical type, intelligence, a moral sense, the dignity of man, the spirit of progress or democracy, the individual—genius or otherwise—the rejection of the father, consciousness of kind, a set of instincts or "drives," social interaction, a basic personality structure, toilet training in infancy, or breast vs. bottle feeding and weaning, to account for the behavior and growth of this great extra-somatic tradition. We explain it in terms of culture itself. A thunder-shower or a tornado is explained in terms of antecedent and con-comitant meteorological events; a clan or a constitution is likewise accounted for by citing its cultural antecedents and concomitants.

Culture is, as we have pointed out repeatedly, a stream of inter-acting elements; one trait reacts upon others and is affected by them in return. Some elements become obsolete and are elimin-ated from the stream; new elements are incorporated into it. New permutations, combinations, and syntheses are continually being formed. Whether we deal with a restricted portion of the cultural continuum such as the evolution of mathematics or the genealogy of the steam engine, or whether we encompass culture in its entirety, the principle of interpretation is the same: cul-ture grows out of culture. In our sketch of the evolution of culture as a whole we deal with large categories: technology, social sys-tems, and philosophies. We break technology down into energy and tool factors. We observe the action of each class of elements, their impact upon others, the effect of technology upon social systems, and the influence of economic and political institutions upon agriculture and steam-driven factories. We note the role that war as a culture process has played in the course of political change. And, finally, we see the fate of civilization delicately balanced in a scales to be tipped this way or that, we know not how, by the modern miracles of nuclear technology.

Culturology is the newest venture of science. After centuries of cultivation in the fields of astronomy, physics, and chemistry; after scores of years of tillage in physiology and psychology, science has at last turned to the most immediate and powerful determinant of man's *human* behavior: his culture. After repeated trials and as many failures it was discovered that culture cannot be explained psychologically; such interpretations are merely anthropomorphisms in scientific clothing. The explanation of culture is and must be culturological. The science of culture is young but full of promise. It is destined to do great things—if only the subject of its study will continue its age-old course: onward and upward.

PART IV CULTUROLOGY

CHAPTER FOURTEEN

THE SCIENCE OF CULTURE

"During the last hundred years, it has become increasingly clear that culture . . . represents . . . a distinct domain . . . that demands for its investigation a distinct science . . ."—R. H. Lowie, *Cultural Anthropology; a Science*

"These specifically human peculiarities which differentiate the race of the *homo sapiens* from all other species of animals is comprehended in the name *culture;* therefore the science of specifically human activities may be most suitably called *culturology* . . ."—Wilhelm Ostwald, *Principles of the Theory of Education*

*E*very living organism must effect a certain minimum adjustment to its environment in order to live and to reproduce its kind. "Understanding" is the name we give to one aspect of this process of adjustment. We do not as a rule use this term in speaking of the lower forms of life, such as plants for example. But plants do the same kind of thing—and, if anything, more surely—that human beings do in contexts to which we apply the word "understanding." Scientific observations and experiments on apes make it quite clear that their behavior possesses qualities that we can only call "insight" and "understanding"; and it is more than likely that other sub-human mammals share these attributes also. But it is in the human species and here alone that we find understanding as a process of adjustment carried on by symbolic means. In the symbol the process of biological evolution attained a metasensory mechanism of adjustment. All sub-human species must effect their adjustments in terms of meanings grasped and interpreted with the senses. But

man can go beyond the reach of sense impressions; he can grasp
and interpret his world with *symbols*. Thanks to this ability, he
may acquire understandings and effect adjustments on a higher
level than any other animal. His understandings may be incom-
parably richer than those of the highest apes, and he can share
them readily with his fellows. Thus a new type of understanding
and adjustment has come into existence in the zoological world.

The use of the neuro-sensory-symbolic faculty in the process
of adjustment finds expression in verbal formulas that we may
call *beliefs*. The sum total of beliefs of a people we term their
philosophy. A philosophy, therefore, is an elaborate mechanism
by means of which a certain kind of animal, man, adjusts himself to the earth beneath him and to the cosmos around him.
A philosophy is of course closely related to other aspects of the
cultural system of which it is itself a part: to technology, to social
organization, and to forms of art. But our concern here is with
philosophy as such, as a technique of interpretation, as a way of
rendering the world intelligible so that articulation with this
world can be effected to the greatest advantage to man.

Philosophy, like culture as a whole, has grown and developed
through all the ages that have elapsed since man began to symbol.
Philosophy is an instrument devised and used for a purpose. In
this respect it is exactly like an axe. One philosophy may be
better—a better instrument of interpretation and adjustment—
than another, just as one axe may be a better chopping instrument than another. There has been a progressive development of
philosophies just as there has been development and progress
of axes or of culture as a whole. The preceding chapters undertake to tell, or at least to exhibit, some of the story of this
development.

The first men interpreted things and events in terms of their
own psyches. They were not aware of their standpoint of interpretation, however; on the contrary, they insisted emphatically
that the minds to which the events of their experience were at-

THE SCIENCE OF CULTURE 399

tributed were not their own, but those of spirits, of gods or demons. They were, however, merely the projection of the human ego into the external world. Thus the whole cosmos, the entire range of experience, was interpreted as the expression of mind and spirit, of desire, will and purpose. This was the philosophy of animism and supernaturalism, but above all, of anthropomorphism.

It took time for the human primate to acquire skill and competence in the use of his newly acquired faculty, the symbol. Hundreds of thousands of years elapsed before any advance was made beyond the original—and self-deceptive—premise that the cosmos was and could be only the expression of an ego like man's. In his philosophies primordial man simply created the world in his own image. Nor have we outgrown this point of view even today as the prevalence, vigor and respectability of theologies clearly show.

But after eons of explaining the world of things and events in terms of the desires, wills and plans of supernatural beings, an advance was made to a new level, a new set of premises. Instead of invoking spirits and minds to account for events, entities, essences, principles, etc., were called upon. Instead of saying, for example, that fossils were fashioned by a god, it was now said that they were formed by "stone-making forces," or that they were "the congelation of lapidific juices." This type of explanation, empty and senseless as it may seem today, was nevertheless a great advance over the animistic, supernaturalistic interpretation that had prevailed before. The answers of supernaturalism were complete and final: God did it; it was God's will, and that was that; there was nothing left to say. Actually, of course, these answers told one nothing; they were as empty as they were final. And, worst of all, they shut the door to anything better; what else could one ask or learn after being told that an event was but an act of God? The metaphysical—to use Comte's term—type of interpretation at least freed one from the bondage of anthropomorphism. If fossils were formed by "stone-making forces," one was, by implication, invited to inquire into the nature of such forces and thus come into direct contact with the real world—instead of one's own image reflected therein—and to learn something about it as a consequence. The metaphysical explanations though empty in themselves were nevertheless progressive; they opened the way to something better: science.

We have not yet outgrown the metaphysical type of interpretation even in social science. We still find events explained in terms of "the separatism of the natives," "tendencies of the human mind," "the principle of the equivalence of brothers," "the essential democracy of the Plains tribes," etc. (see p. 65). But we are making progress.

If one accepted the invitation implicit in the metaphysical type of explanation, if, in an endeavor to find out what "stone-making forces" really are, one "went to nature, took the facts into one's own hands, and saw for himself" (Agassiz), he would stand a good chance of achieving the point of view and the techniques of science. At any rate, this is a type of interpretation that grew out of and eventually superseded metaphysical explanations. Things and events were no longer explained in terms of the purpose or plan of spirits, nor yet as caused by principles or essences; they were explained in terms of *other things and events*. Thus, an earthquake is not merely an expression of divine wrath, an act of punishment for our sins; nor is it merely the expression of a "principle of vulcanism." It is a geologic event that is to be explained in terms of other geologic events.

In science the human primate has come at last to a realistic and effective grasp upon the external world to which he must adjust if he is to survive. As an *explanatory* device, animistic, anthropomorphic and supernaturalistic philosophies were worse than worthless, for false knowledge is often worse than none at all. One has only to think of all the men and women who have been put to death as witches and heretics to get some notion of the magnitude of the disadvantages imposed by this type of philosophy. To be sure, primitive philosophies had other functions than explanatory; they sustained man with illusions, they provided him with courage, comfort, consolation, and confidence, all of which had a biological survival value. But as explanatory techniques, primitive philosophies were a total loss.

Metaphysical philosophies did not really explain the external world either, but they paved the way for a realistic and effective interpretation in the point of view and with the intellectual techniques that we call "science." A profile of modern philosophy discloses its genealogy as well as its structure and composition: a new, vigorous and growing component of science; an old, primitive supernaturalism, strong in certain sectors but declining as its field contracts and its nourishment dwindles; a rather lush growth of anthropomorphism and free will in certain sectors, but this, too, giving way to a more virile flora; and odds and ends of metaphysical reasoning here and there.

If philosophy is a mechanism of adjustment of the human animal to his cosmic setting, then man is at the bottom of philosophic concern. As we pointed out in our chapter on "The Expansion of the Scope of Science," we can trace the history and the growth of science from the standpoint of determinants of human behavior. Astrology was an attempt to appraise the role of heavenly bodies in human affairs and to predict the course of human events as determined by the stars. The philosophy of science found its first expression in astronomy because the heavenly bodies, being the least significant of determinants of human behavior, could be dislodged most easily from the anthropomorphic tradition in which self was confused with not-self. The point of view and the techniques of science, once established in the sector of the celestial, began to spread to other areas. The course of expansion of the scope of science was determined by this law: science will advance and develop in inverse ratio to the significance of phenomena as determinants of human behavior. Terrestrial physics and mechanics followed astronomy. The physical sciences took form before the biological because physical phenomena are less significant as determinants of human behavior than are biological phenomena. Within the biological realm, anatomy develops first, then physiology and psychology. The point upon which these three sciences focused was the individual organism. But it came eventually to be realized that there is a class of phenomena outside and beyond the individual that is nevertheless powerful and significant in the determination of his behavior. Sociology and social psychology were the organizations of scientific techniques to grapple with this class of meta-individual determinants. In the organization of these sciences it was assumed that the categories of determinants of human behavior had now been exhausted. Astronomy and terrestrial physics would take care of the inanimate determinants; anatomy, physiology, and psychology would encompass the individual determinants; and sociology, the science of society, would deal with the supra-individual determinants: what other determinants were there to be reckoned with?

As we have already shown, the assumption of the founders of sociology was far from adequate. True enough, a man behaves differently in the company of his fellows than when alone, just as roosters, dogs, ducks, and apes do. A *sociology* of man—or ape, rat, dog, or duck—is in order, therefore, *in addition* to a *psychology*. But to go no further would be to overlook a fundamental difference between man and all other species. A monkey, dog, or rat, as we have just noted, behaves differently when in the company of his fellows than when alone. We distinguish therefore *individual* and *social* aspects of this individual's behavior. We can go farther and recognize a *social system* of behavior in which the system as such is the focus of attention and interpretation. Thus we distinguish both individual and social systems. But—and here we come to the fundamental difference between man as a human being and all other species—whether we consider rat, dog, or ape behavior in its individual or its social aspects, whether we regard it in the form of individual systems or social systems, *the determinant is the biological organism*. We find one type of social system or behavior in one species of animal, another type in another species; ducks will have one type of social system or behavior, eagles another; lions one type, bison another; sharks one kind, herring another, etc. Among the lower species, *social systems are functions of their respective biological organisms*: $S = f(O)$. But in the human species, on the level of symbolic behavior, this is not the case. Human behavior, either in its average individual or its social aspects, is nowhere a function of the organism. *Human behavior does not vary as the organism varies*; it varies with the extra-somatic factor of culture. *Human behavior is a function of culture: $B = f(C)$*. As the culture varies so will the behavior.

Thus it is not society, or the group, that constitutes the last of a series of categories of determinants of human behavior. Among the lower species, the group is properly regarded as a determinant of the behavior of any one of its members. But in the human species, the group is *itself* determined by the cultural tradition: whether we find a guild of artisans, a clan, a polyandrous household, or an order of knights in a human society will depend upon its *culture*. The discovery of this class of determinants and the isolation, in logical analysis, of these extra-somatic cultural determinants from the biological—in their group aspect as well as individual—has been one of the most significant advances in science in recent times. This assertion will no doubt strike some as extravagant. We are so accustomed to being regaled with accounts of the marvels of modern science—meaning physics, chemistry, and medicine—and so used to disparagements of social science, that to claim that the achievement of the concept of culture is one of the most significant advances in modern science may well seem preposterous to some. We have no desire whatever to minimize the significance of recent advances in physics, chemistry, genetics, or medicine. Some of them, such as quantum mechanics in physics and genetics in biology, may quite properly be called revolutionary. But such advances have taken place in fields that have been cultivated by science for generations or even centuries. But with the achievement of the concept of culture *a whole new field was opened to science.* The lack of significant achievement so far in the new science of culture is therefore not an indication of extravagance of claim on our part. The very newness of our science, the fact that this new sector of experience was discovered, isolated and defined only yesterday, in itself means that there has not yet been time for much accomplishment. It is the discovery of a new world that is so significant, not the relative magnitude or value of achievements won so far in this new world. We are so impressed with the achievements of physics and astronomy that it is hard for some to believe that the lowly "social" sciences can ever match them. This point of view is of course understandable in a day when science can map the distribution of galaxies in the cosmos and measure the mass and temperature of stars a million of light years away, whereas in another field, science has no adequate answer to the question of the prohibition of polygamy in certain societies. But the lot and destiny of man on this planet embrace more than measuring galaxies, splitting atoms, or discovering a new wonder drug. The socio-political-economic systems—in short, the cultures—within which the human species lives and breathes and propagates have much to do with the future of Man. We are just beginning to realize this. And we may look forward to a time when the scientific comprehension of such cultural processes as polygamy and inflation will be considered quite as significant as the measurement of distant stars, the splitting of atoms, or the synthesis of organic compounds. The "discovery" of culture may one day rank in importance in the history of science with the heliocentric theory of Copernicus or the discovery of the cellular basis of all living forms.

This is not to say, as we have tried to make clear earlier, that man is going to win control over the course of cultural development through a scientific comprehension of its structure and processes, any more than we have won control over the sun or distant galaxies by coming to a considerable understanding of them. Understanding, scientific understanding, is *itself* a cultural process. The growth of science is a culture process just as the development of a musical style, a type of architecture, or forms of corporate organization in business are culture processes. The development of understanding in astronomy, in medicine, and in culturology alike will make possible a more realistic and effective adjustment of the human species to the earth and cosmos.

Profound advances in science make their way slowly. It took many years for mankind, even the educated stratum of society, to accept the heliocentric theory of the solar system and to exploit the resources of this point of view. It took considerable time also for the idea of the biological evolution of man to win its way against older conceptions. The discovery and exploration of the unconscious by psychoanalysis met with hostility and resistance. It is not particularly surprising, therefore, to discover that the present advance of science into the new field of culture is meeting with considerable resistance and opposition.

We discover a common basis for all of these resistances and oppositions to the advances of science. Scientific interpretation is non-anthropomorphic, non-anthropocentric. Opposition to the theories of Copernicus, Galileo and Darwin proceeded from an anthropomorphic and anthropocentric as well as a supernaturalistic conception of man and the cosmos: man was the chief work of the Creator of all; he was created in God's image; the world was made for him; it was motionless and in the center of the universe; everything revolved about the earth; everything was interpreted in terms of man. Scientific interpretation is *deterministic*, and as such evokes the hostility of all who are activated or directed by a philosophy of Free Will.

The social sciences of man have been purged of supernaturalism to a very great degree—but not wholly as the existence and respectability of the anthropological school of Father Wilhelm Schmidt, to mention but one example, proves. But they are still anthropomorphically and anthropocentrically oriented to a very high degree. They are furthermore animated by the philosophy of Free Will to a considerable extent. Opposition to the science of culture is thus readily understood. An anthropocentric point of view cannot, of course, tolerate the thesis that it is culture, not man, that determines the form and content of human behavior. The philosophy of Free Will cannot accept a theory of cultural determinism. To many sociologists and cultural anthropologists the notion that culture constitutes a distinct order of phenomena, that it behaves in accordance with its own principles and laws, and is, therefore, explainable only in culturological terms, is a "mystical metaphysics."

Those who oppose the culturological point of view feel however that their position is thoroughly realistic. It is so plain, so obvious, to them that culture could not exist without man, and that it is people, real flesh and blood human beings—not a reified entity called "culture"—who do things; anyone can see this for himself.

As we have previously tried to make clear, one cannot always rely in science upon the "self-evident" features of common sense observation and reasoning. Of course culture could not exist without human beings. Obviously men cast votes, drink or loathe milk, speak English or some other language, believe in witches or other causative agents, build ships, make war, play pinochle, etc. The anti-culturologists confuse *the existence of things* with a *scientific interpretation of things*. To say that a man loathes or prizes milk as a beverage is merely to recognize an event, not to explain it. The culturologist knows full well that it is man, a human organism—and not "a rarefied or reified entity called 'culture'"—that drinks the milk or rejects it as loathsome. But he knows also that observation of an event is not the same thing as an explanation thereof. Why does the man prize or loathe the milk, believe in witches or bacteria, etc.? The culturologist explains the behavior of the human organism in terms of external, extra-somatic cultural elements that function as stimuli to evoke the response and give it its form and content. And the culturologist knows also that the culture process is explainable in terms of itself; the human organism, collectively and individually, is irrelevant—not to the culture process itself—but to an *explanation* of the culture process. We need not consider the neuro-sensory-muscular-glandular-etcetera organization that is man in interpretations of such things as clans, codes of law, grammars, philosophies, etc.

From the standpoint of an explanation of human behavior, we proceed as though culture had a life of its own, even as if it had an existence of its own independently of the human species. "This is not mysticism" as Lowie observed long ago, "but sound scientific method"; a procedure, we might add, that is taken for granted in the more mature fields of science such as physics. The law of falling bodies treats them as if they pass through a perfect vacuum. Physicists frequently attack and solve problems by considering vehicles that move without friction. In my physics textbook I read: "A rigid body is one whose shape is not altered by any forces that are applied to it." But the next sentence goes on to say: "Such a body is only an ideal conception, for *rigid bodies do not exist*." A person with the philosophic outlook of our anti-culturologists would find these physicists "unrealistic," too. They would reject the law of falling bodies because it describes an event that never actually occurs.* They would dismiss frictionless vehicles as "mystical" and reject rigid bodies as "abstractions." The point of view of the anti-culturologist simply cannot realize that it is precisely because he works in this way that the physicist is able to achieve significant results. It is precisely because the law of falling bodies does *not* describe any particular event that it has universal significance and validity. "The paradox is now fully established," says Whitehead, "that the utmost abstractions are the true weapon with which to control our thought of concrete fact." [1]

The culturologist proceeds along the same lines, with the same outlook and the same techniques of interpretation, as the physicist. Cultures can no more exist without men than vehicles can move without friction. But one may regard culture as if it were independent of man just as the physicist may consider vehicles as if they were independent of friction, or deals with bodies as if they actually were rigid. These are effective techniques of interpretation. The realism of those to whom the sun obviously moves around the earth, for whom falling bodies must pass through an atmosphere, for whom frictionless vehicles and rigid bodies do not exist; the realism of those who insist that it is people not

---

* We have, in a recent work by R. H. Lowie, a good example of the confusion of thought that results from a failure to understand one of the elementary techniques of science due to this attitude of pseudo-realism. In a consideration of laws of cultural evolution he says that "there are bound to be so many 'deviations from uniformity . . . produced by special causes [quoting Lewis H. Morgan]' that a law, if operative, could hardly be discovered by human reason" (*Social Organization*, p. 53). The significance of Newton's work finds no appreciation here. No two bodies fall alike; the "deviations from uniformity" are as numerous as the falling bodies themselves. Yet the human mind was quite able to discover a principle common to all particular events and to express it in the form of a thoroughly adequate scientific law. Of course, a law of cultural evolution would describe *no actual series of events* any more than the law of Newton describes any particular falling body. But infinite variety of particulars does not preclude universals; on the contrary, particulars *imply* and *presuppose* universals. How quaint then to expect a scientific law, a statement of the *universal*, to describe this and that *particular*.

culture who vote, speak English, enamel their nails, loathe milk, etc., is a pathetic form of pseudo-realism that has no place in science.

"During the last hundred years," writes Lowie, "it has become increasingly clear that culture . . . [is] a distinct domain . . . that demands for its investigation a distinct science." [2] But what are we to call our new science? We have taken much pains to demonstrate the fundamental difference between a science of culture and the sciences of *psychology* and *sociology*; these terms are therefore quite unsuitable. 'Anthropology' also is unsuitable for many reasons. The term is used to designate so many things as to be almost meaningless. It includes Physical Anthropology, which in turn embraces human paleontology, comparative morphology of primates, human genetics, physiology and psychology, etc. *Cultural* anthropology is variously conceived as psychology, psychoanalysis, psychiatry, sociology, applied anthropology, history, and so on. It would not be facetious at all to define anthropology as the activity that a person, bearing the professional label "anthropologist," engages in. As a matter of fact, the late Franz Boas once suggested that "the whole group of anthropological phenomena may be evanescent, that they may be at bottom biological and psychological problems, and that the whole field of anthropology belongs either to the one or to the other of these sciences." Thus, Boas not only failed to recognize a science of culture but even suggested that anthropology itself "will become more and more a *method* that may be applied by a great number of sciences, rather than a science by itself." [3] The term "anthropology" is therefore quite unsuited to our purpose.

But is not the answer to our problem obvious? Does not the solution lie right before our eyes? What else could one call a science of culture but *culturology*? If a science of mammals is *mammalogy*, of music, *musicology*, of bacteria, *bacteriology*, etc., why should not a science of culture be *culturology*? Our reasoning seems perfectly legitimate and proper, our conclusion sensible and sound. Yet, so conservative, timid, or indifferent are many of the workers in the sciences of man that so radical and revolutionary an innovation as a new suffix for an old familiar word seems pretentious, absurd, or objectionable in some other way. We recall the objections that were raised to Spencer's use of the term "sociology." As he tells us in the introduction to his *Principles of Sociology*, his friends tried to dissuade him from using the word on the ground that it was a "barbarism." Similarly today, some scholars find that *culturology* grates harshly upon their ears. Thus, V. Gordon Childe writes that "the prejudices engendered by *Literae Humaniores* are too strong to allow [him] to adopt White's term 'culturology'." [4] Similarly J. L. Myres, in a review of "The Expansion of the Scope of Science," calls "culturology" a "barbarous name." [5]

It appears that those who condemned Spencer's use of "sociology" as a "barbarism" did so on etymological grounds: it is derived from both Latin and Greek. This, it seems, is enough to make a purist's flesh crawl. But, for better or for worse, the trends and processes of living languages have little regard for such sensibilities. The Anglo-American language readily absorbs words from foreign languages—*taboo, shaman, coyote, tobacco*—and creates new words ("kodak") or new forms ("trust-buster") rather easily. Nor does it hesitate to resort to hybridizations and other improvisations upon occasion, such as numerology, thermocouple, thermopile, automobile, etc., as well as sociology. "Television" is one of the most recent offspring of linguistic miscegenation. Although Professor Childe does not like "culturology" he remarks that "such hybrids seem to accord with the general tendency of linguistic progress." H. L. Mencken, the distinguished authority on the American language, finds "culturology" a "rather clumsy word, but nevertheless logical," and he feels that we have "established the fact that it ought to be used." [6] We feel as did Spencer that "the convenience and suggestiveness of our symbols are of more importance than the legitimacy of their derivation."

We may call attention, in this connection, to the fact that the departments of anthropology at the University of Chicago and at the Chicago Natural History Museum have been using the term "museology" for some time to designate the art of museum organization, equipment, and management. If "-ology" is interpreted in the sense of "science of," then museology is a misnomer, for "museum science" is no more a *science* than "library science," "military science," or "domestic science" are sciences; they are *arts*, not sciences. If "museology" can become respectable, why not "culturology," for which there is more justification on etymological grounds?

The concept of a *science of culture* is, as the preceding pages have made clear, an old one; it goes back at least to Tylor's first chapter of *Primitive Culture* in 1871. The term "culturology" has been used relatively very little, but it was employed in the exact and specific sense in which we use it, over a third of a century ago, and today it is being used on at least three continents.

In his address, "The System of the Sciences," delivered in 1915 (see p. 116), the distinguished German chemist and Nobel prize winner, Wilhelm Ostwald, said "I proposed, therefore, a *long while ago* [emphasis ours] to call the field in question the science of civilization or culturology (*Kulturologie*)." [7] We have not been able as yet to discover this earlier use, or uses, of this term by him.

Fourteen years after the publication of Ostwald's "The System of the Sciences," Read Bain, a sociologist, speaks of "culturology" in a chapter written for *Trends in American Sociology*, edited by Geo. A. Lundberg and others.[8] The sense in which he used the term is not wholly clear, however; he seems to equate "culturology" with sociology in one place and with human ecology in another. He also speaks of the "close kinship between social psychology and culturology." I first used "culturology" in print in 1939, I believe, in "A Problem in Kinship Terminology," [9] although I had employed it in my courses for years prior to this time. Dr. Cheng Che-Yu subtitled his *Oriental and Occidental Cultures Contrasted,* published in Berkeley in 1943, "An Introduction to Culturology." He has written me that he had previously used not only "culturology," but "culturosophy," in publications in Chinese. Professor Huang Wen Shan, of the Institute of Anthropology, National Sun Yat Sen University, Canton, has published a number of articles on culturology in Chinese, and he has informed me that he has a book on culturology now in progress. I have recently seen an advertisement for a book entitled *Epitome de Culturologia,* by J. Imbelloni, published in Buenos Aires. And, of course, there may be other instances that have not come to my attention.

The Chinese language is apparently more congenial to such innovations as "culturology" than is English. "Culturology" in Chinese is *wen wha* (culture) *hsüeh* (science of). Both words are common Chinese terms and their combination seems not to grate upon the ears of Chinese scholars or to wound their sensibilities.

But the objections to "culturology" are not wholly philologic by any means. Linguistic objections come readily to the surface; but deep down underneath lie views and values that will oppose the adoption and use of this term even more strongly than will the classicist nourished in the *Literae Humaniores.* "Culturology" specifies a sector of reality and defines a science. In so doing it trespasses upon the prior claims of psychology and sociology. It does more than trespass, of course; it expropriates as well. That is, it makes it clear that the solution of certain scientific problems does not properly lie within the provinces of psychology and sociology as previously supposed, but belong to—i.e., can be solved only by—a science of culture. Psychologists and sociologists alike are loath to admit that there are problems pertaining to the behavior of man that lie outside their domains; and they are inclined to resent and oppose an upstart science that claims them for itself.

But most of all, perhaps, culturology repudiates and rejects a philosophy that has been dear to the hearts of men for ages, and still inspires and nourishes many a social scientist as well as layman. This is the ancient and still respectable philosophy of anthropocentrism and Free Will. "What nonsense to say that culture does this or that! What is culture but an abstraction? It is not culture that does things; it is people, real flesh and blood human beings. It is always the individual who really thinks, and feels, and acts. Anyone can see this for himself! How absurd then to talk of a science of culture; what a distortion of reality!" As the preceding pages have shown, this view is all too prevalent and vigorous in American anthropology today.

Culturology means determinism, also. The principle of cause and effect operates in the realm of cultural phenomena as it does everywhere else in our experience of the cosmos. Any given cultural situation has been determined by other cultural events. If certain cultural factors are operative, a certain result will eventuate. Contrariwise, certain cultural consummations cannot be realized, however devoutly they may be wished, unless the factors requisite to the consummation are present and operative. This is self-evident in meteorology and geology, but in the interpretation of human behavior it is still called "fatalism" and "defeatism"; or, it is regarded as immoral-and-therefore-false.

The sweet soothing illusion of omnipotence still finds a ready market and a great demand. We can lay hold of our own destiny and shape it as we will. "Mankind under God controls his own cultural destiny and is free to choose and realize the ends . . ." Educators can control the culture process by "establishing certain value systems in his pupils." Psychologists will "study scientifically the sources of . . . [war] in men's minds and scientifically remove them." Social scientists will perfect formulas for controlling cultural forces and the mastery of our destiny if only the

federal government will give them anything like the financial support given the makers of the atomic bomb, etc., etc. Science, it
appears, is to become the handmaiden of a species of modern
magic; the social scientist, to assume the role of a super-shaman.
It is against the weight and force of this passion of free will,
this premise of anthropocentrism, that a science of culture must
make its way.[10]

But these non-linguistic objections to "culturology" serve also
effectively to emphasize the need for a special term with which to
designate our new science and to reveal the peculiar fitness of
"culturology" for this purpose. The "distinct domain" that is culture "demands for its investigation a distinct science," as Lowie
has argued for over two decades. Durkheim, too, saw the "need to
formulate entirely new concepts . . . [and to express them] in an
appropriate terminology." We think and work in science only by
means of concepts made explicit in symbolic form. To think
effectively, to make fundamental distinctions, without which
science is impossible, we must have precision tools, exact concepts.[11]

"Psychology" labels a distinct class of phenomena: the reactions
of organisms to external stimuli. But it does not distinguish cultural phenomena from non-cultural, and the interpretation of the
interaction of extra-somatic elements in the culture process lies
beyond its proper boundaries. "Sociology," too, suffers from the
"fatal defect" of failure to distinguish the cultural from the social,
as Ostwald and Kroeber pointed out long ago. It assimilates culture to its basic concept of interaction, making culture an aspect,
or a by-product, of the social process of interaction whereas the
structures and processes of human society are functions of culture.
As a matter of fact, we have in "sociology" a good example of
the confusion of thought that flows from the use of an ambiguous
and equivocal terminology.[12]

The term "anthropology" has been used to designate so many
different kinds of activities—measuring crania, excavating pot-

sherds, observing ceremonies, studying clans, psychoanalyzing natives, psychoanalyzing whole civilizations, tracing histories of arts and crafts—that it could not well be restricted now to the specific and particular task of interpreting the culture process and that alone. "Cultural anthropology" also has been used to designate a great variety of kinds of interpretation. And "social anthropology" is virtually indistinguishable from "sociology."

With the expansion of the scope of science, a class of phenomena was distinguished from the psychological and the social. It was named "culture" by those who discovered and isolated it. The analysis and interpretation of this distinct class of events has been called *the science of culture* by numerous anthropologists— Kroeber, Lowie, Murdock, and others—since Tylor first coined the phrase in 1871.

And what is a science of culture but *culturology?* With this term we shall make it plain, to even the least discerning mind, that the extra-somatic continuum of symbol-borne events is not the same thing at all as a class of reactions of human organisms considered individually or collectively; that the interaction of cultural elements is not the same thing as the reactions, or interaction, of human organisms. We may seem to exaggerate when we claim that a change in terminology can and will produce a profound change in thinking and point of view. But, as Poincaré pointed out, until the distinction between "heat" and "temperature" was made clear, it was impossible to think effectively of thermal phenomena. "The true discoverer," says Poincaré, "will not be the workman who has patiently built up some of these combinations, but the man who has brought out their relations . . . *The invention of a new word will often be sufficient to bring out the relation, and the word will be creative.*" [13] This is, of course, the significance of "culturology": it brings out the relation between the human organism, on the one hand, and the extra-somatic tradition that is culture on the other. It is creative; it establishes and defines a new science.

CHAPTER REFERENCES

CHAPTER 1. SCIENCE IS *SCIENCING*

1. Shapley, 1920, 1924.
2. Douglass, 1929.
3. Einstein, 1929, p. 107.
4. Minkowski, p. 75.
5. Einstein, 1936, p. 350 ff.; 1934, p. 33.
6. Kroeber, 1931.
7. J. Jeans et al., 1931a; Russell, 1929.

CHAPTER 2. THE SYMBOL

1. Hankins, pp. 56, 327; Linton, 1936, pp. 79, 68, 60; Goldenweiser, 1937, p. 39.
2. Descartes, p. 189.
3. Carlson, pp. 477-79.
4. Locke, Book III, Ch. 9.
5. *ibid.*, Book IV, Ch. 11.
6. Kellogg, p. 289.
7. Locke, Book II, Chs. 11, 10.
8. Tylor, 1881, pp. 54, 123.
9. Carlson, p. 477; Bernard, L. L., 1927a, p. 399; Yerkes, p. 301; Hooton, 1931, p. 167.
10. Hooton, 1931, p. 153.
11. Cf. Thomas, pp. 50-54, 776-777.
12. Keller, 23-24, 303-317, passim.

CHAPTER 3. ON THE USE OF TOOLS BY PRIMATES

1. Argyll, p. 147.
2. Clodd, p. 217.
3. Schmidt, 1934, p. 41.
4. Schnierla, 1948.
5. Hooton, 1931, pp. 138-39.
6. Lowie, 1929, p. 5.
7. Yerkes, p. 347.
8. Tylor, 1881, p. 51.
9. Hooton, 1931, pp. 139, 136.
10. Köhler, p. 295.
11. *ibid.*, p. 277.

12. Dewey, p. 1.
13. Kroeber, 1928, p. 340.

CHAPTER 4. MIND IS MINDING

1. Newman, p. 164.
2. Case, p. 3.
3. Huxley, p. 35.

CHAPTER 5. THE EXPANSION OF THE SCOPE OF SCIENCE

1. Gumplowicz, p. 74.
2. Giddings, 1896, pp. 24, 25.
3. Cattell, p. 597; Baldwin, p. 621.
4. Allport, F. H., pp. 12, 4; Washburn, 1946; Gault, 1927.
5. Blackmar, p. 786; Ward, 1903, p. 59; Giddings, 1906, pp. 788, 794 and 1896, Preface; Hobhouse, p. 130; Salomon, p. 140; Ellwood, 1906, p. 859; Small, pp. 35, 622; Giddings, 1932, p. 402; Bernard, L. L., 1927b, p. 348.
6. Ross, p. 869; MacIver, 1937, p. vii.
7. Young, 1934, p. 19; Bain, 1942, p. 87 and 1929, p. 110; Ogburn and Nimkoff, p. 63; Ellwood, 1944, p. 6.
8. Groves, p. 23; Groves and Moore, pp. 13-14; Young, 1942, p. 36.
9. Lynd, pp. 72, 186 et passim; Bernard, J., p. 68.
10. Simmel, p. 665; Spykman, p. 27.
11. Gary, p. 182.
12. Ellwood, 1944, pp. 6, 14, 13; Willey, p. 208; Willey and Herskovits, p. 191.
13. MacIver, 1930, p. 181 and 1934, p. 243; Lynd, pp. 22, 27; Bernard, L. L., 1942, p. 800.
14. Kroeber, 1936, pp. 331, 333.
15. Tylor, 1871, pp. 5, 8.
16. Durkheim, 1938, p. lvi and 1915, p. 16.
17. Durkheim, 1897, p. 354.
18. Durkheim, 1938, p. li.
19. Durkheim, 1915, p. 16 and 1938, pp. 110, 102.
20. Kroeber, 1917, pp. 192, 206.
21. Kroeber, 1919, p. 263 and 1928, p. 325.
22. Kroeber, 1923, p. 325.
23. Kroeber, 1936, pp. 338, 337.
24. Lowie, 1917, pp. 17, 66, 95 and 1936, pp. 301, 307.
25. Wissler, 1923, pp. 99, 247, 363 and 1927, pp. 75, 87.
26. Wissler, 1927, pp. 62-63, 73, 84.
27. Wissler, 1923, pp. 333-334.
28. Durkheim, 1933, pp. 285-286.
29. Goldenweiser, 1927, pp. 85, 86.
30. Boas, 1928, p. 235; Benedict, 1934, p. 231 and 1943, p. 31.

31. Schmidt, 1939, p. 7.
32. Bidney, 1944, p. 42.
33. Radcliffe-Brown, 1940, pp. 10-11 and 1937, pp. 21, 71.
34. Hallowell, pp. 175, 174.
35. Linton, 1936, pp. 288-89, 363.
36. Herskovits, 1945, pp. 150, 158.
37. Hooton, 1937, pp. 272, 223; 1939, p. 370 and 1943a, p. 5.
38. Hart, 1938.
39. Meggers, pp. 195-97.
40. Gillin, 1939, p. 45.
41. Goldenweiser, 1933, p. 59; Boas, 1936, p. 137 and 1932, p. 612; Sapir,
1917, p. 442; Benedict, 1939, p. 467; Hallowell, p. 174; Linton, 1936, p. 464.
42. See, especially, 1937, pp. 16, 154, 269-70, 294-95.
43. Kroeber, 1944, pp. vii, 763.
44. Tylor, 1871, p. 2.
45. Durkheim, 1938, p. lviii.
46. Kroeber, 1919, p. 263.
47. Mead, p. 13.

CHAPTER 6. CULTUROLOGICAL VS. PSYCHOLOGICAL INTERPRETATIONS OF HUMAN BEHAVIOR

1. Durkheim, 1893, p. 390; 1938, p. 104.
2. Seligman, p. 238.
3. Havens, pp. 21-22.
4. Rivers, p. 2.
5. Williams, p. 83.
6. Morgan, p. 505.
7. Allport, G. W., p. 22.
8. Sheen, 1948.
9. Breasted, 1909, pp. 516, 449.
10. Boas, 1945, p. 101.
11. Benedict, 1942, p. 763.
12. Boas, 1945, pp. 77-78.
13. Kroeber, 1936, pp. 331, 333.

CHAPTER 7. CULTURAL DETERMINANTS OF MIND

1. Durkheim, 1938, pp. 1-2; Radcliffe-Brown, 1934, p. 531.
2. Kroeber, 1944, p. 224.
3. Linton, 1945, p. 5.
4. Goldenweiser, 1933, p. 59.
5. Sapir, 1916, p. 43.
6. Benedict, 1934, p. 253.
7. Wissler, 1927, p. 87.
8. Linton, 1938, p. 248.
9. Hallowell, p. 174.

10. Goldenweiser, 1935, p. 75; Malinowski, 1939, p. 964.
11. Sapir, 1917, p. 442.
12. James, 1880.
13. Newton, p. 544.
14. Breasted, 1909, p. 357.
15. White, L. A., 1942, p. 82.
16. Tylor, 1871, pp. 306-07.
17. quoted by Gumplowicz, p. 45.
18. Gumplowicz, pp. 156-57.
19. Novicoff, pp. 210-211.

CHAPTER 8. GENIUS: Its Causes and Incidence

1. Galton, p. 40.
2. Galton, p. 342.
3. Spencer, 1873, p. 28 ff.
4. James, 1880, p. 453.
5. ibid., p. 449.
6. Hewett, p. 140; Hooton, 1943b, p. 4; Frank, p. 476; Millikan, p. 214; Goldenweiser, 1922, p. 26; Boas, 1945, p. 76; Wissler, 1923, p. 331; Linton, 1936, p. 95.
7. James, 1880, p. 453.
8. ibid., pp. 445, 457, 453.
9. Cooley, p. 346.
10. James, 1880, p. 454.
11. Kroeber, 1917, p. 200.
12. idem.
13. Bell, 1937, p. 532.
14. Hecht, pp. 98-99.
15. Quoted in Shapley, 1943, p. 147.
16. Cooley, pp. 352-53.
17. Ostwald, 1910, p. 185.
18. White, L. A., 1945.
19. Kroeber, 1917; Sapir, 1917.

CHAPTER 9. IKHNATON: The Great Man Vs. the Culture Process

1. Kroeber, 1944, p. 839; 1923, p. 133.
2. Breasted, 1909, p. 357.
3. Breasted, 1912, p. 339.
4. Breasted, 1909, p. 362; 1912, p. 342; 1929, p. 78; Weigall, p. 68; Hall, p. 58; Breasted, 1912, p. 342; Gardiner, p. 858; Moret, 1912, p. 45.
5. Budge, pp. 106, 77-78; Baikie, p. 315; Steindorff and Seele, pp. 201, 80; Pendlebury, p. xiv.
6. Breasted, 1929, pp. 79, 78.
7. Breasted, 1929, p. 80; Weigall, pp. 46, 51, 91.

8. Moret, 1927, p. 441.
9. Moret, 1927, p. 319.
10. Weigall, pp. 69, 70; Moret, 1927, p. 319.
11. Roosevelt, p. 114.
12. Harrington, p. 413.
13. Breasted, 1909, p. 62.
14. ibid., p. 171.
15. ibid., p. 247.
16. idem.
17. Breasted, 1909, p. 272.
18. Glanville, p. 135; Peet, 1926, pp. 202-03.
19. Breasted, 1909, p. 362; Peet, 1926, pp. 202-03.
20. Budge, p. 76; Glanville, p. 124; Steindorff and Seele, pp. 77-80.
21. Steindorff and Seele, p. 221; Glanville, pp. 134-36.
22. Steindorff and Seele, pp. 223-26.
23. ibid., p. 242.
24. Baikie, pp. 426-27.
25. Scharff, p. 144.
26. Breasted, 1909, p. 401.
27. ibid., pp. 402, 403.
28. ibid., pp. 475, 489, 490.
29. ibid., pp. 491-92.
30. ibid., p. 494.
31. ibid., p. 496; Steindorff and Seele, p. 254.
32. Steindorff and Seele, pp. 256, 269; Breasted, 1909, pp. 506-07.
33. Steindorff and Seele, p. 270; cf. Edgerton, p. 153, who alludes to a new and different interpretation of Hrihor's role in this political drama.
34. Breasted, 1909, p. 359.
35. ibid., pp. 170-71.
36. Breasted, 1933, p. 145.
37. Breasted, 1912, pp. 312, 315.
38. Breasted, 1933, p. 296; Peet, "Akhenaten, Ty, etc.," pp. 93, 96-97, 102; Peet, 1926, p. 205.
39. Breasted, 1909, p. 362; Moret, 1912, p. 45.
40. Moret, 1927, p. 324.
41. Peet, 1926, p. 203.
42. Peet, "Akhenaten, Ty, etc."
43. Peet, 1926, p. 207.
44. Budge, p. 152.
45. ibid., p. 41.
46. Peet, "Akhenaten, Ty, etc.," p. 86; see, also, Derry, p. 115, and Engelbach, p. 99.
47. Peet, "Akhenaten, Ty, etc.," p. 86.
48. Newberry, p. 51; Steindorff and Seele, p. 223; Pendlebury, p. 29.
49. Breasted, 1909, p. 272.
50. Breasted, 1909, pp. 367, 399; Weigall, pp. 71, 144, 139.
51. Weigall, p. 71; Breasted, 1909, p. 369.

52. Weigall, p. 98.
53. ibid., pp. 46, 51, 91.
54. Moret, 1927, p. 319; Ruffer, pp. 168, 170, 336; Gardiner, p. 858.
55. Weigall, p. xvii; Smith, 1912, pp. 51, 54; Sethe, pp. 127-28; Engel-bach, 1931; Derry, 1931; Peet, "Akhenaten, Ty, etc."; Pendlebury, p. 9.
56. Smith, 1923, p. 84; 1912, pp. 54-55; Derry, p. 117.
57. Weigall, p. 69; Ruffer, p. 332; Breasted, 1909, p. 329.
58. Smith, 1912, p. 55.
59. Ruffer, pp. 332-333.
60. Ruffer, pp. 170, 333.
61. Newberry, pp. 51, 50; Steindorff and Seele, p. 222.
62. Weigall, p. 52.
63. Peet, 1926, p. 205.
64. Baikie, pp. 304, 311, 313-14.
65. Pendlebury, pp. xiv, 7, 148, 126; Frankfort, p. 29.
66. Weigall, p. 106.
67. Breasted, 1912, p. 334; 1909, p. 377.
68. Breasted, 1929, p. 80; 1912, p. 342.
69. Weigall, p. 175.
70. Breasted, 1909, pp. 356, 385; Peet, "Akhenaten," pp. 106-07.
71. Weigall, pp. 196, 202, 207.
72. Breasted, 1909, p. 377; 1933, p. 296.
73. Weigall, p. 101.
74. Hyvernat, p. 339.
75. Pohle, p. 410.
76. Hyvernat, p. 345.
77. Slochower, p. 46.
78. Mann, 1942, p. 13.
79. Freud, 1939.

CHAPTER 10. THE LOCUS OF MATHEMATICAL REALITY

1. Somerville, pp. 140-41.
2. Somerville, p. 375; White, A. D., I, p. 225, ftn.
3. Quoted by Bell, 1931, p. 20.
4. Hardy, 1941, pp. 63-64.
5. Bridgman, p. 60.
6. Kasner and Newman, p. 359.
7. Descartes, Pt. I, Sec. XVIII, p. 308.
8. N. Altshiller-Court refers to Durkheim's treatment of this point in "Geometry and Experience," (Scientific Monthly, January, 1945).
9. White, L. A., 1943.
10. Einstein, 1929.
11. Kasner and Newman, p. 359.
12. Schrödinger, p. 143.
13. "On the Nature of Axioms," in Science and Hypothesis, Poincaré, 1913.

14. Quoted by Bell, 1937, p. 16.
15. Durkheim, 1938, p. lvi.
16. Durkheim, 1915, p. 424; see, also, 1938, p. li.
17. Einstein, 1934, pp. 58, 69, 57.
18. Hadamard, p. 50.
19. "Mathematical Creation," in Science and Method, in Poincaré, 1913, p. 387.
20. ibid., p. 393.
21. Quoted by Leuba, p. 240.
22. Goncourt, p. 98.
23. Leuba, p. 241.
24. Hardy, 1941, p. 63.
25. Hardy, 1929, p. 4.
26. Hardy, 1941, pp. 62-63, 65.

CHAPTER 11. THE DEFINITION AND PROHIBITION OF INCEST

1. Tylor, 1888, p. 267.
2. Lowie, 1920, p. 15.
3. Goldenweiser, 1937, p. 303.
4. Morgan, pp. 69, 378, 424.
5. Mahaffy, p. 1.
6. Cf. Montagu for discussion of this point as well as for extensive bibliography.
7. Malinowski, 1929a, pp. 153 ff., 3, 171.
8. Freud, 1931, p. 247.
9. Westermarck, table of contents for Chapter XX.
10. Durkheim, 1898, p. 50 ff.
11. Linton, 1936, pp. 125-26.
12. Goldenweiser, 1922, p. 242; 1937, p. 303.
13. Young, 1942, p. 406.
14. Wissler, 1929, p. 145.
15. Goldenweiser, 1922, p. 242; 1937, p. 303.
16. Lowie, 1920, p. 15.
17. Wissler, 1927.
18. Lowie, 1920, pp. 65-66.
19. Radcliffe-Brown, 1930, p. 435.
20. Ogburn, 1933, pp. 661-62.
21. Freud, 1920, p. 269.
22. Lowie, 1940, p. 233; Fortune, 1932, p. 622.
23. Young, 1942, p. 406.
24. Fortune, p. 620.
25. Malinowski, 1931, p. 630; 1929b, p. 407.
26. Seligman, pp. 243-44, 247, 268-69; Gillin, 1936, p. 93; Firth, p. 324 et seq.; Thomas, p. 197.
27. Freud, 1931, pp. 250-51.

28. Freud, "Contributions to the Theory of Sex," in 1938, pp. 616-17.
29. Freud, 1930, pp. 63, 68, 72.
30. Cooper, p. 20.
31. Freud, 1930, p. 74.

CHAPTER 12. MAN'S CONTROL OVER CIVILIZATION

1. Durkheim, 1938, p. lviii.
2. Ogburn, 1922, p. 346.
3. Jeans, 1931b, p. 109.
4. Field, p. 9.
5. Westgate, p. 165.
6. Schmidt, 1939, p. 8; Sieber and Mueller, pp. 119-120.
7. Childe, 1936, p. 19.
8. Kroeber and Richardson, p. 148; Kroeber, 1919.
9. Durkheim, 1938, p. xlvi.
10. Kroeber and Richardson, p. 152.
11. Durkheim, 1915, p. 27.
12. Bassett, pp. 25-26.
13. G. W. Allport, p. 23.
14. Wissler, 1923, p. 8.
15. ibid., pp. 8-10.
16. Durkheim, 1897, pp. 427-28.
17. Kroeber, 1919, p. 263.
18. James, 1890, p. 2439; 1880, p. 442.
19. Tylor, 1871, pp. 2, 24.
20. Whitehead, p. 94.
21. Frank, p. 475.

CHAPTER 13. ENERGY AND THE EVOLUTION OF CULTURE

1. MacCurdy, II, p. 134; Ostwald, 1907, p. 511.
2. Childe, 1936, pp. 7, 9.
3. Schlesinger, pp. 247-48.
4. Compton, p. 576.

CHAPTER 14. THE SCIENCE OF CULTURE

1. Lowie, 1936, p. 301 and 1917, p. 17; Ostwald, 1915b, p. 192; Whitehead, p. 48.
2. Lowie, 1936, p. 301; 1917, p. 17.
3. Boas, 1908, pp. 7, 10.
4. Childe, 1946, p. 251.
5. Myres, p. 11.
6. Mencken, personal communication.
7. Ostwald, 1915a, p. 167; see, also, pp. 168-69; 1915b, pp. 192-94, 205.
8. Bain, 1929, pp. 108, 110-11.

9. White, L. A., 1939, p. 571.
10. Bidney, 1946, p. 541; Linton, 1941, pp. 9, 16-17; G. W. Allport, p. 22.
11. Lowie, 1917, p. 17; 1936, pp. 301, 307; Durkheim, 1938, p. 37.
12. Ostwald, 1915a, p. 167; 1915b, p. 192; Kroeber, 1918, p. 641.
13. Poincaré, 1913, p. 371.

BIBLIOGRAPHY

The following abbreviations are used for those serial publications, handbooks, and encyclopedias that are cited two or more times.

AA   American Anthropologist
AAA-M   American Anthropological Association, Memoirs
AJS   American Journal of Sociology
AM   Atlantic Monthly
AS   Annales du Service des Antiquités de L'Égypte
CE   Catholic Encyclopedia
EB   Encyclopedia Britannica, 14th ed.
ESS   Encyclopedia of the Social Sciences
JEA   Journal of Egyptian Archaeology
JRAI   Journal of the Royal Anthropological Institute
P-CAS   Proceedings, Congress of Arts and Sciences, St. Louis, 1904, Vol. 5, Boston, 1906.
P-MA   Papers of the Michigan Academy of Science, Arts, and Letters
S   Science
SF   Social Forces
SM   Scientific Monthly
SWJ   Southwestern Journal of Anthropology

Abel, Th.
   1929. "Is a Cultural Sociology Possible?" (AJS 35:739-52).
Allport, F. H.
   1924. Social Psychology. Boston.
Allport, G. W.
   1947. "Guide Lines for Research in International Cooperation," (Journal of Social Issues, 3:21-37).
Argyll, Duke of
   1872. Primeval Man. New York.
Baikie, James
   1926. The Amarna Age. London.
Bain, Read
   1929. "Trends in American Sociological Theory," (in Trends in American Sociology, G. A. Lundberg, et al., eds., New York).
   1942. "A Definition of Culture," (Sociology and Social Research, 27: 87-94).
Baldwin, J. M.
   1906. "The History of Psychology," (P-CAS).

Bassett, Raymond E.
    1946. Letter to Editor, (S, 103:25-26).
Bell, E. T.
    1931. The Queen of the Sciences. Baltimore.
    1937. Men of Mathematics. New York.
Benedict, Ruth
    1934. Patterns of Culture. New York.
    1939. "Edward Sapir," (AA 41:465-468).
    1942. "Primitive Freedom," (AM, 169:756-763).
    1943. "Franz Boas as an Ethnologist," (in Franz Boas, 1858-1942, by
      A. L. Kroeber et al., AAA-M 61).
Bernard, Jessie
    1929. "History and Prospects of Sociology," (in Trends in American Soci-
    ology, G. A. Lundberg et al, eds. New York).
Bernard, L. L.
    1927a. "The Psychological Foundations of Society," (in An Introduction
    to Sociology, J. Davis and H. E. Barnes, eds., Boston).
    1927b. "Sociology and Psychology," (in The Social Sciences and their In-
    terrelations, Wm. F. Ogburn and Alexander Goldenweiser, eds. New
    York).
    1942. Introduction to Sociology. New York.
Bidney, David
    1944. "On the Concept of Culture and Some Cultural Fallacies," (AA 46:
    30-44).
    1946. "The Concept of Cultural Crisis," (AA 48:534-552).
Boas, Franz
    1908. "Anthropology," (in Columbia University Lectures in Science, Phi-
    losophy and Art. New York).
    1928. Anthropology and Modern Life. New York.
    1932. "Aims of Anthropological Research," (S, 76:605-613).
    1936. "History and Science in Anthropology: a Reply," (AA 38:137-141).
    1940. Race, Language and Culture. New York.
    1945. Race and Democratic Society. New York.
Breasted, J. H.
    1909. A History of Egypt, revised edition. New York.
    1912. The Development of Religion and Thought in Ancient Egypt. New
    York.
    1929. "Ikhnaton," (EB).
    1933. The Dawn of Conscience. New York.
Brett, G. S.
    1929. "History of Psychology," (EB).
Bridgman, P. W.
    1927. The Logic of Modern Physics. New York.
Budge, E. A. Wallis
    1923. Tutankhamen, Amenism, etc. London.
Carlson, Anton J.
    1926. "The Dynamics of Living Processes," (in The Nature of the World
    and Man, H. H. Newman, ed. Chicago).

Case, E. C.
  1934. "The Modern Biologist's Attitude Toward the Problem of Life," (The Michigan Alumnus Quarterly Review, 40:1-13).
Cattell, J. McK.
  1906. "Conceptions and Methods of Psychology," (P-CAS).
Childe, V. Gordon
  1936. Man Makes Himself. London.
  1946. "Archeology and Anthropology," (SWJ 2:243-251).
Clark, Grahame
  1946. From Savagery to Civilization. London.
Clodd, Edw.
  1888. The Story of Creation. London.
Compton, A. H.
  1940. "Science Shaping American Culture," (Proceedings, American Philosophical Society, 83:573-582).
Comte, Auguste
  no date. Positive Philosophy, translated by Harriet Martineau, one volume edition, Peter Eckler, publisher. New York.
Cooley, C. H.
  1897. "Genius, Fame, and the Comparison of Races," (Annals, American Academy of Political and Social Science, 9:317-358).
Cooper, John M.
  1932. "Incest Prohibitions in Primitive Culture," (Primitive Man, 5: 1-20).
Derry, D. E.
  1931. "Note on the Skeleton Hitherto Believed to be that of King Akhenaten," (AS, 31:115-119).
Descartes, R.
  1901. Discourse on Method (in The Method, Meditations and Philosophy, translated and edited by John Veitch. New York).
Dewey, John
  1920. Reconstruction in Philosophy. New York.
Douglass, A. E.
  1929. "The Secret of the Talkative Tree Rings," (National Geographic Magazine, 56:737-770).
Durkheim, Emile 1893. La Division du Travail. Paris.
  1897. Le Suicide. Paris.
  1898. "La Prohibition de L'Inceste et ses Origines," (L'Année Sociologique, 1:1-70).
  1915. The Elementary Forms of the Religious Life, translated by J. W. Swain. London.
  1933. The Division of Labor in Society, translated by George Simpson. New York.
  1938. The Rules of Sociological Method, translated by S. A. Solvay and J. H. Mueller. Chicago.
Edgerton, Wm. F.
  1947. "The Government and the Governed in the Egyptian Empire," (Journal of Near Eastern Studies, 6:152-160).

Einstein, A.
  1929. "Space-Time," (EB).
  1934. The World as I See It. New York.
  1936. "Physics and Reality," (Journal of the Franklin Institute, 221: 349-382).
Ellwood, C. A.
  1906. Remarks (P-CAS).
  1944. "Culture and Human Society," (SF, 23:6-15).
Engelbach, R.
  1931. "The So-Called Coffin of Akhenaten," (AS, 31:98-114).
Field, Stanley
  1943. "Fifty Years of Progress," (Field Museum News, Vol. 14).
Firth, Raymond
  1936. We, the Tikopia. New York.
Fortune, Reo
  1932. "Incest," (ESS).
Frank, L. K.
  1944. "What is Social Order?" (AJS, 49:470-477).
Frankfort, H.
  1929. "The Affinities of the Mural Painting of El-Amarneh," (in The Mural Painting of El-Amarneh, H. Frankfort, ed., London).
Freud, S.
  1920. General Introduction to Psychoanalysis. New York.
  1930. Civilization and its Discontents. New York.
  1931. Totem and Taboo, New Republic ed. New York.
  1938. The Basic Writings of Sigmund Freud, A. A. Brill, ed. (Modern Library ed. New York).
  1939. Moses and Monotheism. New York.
Galton, Francis
  1869. Hereditary Genius. London.
Gardiner, Alan H.
  1917. "Philosophy, Egyptian," (Encyclopedia of Religion and Ethics, James Hastings, ed. Edinburgh and New York).
Gary, Dorothy
  1929. "The Developing Study of Culture," (in Trends in American Sociology, G. A. Lundberg et al., eds. New York).
Gault, R. H.
  1927. "Recent Developments in Psychology Contributory to Social Explanation," (in Recent Developments in the Social Sciences, E. C. Hayes, ed. Philadelphia).
Giddings, F. H.
  1896. The Principles of Sociology (1921 printing. New York).
  1906. "The Concepts and Methods of Sociology," (P-CAS).
  1932. Civilization and Society. New York.
Gillin, John
  1936. The Barama River Caribs of British Guiana, (Papers, Peabody Museum, Vol. 14, No. 2. Cambridge).

1939."Some Unfinished Business of Cultural Anthropology," (Ohio Archeological and Historical Quarterly, 48:44-52).

Glanville, S. R. K.
1929. "Amenophis and his Successors in the XVIIIth Dynasty," (in The Great Ones of Ancient Egypt, W. Brunton et al., London).

Goldenweiser, A.
1917. "The Autonomy of the Social," (AA, 19:447-449).
1922. Early Civilization. New York.
1927. "Anthropology and Psychology," (in The Social Sciences and Their Interrelations, Wm. F. Ogburn and A. Goldenweiser, eds. New York).
1933. History, Psychology and Culture. New York.
1935. "Why I Am Not a Marxist," (Modern Monthly, 9:71-76).
1937. Anthropology. New York.

Goncourt, Journals
1937. L. Galantière, ed. Garden City, New York.

Groves, E. R.
1928. Introduction to Sociology. New York.

Groves, E. R. and Moore, H. E.
1940. Introduction to Sociology. New York.

Gumplowicz, Ludwig
1899. Outlines of Sociology. Translated by F. W. Moore. Philadelphia.

Hadamard, Jacques
1945. The Psychology of Invention in the Mathematical Field. Princeton.

Hall, H. R.
1929. "Egypt, Religion," (EB).

Hallowell, A. Irving
1945. "Sociopsychological Aspects of Acculturation," (in The Science of Man in the World Crisis, Ralph Linton, ed. New York).

Hankins, F. H.
1928. An Introduction to the Study of Society. New York.

Hardy, G. H.
1929. "Mathematical Proof," (Mind, 38:1-25).
1941. A Mathematician's Apology. Cambridge, England.

Harrington, H.
1929. "Roman Catholic Church" (in part; EB).

Hart, C. W. M.
1938. "Social Evolution and Modern Anthropology" (in Essays in Political Economy, H. A. Innis, ed. Toronto).

Havens, R. D.
1944. "The Burden of Incertitude," (University of Rochester).

Hecht, Selig
1947. Explaining the Atom. New York.

Herskovits, M. J.
1940. The Economic Life of Primitive Peoples. New York.
1945. "The Processes of Cultural Change," (in The Science of Man in the World Crisis, Ralph Linton, ed. New York).

Hewett, Edgar L.
1942. "From Culture to Civilization," (El Palacio, 49:133-142).

Hobhouse, L. T.
  1924. Social Development. London.
Hooton, E. A.
  1931. Up From the Ape. New York.
  1937. Apes, Men and Morons. New York.
  1939. Crime and the Man. Cambridge.
  1943a. "Why We Study Apes and Monkeys," (Fauna, 5:2-6).
  1943b. "Morons into What?" (Woman's Home Companion, 70:4, 96).
Huxley, T. H.
  1870. The Physical Basis of Life. New Haven.
Hyvernat, Henry
  1909. "Egypt," (CE).
James, Wm.
  1880. "Great Men, Great Thoughts and the Environment," (AM, 46: 441-459).
  1890. "The Importance of Individuals," (The Open Court, 4:2437-2440).
Jeans, James et al
  1931a. "The Evolution of the Universe," (Appendix, Report of the Centenary Meeting, British Association for the Advancement of Science).
  1931b. Essay in Living Philosophies. New York.
Kasner, Edw. and Newman, James
  1940. Mathematics and the Imagination. New York.
Keller, Helen
  1903. The Story of My Life. New York.
Kellogg, W. N. and L. A.
  1933. The Ape and the Child. New York.
Köhler, W.
  1926. The Mentality of Apes. New York and London.
Kroeber, A. L.
  1917. "The Superorganic," (AA, 19:163-213).
  1918. "The Possibility of a Social Psychology," (AJS, 23:633-650).
  1919. "On the Principle of Order in Civilization as Exemplified by Changes in Fashion," (AA, 21:235-263).
  1923. Anthropology. New York.
  1928. "Sub-Human Cultural Beginnings," (Quarterly Review of Biology, 3:325-342).
  1931. "The Culture-Area Concepts of Clark Wissler," (in Methods in Social Science, S. A. Rice, ed. Chicago).
  1936. "So-Called Social Science," (Journal of Social Philosophy, 1:317-340).
  1944. Configurations of Culture Growth. Berkeley.
  1948. "White's View of Culture," (AA, 50:405-415).
Kroeber, A. L. and Richardson, Jane
  1940. Three Centuries of Women's Dress Fashions; a Quantitative Analysis (Anthropological Records, Vol. 5, No. 2, University of California, Berkeley).
Leuba, J. H.
  1925. The Psychology of Religious Mysticism. London.

Linton, Ralph
  1936. The Study of Man. New York.
  1938. "The Present Status of Anthropology," (S, 87:241-248).
  1941. "Potential Contributions of Cultural Anthropology to Teacher Education," (in Culture and Personality, American Council on Education. Washington, D. C.).
  1945. The Cultural Background of Personality. New York.
Locke, John
  1894. An Essay Concerning the Human Understanding. London.
Lowie, R. H.
  1917. Culture and Ethnology. New York.
  1920. Primitive Society. New York.
  1929. Are We Civilized? New York.
  1933. "The Family as a Social Unit," (P-MA, 18:53-69).
  1936. "Cultural Anthropology: a Science," (AJS, 42:301-320).
  1940. Introduction to Cultural Anthropology, 2nd ed. New York.
Lynd, Robert S.
  1939. Knowledge for What? Princeton.
MacCurdy, Geo. G.
  1933. Human Origins, 2 vols. New York.
MacIver, R. M.
  1930. "The Trend to Internationalism," (ESS, Vol. 1).
  1934. "Sociology," (ESS).
  1937. Society: A Textbook of Sociology. New York.
Mahaffy, J. P.
  1915. "Cleopatra VI," (JEA, 2:1-4).
Malinowski, B.
  1929a. The Sexual Life of Savages. London.
  1929b. "Kinship," (EB).
  1931. "Culture," (ESS).
  1939. "The Group and Individual in Functional Analysis," (AJS, 44:938-964).
Mann, Thomas
  1942. "The Theme of the Joseph Novels." Washington.
Maxwell, J. Clerk
  1892. Matter and Motion. New York.
Mead, Margaret
  1943. Introduction to Is Germany Incurable? by R. M. Brickner. Philadelphia.
Meggers, Betty J.
  1946. "Recent Trends in American Ethnology," (AA, 48:176-214).
Millikan, R. A.
  1939. "Science and the World Tomorrow," (SM, 49:210-214).
Minkowski, H.
  1923. "Space and Time," (in The Principles of Relativity, H. Lorentz et al. London).
Montagu, M. F. Ashley
  1937. "Physiological Paternity in Australia," (AA, 39:175-183).

Moret, Alexandre
  1912. Kings and Gods of Egypt. London and New York.
  1927. The Nile and Egyptian Civilization. New York.
Morgan, L. H.
  1877. Ancient Society. New York.
Murdock, Geo. P.
  1932. "The Science of Culture," (AA, 34:200-215).
Myres, John L.
  1948. Review of White, "The Expansion of the Scope of Science," (Man, 48:11).
Newberry, P. E.
  1932. "King Ay, the Successor of Tutankhamun," (JEA, 18:50-52).
Newman, H. H.
  1926. "The Nature and Origin of Life," (in The Nature of the World and Man, H. H. Newman, ed. Chicago).
Newton, Isaac
  1934. Principia Mathematica, F. Cajori, ed. Berkeley.
Novicoff, Alexander B.
  1945. "The Concept of Integrative Levels and Biology," (S, 101:209-215).
Ogburn, Wm. F.
  1922. Social Change. New York.
  1933. "The Family," (in Recent Social Trends in the United States, one volume edition. New York).
Ogburn, Wm. F. and Nimkoff, Meyer F.
  1940. Sociology. Boston.
Ogburn, Wm. F. and Thomas, Dorothy
  1922. "Are Inventions Inevitable?" (Political Science Quarterly, 37:83-98).
Ostwald, Wilhelm
  1907. "The Modern Theory of Energetics" (The Monist, 17:481-515).
  1910. Natural Philosophy. New York.
  1915a. "The System of the Sciences," translated by Thomas L. Blayney (The Rice Institute Pamphlet, 2:101-190. Houston, Texas).
  1915b. "Principles of the Theory of Education," English translation (ibid., 2:191-221).
Peet, T. E.
  1926. "Contemporary Life and Thought in Egypt," (Cambridge Ancient History, Vol. 2. New York).
  no date. "Akhenaten, Ty, Nefertete, and Mutnezemt," (in Kings and Queens of Ancient Egypt, W. Brunton et al. New York).
Pendlebury, J. D. S.
  1935. Tell el-Amarna. London.
Pohle, Joseph
  1911. "Priesthood," (CE).
Poincaré, H.
  1913. The Foundations of Science. New York.
Radcliffe-Brown, A. R.
  1923. "The Methods of Ethnology and Social Anthropology," (South African Journal of Science, 20:124-147).

1930-31. "The Social Organization of Australian Tribes," (Oceania, Vol. 1, Pts. 1 to 4).
1934. "Sanction, Social," (ESS).
1937. "The Nature of a Theoretical Natural Science of Society," (University of Chicago, mimeographed notes).
1940. "On Social Structure," (JRAI, 70:1-12).
Rivers, W. H. R.
1916. "Sociology and Psychology," (The Sociological Review, 9:1-13).
Roosevelt, Franklin D.
1934. Public Addresses. Compiled by M. W. Hunt. Los Angeles.
Ross, E. A.
1906. "The Present Problems of Social Psychology," (P-CAS).
Ruffer, Marc A.
1921. Studies in the Palaeopathology of Egypt. R. L. Woodie, ed. Chicago.
Russell, H. N.
1939. "Stellar Evolution." (EB).
Salomon, Gottfried
1934. "Social Organism," (ESS).
Sapir, E.
1916. Time Perspective in Aboriginal American Culture (Canada Dept. of Mines, Memoir 90. Ottawa).
1917. "Do We Need a Superorganic?" (AA, 19:441-447).
Scharff, Alexander
1929. "Haremhab," (in The Great Ones of Ancient Egypt, W. Brunton et al. London).
Schlesinger, A. M.
1922. New Viewpoints in American History. New York.
Schmidt, W.
1934. "Primitive Man," (in European Civilization, Ed. Eyre, ed. London).
1939. The Culture Historical Method of Ethnology. New York.
Schnierla, T. C.
1948. "Psychology, Comparative," (EB).
Schrödinger, Erwin
1935. Science and the Human Temperament. New York.
Seligman, B. Z.
1929. "Incest and Descent: Their Influence on Social Organization," (JRAI, 59:231-272).
Sethe, Kurt
1921. "Beiträge zur Geschichte Amenophis IV," (Nachrichten von der Königlichen Gesellschaft der Wissenschaften zu Göttingen, Philologisch-historische Klasse aus dem Jahre 1921. Berlin).
Shapley, Harlow
1920. "Thermokinetics of Liometopum apiculatum Mayr," (Proceedings, National Academy of Sciences, 6:204-211).
1924. "Note on the Thermokinetics of Dolichoderine Ants," (ibid., 10: 436-439).
Shapley, Harlow, ed.
1943. A Treasury of Science. New York.

Sheen, Fulton J.
   1948. "The Psychology of a Frustrated Soul," (The Catholic Hour, National Broadcasting Company, January 4).
Simmel, Georg
   1898. "The Persistence of Social Groups," (AJS, 3:662-698).
Slochower, Harry
   1938. Thomas Mann's Joseph Story.
Small, Albion W.
   1905. General Sociology. Chicago.
Smith, G. Elliot
   1912. The Royal Mummies. Cairo.
   1923. Tutankhamen. London.
Somerville, Martha, ed.
   1874. Personal Recollections of Mary Somerville. Boston.
Spencer, Herbert
   1868. "On the Genesis of Science," (Essays: Scientific, Political and Speculative, Vol. 1. London).
   1873. The Study of Sociology. New York.
Spykman, N. J.
   1925. The Social Theory of Georg Simmel. Chicago.
Steindorff, Geo. and Seele, K. C.
   1942. When Egypt Ruled the East. Chicago.
Stern, Bernhard J.
   1929. "Concerning the Distinction between the Social and the Cultural," (SF, 8:264-271).
Swanton, John R.
   1943. Are Wars Inevitable? (Smithsonian War Background Studies, No. 12. Washington).
Thomas, Wm. I.
   1937. Primitive Behavior. New York.
Tylor, E. B.
   1871. Primitive Culture. Fifth edition, 1929 printing. London.
   1881. Anthropology. London.
   1888. "On a Method of Investigating the Development of Institutions; Applied to Laws of Marriage and Descent," (JRAI, 18:245-269).
Ward, Lester F.
   1895. "The Place of Sociology among the Sciences," (AJS, 1:16-27).
   1896. "The Filiation of the Sciences," (report by W. C. Winlock, S, 3:292-294).
   1903. Pure Sociology. New York.
Washburn, Margaret F.
   1946. "Social Psychology," (in Encyclopedia Americana).
Weigall, Arthur
   1923. The Life and Times of Akhnaton. London.
Westermarck, Edw.
   1921. The History of Human Marriage, 3 vols. London.
Westgate, Lewis G.
   1943. "Man's Long Story," (SM, 57:155-165).

White, A. D.
1896. A History of the Warfare of Science with Theology in Christendom, 2 vols, 1930 printing. New York.
White, Leslie A.
1939. "A Problem in Kinship Terminology," (AA, 41:566-573).
1942. The Pueblo of Santa Ana, New Mexico, AAA-M 60.
1943. "Keresan Indian Color Terms," (P-MA, 28:559-563).
1945. "History, Evolutionism and Functionalism: Three Types of Interpretation of Culture," (SWJ, 1:221-248).
Whitehead, Alfred N.
1933. Science and the Modern World. Cambridge, England.
Willey, Malcolm M.
1929. "The Validity of the Culture Concept," (AJS, 35:204-219).
Willey, M. M. and Herskovits, M. J.
1923. "The Cultural Approach to Sociology," (AJS, 29:188-199).
Williams, Mary W.
1934. "Slavery, Modern," (ESS).
Wissler, Clark
1923. Man and Culture. New York.
1927. "Recent Developments in Anthropology," (in Recent Developments in the Social Sciences, E. C. Hayes, ed. Philadelphia).
1929. An Introduction to Social Anthropology. New York.
Yerkes, R. M. and A. W.
1929. The Great Apes. New Haven.
Young, Kimball
1934. An Introductory Sociology. New York.
1942. Sociology, a Study of Society and Culture. New York.

NAME INDEX

Abel, Th., 84-85, 425
Allport, F. H., 75, 425
Allport, G. W., 130, 342-43, 425
Argyll, Duke of, 40, 425
Aristotle, 52
Augustine, Saint, 322-23

Baikie, James, 238, 271, 425
Bain, Read, 83, 411, 425
Baldwin, J. M., 75, 425
Barnes, Harry E., xv
Bassett, Raymond E., 342, 426
Bastian, Ad., 182
Bell, E. T., 211, 426
Benedict, Ruth, 95, 130-31, 162, 426
Bernard, Jessie, 83, 426
Bernard, L. L., 32, 82, 86, 426
Bidney, David, 95, 108-09, 347, 426
Blackmar, F. W., 82
Boas, F., 65, 95, 104, 136, 194, 409, 426
Breasted, J. H., 130, 237, 238, 239, 245, 247, 251, 253, 255, 256, 257, 261, 266, 273, 274, 275, 426
Brett, G. S., 52, 426
Bridgman, P. W., 284, 426
Budge, E. A. Wallis, 238, 247, 258-59, 426
Burgess, E. W., 20

Carlson, A. J., 24, 32, 426
Carroll, Lewis, 282

Case, E. C., 53, 427
Cattell, J. McK., 75, 427
Cheng Che-Yu, 412
Childe, V. Gordon, 203, 332, 365, 410, 427
Clark, Grahame, 41, 427
Clodd, Edw., 40, 427
Compton, A. H., 386-87, 427
Comte, Auguste, 56, 59, 69-70, 427
Condon, E. U., xii
Cooley, C. H., 196, 218, 427
Cooper, John M., 326, 427

Darwin, Charles, 14, 27, 40, 229, 296
Day, Clarence, 123
Derry, D. E., 264, 265, 427
Descartes, R., 30, 68, 285, 427
Dewey, John, 46, 427
Douglass, A. E., 4, 427
Durkheim, Emile, xix, 72, 78, 79, 88-90, 97, 106, 121, 146, 286, 290, 291, 309, 330, 336, 342, 346, 414, 427

Edgerton, Wm. F., xiii, 252, 427
Einstein, A., 6, 185, 284, 288-89, 291, 428
Eliot, George, 298
Ellwood, C. A., 82, 83, 85, 428
Emerson, Ralph Waldo, 279
Engelbach, R., 264, 428

SUBJECT INDEX

Agricultural Revolution, 372
Agriculture, a means of harnessing energy, 371; and population increase, 378
Animism, 66
Anthropocentrism, 177, 338, 357-58, 406
Anthropology, and psychiatry, 105; regression of, 103ff., 110; scope of, 409, 415
Anthropomorphism, 65, 106, 183, 234, 406, 413
Apes, imitation among, 42-43; lack culture, 42; mentality of, 23, 43, 45, 212; size of brain, 32-33; and speech, 32, 35-36; use of tools, 41ff.
Art, nature of, 3
Astronomy, 4-5
Atomic energy, 389

Brain, size and weight of, 32-33
Bride-price, 317

Cereals and cultural development, 371
Chance, and the course of history, 228-29; and genius, 202
Church, political functions of, 159-60, 242-44; vs. state, 242-44, 258, 266-67
Class structure, 380, 382-83, 384-85
Complexity of phenomena, 61-63
Conscience, nature of, 156-58

Co-operation, and social evolution, 313-16; among lower primates, 314
Culture, an "abstraction," 96; anatomy of, 364; belief in man's control over, 234, 330ff.; defined by Tylor, 87; depends upon symbolling, 15, 33; a distinct class of phenomena, 73, 92, 397, 409; evolution of, 221, 241, 364ff., 390-93; explained in terms of culture, 92, 100, 105, 167, 181, 201, 339, 351, 392; felt as "outside force," 297-98; has a life of its own, 358, 407; importance of concept of, 403-05; "intangible," 101-02; interpretations of, xvii-xix, 84; nature of, 15-16, 140, 240-41; a "psychological" phenomenon, 104-05; rate of growth of, 385; rate of growth and mental ability, 218-22; reality of questioned, 101; science of, see "Science of culture"
Culture pattern and achievement, 215-17
Culture process, 166, 181, 328; and individual, 161ff., 183-84; and inventions, 168-70, 292
Culture, and cereals, 371; and dreams, 179-81; and energy, 166, 363ff.; and environment, 339; and genius, 215-18; and human behavior, 79, 287, 328,

440

351-52; nature of, 18, 121-23, 146
Human nature, 126, 131, 149ff.; and culture, 287
Human vs. non-human behavior, 34-36, 171
Human organism, locus of culture process, 226, 231, 293

Idealism, philosophy of, 46, 233
Ideas, syntheses of, 291, 293, 297
Ikhnaton, age of, 260, 264; alleged foreign blood, 239, 266; art under, 238-39; Catholic view of, 276-77; death of, 249; Freud on, 278; God reveals himself to, 273; our ignorance concerning, 269-70; innovations of, 256; instrument of Divine Purpose, 276; Jewish view of, 277; loses Asiatic empire, 269, 274-75; Mann on, 277-78; and Moses, 276-78; supposed mummy of, 264; pathology of, 239, 263, 265; alleged personal characteristics, 237-39; vs. the priests, 248, 257-58, 266; reign of, 235; resembles Jesus, 263, 274-75; rewards his followers, 261-62; revolution of, interpreted, 258-59
Inbreeding, 305-07; among lower primates, 315
Incest, 158-59, 303ff.; instinct theory of, 304; and physical deterioration, 305-07
Incest taboos, interpreted by: Cooper, 326; Durkheim, 309; Firth, 325; Fortune, 324-25; Freud, 307-08, 325-26, 328; Gillin, 325; Goldenweiser, 310; Linton, 310; Lowie, 303-04; Malinowski, 325; Morgan, 305; Ogburn, 312; Saint Augustine,

322-23; Seligman, 325; Thomas, 325; Tylor, 313; Westermarck, 309; Wissler, 311; Young, 310-11

Individual, and culture process, 161ff., 183-84, 295, 369; a catalytic agent, 181, 294; differences, 174, 199, 294; the instrument of culture forces, 298; a neural locus of events, 226, 231, 296; the originator of culture, 161ff.; as prime mover, 161ff., 175, 181; vs. social achievement, 225
Inquisition and mental ability, 221
Intra-, extra-organismal contexts, 51, 81
Inventions and discoveries, as cultural syntheses, 168-70, 203-04, 292; inevitability of, 205-09; made simultaneously but independently, 169-70, 205-07, 209-11, 292-93; and social stratification, 223-24; and technology, 224

Kinship, 241, 327, 377, 381; sociological vs. biological, 307
Kissing, 153

Language, and the science of culture, 141; and sensory experience, 288
Law, of cultural evolution, 368, 374-75; of development of philosophy, 69, 111; everywhere, 107
Laws of thought, 299 ftn.
Levirate, 317
Liberals, 179
Living vs. non-living systems, 51
Love, marriage and the family, 321

Man, behavior of, 34; a constant, culture a variable, 200, 226, 294,